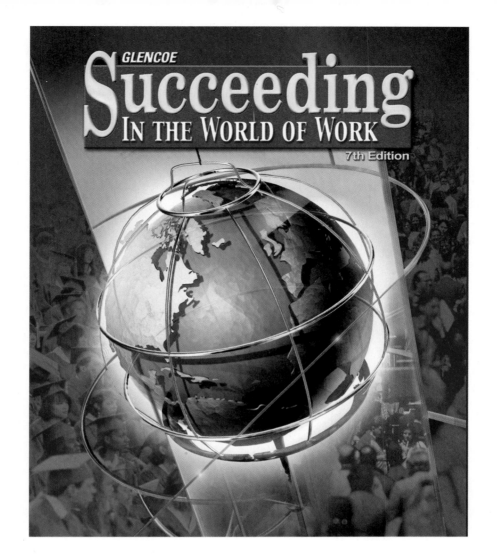

GLENCOE
Succeeding
IN THE WORLD OF WORK
7th Edition

Grady Kimbrell
Educational Consultant
Santa Barbara, California

Ben S. Vineyard
Professor and
Chairman Emeritus

Vocational and
Technical Education

Pittsburg State University
Pittsburg, Kansas

Glencoe
McGraw-Hill

New York, New York   Columbus, Ohio   Chicago, Illinois   Peoria, Illinois   Woodland Hills, California

Glencoe/McGraw-Hill

A Division of The McGraw·Hill Companies

Printed in the United States of America.

Send all inquiries to:
Glencoe/McGraw-Hill
21600 Oxnard Street, Suite 500
Woodland Hills, California 91367

ISBN 0-07-828033-8 (Student Text)
ISBN 0-07-828034-6 (Teacher Wraparound Edition)

4 5 6 7 8 9 058 06 05 04 03

Advisory Board

To best research and address the needs of today's workplace, Glencoe/McGraw-Hill assembled an advisory board of industry leaders and educators. The board lent its expertise and experience to establish the foundation for this innovative, real-world, career education program. Glencoe/McGraw-Hill would like to acknowledge the following companies and individuals for their support and commitment to this project:

Mark Ballard
Director of Human Resources
Recruitment and Development
The Limited, Inc.
Columbus, OH

Michele Bina
Michele Bina and Associates
former Manager of
Organizational Effectiveness
The Prudential Healthcare Group
Woodland Hills, CA

Joe Bryan
Industrial Cooperative Training Coordinator
Warsaw Community Schools
Warsaw, IN

Mary Sue Burkhardt
Career Specialist
Family and Consumer Sciences
Twin Lakes High School
Monticello, IN

Mable Burton
Career Development Specialist
Office of Education for Employment
Philadelphia, PA

Lolita B. Hall
Specialist, Program Improvement
Virginia Department of Education
Richmond, VA

Liz Lamatrice
Career Education Coordinator
Jefferson County, OH

Keith Mitchell
Manager
Testing and Assessment
Abbott Laboratories
Abbott Park, IL

James Murphy
Education Relations Manager
The Boeing Company
Seattle, WA

William M. Pepito
Manager, Lake County
Skills Development Program
Abbott Laboratories
Abbott Park, IL

William J. Ratzburg
Director
Education for Work and Careers
Racine School District
Racine, WI

Gary Schepf
Business Education Department Chair
Nimitz High School
Irving, TX

Reviewers

Debra Brewster
Local Vocation Educator/Coordinator
DeForest High School
DeForest, WI

Annie Hunter Clasen
Program Manager/Instructor
Learey Technical Center
Tampa, FL

Robert P. Dasco
Occupational Work Experience
Coordinator
McKinley Senior High School
Canton, OH

Karen Ann Altfilisch Ellis
Career and Technology Education
Manager
Denver Public Schools
Denver, CO

David Haar
Marketing Education Teacher
Eaglecrest High School
Aurora, CO

Anthony M. Kemps
Technology Education Supervisor
Ramsey Public Schools
Ramsey, NJ

Priscilla McCalla
Professional and Program
Development Director
DECA
Reston, VA

Lyn Flammia McMillan
Industrial Cooperative Training Teacher
Millbrook High School
Raleigh, NC

Pam Schaffer
Vocational Education Coordinator
Utica Schools
Sterling Heights, MI

Scott Taylor
Business Teacher
Rancho Buena Vista High School
Vista, CA

Table of Contents

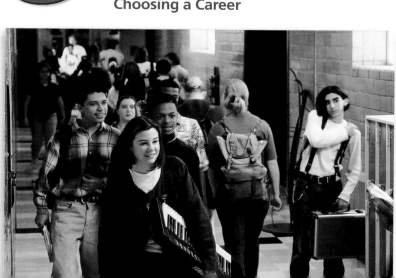

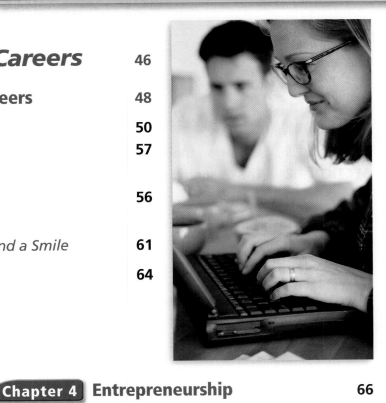

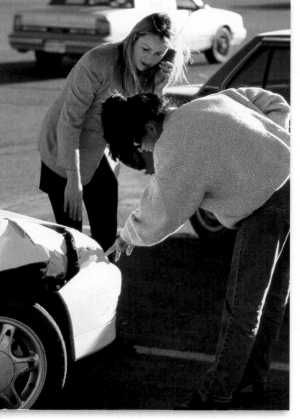

Welcome to
Succeeding in the World of Work!

What do you want to do with your life? What do you dream of becoming? What are you good at? What do you enjoy? This book will help you find the answers to these questions.

If you really think about it, there is at least one thing, if not several things, you really enjoy—things that make the time fly and make you feel good about yourself. Maybe you love playing sports or acting in plays. Maybe you like working with computers or writing stories. Throughout this course, your challenge is to convert the things that interest you into a satisfying career. This book will help you do just that.

First, you'll take a look at yourself. You'll determine your interests, values, and ideal lifestyle and consider how they will influence your career choice. You'll then explore the many career areas and decide which careers best suit you. For example, if you love animals and value education, you may decide a career working as an exhibit interpreter at a zoo or aquarium is right for you.

Next, you will develop your individual career plan. You will look at the type of education you will need, and how to find, apply, and interview for a job.

From there, you'll take a good look at the skills you'll need on the job and gain valuable insight into how to develop these professional skills.

You'll also take an in-depth look at what to expect once you're living on your own. You'll learn how to manage your money, make wise consumer purchases, and meet your adult responsibilities.

Finally, you'll focus on the importance of lifelong learning. You'll receive valuable advice on how to get ahead on the job and how to put your career on the fast track. You'll also learn tips on how to balance your work and personal life to achieve career and personal success.

Understanding the Text Structure

You'll find the structure of *Succeeding in the World of Work* easy to follow. The text is divided into seven units. Each unit covers a distinct area of career exploration: Self-Assessment, Exploring Careers, Finding a Job, Joining the Workforce, Professional Development, Life Skills, and Lifelong Learning.

Within each unit there are chapters. Each chapter is broken down into two or three short sections. The sections begin with **What You'll Learn** and **Why It's Important**. This tells you the skills and knowledge you will have mastered once you complete the section. The section's **Key Terms** are also listed. Each section concludes with a **Key Concept**

Checkpoint that helps to reinforce your understanding of section concepts.

At the end of the chapter, a **Summary** page summarizes the chapter information. You can use this summary to review chapter content. A two-page **Chapter Review** follows the **Summary** page. The review provides extensive questions and activities designed to help you check your understanding of the chapter.

Chapter Features

Text features provide further insight into career topics and challenge your creativity and imagination.

- The **Portfolio Project** gives you the opportunity to develop a portfolio of successful projects and outstanding work.
- The **Career Lab** gives you an opportunity to undertake all aspects of career exploration.
- **Journal: Personal Career Plan** and **Personal Career Project** give you an opportunity to do some creative thinking and journal writing as you apply chapter content to your own career explorations. This activity appears on the opening pages of each chapter.

- **Career Focus** presents information about various career clusters and individuals who work in them.
- **Creative Business Practices** highlights innovative business practices of specific business organizations.
- **Career Checklist** provides helpful tips to use in real-life situations.
- **Ethics in Action** gives you the opportunity to consider what ethical decision you would make in specific real-life situations.
- **Internet Connection** gives you real-world research and investigation projects to conduct on the World Wide Web.
- The **Glossary** and **Index** allow you to quickly access definitions to terms and locate career subjects. The **Glossary** provides definitions for more than 200 terms. Following each definition, in parentheses, is the page number on which the term is explained. The **Index** lists key terms and concepts along with important graphs, charts, and other chapter illustrations.

Get ready for an exciting career exploration adventure with *Succeeding in the World of Work*. An adventure that will prepare you for a lifetime!

UNIT 1

Self-Assessment

Chapter 1
You and the
World of Work

Chapter 2
Getting to Know
Yourself

Portfolio Project

Research Careers Select a career that seems interesting and exciting based on the way it's portrayed on TV or in the movies. Do some research on what that career is like in real life. You can do this by arranging an interview with someone who actually works in the field and by consulting the Internet or traditional library resources. In an essay or presentation, explain how your perception of the career changed as a result of your research. Document your sources in an annotated bibliography.

CAREER LAB PREVIEW

What Type of Career Will Fulfill Your Needs and Interests?

As part of this unit, you will investigate three careers that correspond with your interests and abilities. You'll conduct research on these careers using a variety of resources. After contemplating the information you uncover, you'll decide which career alternative is most appropriate for you. Be prepared to present a career profile on your desired career, along with a two-page essay explaining why this career is a good choice for you.

Chapter 1

You and the World of Work

Section 1.1
Exploring the World of Work

Section 1.2
The Changing Workplace

CHAPTER OBJECTIVES

After completing this chapter, you will be able to

● Explain how a job differs from a career.

● Understand how your career plans will be shaped by your skills and abilities, as well as the job outlook.

● Analyze how the workplace is affected by forces such as changing technology and the global economy.

JOURNAL

Personal Career Plan

Take a look into your future—
it's the day of your retirement
party. As you look back on
your career, what are you
most proud of? What will you
say to the people who have
gathered to celebrate with
you? What do you hope to
hear them say about you and
your work? Write your
answers in a journal entry.

Personal Career Project

Contact a retired person in
your community whose career
spanned 20 years or more.
Interview the person, asking
some of the same questions
that you addressed in your
journal entry. Compare your
subject's answers with your
journal entry.

Exploring the World of Work

WHAT YOU'LL LEARN

- How to distinguish between a job and a career.
- How your job can affect your lifestyle.
- Why people work.

WHY IT'S IMPORTANT

Determining how jobs affect your lifestyle will help you understand the importance of making sound career choices.

KEY TERMS

- **job**
- **career**
- **lifestyle**

Do you wonder what you're going to do after high school? Maybe it's time to think about your options and to prepare for them. Will you go to trade school or college? Will you go to work? What kind of work will you do?

You probably won't be surprised to learn that most people prefer to do work that uses their interests and talents. After all, work takes up a lot of time. With a full-time job, you could spend more than 2,000 hours a year at work. (That's more time than you spend doing anything else except sleeping!)

What kind of job would be right for you? Think about what skills you have and what interests you. To get an idea of what work you'd like to do, compile a list of transferable skills that can be applied in many contexts and a list of your interests.

- Write down your *skills*—the things you feel you're good at—such as being organized, solving math problems, or getting along with people.

- Then write down your *interests*, or favorite activities. You may like to listen to music, dance, play basketball, or work with computers.

When you have finished your lists, make a corresponding list of possible career options that match your skills, interests, and aptitudes, then place your lists in your personal career portfolio.

What Is Work?

Is work something people do simply to earn money, or is it something much more? Here's what Robert Lombardi, a graphic production artist, has to say about the meaning of work.

"I've found that work can be an enjoyable experience, not just the thing you do to make money. If you have a job you like, work means much more than just paying your bills. It means using your talents, being with people who have similar interests, making a contribution, and getting a real sense of satisfaction from doing a good job."

Robert uses desktop publishing software to arrange the words and artwork in magazines, books, and print advertisements. He finds his work satisfying because it suits his interests, skills, and talents.

Jobs and Careers

Is a job the same thing as a career? What's the difference between the two?

A **job** is work that people do for pay. The work usually consists of certain tasks. Often a job is a position with a company. For example, Robert has had jobs with advertising agencies and publishing companies. Sometimes jobs lead to careers.

A **career** is a series of related jobs built on a foundation of interest, knowledge, training, and experience. Robert developed his career by working at different graphic production jobs. As he gained experience, he found more challenging—and better-paying—work with each new job.

Like Robert, many people work at several jobs during their careers. According to current estimates by the U.S. Bureau of Labor, the average American will have

Rewarding Work Robert wanted to be a graphic production artist because he had a talent for visual arts. *Why is following your skills and interests so important in choosing a career?*

more than eight different jobs by the age of 32. Experience working at different jobs can help you find the employment opportunities that best suit your needs.

Impact on Lifestyle

Your **lifestyle** is the way you use your time, energy, and resources. Many people use much of their time and energy and many of their resources at work. The work you do affects other parts of your life. It can determine how much time you have to spend with friends and family and how much money and energy you have to pursue your favorite activities. Your lifestyle may vary according to changes in your career.

To see how work affects lifestyle, read about Amelia. Amelia Sanchez is studying for her associate degree in early childhood education. Her goal is to work at a day care center, but for now she baby-sits for two

ETHICS *in Action*

Summer Job Your guidance counselor announces a summer job opening at the local newspaper. You want to be a journalist, so the job would be good experience. Your friend is interested in the job because it pays more than her job at a retail shop. You both get good grades and take honors classes, so there is a good chance either of you could get the job.

THINK ABOUT IT
Will you ask your friend not to apply for the position at the newspaper? Why or why not?

elementary school children in the afternoons and on weekends.

Amelia's baby-sitting schedule frees her to take classes in the morning. She also is gaining experience working with children. Between going to school and working, though, she doesn't have much free time to spend with her friends and family. In

Job Demands Amelia uses her part-time job to gain work experience and to earn money to pay for schooling. *How can your job affect your lifestyle?*

addition, she spends most of her income and energy on getting her training. However, Amelia knows that she's willing to make temporary sacrifices to get the career she wants.

What kind of lifestyle do *you* want in the future? Make a list of how you'd like to spend your time, resources, and energy. Look back at the lists you made earlier about your skills and interests. These lists can help you find out the kind of work you'd like to do and the kind of lifestyle you'd like to have.

Why People Work

Why do people work? Why do your family members work? Why do your friends work? If you have an after-school job, why do *you* work?

That's a no-brainer, you say—to make money! That's the most basic reason, of course, but can you think of other reasons for having a job? Here's a short list of why people work:

- People work to earn money to pay for housing, transportation, food, clothes and other expenses, such as health care, insurance, education, taxes, and recreation. Look at ***Figure 1.1*** below to see how consumers spend their money.

- People also work because they want to be with other people. They may enjoy being in an environment with people who have similar interests.

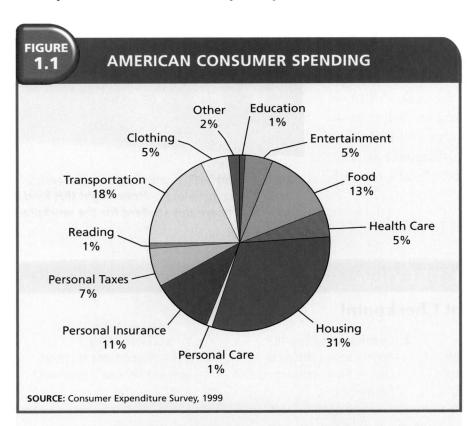

FIGURE 1.1 **AMERICAN CONSUMER SPENDING**

Other 2%
Education 1%
Clothing 5%
Entertainment 5%
Transportation 18%
Food 13%
Reading 1%
Health Care 5%
Personal Taxes 7%
Personal Insurance 11%
Personal Care 1%
Housing 31%

SOURCE: Consumer Expenditure Survey, 1999

▲ **Spending Habits** American consumers spend more than half their money in three areas. *What are the areas? Why might this fact serve as an eye-opener to people just starting out on their own?*

- Self-fulfillment is another reason why people work. They feel good about themselves when they do a job well. Working at a job that suits them gives them a feeling of accomplishment.

If people do their work well, others repect them. When this happens they feel proud and respect themselves.

People can find satisfaction in their jobs for many reasons. Herminio Fernandez, a video-game programmer, loves to create video games. He gets a real sense of satisfaction when he writes programs that help artists assemble the pictures for video games.

What task or job have you done recently that gave you a feeling of accomplishment? Perhaps it was illustrating a poster for a school fund-raising project or coaching basketball to younger children in your neighborhood. Write a brief entry in your journal describing the task and how you felt after completing it. What else could you do that might give you that feeling again? Finding self-fulfillment has lasting effects. You feel good about yourself and about what you do.

Reaching Out Helping others gives some people a sense of accomplishment. *How might this kind of activity prepare this student for the workplace?*

SECTION 1.1 REVIEW

✓ Key Concept Checkpoint

Comprehension

1. Give an example of one job that a high school graduate with each of the following skills or interests might do: math, music, computers.

2. Describe a situation that might cause a person to change his or her main reason for working.

Critical Thinking

3. Why is it a bad idea to choose a job just because it pays well?

CAREER FOCUS

CAREER FACTS

Education or Training A degree from a vocational program or a two- or four-year college is encouraged. Apprenticeship programs offered by professional culinary institutes, industry associations, and trade unions are also helpful.

Aptitudes, Abilities, and Skills
The ability to work as part of a team, good management skills, a keen sense of taste and smell, strong organizational skills, and the ability to create a successful menu are important.

Career Outlook Demand is expected to grow through 2008, especially for those with bachelor's or associate degrees in restaurant and institutional food service management.

Career Path Chefs may work as caterers or restaurant owners, teach in culinary programs, or go on to management positions. There are many opportunities for advancement to executive chef.

What is your key to success?

"The key to my success is surrounding myself with dedicated people who share my focus on establishing a good and consistent restaurant."

What does your job entail?

"For my first five years, I cooked in the kitchen every day. Now instead of cooking, I rely on my staff to re-create the menu that I design. I focus more on promoting the restaurant to attract more business. I also attend classes, trade shows, conferences, and conventions."

What do you like most about your work?

"I enjoy the variety of my job. After working for 18 years as an X-ray technician, I decided to pursue my dream of working in the restaurant business. I began taking cooking lessons and started my own catering company. I achieved success in catering and went on to the New York Cooking School. Over the years, I worked in France, Hawaii, and Guam. In 1993, I became owner of one of the restaurants that I work in today. What I like most about my work is the satisfaction that I can bring to the guests who dine at my restaurant."

What training do you recommend for students?

"Students should take classes in the culinary arts, exploring programs at local community colleges or culinary institutes. I would also encourage students to take advantage of travel opportunities, which allow them to experience the foods and cultures of other countries."

Critical Thinking What are some informal things that students interested in the culinary arts can do to develop their skills?

The Changing Workplace

- How the global economy affects the U.S. job market.
- How technology influences the workplace.
- Why you should consider the job outlook when making career plans.

Familiarity with the workings of the economy and workplace will improve your job prospects.

- economy
- global economy
- job market
- team
- outsourcing
- telecommute

Your place in the world of work will influence every aspect of your life. This is why choosing the kind of work you will do is one of the most important decisions you will ever make. So far, you've been thinking about the kind of work that might fit your interests and skills. You've also been thinking about the kind of lifestyle you'd like to have and how your work would affect it. What else might be important to consider when thinking about the work you'd like to do?

Well, there's the workplace itself. Today, however, the workplace is constantly changing. Changes in the world affect what work is available for people to do and the way in which they do it. Knowing about these changes can help you make sound decisions about your job, your career, and your future. How can you keep up with all these changes?

You can follow trends in the world of work the same way you keep up with what's happening in music, fashion, sports, and entertainment. Which are the up-and-coming industries and occupations? Which ones are on the way out? To find out, read newspapers and magazines and watch the news on television. Talk to people who work in the field that you're interested in and ask them questions about the changes and opportunities in their workplace.

The Global Economy and the Job Market

Look at a few of the things you own—a pair of pants, a book, a CD, a bicycle—and check their labels or packaging. Where were the objects made? At least some of your possessions were probably made in other countries. Because of what you buy, you are part of the global economy. The term **economy** refers to the ways in which a group produces, distributes, and consumes its goods and services. *Goods* are the items that people buy. *Services* are activities done for others for a fee. The term **global economy** refers to the ways in which the world's economies are linked.

The global economy has a direct impact on the **job market**, or the demand for particular jobs, in each country. How does the global economy affect the job market in the United States—the job market you will probably be entering?

Critics of the global economy argue that trade with foreign countries can lead to American workers losing their jobs to overseas workers. For instance, some American computer software companies hire software programmers in Asia—where labor costs are cheaper.

On the other hand, the global economy may be good for the United States for a variety of reasons. Many American businesses export goods (sell goods to other countries), and these exports create jobs. Furthermore, some experts feel that the increased use of overseas workers may help the U.S. economy by holding down costs. U.S.-based offices of foreign firms have also provided jobs for many Americans.

Keeping abreast of the global economy can help you learn more about the worldwide job market. For example, which jobs

Economic Trends As a part of the global economy, consumers can buy products from around the world. *What are other advantages of the global economy?*

will be sent abroad? Which jobs will be created because of the changing economy? Which jobs will involve trade with foreign countries? Which jobs will be available to American workers in foreign countries?

Impact on Today's Workers

The global economy creates stiff competition for businesses. Just as you want to do well in your career, an employer wants his or her business to do well. As a result,

Working Together Many skills that are useful in the workplace can also help you enjoy your life outside of work. *Why is listening an important aspect of communicating?*

the employer will need employees who can do a variety of tasks and who possess a variety of skills.

How can you meet the demands put on workers in a global economy? You can develop transferable skills—many of which you are already learning—and apply them in your job. Certain fundamental skills, necessary for employment in all industries, will help you achieve success on the job:

- *basic skills*, such as reading, writing, mathematics, listening, and speaking;

- *thinking skills*, such as creative thinking, decision making, problem solving, seeing things in the mind's eye (picturing things in your mind), knowing how to learn, and reasoning; and

- *personal qualities*, such as responsibility, self-esteem, sociability, self-management, integrity, and honesty.

Creative
BUSINESS PRACTICES

PepsiCo
CEO Mentors Top Executives

PepsiCo is the corporation that owns top brand products such as Pepsi-Cola and Tropicana beverages, Frito-Lay snacks, and the fast-food restaurants Pizza Hut, Taco Bell, and Kentucky Fried Chicken. PepsiCo's CEO, Roger Enrico, is committed to personally mentoring the company's top managers.

PepsiCo believes that Enrico's personal mentoring—which is a rarity in such a large corporation—is important to help shape effective leaders for the future. Nearly 130 of PepsiCo's executives have been through Enrico's leadership workshops.

Teaching is a passion for Enrico, who hosts the week-long, nine-person workshops, usually at one of his own ranches or retreats. In addition to group discussions, managers each bring an important proposal or issue to the workshop, and they receive one-on-one time with Enrico to go over strategies. Enrico believes that it is important to be involved with the direction of new initiatives in the beginning stages. Outside of the workshops, managers are encouraged to call him for advice.

It's not all work at PepsiCo's leadership workshops, however. Enrico knows the importance of relaxation. While participating in activities such as horseback riding and fishing, Enrico and the managers get to know each other as people, not just as PepsiCo executives.

Critical Thinking
How do you think PepsiCo benefits by having its executives trained by the CEO?

Link and Learn
To read more about PepsiCo and its many divisions, visit the company's Web site via the link on the *Succeeding in the World of Work* Web site at **www.careers.glencoe.com**.

Changing Technology

Not long ago, cell phones, DVDs, and CD-ROMs did not exist, and very few people had access to the Internet. Laptops and desktop computers were just coming into common use in businesses and households. Such advances in technology are constantly—and rapidly—changing how people work. As *Figure 1.2* shows, people working in very different fields use a wide range of technology to help them do their work more quickly and efficiently.

Today's Workplace

Modern technology affects not only what work you do but how and where you do it. Trends that you'll probably encounter in the workplace include the use of teams, outsourcing, and telecommuting.

A **team** is an organized group that sets goals, makes decisions, and implements actions within a company. As companies increase their use of technology, some new jobs are created (such as technical jobs), and others are eliminated. Many companies have eliminated the position of middle manager—a job that involves directing other workers. As a result, workers are collaborating on projects rather than just doing what a manager tells them to do.

Another practice is **outsourcing**. In this practice, businesses hire other companies or individuals to produce their services or goods. For example, airline companies often contract with individuals or other companies to provide baggage handling and meals for their customers.

Roughly 29.7 million workers do not work exclusively at a company's work site. Instead they **telecommute**, work from home, using a computer, fax (facsimile), and telephone to perform their jobs.

FIGURE 1.2 Technology in the Workplace
Modern technology enables a variety of workers to do their jobs quickly and efficiently.

A **Retail Workers** Sales workers in stores wave wands over goods so that lasers can read prices. The sale is instantly fed into a computerized database that tracks the store's inventory. Sales workers can help customers complete their shopping more quickly. Stores keep better track of how each item sells and when they need to reorder.

B **Industry Workers** Repair workers out on calls communicate with the home office via cellular phones. In this way they can quickly learn of homes or offices they must visit to make repairs. The company saves time, and customers get faster service.

C **Office, Manufacturing, and Farm Workers** Today millions of workers in a wide range of industries use computers to perform daily activities. Office workers use computers to prepare letters, design spreadsheets, and create databases. Manufacturing workers use computers to automate production and to test products. Farmworkers use computers to test soil and to keep track of livestock and other commodities.

Impact on Today's Workers

The workplace may be changing, but one thing is certain. You'll be involved with technology in some form—especially computers—in whatever career you choose. Does that mean you need to know what goes on inside a computer? No, says one expert: "After all, you don't have to know how to design a car to drive one." You will need to know how to *use* one, though.

You'll also probably continue learning for as long as you work—not just about new technologies but also about new ways of working. While advanced technology offers you many different opportunities for work, it also means you'll need to keep up with the changes.

The Job Outlook

What job market can you expect when you graduate from high school? The good news is that total employment is projected to increase by 14 percent by the year 2008. However, these jobs will not be evenly distributed across industries. Most of the work will be in the service-producing industries. *Service-producing industries*

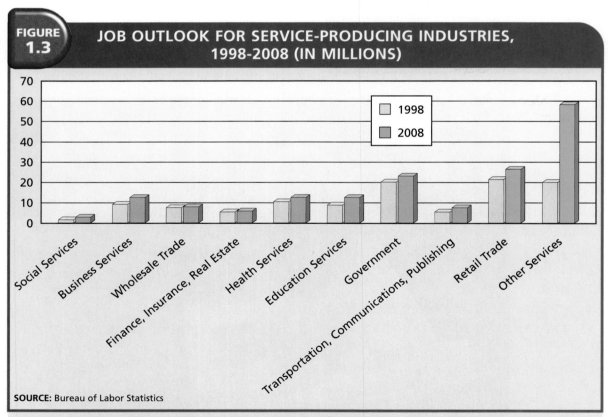

FIGURE 1.3

JOB OUTLOOK FOR SERVICE-PRODUCING INDUSTRIES, 1998-2008 (IN MILLIONS)

Legend: 1998, 2008

Categories: Social Services, Business Services, Wholesale Trade, Finance, Insurance, Real Estate, Health Services, Education Services, Government, Transportation, Communications, Publishing, Retail Trade, Other Services

SOURCE: Bureau of Labor Statistics

▲ **Hot Jobs** Tremendous growth is predicted in the service sector in upcoming years. *Why do you think the service sector—health, business, education, social services—is creating so many jobs?*

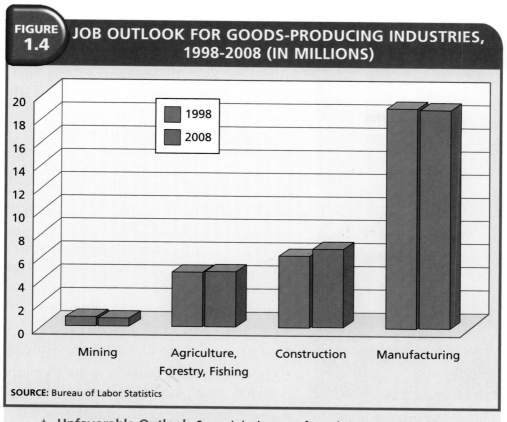

FIGURE 1.4 JOB OUTLOOK FOR GOODS-PRODUCING INDUSTRIES, 1998-2008 (IN MILLIONS)

Legend: 1998, 2008

Categories: Mining, Agriculture, Forestry, Fishing, Construction, Manufacturing

SOURCE: Bureau of Labor Statistics

▲ **Unfavorable Outlook** Some jobs in manufacturing are expected to decline. *Why do you think this is so?*

provide services for a fee. These include medical care, travel accommodations, and education. Fewer jobs are expected in the *goods-producing industries*, which provide goods such as stereo systems, cars, and buildings.

Figure 1.3 and **Figure 1.4** identify these different industries and show expectations for their growth or decline. Read the graphs to find out which industries are growing and which are declining. How does this information affect your ideas about a career? Think about your skills and interests. Which industries do you think would be appropriate for you?

inter**NET**
CONNECTION

Job Outlook
You are thinking of pursuing several different careers but want to know the future demand for these jobs.

Connect
• Pick three jobs that interest you and search the Web site of the United States Bureau of Labor Statistics for information on them.
• Research the career outlook for these jobs in the next five years.
• Write a one-paragraph summary of each job outlook, and explain whether you think it would be worthwhile to pursue these careers.

Personal Qualities A physical therapy aide helps people recover their strength after orthopedic surgery. *Why does a physical therapy aide need to have a sense of responsibility and self-esteem?*

Impact on Today's Workers

You don't have to choose a career just because it seems to offer the best job prospects. Even though you're learning to follow trends in the job market, you still want to find work that matches your interests, skills, personality, and abilities. Whatever occupation you choose, though, you *will* need certain basic skills, thinking skills, and personal qualities. In addition, you'll probably need specific task-related skills.

For example, suppose you decide to become a physical therapy aide. What interests, skills, and personal qualities would you need for this occupation? Here are a few:

- a desire to help and motivate people,
- good listening skills in order to learn what your patients' needs are,
- good speaking skills in order to explain the exercises to your patients, and
- the ability to work under the supervision of a physical therapist.

SECTION 1.2 REVIEW

✔ Key Concept Checkpoint

Comprehension

1. How does the global economy affect the job market?
2. Choose a career you're interested in, and describe how technology may affect it.

3. Which do you consider more important in choosing a career—following your own interests or following the job outlook? Why?

Critical Thinking

4. Why do some employers consider personal qualities more important than experience or special skills?

KEY TERMS
job (p. 5)
career (p. 5)
lifestyle (p. 6)

SECTION 1.1

- Consider your interests and skills when planning the kind of work you'd like to do. (p. 4)

- A job is work that people do for pay. The work usually consists of certain tasks. A career is a series of related jobs built on a person's interests, knowledge, training, and experience. (p. 5)

- Your lifestyle is the way you use your time, energy, and resources. (pp. 6–7)

- Three important reasons why people work are (1) to earn money to pay expenses, (2) to fulfill their need to be with other people, and (3) to receive satisfaction from doing a job well. (pp. 7–8)

SECTION 1.2

KEY TERMS
economy (p. 11)
global economy (p. 11)
job market (p. 11)
team (p. 14)
outsourcing (p. 14)
telecommute (p. 14)

- The global economy has a direct impact on the job market. You need basic skills, thinking skills, and personal qualities to meet the demands of the job market. (pp. 11–13)

- Rapidly advancing technology has changed the workplace. Trends in the workplace include the use of teams, outsourcing, and telecommuting. (pp. 14–16)

- Most of the new jobs predicted for 1998 through 2008 will fall in the service-producing sector. While you need to be aware of trends, seeking job satisfaction is also very important. (pp. 16–18)

Reviewing Key Terms

1. Write a short paragraph about the world of work, using the terms below.
   - job
   - career
   - lifestyle
   - economy
   - global economy
   - job market
   - team
   - outsourcing
   - telecommute

Recalling Key Concepts

2. Work that you do for pay is ____.

   (a) a career (b) an industry (c) a job

3. American consumers spend the most money on ____.

   (a) food (b) housing (c) health care

4. Why do some people think the global economy is good for the United States?

   (a) Some jobs go to workers overseas.

   (b) Foreign products are of a higher quality.

   (c) The U.S. export business creates new jobs here at home.

5. Telecommuting means ____.

   (a) working at home, using a computer, fax, and telephone

   (b) transporting manufactured goods

   (c) communicating by television

6. By 2008, most new jobs will be in ____.

   (a) manufacturing (b) entertainment

   (c) services

Problem Solving

7. Why is it an advantage to have several jobs while you are building your career?

8. How does your job's income affect other aspects of your lifestyle?

9. Explain how the global economy makes businesses more competitive.

10. What is the danger of limiting your career opportunities to only those you have heard about or been trained for?

11. Why do people who telecommute need good organizational and management skills?

Work-Based Learning

Basic Skills Math

12. Your clothing store is open seven days a week from 9 A.M. to 9 P.M. You are the manager of three employees, each of whom wants to work at least 24 hours a week. Each employee can work the 9:00 A.M. to 3:00 P.M. shift or the 3:00 P.M. to 9:00 P.M. shift and at least one weekend day. No one can work both shifts on the same day. Make up a schedule that will meet these requirements.

Interpersonal Skills Teaching Others

13. Sherry works as an administrative assistant for a small law firm. Today she needs to explain to a new lawyer how to use the office's voice mail system. Prepare an outline of one good way for Sherry to teach the lawyer the system so that he fully understands it.

School-Based Learning

Language Arts Write a Report

14. Changes in the world affect what work is available for people to do and the way in which they do it. Knowing about these changes can help you make sound decisions about your job, your career, and your future. Write a report citing examples of change in our society. Explain how each change might affect the job market.

Math Calculate Prep-Time

15. In a restaurant, it takes three workers 20 minutes each to prepare the vegetables for the salad bar. If the salad bar is filled four times a night, on average, how much worker time is required to keep it filled?

Social Studies Research Job Outlook

16. Sarah is a computer troubleshooter for a U.S.-based computer manufacturer. She is interested in living and working in Japan. Research the current job outlook in Japan. Which industries and occupations are growing and which are declining?

Role Play

17. Career Counseling Visit

Situation You have been employed by the Department of Labor to help students understand the importance of transferable skills. For your job, you are required to visit high school classrooms across the country to deliver presentations and answer questions. You hope to encourage students to broaden their horizons by developing their transferable skills.

Activity Make a presentation about transferable skills within your career interest area. In your presentation describe different transferable skills, and present visual aids. Be prepared to answer questions that students pose.

Evaluation You will be evaluated on how well you meet the following performance indicators:

- Explain a variety of transferable skills
- Provide specific and comprehensive information about skills
- Handle a question and answer session

*inter*NET CONNECTION

18. Research Job Outlook
Select an industry that interests you. Locate the most recent Bureau of Labor Statistics report analyzing future employment trends. Find your industry in the report, and note how much jobs in the industry are expected to grow or decline in the future.

Connect Search employment and career Web sites for current job opportunities in an industry that interests you. Note entry-level positions that are available. Contact the companies hiring for these positions and inquire about average salary, work hours, and benefits.

Chapter 2

Getting to Know Yourself

CHAPTER OBJECTIVES

After completing this chapter, you will be able to

- Follow the seven steps in the decision-making process and explain how these steps are helpful in choosing a career.

- Identify your values, interests, aptitudes, personal preferences, and abilities and describe how they affect your career choices.

- Identify and match your personality and learning styles to career choices.

JOURNAL

Personal Career Plan

Think about all your activities during a typical week. Which activity do you find most satisfying? What makes that activity especially satisfying for you? What does this tell you about your values and interests? Record your ideas in your journal.

Personal Career Project

Interview a human resources professional to find out what methods companies use to match applicants to jobs. Ask for copies of any tests or surveys used by the company. Take the assessments on your own. Reflect on your results in your journal.

Decision Making

How do you make decisions? Do you flip a coin? Consult friends? Make lists of pros and cons? If you're the kind of person who waits for someone else to make decisions for you, you may not be very happy with the outcome.

Maybe you've been putting off deciding what to do after graduation. If so, keep the following fact in mind: Most people don't plan to fail; they just fail to plan. The truth is, half of all employed people simply fall into their jobs—out of laziness or luck or from being unaware of other options. If you'd rather have a say in your future, it's time to take control of your own life.

A Seven-Step Process

If you've ever made an important decision, you know that good decision making doesn't just happen. The longer a decision will affect your life, the more time you need to think about possible consequences. Decisions that will affect your life for many years should be made carefully and logically. One of the biggest decisions in your life—your career choice—will require serious planning. This will be easier if you follow a **decision-making process**—a logical series of steps to identify and evaluate possibilities and to arrive at a good choice.

Using the Decision-Making Process Some decisions are more important than others. *Why might these newlyweds take a long time to decide which house to buy?*

Breaking It Down

Like learning a new dance, following a decision-making process may feel awkward at first as you work through the basic steps. Once you have learned them, however, you can add variations of your own to adapt the process to different life situations. Here, then, are the seven basic steps in a typical decision-making process:

1. Define your needs or wants.
2. Analyze your resources.
3. Identify your choices.
4. Gather information.
5. Evaluate your choices.
6. Make a decision.
7. Plan how to reach your goal.

Now take a look at *Figure 2.1* on the next page to see how these seven steps can be applied to buying a car.

Careers in Baseball

Baseball is your favorite sport. Even though you don't expect to be a professional baseball player, you would like to work in some capacity for your favorite team.

Connect

• Visit the Web site of your favorite Major League Baseball team and search for career opportunities in marketing, public relations, management, scouting, or other areas.

• Write a description of the positions that interest you and explain how you think these jobs benefit the team.

FIGURE 2.1

HOW TO USE A SEVEN-STEP DECISION-MAKING PROCESS

Step 1: Define Your Needs or Wants	Chances are, you want a car that is not too expensive, and is in reasonably good condition.
Step 2: Analyze Your Resources	Your main resource in this case is money. How much do you have? How much do you need to buy the car?
Step 3: Identify Your Choices	Now it's time to think about where you will get the car. You might make a list of sources, including new-car dealers, used-car dealers, owner-advertised cars in the classified ads, and your second-cousin Ellen, who offered to sell you her 1985 station wagon for "next to nothing."
Step 4: Gather Information	Next, you must take time to evaluate each source on your list. Call each person or place, and make an appointment. Look at each available car, and ask questions. Take notes on such factors as cost, condition, insurance, warranty, and appearance. Take test drives. Draw sketches. At this point, you may eliminate some choices. For example, a new car may be too expensive.
Step 5: Evaluate Your Choices	Now is the time to review your notes. You might make a chart rating each car on the basis of four or five factors. In evaluating your choices, you will need to consider which factors are most important to you.
Step 6: Make a Decision	Working from your notes or chart, decide which car you want to buy.
Step 7: Plan How to Reach Your Goal	Focusing now on the car you have chosen, list the steps you need to take before you can actually drive the car home. These may include informing the dealer that you want the car, making a down payment, arranging a loan, and buying insurance.

▲ **Weighing Your Options** A seven-step decision-making process can help you make informed choices. *Why is it important to make conscious decisions?*

Job Satisfaction What you enjoy doing is an important personal resource that needs to be considered as you plan your career. *What do you think these carpenters enjoy about their work?*

Using the Decision-Making Process to Choose a Career

You can also use the seven-step process in choosing a career. However, since the stakes are much higher than they are in buying a car, the process will be more complex. As you proceed through this and the next three chapters, you will use the steps to create a written career plan.

Creative BUSINESS PRACTICES

Patagonia
Exploring Opportunities

Patagonia, Inc., designer and distributor of technical outdoor clothing and adventure sports gear, allows its employees to take up to two months of paid leave to work as interns with a nonprofit environmental group of their choice.

During internships, Patagonia employees receive their regular salary and benefits for up to 60 days while donating time and energy. Patagonia employees have worked all over the world for causes such as Save the Whales, the Chumbe Island Project, which encourages coral reef protection, and the Mist Preservation Society, which helps preserve the subtropical forests of New Zealand.

The Patagonia internship program is a winning situation for everyone involved.

Nonprofit groups benefit from the experience of talented volunteers, employees get time away from the office to make a difference in the world, and Patagonia gets to support worthy efforts.

Critical Thinking
If you had the opportunity to take part in Patagonia's internship program, which causes would interest you? Why?

Link and Learn
To read more about Patagonia's internship program, visit the company's Web site via the link on the *Succeeding in the World of Work* Web site at www.careers.glencoe.com.

Step 1. Define Your Needs

The path to a career starts with considering your hopes and dreams for the future. Where will you want to live? Do you want a job that will allow you to travel? Do you hope to marry and have children? How much money will you need to earn? How much of your time and energy will you devote to your job? Do you want to start your own business? Later in this chapter, you will explore such questions and generate information about your personal goals.

Step 2. Analyze Your Personal Resources

In choosing a career, your resources relate to who you are and what you have to offer. Such resources include your values, interests, aptitudes and abilities, and personality traits and styles of learning. By being aware of all that you are, you will be more likely to make a realistic career choice. In the next sections of this chapter, you will examine these various aspects of yourself.

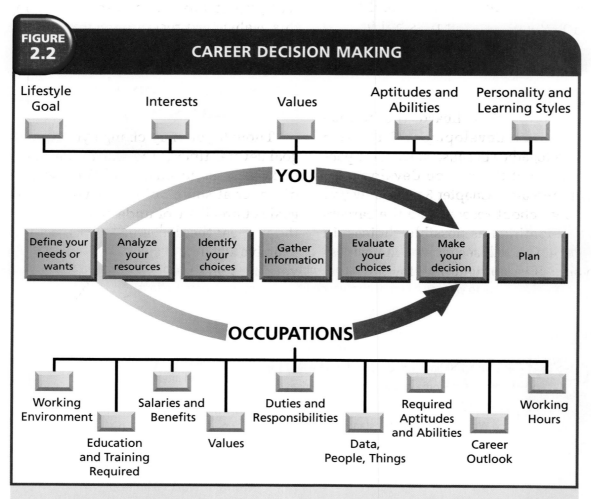

FIGURE 2.2

CAREER DECISION MAKING

| Lifestyle Goal | Interests | Values | Aptitudes and Abilities | Personality and Learning Styles |

YOU

| Define your needs or wants | Analyze your resources | Identify your choices | Gather information | Evaluate your choices | Make your decision | Plan |

OCCUPATIONS

Working Environment — Education and Training Required — Salaries and Benefits — Values — Duties and Responsibilities — Data, People, Things — Required Aptitudes and Abilities — Career Outlook — Working Hours

▲ **Career Course** Over the next few chapters, you will proceed through the seven-step decision-making process, to choose a career for yourself. This diagram previews your course. *What two general areas will you explore before you actually make a career decision and begin to plan for it?*

Step 3. Identify Your Career Choices

This step involves selecting several possible careers that may match your personal goals and resources. If you are like many teenagers, you may not be able to think of a career you would enjoy. You can jump-start your thinking by increasing your awareness of life's possibilities. Keep your eyes and ears open to discover "what's out there." Even if you decide not to follow certain paths, at least you will know your options. Chapters 3 and 4 will help you uncover career possibilities.

Step 4. Research Your Career Choices

Have you ever heard the phrase "research and development"? The two terms go together because successful people know that there is no development without research. Chapter 3 will show you how to go about researching the careers you've identified as possible choices. In Chapter 4, you will see if being in business for yourself is the right path for you.

Step 5. Evaluate Your Career Choices

By the time you reach this fifth step, you will have gathered much information both about yourself and about various career possibilities. Evaluating your career choices involves systematically looking at them to see whether they match your personal goals and resources. *Figure 2.2* shows how the decision-making process is central to career evaluation. If the process looks complicated, don't worry. Chapter 5 will suggest a helpful strategy for making this evaluation process manageable.

Steps 6 and 7. Make Your Decision and Plan How to Reach Your Goal

Though you may change your career goal several times, it is still important to make a decision and a plan. You may also discover at some point that your career goal is unrealistic or undesirable. You can then repeat the decision-making process to arrive at a new goal. Chapter 5 will help you focus on these last two steps.

SECTION 2.1 REVIEW

✔ Key Concept Checkpoint

Comprehension

1. Explain how you would use the decision-making process to decide what to buy if you had $1,000 to spend. In your report, list and explain the seven steps in the decision-making process.

2. Explain the importance of having a strategy for choosing a career.

Critical Thinking

3. Why might you use the decision-making process many times before finding the right career?

Setting Lifestyle Goals

"Know thyself!" This inscription was carved at the Ancient Greek temple in Delphi, where people once traveled seeking advice about their futures. This bit of ancient wisdom is no less valid today. By getting to know yourself, you can plot your future better and choose a career you'll be interested in pursuing. A good place to begin this inward exploration is by considering lifestyle goals.

Lifestyle goals are the way you want to spend your time, energy, and resources in the future. Brainstorm about the lifestyle you'd like to have someday. Ask yourself a few questions.

- What do you want to accomplish in life?
- Do you want to raise a family?
- Where would you like to live—in a house or in an apartment? In a city or in the country?
- How would you like to spend your free time?
- Do you want a high income or just enough money to be comfortable?

Now imagine your life five or ten years from today. Write down or sketch the way you'd like to be living. What career would make this lifestyle possible? To begin to see whether this career would be a realistic choice for you, you'll need to take a closer look at yourself.

Individual Priorities Many people prefer a career that allows them to live near their family and friends. *What kind of career might give you a chance to work in your community?*

What Are Your Values?

Becoming aware of your values is an important way of getting to know yourself. Your **values** are the principles that you want to live by and the beliefs that really matter to you. You can determine your values by taking a close look at what you feel is truly important. For example, if you spend a good deal of time playing your guitar and listening to music, you probably would say that one of your values is artistic expression. If you prefer activities such as after-school tutoring or volunteering at a local hospital or nursing home, then you probably value helping others. Choosing a career that matches your values can help ensure that you enjoy your work. Careers that reflect your own set of values are also likely to bring you a great sense of self-fulfillment.

Besides principles and beliefs, your values may also include concrete things, such as money and fine clothing. As you think about a future career, you should consider how well it suits these values. For example, someone who values the finer things in life would most likely not be happy with a volunteering position.

Six General Values

Your values may change as you go through life. However, you will probably keep a core set of basic values that you learned early on from the people who were most important to you. Most people generally base their value system on that of their parents or the beliefs upheld by their religious faith. To help determine your current values, think about the following list of six general values. Which ones are very important to you, and which ones concern you less? Can you think of any careers especially suited to each of these values? Do any of these careers appeal to you?

1. *Responsibility.* Being responsible means fulfilling obligations in a dependable and trustworthy way. You may decide to take on responsibilities, such as caring for a sick friend. Other responsibilities may be automatically expected of you as part of your position in life, say, as a parent or team leader.

2. *Relationships.* If you value relationships, your family and friends are important to you. You may then make career decisions that will allow you to work with people you like or to live near your family.

3. *Compassion.* Compassion is caring deeply about people and their well-being. You may also feel compassion for other creatures, such as threatened animals. A compassionate person may choose a career that would better people's lives.

4. *Courage.* Courage is the ability to conquer fear or despair. You use courage, for example, when you speak up for an unpopular cause.

5. *Achievement.* Valuing achievement means you want to succeed in whatever you do, whether you are an artist, an auto mechanic, a wilderness guide, or a computer programmer.

6. *Recognition.* If you value recognition, you want other people to appreciate and respect your accomplishments. You want to be rewarded for your work in some noticeable way—with a good salary, through job promotions, or with approval and praise.

Now make your own list, ranking your values in order of importance. You may include some or all of the six general values, and you may add as many others as you wish. (Keep this list for later use.) Can you imagine a career that would satisfy your particular mix of values?

Putting Your Values into Practice

While many people may share the same value—such as believing it is important to help others—each person may put that value into practice in a different way. For example, Chris Watson is a paraprofessional at an elementary school in suburban Chicago. He helps disabled children get around by assisting them with their

Putting Values into Practice Chris works at a school for children with special needs. He makes friends with all the children at the school. This behavior helps students with disabilities become more a part of things. *How else could Chris help the children he works with?*

wheelchairs and walkers. Through his work, Chris helps one person at a time. Janet Gregory, in contrast, helps others indirectly by working as an administrator for a charity organization that shelters the homeless in the Bronx, New York. In trying to match a career to your own set of values, you will probably find that you have a range of choices. Narrowing your choices will mean looking even deeper into yourself.

What Are Your Interests?

In addition to recognizing your values, you need to pay attention to your interests when considering a career. Your interests are the things you enjoy doing. You may, for example, like singing in a choir or doing dissections in biology class. If you aren't sure what your interests are, one way to find out is to try activities you haven't done before. You might try, for example, taking karate classes or volunteering at a hospital or nursing home.

Favorite Activities

You probably already enjoy a variety of activities, so make a list of your ten favorite ones and try to rank them. Think of activities you like to do with friends or quietly by yourself—at school, at home, at work, or outdoors. (Keep this list for later use.)

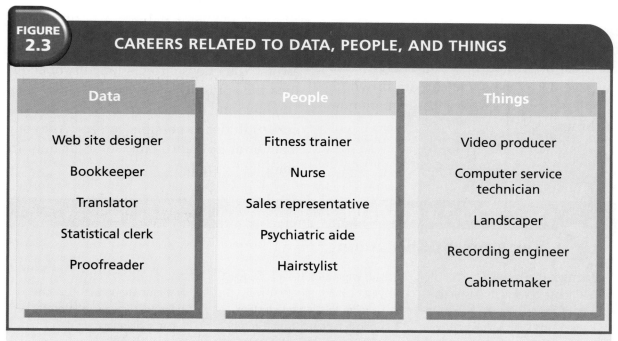

FIGURE 2.3

CAREERS RELATED TO DATA, PEOPLE, AND THINGS

Data	People	Things
Web site designer	Fitness trainer	Video producer
Bookkeeper	Nurse	Computer service technician
Translator	Sales representative	Landscaper
Statistical clerk	Psychiatric aide	Recording engineer
Proofreader	Hairstylist	Cabinetmaker

▲ **Occupation Options** This chart shows some careers in each of three categories. You can find other listings at your library in the U.S. Department of Labor's *Dictionary of Occupational Titles.* *Which career interests you the most? Why?*

Data, People, or Things?

Identifying your interests can help you recognize whether you would prefer to work with data, people, or things. These three categories described below can form the basis for describing different kinds of careers.

- The **data** category involves working with information, ideas, facts, symbols, figures, or statistics.
- The *people* category includes working with people *and* animals.
- The *things* category involves working with physical objects of any size, such as instruments, tools, machinery, equipment, raw materials, and vehicles.

Since any career you choose would probably involve an overlapping of these categories, think about which category you are *most* interested in. Look at *Figure 2.3* on page 33 to see some careers in which people work primarily with data, people, or things.

ETHICS *in Action*

Calling in Sick You recently started a new job at an office supply store, and you cannot take any vacation time until you have been working there for three months. Before you got the job, you and your friends had planned a trip to the beach for tomorrow. You really want to go on the trip, and you have five sick days that can be used immediately.

THINK ABOUT IT
Should you call in sick and go to the beach? Why or why not?

Interest and Aptitude Assessment

Another helpful way to identify and assess your interests is to take a formal career interest and aptitude assessment, which is like a test that has no right or wrong answers. You choose from a long list of activities and aptitudes to determine which ones you have and then you match your interests and aptitudes to possible careers. Ask your teacher or guidance counselor for help in completing such a survey.

SECTION 2.2 REVIEW

✓ Key Concept Checkpoint

Comprehension

1. Choose a value that is important to you. Discuss how you developed this value and how you might put it into practice in a career.

2. Choose one of your interests, and write down reasons why you enjoy this activity. Suggest what career might let you develop this interest further.

3. Choose a career from Figure 2.3. Describe how the categories data, people, and things might overlap for a person working in that career.

Critical Thinking

4. Is it more important to consider your values or interests when making career decisions? Explain.

CAREER FOCUS

CAREER FACTS

Education or Training A BSW, or bachelor's in social work, is required for most jobs. A master's degree (MSW) is recommended for advancement. Training can be obtained through volunteer work.

Aptitudes, Abilities, and Skills Social workers must be sensitive to social issues and people and have a strong desire to help people. They must also be patient, responsible, able to work independently and as part of a team, and emotionally mature. Strong conflict resolution skills as well as stress-management skills are helpful.

Career Outlook Employment in this field is expected to grow much faster than average through 2008.

Career Path A social worker can look to advance to positions of supervisor, program manager, or executive director of an agency, or go into private practice.

What does your job entail?

"As a case manager for Big Brothers, Big Sisters, I help develop the relationships between volunteers—Big Brothers and Sisters—and children—Little Brothers and Sisters. I interview and assess potential Little Brothers and Sisters and their guardians to see if they are a good fit for the program. From there, I conduct matching conferences to establish compatible pairs. I maintain ongoing contact with the volunteers and children. I am responsible for completing annual evaluations of each match."

What skills are most important to you?

"The skills that are most important to me are being an excellent listener and being able to interact well with others. My knowledge of Spanish is also an important asset."

What do you like most about your job?

"I like the opportunity to interact with people on a daily basis. It is also rewarding to see a lasting friendship flourish and to know that I had a part in developing it."

What advice would you offer to students interested in your field?

"I strongly recommend that students volunteer for different agencies. It is important to have a desire to work efficiently until your task is achieved, which requires you to develop a passion for what you do. Finally, in this type of work it is important to develop other interests and to "keep work at work." I strongly recommend that students create a positive outlet for relieving stress."

Critical Thinking Why is emotional maturity a necessity in this field?

Are Your Goals Realistic?

Now that you have identified some of your values and interests, what's next? You'll want to consider your skills and personality.

Aptitudes and Abilities

Aptitude and ability are the "before and after" of a skill. An **aptitude** is your potential for learning a certain skill. An **ability** is a skill you have already developed. Suppose you discover that you have the knack for training your new pet dog. If you continue to study and work with other dogs to become a professional trainer, then your aptitude will become your ability.

How do you discover your own aptitudes and abilities? First, you need to realize that there are many kinds of skills. Thinking creatively, making decisions, knowing how to learn, and seeing things in the mind's eye are skills important to your success. You should also think about your personality traits such as responsibility, friendliness, honesty, self-esteem, adaptability, and self-control. Another part of your personal set of skills is your physical attributes such as grace, speed, and strength. What other skills can you think of?

What Are *Your* Aptitudes and Abilities?

To get a clear picture of your aptitudes and abilities, make a list of all your skills that you can think of. Need help? Try these techniques:

- Make a chart with the headings Mental, Physical, and Social. List your aptitudes and abilities in each category.
- Meet with a friend, family member, or anyone else you trust. Talk about what you think your aptitudes and abilities are, and ask the other person to write them down. After you finish, discuss the list. Does this person agree with your evaluation? What ideas does he or she have about your aptitudes and abilities?

Matching Your Aptitudes and Abilities to Careers

Now review your list of aptitudes and abilities, and try to think of at least one career that requires each of your skills. For example, if one of your aptitudes is caring for children, a good match might be a career as a day care provider or teacher. Finding a realistic career match for your aptitudes and abilities will make your working life more enjoyable.

Once you have identified some of your aptitudes and abilities, you will probably feel that you are really getting to know yourself. Next, look at how your personality influences your career choice.

Your Personality and Learning Styles

All the special qualities that make you an individual form your personality. **Personality** is the combination of your attitudes, behaviors, and characteristics. To explore your personality, you need to examine your self-concept and styles of learning.

Self-Concept

The way you see yourself is your **self-concept**. When you look in the mirror, do you see someone who is confident, curious, dependable, funny, observant, sympathetic? You may have some or all of these traits, and more. Some of your personality traits may even seem to contradict one another. You may, for example, feel shy in new situations but outgoing in familiar surroundings. On some days you may think you're a fairly interesting person, and on other days, you may think you're not that interesting. Everyone has highs and lows. However, you probably do have a fairly consistent self-concept—a feeling that you know the kind of person you are.

Personality Types and Learning Styles

The different ways that people naturally think and learn are called **learning styles** (see *Figure 2.4* on page 38). When you are aware of your own learning styles, you are able to determine the best approach for you to learn something new. You also can judge what kind of field would be good for your particular personality type, because you'd probably do well in a career that used your strongest learning style.

Read the list of the eight styles of learning given in *Figure 2.4*. Which ones apply to you? Which one do you think is your main style of learning?

Being aware of all the aspects of yourself that make you who you are will give you a great advantage as you explore career choices. Look at *Figure 2.5* to see how you can identify your personal qualities on the path to a career. Then write a description of yourself in your journal, adding drawings if you wish. Include at least some of your values, interests, aptitudes and abilities, and personality traits and learning styles.

FIGURE 2.4

LEARNING STYLES

Type of Learner	Likes	Best Ways to Learn
Linguistic	Likes to read, write, and tell stories; good at memorizing names and dates.	Learns best by saying, hearing, and seeing words.
Logical/ Mathematical	Likes to do experiments, work with numbers, explore patterns and relationships; good at math, logic, and problem solving.	Learns best by making categories, classifying, and working with patterns.
Spatial	Likes to draw, build, design, and create things; good at imagining, doing puzzles and mazes, and reading maps and charts.	Learns best by using the mind's eye and working with colors and pictures.
Musical	Likes to sing, hum, play an instrument, and listen to music; good at remembering melodies, noticing pitches and rhythms, and keeping time.	Learns best through rhythm and melody.
Bodily/ Kinesthetic	Likes to touch and move around; good at hands-on activities and crafts.	Learns best by interacting with people and objects in a real space.
Interpersonal	Likes having lots of friends, talking to people, and joining groups; good at understanding people, leading, organizing, communicating, and mediating conflicts.	Learns best by sharing, comparing, and cooperating.
Intrapersonal	Likes to work alone and pursue interests at own pace; good at self awareness, focusing on personal feelings, and following instincts to learn what needs to be known.	Learns best through independent study.
Naturalist	Likes to spend time outdoors and work with plants, animals, and other parts of the natural environment; has keen sensory skills; good at identifying plants and animals and at hearing and seeing connections to nature.	Learns best by recognizing patterns, sorting, and classifying.

▲ **Learning Style Link** Although most people may have a preferred style of learning, they can usually shift between styles to acquire new skills and knowledge. *Can you think of a career that would be especially suited to each type of learner?*

FIGURE 2.5 **The Path to a Career** Knowing your values and interests, aptitudes and abilities, and personality and favorite learning styles will help you choose a career.

A **Values and Interests** Think about what you value and enjoy. Do you like to help people or animals? Are you a wiz with numbers or at fixing things? What do you like to do or read about during your leisure time?

B **Aptitudes and Abilities** Think about the skills that seem to come naturally to you. Do you have a knack for music? For sports? For leadership?

C **Personality and Learning Styles** Consider where you feel most comfortable and what brings out the best in you. Would you like to work outdoors in nature? In high-tech lab? On a busy stock exchange floor?

Determining Your Personality Type

Psychologists, counselors, and human resources professionals use many tests to determine an individual's personality type. One of the most accurate and well-known tests is the Meyers-Briggs Type Indicator (MBTI), which uses a series of yes-or-no questions to classify individuals as having one of 16 different personality types. Each personality type has its own specific characteristics, including strengths and weaknesses.

Knowing about your personality type can help you understand your natural abilities and which careers would suit you best. For example, according to the MBTI, people with the ISFJ personality type make excellent museum curators, librarians, and nurses.

Personality tests can also help you understand how you behave in social situations. People with the ENFJ personality type are born leaders who tend to provide for the welfare and happiness of those in their care.

SECTION 2.3 REVIEW

 Key Concept Checkpoint

Comprehension
1. Name something you feel you have an aptitude for. Write a one-page plan for developing it into an ability.

2. Choose a learning style and name a career that you think would match it. Explain why that career matches the learning style.

Critical Thinking
3. What are some careers that require special aptitudes or abilities?

SECTION 2.1

- Careful planning for your future career will allow you to be in control of one of the biggest decisions in your life. (p. 24)

- The longer a decision will affect your life, the more time you need to think about the consequences beforehand. (p. 24)

KEY TERM
decision-making process
  (p. 24)

SECTION 2.2

- When beginning to think about a career, consider your lifestyle goals. Imagine how you would like to spend your time, energy, and resources in the future. (p. 30)

- Consider your values, or the principles that you want to live by, when you are planning for a career. General values include responsibility, relationships, compassion, courage, achievement, and recognition. (pp. 31–32)

- Your interests are your favorite activities. You probably want to plan for a career that would involve your interests. You need to determine whether you prefer working with data, people, or things (pp. 33–34)

KEY TERMS
lifestyle goals (p. 30)
values (p. 31)
data (p. 34)

SECTION 2.3

- An aptitude is your potential for learning a certain skill. An ability is a skill you have already developed. You want to discover your aptitudes and abilities because you will want to use them in the career of your choice. (pp. 36–37)

- Your personality and main learning style can influence the kind of career that would be right for you. Personality includes your attitudes, behaviors, and characteristics. There are eight learning styles, which relate to how you think and learn. (pp. 37–40)

KEY TERMS
aptitude (p. 36)
ability (p. 36)
personality (p. 37)
self-concept (p. 37)
learning styles (p. 37)

Reviewing Key Terms

1. On a separate sheet of paper, write a yearbook profile of yourself using the following terms as headings.
   - lifestyle goals
   - values
   - data
   - learning styles
   - aptitudes
   - abilities
   - self-concept
   - personality

Recalling Key Concepts

On a separate sheet of paper, tell whether each statement is true or false. Rewrite any false statements to make them true.

2. The first step in the seven-step decision-making process is to gather information.

3. In choosing a career, your resources pertain to who you are and what you have to offer.

4. People who share the same values always practice them in the same way.

5. Your interests are the things you like to do.

6. Working with data means you are working with things.

7. Aptitudes are your developed skills.

8. Learning styles are the different ways that people think and learn.

Problem Solving

9. What role should your instincts play in the decision-making process when considering possible careers?

10. What consequences might result from settling on a career that conflicts with your personal values?

11. Classify the following skills according to data, people, or things and explain your reasoning: supervising, repairing, communicating, designing, organizing, operating.

12. Volunteer to help a friend discover his or her aptitudes and abilities. What questions would you ask to encourage your friend to become better aware of his or her personal skills?

13. Think of three people you know well, and decide which learning styles fit them. Explain your choices.

Work-Based Learning

Basic Skills Speaking

14. Imagine that you have been offered a promotion. Prepare an oral report describing the specific factors considered in the process of making your decision whether to accept the promotion. Practice your oral report at home before speaking to the class.

Information Organizing and Maintaining Information

15. Create a chart to help you keep track of what you have learned about yourself. Use these column headings: Lifestyle Goals, Values, Interests, Aptitudes, Abilities, and Learning Styles. Fill in the chart and add to it as the year goes on.

School-Based Learning

Social Studies Research Values

16. Research another culture's system of values using traditional library resources and the Internet. If possible, interview someone who grew up in a different culture. Name and describe three values. How do these values affect the world of work in that culture? Share your findings in a report to the class.

Math Conduct a Survey

17. Conduct a study on the learning styles in your class. Ask each student to identify his or her main learning style. Make a bar graph showing the number of students for each learning style. Write up a brief report of your class's learning styles. Is there one dominant style? Are all the learning styles represented?

Art Depict Your Interests

18. Draw a picture that reflects one (or some) of your values or interests. Use a pencil, markers, watercolors, or collage techniques. Be prepared to explain your artwork.

Role Play

19. Using Skills and Abilities at Work

Situation Your employer, Roger, feels that a group of new hires lacks basic skills and abilities. As part of a new training program, Roger has asked you and a coworker to perform three brief skits for the new employees. The skits should show work-related scenarios in which essential skills such as decision making, adaptability, friendliness, self-control, and responsibility are modeled.

Activity Create three brief skits that show how skills and abilities can be used in everyday work experiences. Perform your skits for the class. Be sure to provide brief introductory and closing statements to explain your skits.

Evaluation You will be evaluated on how well you meet the following performance indicators:

- Demonstrate preparation and creativity in enacting skits
- Accurately convey skills and abilities
- Provide meaningful background and closing comments

*inter*NET CONNECTION

20. A Perfect Match Create a list of at least ten career opportunities that match your interests and aptitudes.

Connect Search career and employment Web sites to gather information about five of the jobs that you listed. Decide which positions you are interested in investigating further.

Choosing a Career: What Type of Career Will Fulfill Your Needs and Interests?

✓ Overview

You know that choosing a career is a very important decision. However, you still aren't sure what you want to do with the rest of your life. You have decided to use the decision-making process described in Chapter 2 to help you make some preliminary career choices. Based on your personal needs, values, and interests, you've identified three careers that appeal to you. Now you'll perform the research and contemplation necessary to make some solid decisions about your future.

✓ Assignment

Research the three careers that seem compatible with your interests, aptitudes, values, and abilities. Access career information using a variety of resources, including the Internet, trade journals, and personal interviews. Then, write a career critique for each career and decide which career is the best option for you. Create a detailed career critique for that career and write a two-page essay explaining your choice. In your essay, state the steps you plan to take now to prepare for this career. Be sure to include a preliminary education and training plan to achieve your career goal.

✓ Tools/Resources

To complete this project, you must have access to the Internet as well as traditional library resources. You also must interview candidates in the careers that interest you, taking notes throughout the interviews. During interviews, you will need a mini-cassette recorder or a pencil and notepad. You will also need a word processing program to prepare your career profile and essay.

✓ Procedures

Keeping in mind the suggestions offered in Chapters 1 and 2, identify three careers that interest you and follow the steps listed below:

- Perform research using a variety of resources and experiences.
- Take notes on your three career choices, organizing your notes according to the suggestions offered in the Helpful Hints section of this lab.

- When you've accumulated enough research, write your career critiques and decide which career suits you best.
- If your research indicates that your career choices are completely unsuitable choose more careers to research until you find one that is compatible with your interests, aptitudes, values, and abilities.
- Using a clear, coherent format, create a comprehensive career critique of the career you've selected.
- Write a two-page essay explaining why this career is a good choice for you and the steps you would need to take if you decide to pursue this career.

✓ Report

Your final products for this lab should include a typed career critique and a two-page essay explaining why the career you've profiled is a promising option for you.

✓ Presentation and Evaluation

Your career critique will be evaluated based on

- Organization of research
- Comprehensiveness, relevance, and currentness of data
- Evidence of thorough research
- Neatness and presentation

Your two-page essay will be evaluated based on

- Content and thoughtfulness of essay
- Identification of a preliminary education and training plan to achieve the career goal
- Neatness and presentation

✓ Personal Career Portfolio

Print out a copy of your completed report to include in your personal career portfolio.

HELPFUL HINTS

Creating a Career Critique

To create an accurate and complete career critique, you'll need to perform thorough research about the careers you've identified. When creating your profile, include the following information about your career:

- advantages
- disadvantages
- job outlook
- education requirements
- training requirements
- salary
- benefits
- work schedule
- work conditions
- opportunities for advancement
- educational requirements
- personal qualities needed

Exploring Careers

Portfolio Project

Career Timeline Select a career that you are interested in learning more about. Research the career, looking for details about specific requirements in terms of education, training, and work experience. Establish short-term and long-term goals that will help you launch a career in this field. Then think about opportunities for promotion and advancement within this field and set additional goals. Design a timeline on which you plot and label the steps and goals that will help you reach your ultimate career goal.

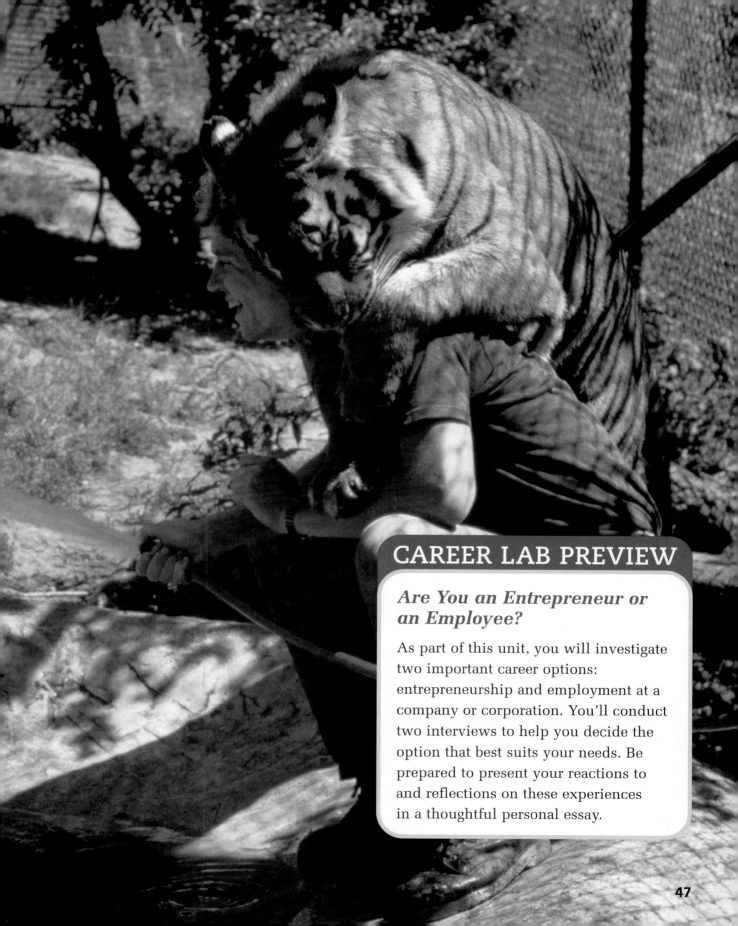

CAREER LAB PREVIEW

Are You an Entrepreneur or an Employee?

As part of this unit, you will investigate two important career options: entrepreneurship and employment at a company or corporation. You'll conduct two interviews to help you decide the option that best suits your needs. Be prepared to present your reactions to and reflections on these experiences in a thoughtful personal essay.

Chapter 3

Researching Careers

Section 3.1
Exploring Careers

Section 3.2
What to Research

CHAPTER OBJECTIVES

After completing this chapter, you will be able to

- Research careers using traditional resources, the Internet, and informal strategies.

- Explain how part-time work can help you gain insight in making future career plans.

- Formulate key questions to ask in assessing a career opportunity.

- Understand the characteristics of a career profile.

JOURNAL

Personal Career Plan

You come into contact daily with people involved in many different careers—teachers, salespeople, police officers, and administrators, to name just a few. In your journal, write a list of the careers represented by the people that you meet or observe in a single day.

Personal Career Project

Review your list, and identify the careers that interest you. Find five employers in your area who hire workers in one of these career fields. Contact three of them to find out how you would go about getting a part-time job with them.

Exploring Careers

- Methods for researching careers formally and informally.
- How part-time work experience can help you explore career choices.

Exploring careers will help you find the employment options that best match your interests, values, and personal needs.

- **Internet job services**
- **exploratory interview**
- **cooperative program**
- **job shadowing**
- **internship**
- **service learning**

Now that you've thought about your own interests and abilities, it's time to learn more about the real world of work. The U.S. Office of Education lends a hand by dividing careers into 16 pathways. Look at *Figure 3.1.* Which cluster—or clusters—seems to fit the kind of person you are? Narrow your search by choosing a cluster. Then start exploring related careers that might be right for you.

Research—It's Right Before Your Very Eyes

You can discover what the world of work has to offer by simply keeping your eyes and ears open. Look around as you travel to school, as you play, eat, shop, or just hang out with friends. During the next week, list all the careers that you notice. You'll be amazed at how effective this kind of informal research can be.

Been There, Done That

Talk to people you know about their career experiences. Just ask a few basic questions.

- What was your favorite job?
- What was your least favorite job?
- What was your most unusual job?
- How do you like your current job?

Put your listening skills to work as you gather first-hand information.

FIGURE
3.1

THE U.S. DEPARTMENT OF EDUCATION CAREER CLUSTERS

Career Cluster	Job Examples
Agriculture and Natural Resources	Food Scientist, Environmental Engineer, Veterinarian, Biochemist
Architecture and Construction	Contractor, Architect, Plumber, Building Inspector
Arts, A/V Technology, and Communications	Actor, Novelist, Musician, Cartoonist
Business and Administration	Administrative Assistant, Bookkeeper, Accountant, Entrepreneur
Education and Training	Teacher, Guidance Counselor, Principal, Coach
Finance	Stock Broker, Banker, Tax Examiner, Insurance Agent
Government and Public Administration	City Manager, Mayor, Parks Director, Urban Planner
Health Science	Pediatrician, Nurse's Aide, Dentist, Chiropractor
Hospitality and Tourism	Chef, Hotel Manager, Cruise Director, Fitness Instructor
Human Services	Social Worker, Substance Abuse Specialist, Psychologist, Child Care Worker
Information Technology	Web Designer, Network Administrator, Software Engineer, Technical Writer
Law and Public Safety	Attorney, Paramedic, Paralegal, Firefighter
Manufacturing	Production Supervisor, Manufacturing Engineer, Welding Technician, Quality Technician
Retail/Wholesale Sales and Service	Sales Associate, Retail Buyer, Interior Designer, Customer Service Representative
Scientific Research and Engineering	Mathematician, Marine Biologist, Ocean Technician, Electric Engineer
Transportation, Distribution, and Logistics	Pilot, Airline Reservations Agent, Railroad Conductor, Truck Driver, Automotive Mechanic

▲ **Career Clusters** The U.S. Department of Education has grouped careers into 16 clusters based on similar job characteristics. *Which areas appeal to you? Why?*

What's Happening?

Have you ever seen a situation in a movie and thought, "Wow, that's the job I want"? Think about movies and TV shows that you've seen and magazines and newspapers that you've read. Are people doing things you'd like to do? If so, learn more about them. That's how Jen Kizer found her career. She never missed her favorite TV program—real-life rescues of people in danger. When she stopped to think about it, she realized that emergency rescue work was exactly what she wanted to do with her life.

Formal Research

Consider yourself a detective, hot on the trail of a satisfying career. While informal research gives you some clues, formal approaches yield even more.

Libraries—Check Them Out

Your first stop might be your school or public library. Many libraries have career information centers. You can search the catalog to find reference books, magazines, videotapes, and other sources of career information.

Books. Look for three useful books published by the U.S. Department of Labor.

- The *Dictionary of Occupational Titles* describes more than 20,000 jobs.

- The *Occupational Outlook Handbook*, updated every two years, describes the type of work, the training and education required, and the future outlook for hundreds of careers.

- The *Guide for Occupational Exploration* groups careers into categories, such as mechanical careers and careers protecting people, and describes many careers within each category.

Library Research Libraries have a broad range of career materials, including videotapes and audiotapes. *Why do you think watching a videotape that shows someone at work might be more engaging than reading about someone at work?*

Additional Print Resources. Libraries also contain other print resources, including magazines, government reports, and newspapers.

- With the *Reader's Guide to Periodical Literature*, locate magazine articles on specific industries and career trends. Business magazines, such as *Forbes, BusinessWeek, Entrepreneur,* and *Wired*, cover the hot topics and inside news of many industries.

- The *Occupational Outlook Quarterly*, published by the Department of Labor, provides up-to-date information on employment trends.

- Job listings in your local newspaper show what is available in your local job market.

- Many labor organizations and industry service groups produce audiotapes and videotapes of workers in action. The library collects them for you, so take advantage of them.

Internet Job Services

The World Wide Web offers a wide range of **Internet job services** such as Web sites, newsgroups, and bulletin boards created by trade organizations, companies, and individuals—all designed for job recruitment and career research. Two helpful sites are Monster.com and Hotjobs.com. You can also search on a specific company's Web site to find career information.

The government also offers career information, information services via the Web, including O*NET, and an online database of the *Dictionary of Occupational Titles* that offers up-to-date information on thousands of jobs.

Most Web sites list job opportunities in different industries according to title, key duties, location, and other criteria. Once you've determined a career that interests you, you can use a Web directory like Yahoo! to get a listing of career-related Web sites. As you search for a job online, choose specific search terms, such as research assistant or marketing, to help you find those jobs that best match your interests. Some Web sites will even e-mail you when jobs in your desired field become available.

Exploratory Interviews

Ask your family, friends, neighbors, teachers, and counselors to help you build a list of people who work in careers that

Search Terms When searching for a job online, it helps to use specific search terms. *If you were searching for sales positions in the medical field, what search terms would you use?*

you find interesting. After doing some initial research into a career, call someone who has the career you are interested in and works in the business or industry you are interested in and arrange an **exploratory interview**. That's simply a short, informal talk with someone who works in a career that appeals to you.

Ask questions such as these:

- How did you start your career?
- What education and training did it require?
- What do you like about your job?
- What do you do on a typical day?

Don't be afraid to ask people for interviews. They may have started out by receiving someone else's help and may be happy to pass the favor along. Take notes during each interview. Afterward, write your reflections on the experience in a journal labeled *career resource file*.

The story of John Liu is a great example. When he was a teenager, John thought he wanted a career in retailing. He asked everyone he knew until he found the perfect contact—a friend's aunt who worked as a department store buyer. "I learned more about buying and selling in an hour with her than I could have imagined. She was smart, savvy, and she loved her work." The interview paid off. John went on to become a well-known marketing consultant. "I'm really grateful for her advice, and I help students today whenever I'm asked."

Part-Time Work

The most direct way to learn about a career is to work. If your schedule allows it, working part-time will enable you to observe a career from the inside. You'll gain experience, make personal contacts, and put some money in your pocket at the same time.

Work Experience Programs

You may find a part-time job through a vocational education program. Such programs are designed to give you a chance to learn job skills while you are still in high school. As a bonus, the work also earns you class credit and a grade.

Some local corporations team up with schools, hiring students to perform jobs that are taught in their high school classes. This is called a **cooperative program**. A high school in California, for example, used math and science classes to prepare students for work at a local chemical company.

Some schools create school-based businesses. One enterprising high school in Minnesota bought a grocery store that was going out of business. Students learned

Experiential Learning You can learn about careers through part-time work. *What job skills might be needed for the job pictured here?*

marketing and retailing in classes and then applied their knowledge working at the school store.

Job Shadowing

You don't need to be a spy to "shadow" someone. **Job shadowing**, which involves following a worker for a few days on the job, means learning the ropes by watching and listening.

Today Elena Kazinski is a television camera operator for a major production company, but when she was a student she didn't know anyone in the industry. As she tells it, "I was always hanging around our local TV studio, and one day I just asked the camera operator if I could talk to her about her job. She offered to let me shadow her. I got the OK from the station, and I stuck to her like glue for a week. I even helped with some equipment. After that, I was hooked. TV production has been my life ever since."

Volunteering and Internships

You may think that volunteers don't get paid. True, they don't usually draw a salary, but they are paid in valuable experience. Don't underestimate the value of volunteering as another way to explore

careers. What you learn can help you make major decisions later. Hospitals, senior citizen centers, and museums are just a few places that use volunteers.

An **internship** is a more formal position and usually requires a longer-term commitment than volunteering. Like volunteers, interns are usually unpaid, but they learn vital job skills. An intern is on the spot, working where the action is. With one foot in the door, interns who work hard can sometimes step into full-time paying positions.

In addition, many communities and schools offer **service learning**. In such programs, community service—for example, cleaning up a neighborhood—becomes part of your schoolwork.

SECTION 3.1 REVIEW

 Key Concept Checkpoint

Comprehension
1. Why are talking to people and using media resources called informal methods of researching jobs?

2. What kinds of career information can you find in libraries and on the Internet?
3. What are some benefits of doing unpaid part-time work?

Critical Thinking
4. Why is it important to consider several career options, even if you're sure of your career choice?

CAREER FOCUS

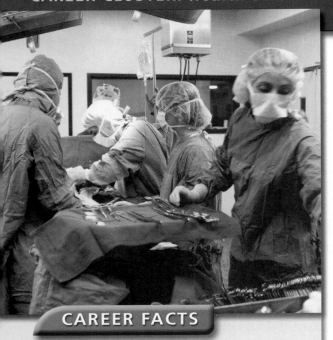

CAREER FACTS

Education or Training Completion of an accredited, formal education program, generally a bachelor's degree program is necessary. Some work experience in the health care field is helpful.

Aptitudes, Abilities, and Skills Good people skills, strong communication skills (both written and oral), patience, ability to work under pressure, and ability to work well with a team are helpful.

Career Outlook Demand is expected to grow much faster than average through 2008, particularly in areas attracting physicians such as rural and inner city clinics.

Career Path Some PAs pursue specialized education. While a PA can advance to a position with a higher salary and more responsibility, he or she is always supervised by a physician.

What is your key to success?

"My key to success is determination and a clear idea of my goals. Upon entering college, I didn't have the requirements for acceptance into the Physician's Assistant (PA) program. Instead of being discouraged, I went to the program director and asked if I could take the PA classes while not officially enrolled. When it came to reevaluate my status, I was accepted into the program."

What does your job entail?

"I obtain and document patients' medical histories. I diagnose and treat illnesses, order and interpret tests, and counsel patients on preventative care. I also perform many clinical procedures including suturing, injections, and cardiopulmonary resuscitation."

What skills are most important to you?

"Communication and interpersonal skills are the most important skills because you must deal with patients who are often vulnerable and upset."

Why do you like being a physician's assistant?

"I like the diversity of my job. I take care of children, adolescents, and adults with many different types of medical problems. Helping people in their time of need is very rewarding. The job can occasionally be tiring and frustrating, but I can walk away at the end of the day and know that I made a difference."

Critical Thinking Why is it necessary to be able to work well under pressure in this field?

What to Research

Once you know *where* to get career information, the next question is *what* information you should get. You'll want to know what the career is like and whether it is right for you. You can find that out by examining careers in terms of these ten characteristics:

1. values,
2. tasks and responsibilities,
3. working with data-people-things,
4. work environment,
5. working hours,
6. aptitudes and abilities,
7. education and training,
8. salary and benefits,
9. career outlook, and
10. international career outlook.

Try to gather information on each of these factors for each career you investigate. This will enable you to compare careers directly and make a wise career decision.

Values

When you look into a career, ask yourself if your values match the values that will help you in that career. What do you really care about? What do people in that career really care about? Justice? Art? Money? Health? Fame?

WHAT YOU'LL LEARN

- Key questions to ask while researching careers.
- Important characteristics that make up a career profile.

WHY IT'S IMPORTANT

Asking the right questions about jobs that interest you will make your career search more productive.

KEY TERMS

- **work environment**
- **flextime**
- **benefits**

Tasks and Responsibilities

When you go to work each day, what will you actually be doing? Find out by asking basic questions, such as these:

- What specific tasks do workers in this career perform?
- Are the workdays repetitive or full of new experiences?
- Is the pace easy, or is the career a high-pressure one?
- Is the work primarily physical or mental?

Working with Data-People-Things

Careers involve working with data, people, and things. Many careers entail working with all three as *Figure 3.2* shows. For any given career, though, one area tends to predominate. Statisticians, for example, work mainly with data, home health aides work primarily with people, and technicians usually work with things.

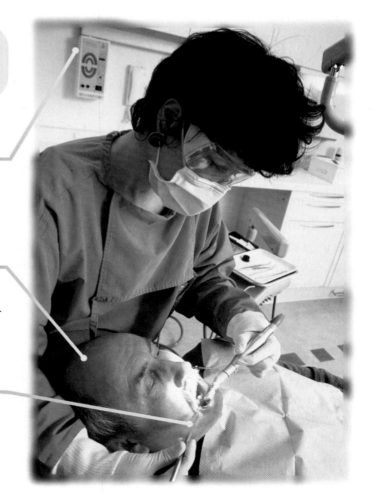

FIGURE 3.2 Data-People-Things Many careers involve working with data, people, and things.

A **Data** The dental hygienist uses information—what she learned in her training plus her knowledge of this particular patient from past cleaning sessions.

B **People** The hygienist spends most of her day working with people. A hygienist with a friendly manner will help patients feel comfortable.

C **Things** The hygienist works with things—the tools she uses to clean the patient's teeth. A hygienist has to use dental tools carefully and keep all equipment clean.

Work Environment

Because you'll be spending about 40 hours a week at work, do yourself a favor: Consider your **work environment**. Your physical and social surroundings can affect your well-being. Do you want to work indoors or outdoors? Would you rather work alone or with other people?

Take a few minutes to visualize your ideal work environment. Then draw a picture or write a paragraph describing what you envisioned. As you research careers, try to find those that match that image.

Working Hours

When you think about work, do you assume you'll be starting at 9:00 A.M. and quitting at 5:00 P.M.? Of course, many people do work those hours—but in the world of work, variety rules. Andrew Barros, a restaurant host, starts work at 3:00 P.M. and leaves after the last guest does at about 11:00 P.M. Andrew's restaurant buys produce from Janet Cho, who works from 4:00 A.M. to noon. Many careers are simply not 9-to-5 careers. When are you at your best? Are you a night owl or a morning person?

Some careers allow flexible scheduling. With **flextime**, workers construct their work schedules to suit their lives. Some people work four ten-hour days and enjoy three-day weekends. Some work from 7:00 A.M. to 3:00 P.M. so that they can be home when their children return from school. Some people telecommute: They work at home and communicate with clients and colleagues by phone, fax, and computer.

Flexible Scheduling Flextime scheduling allows some workers to more easily match their work schedules with the demands of family life. Many employers that offer flextime require workers to be on-site during certain core hours, typically from 10:00 A.M. to 4:00 P.M. *Why do you think this is the case?*

Aptitudes and Abilities

As you know, skills for any kind of work are more easily learned if you have an aptitude for learning them. In Chapter 2 you analyzed your own aptitudes and abilities. As you do your research, find out which aptitudes and abilities are needed for each career. You can then match your natural talents with careers that require those same abilities. Anthony McCabe was a high school student who loved to talk. He talked about anything to anybody, and he had the knack of getting people to relax and open up to him. When it dawned on him that talking was what he was really good at, his career started to take shape, and today he hosts his own radio talk show.

Education and Training

Careers demand different kinds and levels of education and training. You may need a two-year associate degree, a four-year bachelor's degree, or a technical or business school license or certificate. As you research, note how much time, money, and effort it will take to get the necessary education and training for various careers.

FIGURE 3.3

TOP TEN JOB OPPORTUNITIES REQUIRING A BACHELOR'S DEGREE OR HIGHER THROUGH 2005

Occupation	Average Annual Openings
General managers and top executives	100,320
Teachers, secondary school	71,070
Teachers, elementary school	46,490
Systems analysts, electronic data processing	43,710
Financial managers	29,490
Accountants and auditors	28,370
Lawyers	24,370
Teachers, special education	23,850
Marketing, advertising, and public relations manager	19,190
Physicians and surgeons	18,590

SOURCE: U.S. Department of Labor

▲ **Job Opportunities** This chart displays the ten careers that are projected to have the most job openings through 2005. *Why do you think the job outlook is favorable for these careers?*

Salary and Benefits

Occupational directories often include general information on what jobs pay. They list an hourly rate or a weekly or annual salary, as well as salary ranges based on national averages.

Of course, many company employees receive more than their paychecks. **Benefits** may include health insurance, paid vacation and holiday time, and a retirement plan.

Other benefits may include regular bonuses, discounts on merchandise, low interest loans on homes and autos, or even gym memberships

Career Outlook

What will your career area be like in ten years? Many of the research materials described in Section 3.1 can tell you about industry prospects and help you make big decisions. *Figure 3.3* shows the career outlook for those careers requiring a bachelor's degree or higher.

Kathy Silno's research helped her. Kathy was mechanically inclined, and she considered a career in manufacturing. Her research, however, pointed to an upcoming increase in service jobs. Kathy decided on automotive repair and found a service job with a good future.

Creative BUSINESS PRACTICES

Starbucks Coffee Company
Community Service and a Smile

Starbucks may serve a good cup of coffee, but the company is also known for its commitment to the community. The coffee shop that opened in Seattle, Washington, in 1971 now has over 3,300 locations worldwide. Even with this expansion, Starbucks still gives back to its hometown, supporting many local efforts to improve Seattle's quality of life. Contributing positively to its community and the environment is so important to Starbucks that it is part of the company's mission statement.

Starbucks is involved with many local causes, including improving public parks, sponsoring violence prevention and literacy programs, and supporting Seattle's arts. In January 2000, Starbucks started the "Make Your Mark" program, which encourages all Starbucks employees to do volunteer work. Starbucks supports its employees by matching volunteer hours with cash donations to local nonprofit organizations.

Critical Thinking

Would you choose to patronize one business instead of another because of its involvement in the community? Why or why not?

Link and Learn

For more information about Starbucks Coffee Company's community initiatives, visit their Web site via the link on the *Succeeding in the World of Work* Web site at www.careers.glencoe.com.

International Career Outlook

With growth in the global economy, more and more careers involve working internationally. Brainstorm with your friends and family. Do they know someone who has worked in a foreign country? Pool your resources with other students and make a list of international career possibilities, such as English teacher, civil engineer, or health-care worker.

You can find plenty of international jobs by using library resources. Browse the Web as well.

Global Opportunities In today's global economy, many jobs are opening up in foreign countries. *In what foreign country do you think you might like to work? Why?*

SECTION 3.2 REVIEW

✓ Key Concept Checkpoint

Comprehension
1. What aspects of the work environment are important when evaluating a career?

2. Why should you consider a career's outlook?

Critical Thinking
3. What are some skills, abilities, or personality traits that would be important for a person interested in working abroad?

KEY TERMS

Internet job services (p. 53)
**exploratory interview
(p. 54)**
**cooperative program
(p. 54)**
job shadowing (p. 55)
internship (p. 55)
service learning (p. 55)

SECTION 3.1

- The U.S. Office of Education divides careers into 16 pathways. (pp. 50–51)

- You can research careers informally from the world around you, friends and family, and media resources. (pp. 50–53)

- You can research careers formally in books, magazines, and other printed matter; videotapes and audiotapes; and in computerized job resources. (pp. 52–53)

- You can obtain a wealth of up-to-date information on the Internet, especially the World Wide Web. (pp. 53)

- You can research a career and then interview someone who works in that field. (pp. 53–54)

- You can obtain part-time work in many different ways: through educational programs, job shadowing, volunteering, internships, and service learning. (pp. 54–55)

KEY TERMS

work environment (p. 59)
flextime (p. 59)
benefits (p. 61)

SECTION 3.2

- Consider whether the values that a career reinforces match your values. (p. 57)

- Investigate exactly what tasks and responsibilities a career entails. (p. 58)

- Look for a career that balances working with data, people, and things in a way that suits you. (p. 58)

- Evaluate the work environment a career offers. (p. 59)

- Find out what scheduling flexibility is possible within a career. (p. 59)

- Determine what aptitudes and abilities you have that a career requires. (pp. 59–60)

- Investigate what education and training you need for a career. (p. 60)

- Many career resources describe the salary ranges of different careers. (p. 61)

- Consider whether the number of people working in a career is expected to increase or decrease in the future. (p. 61)

- Consider international careers in the growing global economy. (p. 62)

Reviewing Key Terms

1. Work with a partner to practice your vocabulary. On a separate sheet of paper, write an example of each term, and see if you and your partner can match each other's examples with the correct terms.
   - Internet job services
   - exploratory interview
   - cooperative program
   - service learning
   - work environment
   - flextime
   - fringe benefits
   - job shadowing
   - internship

Recalling Key Concepts

2. The *Dictionary of Occupational Titles* is a guide to ____.
   (a) employers (b) job titles
   (c) career magazines

3. The *Reader's Guide to Periodical Literature* helps in finding ____.
   (a) magazine articles (b) career videos
   (c) Internet listings

4. Working in a homeless shelter as part of course work is called ____.
   (a) an internship (b) benefits
   (c) service learning

5. Driving a tow-truck and repairing engines are examples of ____.
   (a) a career outlook (b) values
   (c) tasks and responsibilities

6. One characteristic that makes up a career profile is ____.
   (a) salary (b) internships (c) data

Problem Solving

7. What are some advantages of doing formal career research?

8. What should you do before having an exploratory interview?

9. What might motivate a career professional to allow a student to shadow him or her on the job?

10. What personal values would match someone to a career in the military?

11. How might a compatible work environment contribute to job satisfaction?

Work-Based Learning

Personal Qualities Self-Esteem

12. List qualities that make you a good candidate for a part-time job.

Resources Allocating Time

13. Imagine that you have volunteered for after-school service learning. Estimate how many hours per week and on which days you could work. What factors influenced your estimate?

Technology Selecting Technology

14. Compare searching for career information using the *Reader's Guide to Periodical Literature* with searching on the Internet.

School-Based Learning

Art Design a Flyer

15. Henry is in charge of publicity for a yard sale intended to raise funds for a school club. Design a flyer advertising the event.

Social Studies Conduct Market Research

16. Eriko is an intern at the local radio station, which is doing market research for a station profile. Its listening audience is mostly 30- to 40-year-olds. Eriko must research the major historical and cultural events that occurred when these listeners were teenagers. What five events would you suggest?

Math Calculate Salary

17. A listing in the *Occupational Outlook Handbook* puts the average weekly salary range for a career at $250 to $300. What would the yearly salary range be? If a worker earning the minimum of this range received a 5 percent raise, what would the new weekly salary be?

Role Play

18. **Exploratory Interview**

   Situation You are to assume the role of a real estate agent from a large city. A student from a local high school has asked you to visit his classroom to discuss your career. He is hoping that an exploratory interview will give him a better idea of what is involved in a career in real estate.

   Activity Your task is to research a career as a real estate agent, paying particular attention to those characteristics defined in Section 3.2. You must be prepared to answer those questions that would be addressed in an exploratory interview.

Evaluation You will be evaluated on how well you meet the following performance indicators:

- Explain the nature of the work
- Address the necessary skills and education or training
- Give an overview of realistic expectations in this career

19. **Arrange a Job Shadowing Experience**
   Find someone who will agree to allow you to job shadow over a weekend or a holiday. Make notes on the career in terms of the ten characteristics described in this chapter.

   Connect Find Web sites that are related to this career and research the same ten characteristics. Compare this information to the notes that you have from your job shadow experience. Report your findings to your class.

20. **Research Educational Programs**
   Choose one career from any of the 16 U.S. Office of Education Career Pathways. Find out what kind of education is required for this field.

   Connect Research schools and universities that offer programs on your selected career. Choose one school that has a strong program and, using design software, prepare a brochure highlighting the career benefits of this school's program.

Entrepreneurship

CHAPTER OBJECTIVES

After completing this chapter, you will be able to

- Define entrepreneurship and explain its advantages and disadvantages.

- Identify the four main ways of becoming a business owner and explain the advantages and disadvantages of each.

- Describe basic forms of business ownership.

- Describe the processes and decisions involved in establishing a new business.

JOURNAL

Personal Career Plan

Entrepreneurship is an exciting undertaking—but it's not for everyone. How does entrepreneurship fit your own values, interests, and abilities? In your journal, list the advantages and disadvantages entrepreneurship might offer you.

Personal Career Project

Choose a business that interests you. Research the skills and experience you would need to get into that business and be successful. Then develop short-term and long-term goals for developing the necessary skills and experience.

SECTION 4.1

What Is Entrepreneurship?

WHAT YOU'LL LEARN

- What is meant by the term entrepreneur and what makes a person a good candidate for entrepreneurship
- How to weigh the advantages and disadvantages of entrepreneurship

WHY IT'S IMPORTANT

General knowledge about entrepreneurship and its pros and cons will help you decide if this career option is suitable for you.

KEY TERM

- entrepreneur

Are you a fan of the *Star Trek* movies and TV programs? In this sci-fi adventure, the crew of a starship travels across the universe, exploring places where no one has gone before. The starship is called the *Enterprise*—and for good reason. The word comes from an Old French word, meaning "to take action, take risks, take responsibility."

You might be surprised to learn that the word *entrepreneur* comes from the same root as *enterprise*. An **entrepreneur** is someone who organizes and then runs a business. An entrepreneur's life is challenging. The risks can be high, but the rewards can also be great. Entrepreneurs must make wise decisions and search out inventive solutions.

Does this adventure appeal to you? Are you willing to set off into the unknown and find your way? Maybe your career path leads to entrepreneurship.

Advantages of Entrepreneurship

If you think entrepreneurship would demand a great deal from you, you're right. What, then, are the advantages?

- *You're in charge.* Entrepreneurs decide when and how hard to work and how their businesses will operate.
- *There is great job satisfaction.*
- *Entrepreneurship can lead to a good income.*

Heavy Workload Entrepreneurs can't go home at 5:00 P.M. if there's still work to be done. *What rewards does the entrepreneur reap for all the long hours?*

Disadvantages of Entrepreneurship

Entrepreneurship can be exciting and rewarding, but there are also drawbacks.

- *There is financial risk.* You can lose your investment and sometimes more.

- *Entrepreneurs often work long hours.*

- *Competition can be stiff.*

- *There are no guarantees of success.* Almost two of every three new businesses fail within their first four years.

Traits of Entrepreneurs

Most entrepreneurs share certain behaviors and attitudes. If the ones described below don't quite match traits you see in yourself, you can develop them.

Motivation

Successful entrepreneurs are very self-motivated. They know what they want to achieve, and they believe in their ability.

They keep themselves motivated by setting short- and long-term goals. Then they make and follow a plan for achieving those goals.

Sight and Foresight

Entrepreneurs recognize opportunities (see *Figure 4.1*). They see problems and find a way to build success on them. That's how Daryl Bernstein got his start when he was 17 years old.

FIGURE 4.1

Becoming an Entrepreneur Eve Jones, a college student majoring in business, wants to start an on-campus business. She's confident that she'll derive satisfaction from being her own boss, but she's not sure she's ready for the financial risk and long hours involved. Before she makes any decisions, Eve makes sure she is thoroughly prepared.

A **Vision** As an aspiring entrepreneur, Eve is alert to situations around her. She keeps up with business trends, noticing that lecture-notes services are becoming big business on college campuses nationwide. This gives her an idea for an on-campus business videotaping class lectures and renting copies of the tapes to fellow students.

B **Research** Will her idea work? Eve talks to other students to find out if they would be interested in renting videotapes of class lectures, and she asks for input from people who have started their own on-campus businesses. She asks all the relevant questions: What equipment and personnel will she need for her business? What problems is she likely to face? What kind of competition will she have? How much will she need to charge students for renting the lecture videos?

C **Planning** Using the results of her research, Eve evaluates the pros and cons of starting her business. Is she prepared for the financial and personal risks involved in entrepreneurship? How will she obtain financing? Where will her business be located? Eve plans all the steps necessary to put her idea into action.

D **Going For It!** Eve takes out a loan for equipment, recruits two film students to help her tape the class lectures, and rents space in the college library to store her videotapes. As her business takes off, she elicits feedback from her customers so she can anticipate and solve problems and attract more business.

Daryl noticed that large companies used logos to promote their services and products. He thought logos would also benefit small companies. As a result, he started a business creating logos for small companies. It took a while, but his business became a success. In the process, he helped his clients increase their profits by giving them a greater identity and ultimately more recognition.

Recognizing opportunities is part of a process. *Figure 4.1* on pages 70–71 shows how one entrepreneur capitalized on an idea and an opportunity. Eve Jones saw a need, researched the possibilities, evaluated the risks and rewards, and decided to take the leap and start her own business. Notice that her research did not end when the business started. Successful entrepreneurs constantly evaluate their businesses and their customers' needs in order to achieve success.

Decision Making

Entrepreneurs make business decisions every day, and the decisions must be good ones. Refer back to Section 2.1 of Chapter 2 for more information on how to make decisions.

CAREER CHECKLIST

When Starting Your Own Business...

- ✔ Talk to entrepreneurs who have started their own businesses, especially if they work in your area of interest.
- ✔ Take a good look at yourself. Do you possess the personal qualities that an entrepreneur needs? If not, brainstorm ways that you can start developing these important qualities.
- ✔ Perform further research about business plans and create one for your business.
- ✔ Be creative—sometimes the craziest idea can be a booming success in the business world.
- ✔ Investigate the unfulfilled business needs of your own community.
- ✔ Brainstorm with friends and find a partner that you work well with.
- ✔ Be persistent! It may take some time for your plan to become a success.

SECTION 4.1 REVIEW

Key Concept Checkpoint

Comprehension

1. Give an example of a successful business in your community. How might the traits of an entrepreneur have helped this business succeed?

2. Are the advantages or the disadvantages of entrepreneurship more important to you? Why?

Critical Thinking

3. Why might entrepreneurship offer greater job satisfaction than working for someone else?

Ways of Becoming a Business Owner

If you decide entrepreneurship is for you, you'll have to decide how you're going to get your own business. Here are the four main ways of doing so:

1. starting a new business,
2. buying an existing business,
3. buying a franchise, and
4. taking over the family business.

Starting a New Business

Starting a new business is a dream many people share. What an exciting adventure! If you start a new business, look for challenges as well as rewards.

The Challenges

No matter how you get into business, you will face challenges. If you're starting a new business, you'll face a few additional ones.

- A new business requires more time and effort than an established business.

- Start-up costs are often high. **Start-up costs** are the expenses involved in going into business. Examples include renting or buying space and buying equipment, office supplies, and insurance.

- If you borrow money, you'll have to convince lenders that your business idea will work.

- It's risky. No matter how well you plan, you won't know if the business will succeed until you've tried it.

WHAT YOU'LL LEARN

- The four main ways of becoming a business owner
- The advantages and disadvantages of each major route to business ownership

WHY IT'S IMPORTANT

Awareness of the advantages and disadvantages associated with launching a business will help you make informed choices should you decide to become an entrepreneur.

KEY TERMS

- start-up costs
- lease
- goodwill
- market outlook
- franchise

Sole Authority When you start a new business, you have to take care of all the business details. *How would you feel about making all the necessary decisions?*

The Rewards

Tough challenges await those who build a business, but there are also many rewards:

- You don't inherit a previous owner's mistakes. You can develop a name for your business without worrying about an existing reputation.

- You can build your business your way, using your experiences and the information you've gained from studying other businesses.

- You get personal satisfaction from knowing you built the business.

Buying an Existing Business

If you don't want to start a new business, you might buy an existing one. A successful business may be for sale because the owners are retiring or entering a new business or even because business is so good, the owners can't handle it anymore. An owner of a business might also be motivated to sell because he or she wants more free time.

There are many reasons why an unsuccessful business might be for sale. Take a close look at the reasons that caused the business's failure. The business may still be a good investment if you are fairly certain that it can be a turned around. The bottom line, however, is that the business is now losing money. Before buying, determine whether the business's problems can be fixed, and at what cost. You can often purchase a failing business at a reduced rate. Be sure to take advantage of such savings opportunities, because you may need a great deal of capital to restore the profitability of the business.

A Fast Start

Buying an existing business can put you several steps ahead. First, you can save on start-up costs by taking advantage of the previous owner's business agreements, such as a lease signed when rents were lower. A **lease** is a contract to use something for a specified period of time. You may also not have to worry about buying or renting office furniture or equipment. Furthermore, the person selling the business might be a good source of advice.

If the business has been successful, you can build on that success. The **goodwill**, or loyalty, of customers is one of a business's most valuable assets. You may also benefit from an established reputation and a trained staff.

Drawbacks

An existing business may come with its own existing problems:

- The location may be poor.
- The competition may be taking business away.
- The **market outlook**, or potential for future sales, may have changed.
- The building or equipment may need expensive repairs or replacement.
- The business may have a reputation for poor products.

Buying a Franchise

A type of existing business that offers specific advantages is the franchise. A **franchise** is the legal right to sell a company's goods and services. Many fast-food restaurants and real estate offices are franchises.

When you buy a franchise, you are actually buying the right to sell another company's products. In addition to paying for the franchise, you will continue to pay a percentage of your profits to the parent company.

Like any business owner, you are in charge. However, you must follow the parent company's guidelines. These may dictate how to make or distribute the goods or services.

Less Risk

A franchise may be a wise choice for people with limited business experience. Here are some other benefits you'll gain:

- a recognized product name,
- established management systems,
- a business reputation and customer goodwill,
- training and support services,
- advertising, and
- financing.

Less Gain

A franchise is not the right choice for everyone. A franchise may be less profitable because you pay a portion of your profits to the parent company. Since you didn't build the company from scratch, there may be less satisfaction.

Taking Over the Family Business

Does your father, mother, or another relative own a business? If so, it might be a shortcut into entrepreneurship.

Smoothing the Way

Taking over a family business can have the advantages of the franchise without the fees.

- Your relatives might help you finance the business.

- Family members tend to be loyal and to trust each other.

- Family members working as a team can achieve more than individuals.

- Relatives can teach you the business.

- Customers are likely to give the same trust and goodwill to a new owner who is part of the family they are accustomed to doing business with.

Bumps in the Road

In addition to the usual hazards of business ownership, a family business presents special ones. To begin with, it's sometimes hard to have normal business relationships with relatives. Moreover, when the family is part of the business, you can't always go home and leave the business behind.

The Family Business Joining a family business can be an easy entry into business. Relatives provide emotional as well as professional support. *What do you think would be the hardest part of joining a family business?*

SECTION 4.2 REVIEW

 Key Concept Checkpoint

Comprehension

1. Describe four ways to enter the fast-food business. Which one do you think would offer you the best chance for success? Why?

2. State the advantages and disadvantages of buying an existing business rather than starting a new business.

Critical Thinking

3. Why should you think twice about buying a business that has a bad reputation?

CAREER FOCUS

Heather Lynch
Real Estate Agent

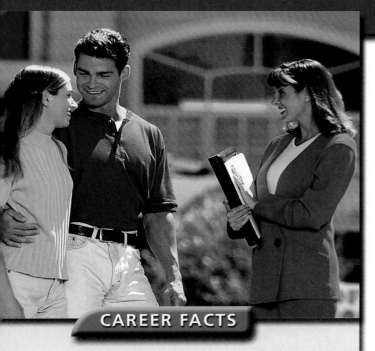

CAREER FACTS

Education or Training To receive the mandatory real estate license, candidates must have a high school diploma and pass a test. College courses in real estate, finance, business administration, statistics, economics, and law are helpful.

Aptitudes, Abilities, and Skills A pleasant personality, solid communication and people skills, honesty, maturity, tact, self-motivation, and enthusiasm are required

Career Outlook Average job growth expected through 2008.

Career Path As agents advance, they make higher commissions and can rise to management positions in large firms. Other agents may become real estate brokers, appraisers, property managers, or investment counselors.

What is your key to success?

"Providing good customer service is a major key to my success. It's important to be patient and attentive to clients' needs. It's also important to know what clients are looking for in a property. Networking is important, because Realtors work strictly on commission. If real estate agents don't find their own clients through networking or cold calling, they won't make any money."

What does your job entail?

"My job involves making phone calls, preparing daily updates for clients, going to home inspections, finding listings for prospective home buyers, meeting with appraisers, showing houses, and preparing contracts. I also make some cold calls every day. Because my job involves catering to the needs of my clients, I end up doing a lot of work on weekends and evenings."

What kind of training did you have?

"I took a class to help me prepare for the real estate licensing exam. The class taught me about all aspects of the real estate industry. After I got my license, I worked with a mentor, who gave me a lot of helpful advice and guidance. Now I attend continuing education seminars to keep my license valid. I'm required to complete 15 hours of class every two years."

What do you like most about your work?

"I enjoy setting my own schedule. I also enjoy working with people. It's rewarding and exciting to help my clients find homes."

> **Critical Thinking** Why is it important for Realtors to be self-motivated?

Getting Started in Your Own Business

Let's say that you've decided to become an entrepreneur. Will you own the business by yourself, or do you want someone to share the work and the risks? Where will you locate your business—in your home or in a building elsewhere? Think about the business you'd like to start. How would you answer these questions?

Forms of Legal Ownership

If you decide that you want to own a business you must also decide what legal form the ownership will take. You have three choices: sole proprietorship, partnership, or corporation. *Figure 4.2* compares the advantages and disadvantages of each form of ownership.

Sole Proprietorship

Most businesses begin as a **sole proprietorship**. This means the business is completely owned by one person. About 75 percent of all U.S. businesses are sole proprietorships.

Partnership

A **partnership** is a legal arrangement in which two or more people share ownership. Control and profits are divided among partners, according to a partnership agreement. A partnership is the least common of the three forms of business ownership.

FIGURE
4.2

FORMS OF BUSINESS OWNERSHIP

Form of Business Ownership	Advantages	Disadvantages
Sole Proprietorship	• Owner makes all decisions • Easiest form of business to set up • Least regulated of the three forms of business	• Limited by the skills, abilities, and financial resources of one person • Difficult to raise funds to finance business • Owner has sole financial responsibility for company; personal assets sometimes at risk
Partnership	• Can draw on the skills, abilities, and financial resources of more than one person • Easier to raise funds than in sole proprietorship	• More complicated than sole proprietorship • Tensions and conflicts may develop among partners • Owners liable for all business losses; personal property sometimes in jeopardy
Corporation	• Easier to finance than other forms of business • Financial liability of shareholders limited (usually, can lose only what they've invested)	• Expensive to set up • Record keeping often time-consuming and costly • Often pays more taxes than other forms of business

▲ **Ownership Options** Every form of business ownership has its advantages and disadvantages. *What business do you know of that is owned as a sole proprietorship? A partnership? A corporation?*

Corporation

A **corporation** is a business, chartered by a state, that legally operates apart from the owner(s). The owners buy shares, or parts, of the company. They are called *shareholders* and earn a profit based on the number of shares they own.

Corporations often have an easier time getting financing, but are required to maintain significant records that are not required for other forms of ownership.

Location, Location, Location

Suppose you want to open a fast-food restaurant. Is location important? Of course! You've got to be near your customers. What about a mail-order business? As long as a good postal service is available, you can ship goods from anywhere. In this case, location may not be so important.

interNET
CONNECTION

Be Your Own Boss
You would like to open your own shop to sell your handmade decorated T-shirts, as well as other clothing.

Connect
- Visit the Small Business Administration's Web site and read about the steps you need to take to own your own business.
- Make a list of the pros and cons of being a small business owner and explain whether you think being your own boss and running your own shop would suit you.

Worth the Price? Good locations are usually expensive, yet business owners want the best location they can afford. *What advantages does this site offer the business owner?*

When location is important, consider these factors:

- the type of businesses in the area,
- the condition of streets and buildings,
- the cost of property,
- the location of the competition, and
- the location of your customers.

Working at Home

What about working out of your home? It's cheaper than leasing a location, and more convenient. You'll also enjoy more flexibility and a relaxed atmosphere.

What about the problems? First, some communities restrict the kinds of businesses that can operate in residential areas. In addition, the isolation of working at home troubles many business owners. Jean Ainsworth left a large office to start a home-based business. "I hadn't realized how much I enjoyed saying 'Good morning' to people, sharing the weekend, hearing about the football games," says Ainsworth. "I had a grandchild last August and I didn't have a set of people to show the pictures to."

Financing

Whatever type of business you launch, you'll need money to get it going. You might draw on your savings or get a loan from friends. More likely, you'll need to borrow money from a commercial lender. To apply for a loan, you'll need a business description and a financial plan.

A *business plan* gives specific information about your business. It describes your product and states where your business will be located. It specifies how many employees you will hire and what their salaries will be. It describes your competitors and points out their strengths and weaknesses. It also describes your marketing plan and your timetable for starting the business.

A *financial plan* spells out your start-up costs, operating expenses, and other costs for the first few months. **Operating expenses** are the costs of doing business, such as the costs of manufacturing and selling the product.

Operating Your Own Business

Whatever business you choose to enter as an entrepreneur, you will need a variety of skills and competencies. These include reading, writing, math, listening, and speaking skills.

Africa Brown started a business called Africa's Clothing when she was a 16-year-old high school student in Washington, D.C. She got the idea after participating in an entrepreneurship program offered by the Business Kids Institute and the city of Washington, D.C. Brown makes clothing to order, mainly for her classmates. She must listen effectively to take orders accurately and to get the job done right. She must speak well so that she can explain her service. Think about the business you'd like to start. How will you use listening, speaking, reading, writing, and math skills?

Creative BUSINESS PRACTICES

HBO
Encouraging Employees to Mentor

HBO, the cable television network, sponsors a mentoring program for young people in both Los Angeles and New York, in which HBO employees mentor underprivileged children. The program encourages long-term relationships, with the hope that mentor pairs will be together for several years. The children visit their mentors at the HBO offices for a minimum of two hours every other week.

The mentor program gives HBO employees a chance to give back to the community. It offers young people hope for the future and gets them interested in finding a career.

HBO recruits mentors with posters, e-mails, and a promotional video. HBO sup-ports the program by paying for transportation, food, and special activities such as bowling, softball games, picnics, holiday gifts, and other special presents throughout the year.

Critical Thinking
Do you or does anyone you know participate in a mentoring program? What are the benefits of being mentored? Would you ever consider becoming a mentor? Why or why not?

Link and Learn
Search the Web for more information about mentoring programs.

You'll need math skills for almost every aspect of business, from setting prices to calculating payroll.

One essential record for business owners is the **income statement**, which is a summary of your business's income and expenses during a specific period, such as a month, a quarter, or a year. The first item in an income statement is **revenue**, or income from sales. Another item is **gross profit**, or the difference between the cost of goods and their selling price. **Net profit** is the amount left after operating expenses are subtracted from the gross profit.

Another important business record is a *balance sheet*, which summarizes a business's assets, liabilities, and owner's equity. *Assets*, which can be classified as current or fixed, are anything of monetary value that you own. Money in the bank and inventory are current assets. Fixed assets include land, equipment, furniture, and fixtures.

Liabilities are debts a business owes. Current liabilities must be paid during the current year. Long-term liabilities are not due in the next 12 months.

The savings you invest in your business is your *equity*, or ownership interest, in the business. *Net worth* is the difference between the assets of a business and its liabilities.

A *cash flow statement* is also an essential business record. This statement is a monthly plan that shows when you anticipate cash coming into the business and when you expect to pay out cash. A cash flow statement helps you see if you will have enough money when you need it to pay your bills.

SECTION 4.3 REVIEW

✔ Key Concept Checkpoint

Comprehension

1. Imagine that you are starting a trucking company. What form of ownership will you choose? Why?
2. What should you consider in choosing a location for this business?
3. You have decided to organize your trucking company as a corporation. How will you go about financing it?

Critical Thinking

4. Why might you choose to take a business loan from a bank, even if a relative has enough money to finance your venture?

KEY TERM
entrepreneur (p. 68)

SECTION 4.1

- Entrepreneurship offers you the chance to run your own business, to enjoy job satisfaction, and to earn a high income. The downside is financial risk, long hours, and no *guarantee* of success. (pp. 68-69)

- Entrepreneurs are self-motivated and recognize opportunities around them. (pp. 70-72)

KEY TERMS
start-up costs (p. 73)
lease (p. 74)
goodwill (p. 75)
market outlook (p. 75)
franchise (p. 75)

SECTION 4.2

- If you start a new business, you don't inherit problems. However, it's risky, and takes time, effort, and money. (pp. 73–74)

- If you buy an existing business, you may have low start-up costs, an operating business, and goodwill. However, you may inherit a poor location, stiff competition, a dwindling market, bad equipment, or a poor reputation. (pp. 74–75)

- When you buy a franchise, you get a proven product, established systems, and company support. However, a franchise can be expensive, and you must pay part of your profits to the parent company. (p. 75)

- If you enter a family business, relatives may help you finance it and may teach you the business. However, having normal business relationships with relatives is often difficult. (pp. 75–76)

KEY TERMS
sole proprietorship (p. 78)
partnership (p. 78)
corporation (p. 79)
operating expenses (p. 81)
income statement (p. 82)
revenue (p. 82)
gross profit (p. 82)
net profit (p. 82)

SECTION 4.3

- There are three legal forms of business ownership: sole proprietorships, partnerships, and corporations. (pp. 78–79)

- Location is extremely important for many businesses. (pp. 79–80)

- A home-based business has low costs and flexible working conditions. However, you may feel isolated. (p. 80)

- A business loan application requires a business plan and a financial plan. (pp. 80–82)

Reviewing Key Terms

1. Describe a business you would like to own. Use the following key terms in your description.
   - entrepreneur
   - start-up costs
   - lease
   - goodwill
   - market outlook
   - franchise
   - sole proprietorship
   - partnership
   - corporation
   - operating expenses
   - income statement
   - revenue
   - gross profit
   - net profit

Recalling Key Concepts

For each of the following statements, determine if it is true or false. Rewrite any false statements to make them true.

2. Entrepreneurs often work long hours, but they enjoy great job satisfaction.

3. Once a franchise is paid for, all profits go to the entrepreneur.

4. Entrepreneurs who plan to work out of their homes should consider whether they can handle the isolation.

5. In a partnership, the owners can never lose their personal property if the business fails.

6. A financial plan shows how much a business has earned or lost.

Problem Solving

7. Is a family business more like a franchise or more like a new business? Explain your answer.

8. Why would someone wish to enter into a partnership instead of operating as a sole proprietor?

9. After six months of operation, an entrepreneur prepares an income statement. It shows that while he has had strong sales and high revenue, instead of a gross profit, he has a gross loss. What should he understand about the cost of the goods he is selling?

Work-Based Learning

Basic Skills Listening Skills

10. Work with a group of four or five other students. Individually, prepare a detailed message. Give the message orally to a group member, who should pass it on to the next group member, who should also pass it on. When you receive a message, write it down before passing it on. When all messages have returned to their authors, discuss with your group the accuracy of the messages given and received. Write a one-paragraph summary of your conclusion.

Interpersonal Skills Serving Clients/Customers

11. Alicia owns a bakery. During busy hours, she and her one employee cannot serve customers quickly enough. The customers become upset when she waits on them out of order. Sometimes they leave if the line is too long. Without hiring more employees, what might Alicia do to keep her customers happy?

School-Based Learning

Math Calculate Net Profit

12. Brad sells ice cream and soft drinks at outdoor festivals. He buys soft drinks for 50 cents per can and ice-cream bars for $75 per hundred. He marks up all items by 100 percent, selling the drinks for $1.00 and ice-cream bars for $1.50. One day, he sold 100 cans of soft drinks and 90 ice-cream bars. His expenses totaled $31.50. What was his net profit?

Social Studies Research Community

13. Carlos wants to operate a landscaping business out of the garage behind his house. In your neighborhood, would it be legal to run such a business at home? Research your community's guidelines for home businesses.

Human Relations Utilize Resources

14. Because of a downturn in business, Christy must lay off three employees. Research what local or state agencies can help them find new jobs or provide training for new careers.

Role Play

15. Retaining Employees

Situation Lately your employer, a small catering company, has lost a lot of key employees. Customers have begun to notice the high turnover and have complained about the service. The business's owner can't afford to give employees a raise, so she has asked you to come up with a comprehensive plan to improve employee retention that does not involve raising wages.

Activity Research how major corporations and small businesses keep good employees from resigning. Then develop an employee retention plan. Present your plan to the company's owner, using visual aids and statistics to enhance your presentation.

Evaluation You will be evaluated based on how well you meet the following performance indicators:

- Demonstrate thorough research
- Propose practical, yet innovative solutions
- Enhance the presentation with effective visual aids

*inter*NET CONNECTION

16. Write a Small Business Plan
Use career information to apply entrepreneurial skills. Choose a business that you would like to start. Then research how to write a business plan.

Connect Search the Internet for web sites for entrepreneurs launching their own businesses. Find information about writing business plans and use that information to develop your own small business plan.

Chapter 5

Developing an Individual Career Plan

Section 5.1
Evaluating Career
Choices

Section 5.2
Your Plan of Action

CHAPTER OBJECTIVES

After completing this chapter, you will be able to

- Evaluate various career possibilities.

- Develop an individual career plan and set intermediate career goals.

- Identify the education and training you will need to reach your career goals.

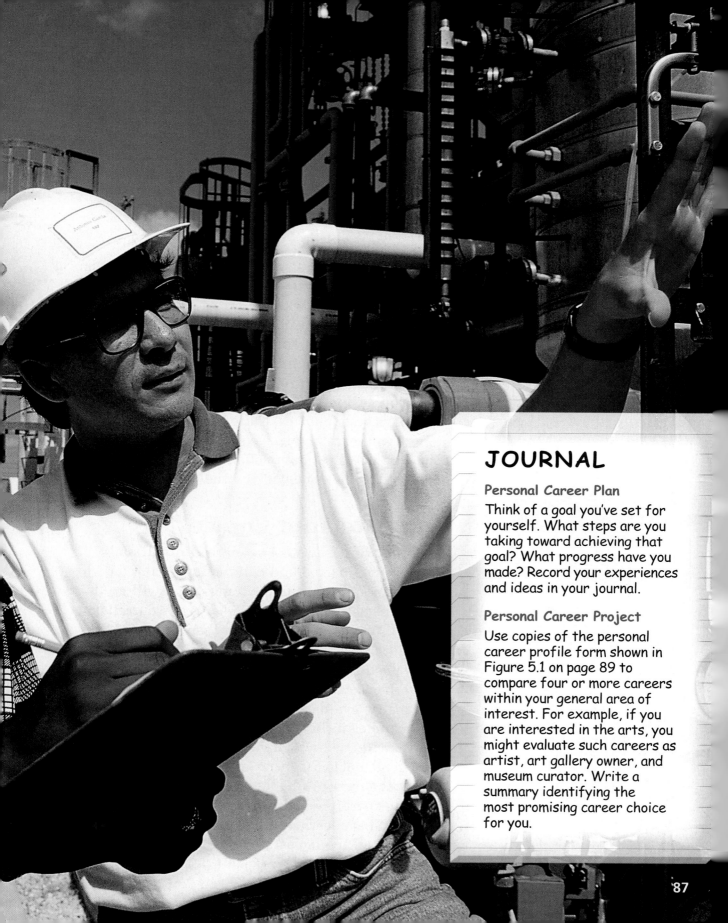

JOURNAL

Personal Career Plan

Think of a goal you've set for yourself. What steps are you taking toward achieving that goal? What progress have you made? Record your experiences and ideas in your journal.

Personal Career Project

Use copies of the personal career profile form shown in Figure 5.1 on page 89 to compare four or more careers within your general area of interest. For example, if you are interested in the arts, you might evaluate such careers as artist, art gallery owner, and museum curator. Write a summary identifying the most promising career choice for you.

Evaluating Career Choices

WHAT YOU'LL LEARN

- How to evaluate career possibilities

WHY IT'S IMPORTANT

After choosing a career that seems right for you, you can begin planning the steps you will take to achieve that goal.

KEY TERMS

- **evaluation**
- **personal career profile form**

Throughout Chapters 2, 3, and 4, you have been completing the first four steps in the decision-making process to explore career possibilities. In Chapter 2, you took a close look at your own personal needs and resources. You then identified your choices and began gathering information as part of your career research.

If you've done your research well, you've turned up many career choices. Narrowing these choices to a few "winners" involves comparing your personal data with the career information you've gathered. This step needs to be done with special care.

Evaluate Your Choices

Evaluation can take several forms. Usually it involves comparing and contrasting sets of data to rank them and determine winners. You will do this to find the best possible match between yourself and a career. Why is choice A better than choice B? Why is choice C less realistic than choice D?

Evaluation can also involve weighing possible outcomes. If I take this course of action, what will happen?

Finally, evaluation can involve thinking about your choices in light of your values. If I make this choice, will I be living up to what I truly believe in?

A good tool to use in evaluating your choices is the **personal career profile form** shown in *Figure 5.1.* This is a chart in which you can arrange side by side what you have learned about yourself and what you have learned about a career possibility.

FIGURE
5.1

PERSONAL CAREER PROFILE

Name *Gloria Perry* Date *December 14* Career *Fashion Industry Publicist*

Personal Information	Career Information	Match (1-10)
Your Values *I believe in equal opportunities for all people, especially women! I like to do creative things, too.*	**Career Values** *All kinds of people work in fashion. As a publicist, I would be able to use my creativity, as well as work with other people.*	9
Your Interests *My hobbies include reading Victorian novels. I love fashion and keep very up-to-date on the new styles, but I hate sewing! I also enjoy parties.*	**Career Duties and Responsibilities** *As a fashion publicist, I would make contacts with stores and buyers, arrange fashion shows and launch parties, and send out press releases.*	8
Your Personality *I'm very outgoing and enjoy having lots of friends. I get bored just sitting in class, unless there are open discussions. I have a good imagination.*	**Personality Type Needed** *A publicist must be outgoing and friendly. She must also be responsible and stay on top of things. Communication skills are important.*	6
Data-People-Things Preferences *I like being with people best of all. I find people fascinating. Sometimes facts interest me, too, but I prefer spending time with people!*	**Data-People-Things Relationships** *Publicists work mostly with people. In the fashion industry, you must be on top of trends, which are constantly changing. You don't work much with things—except for clothes and accessories!*	9
Skills and Aptitudes *My best subject is history. I have a natural sense of design and color, but I'm average at actually drawing. My teacher says I'm "excellent" at reading comprehension, but I hate grammar.*	**Skills and Aptitudes Required** *Good verbal and writing skills are essential for a publicist. You also must be a good "people person." History doesn't matter so much, but you never know–it could help.*	7
Education/Training Acceptable *I would love to go to fashion school in New York City. I suppose I need some business training as well.*	**Education/Training Required** *I guess a four-year fashion school would be best– one that has a good business department.*	9

▲ **Evaluating Careers** Gloria Perry completed a personal career profile form for each career possibility that she researched. *Do you think Gloria would be successful as a fashion industry publicist?*

In the third column, you are asked to use a 1-to-10 rating system to express how closely your personal and career information match. A perfect 10 (or as close as possible) in all six categories wins the gold.

Use the following questions to help you assign a score for each category:

- *Values*   Does this career match up well with my values?

- *Interests Versus Responsibilities* Will the day-to-day responsibilities interest me? Will I be good at them?

- *Personality*   Will I be happy with the work environment and hours?

Making Decisions Choosing the right career path can seem bewildering. *Why is it important to keep your career plans flexible at this stage of your life?*

- *Data-People-Things* Do the data-people-things requirements of this career match up well with my own preferences?

- *Skills and Aptitudes* Do I have the skills I need for this career—or the aptitudes to develop them?

- *Education/Training* Am I willing to get the education and training necessary for this career?

You should complete a personal career profile form for each career choice you have identified for yourself. Then you should tally the scores on all the forms and see which career choice ranks the highest. You are now ready for the next step.

Make Your Decision

Now's the time to make a choice. Which career will you pursue? You may be afraid to commit yourself, but try to have confidence in your research and evaluations. Remember: Unless you define a goal, you are unlikely to reach it. Also, remember that your choice is flexible—one that you will probably change as your life develops.

In the next section, you will work on the final step in the decision-making process: drawing up your plan of action.

interNET CONNECTION

Internships
Many companies offer paid and unpaid internships to students who want to gain experience. You would like to be a news anchor and are looking for an internship at a television station.

Connect
- Visit the Web sites of local television stations or cable news stations and research internship opportunities.
- Write a paragraph or two comparing internships at two different stations. Some points to compare are pay, full- or part-time status, length of internship, and job responsibilities.

SECTION 5.1 REVIEW

✔ Key Concept Checkpoint

Comprehension

1. Your uncle has been urging you to pursue a career as a real estate broker. However, you feel you'd prefer working as a sales representative for a sporting goods manufacturer. How would you go about evaluating these two career possibilities to see which one might be better for you?

Critical Thinking

2. Why is it important to evaluate and determine the career that suits you best?

CAREER FOCUS

CAREER CLUSTER: Government and Public Administration

Felix W. Ortiz
Assemblyman

CAREER FACTS

Education or Training Candidates for public office must meet age requirements and be U.S. citizens. Political experience on government bureaus, boards, or commissions is recommended, as well as a master's degree in public administration.

Aptitudes, Abilities, and Skills Strong writing and public speaking skills, knowledge of local issues, good people skills, management skills, and strong fundraising, budgeting, and problem-solving skills are needed.

Career Outlook Little growth is expected in this field through 2008, but there may be an increase in positions at the local level.

Career Path Public officials often gain experience as assistants to elected officials, or as aides to government bodies or committees.

What is your key to success?

"The foundation to any success is a solid education. Without the proper education, it would not have been possible for me to make the achievements I have made."

What does your job entail?

"The main part of my job deals with legislation; I propose new bills, amend old ones, offer support to bills that I believe in, and oppose those I find detrimental. Meetings with organizations and lobbyists associated with issues that I am working on are also part of my day. I attend sessions along with the rest of the Assembly, primarily during the first half of the year. I also attend conferences, meetings, and functions throughout the year."

What skills are important to you?

"As I am here for the people, it is crucial that I have strong people skills. Writing and communication skills are vital, as they are necessary for clear communication with others. An internship with the government can help students develop these skills."

What do you like most about your job?

"Perhaps the most rewarding aspect of my job is the fact that I have the chance to make a difference in the lives of my constituents. I truly enjoy the opportunity to help people, especially children. It is great to know that I have the ability to make a positive impact on the daily lives of people through legislation."

Critical Thinking Why might government officials advance to other offices in their hometown jurisdiction more quickly than in a new area?

Your Plan of Action

Making your career goals a reality means planning a course of action, called an **individual career plan**. This is the seventh and final step in the decision-making process leading to a career. There is no substitute for planning if you want to be successful and happy. Having a plan doesn't guarantee success, but it greatly improves your chances. You may get help from many sources, but the most workable plan will probably be the one you design yourself. Consider, for example, how Ronald Jones of Chelsea, Massachusetts, is planning for his future.

Since graduating from high school, Ron has been working five nights a week as a waiter at a French restaurant in Boston. During the day, he attends a culinary arts institute, where he is learning to become a gourmet chef. He describes his job as follows:

"It's a little hectic most of the time, but when things slow down, I can watch how the kitchen is run and how various dishes are prepared. I'm making good tips, which is helping me pay for school. I wouldn't want to have this waitering job forever, but the restaurant experience I'm getting—not to mention the cash—is helping me prepare for the career I really want."

Like Ron, it's time for you to start making plans. How will you begin?

WHAT YOU'LL LEARN

- How to establish an individual career plan and set intermediate career goals
- How to determine the education and training you will need

WHY IT'S IMPORTANT

Planning a course of action early is essential in achieving your career goals.

KEY TERMS

- **individual career plan**
- **on-the-job training**
- **apprentice**
- **vocational-technical center**
- **trade school**
- **continuing education**

Plan How to Reach Your Goal

To reach your ultimate career goal, you will first need to establish some intermediate planning goals. These are the steps you will take to get from where you are now to where you want to be. For example, if your career goal is to become a real estate broker, one intermediate goal would be to find out what training you need to qualify for a real estate license.

A good first step in planning how to reach your goal is to identify high school courses related to specific career choices in your career interest area. Selecting high school courses and experiences should be a part of your *graduation plan* that can lead you to a specific career choice in your career interest area.

Intermediate planning goals are important because they allow you to break your career plan into manageable steps. In this way, the prospect of striving toward a particular career goal doesn't seem so overwhelming. Intermediate goals can also help you feel confident and focused.

Taking Aim

The more specific your intermediate career targets, the more likely you are to hit the bull's-eye. Vague intermediate goals will not help you gain relevant experience. For example, if your ultimate career goal is to become a medical technician, it is not enough to say your intermediate goal is "to get a job working in a hospital." That's like throwing a dart in the general direction of the board. Instead, a goal such as "to enroll in a program that will train me to be an emergency room technician" is much closer to the mark.

In your journal, write down a few intermediate goals for your particular career choice. Then see if you can make each one more specific.

With Your Feet on the Ground

Besides being specific, your planning goals should be realistic. To plan realistic goals for the future, you must think about who and where you are today.

Plan of Action Ron dreams of becoming a great chef. *How do you plan to get from where you are now to your ultimate goal?*

It would be almost impossible to hit that bull's-eye if you didn't know where you were standing in relation to the dartboard. It would be just as difficult to reach your career goals if you were not honest with yourself about where you are starting from on your career path.

For example, if you dislike math, you may not be happy as an engineer. On the other hand, even if your math skills are weak right now, you may still strongly believe that you would enjoy being an engineer. Therefore, a realistic—and necessary—intermediate goal would be to strengthen your math skills in the near future.

An important note: Be careful not to confuse the words *realistic* and *traditional*. For example, women were traditionally more limited in their job options than men. Today, however, it is realistic for women to consider all jobs. Also, since you will be developing your career in the years to come, do not limit yourself by the current reality of the world. Be creative in your thinking. You may end up starting a trend-setting business, as Meredith Hunter has done. (See *Figure 5.2* on page 96).

Creative BUSINESS PRACTICES

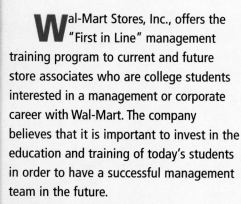

Wal-Mart
Recruiting Students for Management

Wal-Mart Stores, Inc., offers the "First in Line" management training program to current and future store associates who are college students interested in a management or corporate career with Wal-Mart. The company believes that it is important to invest in the education and training of today's students in order to have a successful management team in the future.

Applicants for First in Line must be full-time juniors or seniors in an accredited college or university with a grade point average of 2.5 or higher. They must be willing to work at least 16 hours per week while in school and relocate after graduation.

Student associates are paired with a management sponsor who assists them during the training period. After completing the training, many graduates are promoted to assistant store manager positions. Other program graduates move on to Wal-Mart's corporate office in Bentonville, Arkansas, where they work in merchandising, loss prevention, and information technology.

Critical Thinking

What benefits could current employers offer you to make you consider employment with them after graduation?

Link and Learn

To read more about careers with Wal-Mart, visit the company's Web site via the link on the *Succeeding in the World of Work* Web site at **www.careers.glencoe.com**.

Stepping-Stone Goals

Think of your ultimate goal as a green meadow on the far side of a river. If you simply plunge into the river, chances are you will be carried way off course. Now imagine a series of stepping-stones. By using each one in turn, you will be able to cross the river safely—and relatively quickly. Think of the stepping-stones as your short-, medium-, and long-term planning goals.

Ronald Jones, whom you read about earlier, has established several stepping-stone goals. While his ultimate career goal is to be executivie chef of a fine restaurant, he is currently working on a short-term goal: to get practical restaurant experience while serving as a waiter. He is also working on a medium-term goal: to earn a certificate within a few years from the culinary institute he attends. One long-term goal he has is to study with a master chef in France.

Having stepping-stone goals will also allow you to make a "course correction" if you decide your ultimate goal is not right for you. At any point along the way, you can change your mind and head off in a different direction. On the basis of his waitering experience, for example, Ron might decide he would prefer to own and operate a restaurant. He could then revise his medium- term goals to include taking business courses.

FIGURE 5.2 Setting Planning Goals
Stepping-stone goals are short-, medium-, and long-term goals that can help you reach your ultimate career goal in realistic stages.

A Career Decision Several years ago, Meredith Hunter made a career decision. She wanted to start a company that would create computer games based on well-known, high-quality children's books. Since she had little experience with business or computers, she knew that she had a long way to go before she could achieve her goal. However, she also knew that listing specific planning goals was a good place to start.

B Short-Term Goals Meredith's first short-term goal was to attend business school to acquire the knowledge and skills she would need to start her own business. She planned to take courses in business incorporation, management, and law, as well as in computer programming.

C Medium-Term Goals One of Meredith's medium-term goals was to get a job with a successful computer game company—preferably one in which she could have some creative input. She accomplished that goal. At this job, she learned as much as she could about how games are researched, developed, manufactured, and distributed.

D Long-Term Goal Meredith has reached her **long-term goal.** Having found business people willing to invest in her idea, she hired a creative team of artists. Today she runs a company that creates computer games.

Deciding on Education and Training

One of your first stepping-stone goals should be receiving the education and training you will need to achieve your ultimate career goal. *Figure 5.3* shows that workers who have more than a high school diploma are generally better prepared to succeed at their jobs than those who do not.

Make a list of several careers in your interest area. Then develop a chart classifying employment opportunities based on educational and training requirements.

Many options are available for getting the education and training you will need, including online learning apprenticeships and schools.

Online Learning

One of the newest ways to receive advanced education and training is online. Although it is relatively new, online education is quickly becoming popular. Many people are attracted by the convenience and flexibility of online classes, which allow them to work when and where they want to and at their own pace. Another advantage of online learning is the cost, which is typically less than traditional education programs.

Before opting for an online education, however, remember that interaction with a teacher, discussion, and the stimulation of class participation are strong motivators and among the most powerful educational tools.

FIGURE 5.3

BUSINESS SATISFACTION
Percent of businesses* ranking the skills of recent hires as excellent or very good

Legend:
- Recent hires with high school diploma or equivalent
- Recent hires with more than a high school diploma

Categories: Basic skills, Personal qualities, Thinking skills, Interpersonal skills, Technology skills, System skills, Information skills, Resource skills

*Racine Area Manufacturing and Commerce (RAMAC) Members, Racine County, Wisconsin
SOURCE: RAMAC Education Committee Workforce Survey

▲ **Advanced Education** A survey by the Racine Area Manufacturing and Commerce Education Committee found that employers tend to be more satisfied with workers who have received some post-high school training. *How do you suppose such extra training affects an employee's wages over the course of a career?*

On-the-Job Training: Learning by Doing

Offered by many companies, **on-the-job training** is on-site instruction in how to perform a particular job. It may consist of a few days of orientation for new employees or more formal long-term instruction. Workers at nuclear power plants, for example, undergo continual training in technical and safety procedures.

The need to be on the cutting edge of new trends leads many large companies to stress ongoing training for their employees. For instance, companies that use computer networks generally offer courses to keep their workers up-to-date with the latest software and computer technology.

Apprenticeships

The practice of training young people through apprenticeships to master a craft goes back many hundreds of years. Today an **apprentice** is someone who learns how to do a job through hands-on experience under the guidance of a skilled worker. Apprenticeships are still a fairly common way for unions to train skilled workers, especially in construction and manufacturing.

Kattai Wendall of Pittsburgh, Pennsylvania, for example, found her apprenticeship as a sheet-metal worker through her state apprenticeship agency. Although she does not make very much money now working at a manufacturing plant, she feels lucky because she is getting paid to learn a trade that will eventually earn her a better position and salary.

Apprenticeship The practice of serving as an apprentice to learn a craft from a master is centuries old. *What are advantages of this form of training?*

Vocational-Technical Centers

You can prepare for many careers by attending a **vocational-technical center.** This is a school that offers a variety of skills-oriented programs, such as courses in automotive or computer technology. Most vocational-technical centers have evening classes and are relatively inexpensive.

Trade Schools

The culinary arts institute that Ronald Jones attends in Massachusetts is an example of a trade school. A **trade school** is a privately run institution that trains students for a particular profession. Trade schools are usually more expensive than vocational-technical centers. However, they sometimes offer specialized programs that vocational-technical centers do not.

Community and Technical Colleges

Community colleges and technical colleges offer two-year and certificate programs in many occupational areas, such as accounting, tourism management, paralegal work, retailing, and desktop publishing. These colleges usually offer night and weekend classes and are less expensive than trade schools or four-year colleges. A graduate from a community or technical college with a two-year associate degree can usually transfer his or her credits to a four-year college or university.

Four-Year Colleges and Universities

Some careers—such as teacher and physical therapist—require a minimum of a bachelor's degree from a four-year college or university. Other careers—such as those in law, architecture, and medicine—require even more advanced degrees. In choosing a college, you will want to consider such factors as location, size, cost, the quality of your particular program, entrance requirements, and the availability of financial aid.

Military Service

Did you know that the military is the largest employer in the United States? If you think you might be cut out for the military, you may be able to receive training in one of more than 200 different occupations, including health technician and air-traffic controller. Depending on the career you choose, you must enlist for up to six years of active duty.

Sometimes you can attend school before or during your service. At other times, the military will pay for your education after you serve.

Committing Yourself on Paper

Are you feeling overwhelmed? That's only natural when faced with so many career options, but don't waste your energy worrying. Instead, take out a notebook and begin formulating your individual career plan on paper.

Questions and Answers

Start by creating a list of questions to answer about your career goals, education, and training. You might begin with these questions:

- What is my ultimate career goal?
- What is my first "stepping-stone" or short-term goal?
- Which educational programs offer the training I need?
- How much money will I need to pay for my education and training? Where will this money come from?

Careers in the Military The military is one place you can get post-high school training. *Why might the armed forces be a good career choice for some and not for others?*

Continuing Education

Many adults return to school at some point in their lives to complete their education, brush up on old skills, or pursue new paths. Many high schools, colleges, and universities offer **continuing education**—programs geared toward adult students. Many colleges and universities offer online and correspondence courses. Some of these programs lead to academic degrees.

Where Do You Go from Here?

Use print and online resources to complete an educational and training plan for a career pathway in your career interest area. Your plan should begin with entry into high school and continue through a postsecondary educational and/or training program. Then write up your educational and career plan as a timeline, similar to Ronald Jones's shown in *Figure 5.4* below. In chronological order, write your short-, medium-, and long-term goals. Include your projected starting and ending dates. Be sure to list and explain educational and/or training alternatives after high school. You can modify the goals and dates as you get closer to your ultimate goal. When you are finished, place your educational and career plan and timeline in your personal career portfolio.

Your decisions and plans are flexible. Expect to change them. The advantage to having a plan is that you will continue to move ahead until you find the right career.

FIGURE 5.4

EDUCATIONAL AND CAREER PLAN

	Now	1 year	2 years	3 years	4 years
Short-term	Work as a waiter and get practical restaurant experience				
Medium-term		Earn certificate from culinary institute			
Long-term				Study in France	
Ultimate goal					Executive chef

◀ **Setting Goals**
Putting his short-, medium-, and long-term plans in chronological order allowed Ronald Jones to visualize his career goals. *Which plans will Ronald be working on simultaneously for a while?*

SECTION 5.2 REVIEW

Key Concept Checkpoint

Comprehension

1. Explain why having "stepping-stone" planning goals is important for reaching your ultimate career goal.

2. Suppose that you have a friend who wants to be a fashion designer. How would you advise your friend to explore education or training options?

3. What is the advantage of committing your career plans to writing?

Critical Thinking

4. How often should you review your individual career plan and the goals that you have established? Why?

SECTION 5.1

- In evaluating possible careers, you should match the career information you've gathered to your personal interests and resources. (p. 88)

- Using a personal career profile form allows you to analyze career possibilities in a systematic way. (pp. 88–91)

KEY TERMS
evaluation (p. 88)
personal career profile form (p. 88)

SECTION 5.2

- The most workable career plan will probably be the one you design for yourself. (p. 93)

- Establishing intermediate career goals will make your ultimate goal easier to reach. (p. 94)

- For your planning goals to be realistic, you must be honest with yourself about your personal strengths. (pp. 94–95)

- Setting short-, medium-, and long-term goals will enable you to evaluate your career path as you go along. (pp. 96–97)

- Acquiring more education and training means having more career opportunities to choose from. Your options include online learning, on-the-job training, apprenticeships, vocational-technical programs, trade schools, community and technical colleges, four-year colleges and universities, continuing education programs, and military service. (pp. 98–101)

- Committing your plan of action to paper will help you develop specific career plans. It will also allow you to revise your plans while you continue to move ahead toward a career that will be right for you. (pp. 101–102)

KEY TERMS
individual career plan (p. 93)
on-the-job training (p. 99)
apprentice (p. 99)
vocational-technical center (p. 100)
trade school (p. 100)
continuing education (p. 101)

Reviewing Key Terms

1. Write a one-page article about making a career decision. Use the following terms in your article:
   - evaluation
   - personal career profile form
   - individual career plan
   - apprentice
   - on-the-job training
   - vocational-technical center
   - trade school
   - continuing education

Recalling Key Concepts

Determine whether each of the following statements is true. Rewrite any false statements to make them true.

2. You can use a personal career profile form to match what you know about yourself with what you know about different careers.

3. Once you establish an individual career plan, you should not change it.

4. Vocational-technical centers are more expensive than trade schools.

5. An individual career plan should include short-, medium-, and long-term goals.

Problem Solving

6. What consequences might result from settling on a career that conflicts with your personal values?

7. When evaluating your hopes and dreams, it helps to visualize your future. How might good visualization skills help you in your job or career?

Work-Based Learning

Basic Skills Writing

8. Determine your top three career choices. Research the education and training needed for each career. Summarize your findings in a 150-word report.

Thinking Skills Decision Making

9. Andrew just graduated from high school. His interests are radio and television, and he plans to build a career in the communications industry. He has just been offered an excellent job as publicity coordinator for a local radio station. The problem is that it is a full-time job with irregular hours and Andrew has been planning to attend college full-time. How should Andrew reach a decision? What do you think a good decision might be?

Interpersonal Skills Participating as a Team Member

10. As a class, make a list of the names and addresses of vocational-technical centers, trade schools, community and technical colleges, and four-year colleges and universities. Then, break the class down into teams of three students. Each team should select a different institution. As a team write a letter requesting information from the institution you have selected. Send your letter to the institution. When you receive the material, use it to create a class display.

School-Based Learning

Vocational Education Select Training Program

11. Lynn recently graduated from high school. Her career goal is to become a computer programmer. She is interested in learning computer programming, however, she must stick to a very strict budget. Using the library, the Internet, or the telephone, research the costs of computer-training programs in your area. Determine which program offers the best training for the lowest cost.

Art Seek Careers

12. You have been told you have excellent art skills and should pursue a career in the art field. Using resources in your school library, develop a list of five careers that require artistic skills. Explain the tasks involved in each career that would require your art skills.

Science Set Goals

13. You are interested in becoming a physical therapist. Research the career to find out more about it. Then develop a list of short-, medium-, and long-term goals that would help you reach this ultimate career goal.

Role Play

14. Securing an Internship

Situation You'd like to be a graphic artist and want to spend your summer vacation working at a business that will allow you to gain relevant experience. You know of an ideal local business that produces brochures, business cards, and advertisements. However, you've heard that the company's owner, Rachel Williams, is very busy and can be intimidating.

Activity Prepare a brief presentation and portfolio that will enable you to convince Rachel of your commitment to securing an internship. Choose specific skills and talents to highlight, and explain how your internship will benefit the company.

Evaluation You will be evaluated based on how well you meet the following performance indicators:

- Demonstrate preparation while presenting personal qualifications
- Create and use a professional portfolio to enhance your presentation
- Convey maturity and enthusiasm throughout your presentation

*inter*NET CONNECTION

15. Conduct an Interview
Interview a woman who has been successful in a predominantly male field. Ask her about her career, especially about difficulties she encountered because of her gender. Present your findings to the class in an oral report.

Connect Search the Web for current information about women in the workforce. Determine if the "glass ceiling" is still a reality and find statistics that compare average male and female salaries.

CAREER LAB

Real-World Workshop

Are You an Entrepreneur or an Employee?

✓ Overview

You've come up with a great idea for launching your own business, but you aren't sure how you feel about the risks of entrepreneurship. After all, you've read that two of every three businesses fail within their first four years of operation. On the other hand, you have confidence in your ideas and willingness to work hard. You've decided to talk with a successful entrepreneur and a successful corporate employee to get a better sense of what career choice will work best for you.

✓ Assignment

Identify a successful entrepreneur and corporate employee in your community to interview. Ideally, both interviewees should work in a field that interests you (preferably one of the careers that you researched in Career Lab 1). Brainstorm a list of questions to ask each individual. Then arrange an interview with both of your candidates. Hold the interview and take detailed notes.

✓ Tools/Resources

To complete this assignment, you must research companies and professionals in your area to identify your two interview candidates. During your interviews, you will need a mini-cassette recorder or a pencil and pad of paper. You will also need a word processing program to prepare a report afterwards.

✓ Procedures

Think about the careers and interests you identified in Career Lab 1. Consult the Internet, traditional library resources, your parents, and teachers and guidance counselors to identify appropriate individuals. Then arrange a specific time and place to interview your subjects. Before your interviews, create a list of thorough, thoughtful questions to pose. Such as:

- Why do you like being self employed/an employee of a company?
- How many hours do you generally work during a week?

- What is your top job priority?
- Would you recommend your career choice to another? Why or why not?
- What types of qualities do you think that a person in your line of work should possess?
- What are the advantages/disadvantages of your line of work?
- How has changing technology affected your career?
- How does the global economy affect your career?
- Why did you choose to work for a company/start your own business?
- What do you feel is the best advice you can offer to someone who wants to follow in your footsteps?
- What are your keys to success?

During your interviews, take notes or record responses. After your interviews, reflect on the matters discussed. Decide which type of career best suits you. Incorporate the insights you gained into a personal essay in which you discuss the specific things that you learned.

☑ Report

Your final product for this lab should include a typed copy of the transcripts of your interviews and a personal essay. Be sure to state your opinion about which career option best suits your needs and personality. Finally, discuss how the overall experience affected your long-term plans for the future.

☑ Presentation and Evaluation

Your report will be evaluated based on

- Subjects interviewed
- Depth of interview
- Questions asked
- Content and thoughtfulness of your personal essay
- Presentation and neatness

☑ Personal Career Portfolio

Print out a copy of your completed report to include in your personal career portfolio.

HELPFUL HINTS

Interview Etiquette
- Schedule a time that's convenient for your subjects—after all, they are taking time out of their day to help you.
- If you plan on recording a person during an interview, always ask for permission first.

- Show up at the interview prepared; have your questions and other materials ready.
- To make the most of your interview, do not ask questions that can be answered by a simple yes or no.
- After the interview, send your subject a brief written note expressing your thanks.

Chapter 6
Finding and
Applying for
a Job

Chapter 7
Interviewing

Portfolio Project

Résumé Reference Collection Collect at least ten current résumés prepared by adults. Ask your parents, relatives, or other adult friends for copies of their résumés. If you have trouble collecting enough résumés from people you know, you can also look for résumés on the Internet. Create a reference folder that displays your ten résumés, and write a brief paragraph explaining the strengths of each résumé. Think about how you can use the résumés you've collected to gather ideas for creating your own résumé. Keep your reference folder so that you can refer to it whenever you update your résumé.

CAREER LAB PREVIEW

Making a Good Impression

As part of this unit, you will work on improving your communication and presentation skills by role-playing and recording two interviews. You and a partner will devise, enact, and record two interviews using the skills and techniques described in Chapters 6 and 7. Once you've completed your interviews, you'll critique your performance and present your ideas and interviews to the class.

Chapter 6

Finding and Applying for a Job

Section 6.1
Exploring Sources of Job Leads

Section 6.2
Applying for a Job

CHAPTER OBJECTIVES

After completing this chapter, you will be able to

● Explain why networking is effective for developing job leads.

● Create and maintain a career network and contact list.

● Use the Internet and other resources to search for career opportunities.

● Prepare written materials necessary for job-hunting, including applications, résumés, and cover letters.

JOURNAL

Personal Career Plan

During the next week, explore as many sources of job leads as possible. Record your explorations in your journal, noting details about each job opening and how you learned about it.

Personal Career Project

Research the skills and qualifications for the job opening that interests you most. Then contact the company to find out the name of the person who is in charge of hiring for this position. Design a cover letter and résumé tailored to this job, incorporating the skills-specific information.

Exploring Sources of Job Leads

WHAT YOU'LL LEARN

- Why networking is an effective strategy for developing job leads
- How to create and maintain a career network and contact list
- How to use networking and Internet research skills to identify job leads

WHY IT'S IMPORTANT

Using a variety of strategies, including networking and Internet research, will enable you to find many career opportunities.

KEY TERMS

- job lead
- networking
- contact list
- referral
- school-to-work programs
- Internet

Getting a job is the beginning of a new lifestyle. There will be new friends, new surroundings, new challenges, and your own income. Think of the possibilities! To get started on this adventure, you need a job. Not just any job will do, though. You need the right job. This is the one that you will enjoy and do well at.

Finding the right job usually begins with a job lead. A **job lead** is information about a job opening. It can be a tip from a friend, a classified (help-wanted) ad in the newspaper, or information from a teacher or school guidance counselor.

Networking

How do you go about developing job leads? One of the best ways is by networking. **Networking** is communicating with people you know or can get to know to share information and advice.

How well does networking work? Compare it to other ways of getting a job shown in *Figure 6.1.*

What makes networking so useful is that your contacts may be "insiders." Often, they work at the company that is hiring. They can tell you what the company is looking for and give you a recommendation that really counts.

Creating Your Own Network

Networking is not as difficult as you might think. You know people, don't you? Those people will form the basis for your network.

To get started, make a **contact list**. This is simply a list of people you know who might be helpful in your job search. For example, do you have any friends who have started new jobs recently? Ask them if they have any leads. Do any family friends own or manage their own businesses? They may need someone with your qualifications or may have a business contact who is looking for a good worker.

List friends who work for companies where you would like to work. Then add the names of school friends and neighbors who are somehow connected with a business that interests you. Most businesses welcome applications from friends of their employees because they trust the opinions of current employees. Valued company employees are good people to make recommendations because they understand the skills, values, and work ethic necessary to work for their company.

Professional people can also provide opportunities for networking. You probably have periodic contact with professional people—doctors, lawyers, or business people. If you have established a good rapport with these people, they will be happy to provide you with referrals. A **referral** is someone to whom you've been directed by a contact who is already part of your network.

Former employers are another source of job leads. It is likely that a former employer will want to help you find a job if he or she was pleased with your work.

FIGURE 6.1 — WAYS THAT PEOPLE GET JOBS

Percent of total job seekers using the method	Method	Effectiveness Rate*
66.0%	Applied directly to employer	47.7%
50.8	Asked friends about jobs where they work	22.1
41.8	Asked friends about jobs elsewhere	11.9
28.4	Asked relatives about jobs where they work	19.3
27.3	Asked relatives about jobs elsewhere	7.4
45.9	Answered local newspaper ads	23.9
21.0	Private employment agency	24.2
12.5	School placement office	21.4
10.4	Asked teacher or professor	12.1

* A percentage was obtained by dividing the number of job seekers who actually found work using the method by the total number of job seekers who used that method, whether successfully or not.

▲ **Job Hunting** The graph shows the effectiveness of different job search methods. *Why do you think most people get jobs by networking and contacting employers directly?*

FIGURE
6.2

ASSOCIATIONS IN SUCCESSFUL NETWORKS

Associations	Description	Examples
Personal	All the people you know personally; according to a recent MTV poll, 85 percent of young workers found jobs through personal associations	Classmates, neighbors, family, friends
Professional	The people you work with or know because of the business you're in or professional organization you belong to	Coworkers, supervisors, customers, colleagues in other companies
Organizational	People you know because of organizations or clubs you belong to	Members of your Sierra Club chapter, computer club, softball team, church or synagogue
Opportunistic	People you bump into by chance	The clerk at the music store, the woman sitting next to you on the train, the contractor who's repairing a neighbor's house
Technological	People you communicate with on the Internet	The friends you talk to in a chat room, news group, discussion group

▲ **Using Connections** Successful networks include five types of associations: personal, professional, organizational, opportunistic, and technological. *Why should you try to include all five types of associations in your network?*

You can also receive job leads by joining professional or community organizations. By joining such groups, you'll meet new people and build your network (see **Figure 6.2**). *Listservs*, which are e-mail networks that link professionals who work in a specific industry, often provide useful job leads and contacts. Although membership to some listservs costs money, the opportunities that a good service will supply may make the fee worthwhile.

Using Your School's Resources

When planning your job search, don't overlook resources at your school. Your school has a counselor or teacher who can guide you in your job hunt. Your school may even have a placement office.

A counselor can set up interviews with employers. He or she can help you identify and follow leads in specific career areas.

Your school counselor may also be able to help you get into **school-to-work programs**. These programs bring schools and local businesses together. Students gain work experience and training. When they graduate, they usually get preference for jobs at the businesses.

Printed Job Advertisements

The classified ads can be one part of your job search, but it should not be the only one. Only a small percentage of job seekers find their jobs through ads.

In pursuing this method of job hunting, don't limit yourself to newspaper classifieds. There are many other sources. Check these out:

- *National Business Employment Weekly*,

- *Black Enterprise*, *Hispanic Business*, and similar publications that are geared to specific ethnic groups, and

- magazines that specialize in particular industries, such as *Advertising Age* and *Computerworld*.

Using the Telephone

The telephone is one of your most useful job-hunting tools. Use it to make hot calls. A *hot call* is a call to a referral or a call to follow up a lead. It's *hot*

CAREER CHECKLIST

When Looking for a Job...

- ☑ Search the newspaper and the Internet for available jobs in your field of interest.
- ☑ Take advantage of resources available through teachers or your school's guidance counselor.
- ☑ Create a résumé that highlights your professional and personal strengths.
- ☑ Write a cover letter that advertises your best qualities.
- ☑ Utilize all of your contacts for networking, including friends and family members.
- ☑ Prepare for the interview.
- ☑ Have confidence in yourself and your abilities to succeed in a new job.

Starting a Network You can begin networking with your friends. *How can friends help you find a job?*

Cold Calls When making cold calls, plan your conversation carefully. *Why is it helpful to write a script?*

because you know whom you're calling and you know there's a job or information at the other end of it.

You may also make *cold calls*. These are blind calls. You're not calling to follow up on a specific job lead or a referral but just to get information. Does the company have any openings? Whom can you talk to there? If you make cold calls, plan them carefully.

- Scan the Yellow Pages for companies you might want to work for, and call them. Ask for the personnel director or the supervisor of a department.

- Write an introductory script to use when calling. Tell who you are, why you're calling, and what you want.

- Write questions that will get you information about job openings. Be sure to request referrals.

A telephone call may be your first personal contact with an employer. Make it effective. Practice the skills of speaking and listening.

Employment Agencies

An employment agency is a matchmaker between job seekers and companies with job openings. Job seekers fill out applications at the agency. Businesses call the agency when they have openings. The agency brings the two together.

There are two kinds of employment agencies—public and private. Public agencies provide free placement services. Private agencies charge a fee, which may be paid by either the job seeker or the employer. Private agencies may give more personal service and list jobs not on file with the public agency.

Using the Internet

Using the job-hunting tactics discussed so far, you can contact hundreds of potential employers. That's not bad, but the **Internet**, an international network of computer networks, offers you the ability to contact an unlimited number of employers worldwide.

Finding the Right Web Sites

Many Web sites are created for the sole purpose of linking job seekers with employers. Web sites such as *www.monster.com* and *www.careerbuilder.com* are two of the most popular sites visited by people in search of jobs. At such sites, you can search for jobs according to job title, the city in which you'd like to work, and other important criteria. Once you've found an interesting opportunity, you can e-mail your résumé directly to the person who is in charge of hiring for that position. Using the Internet, you can feasibly send out hundreds of copies of your résumé in just one day—without paying for expensive paper or postage!

Most career Web sites provide more than job listings. Some sites permit you to

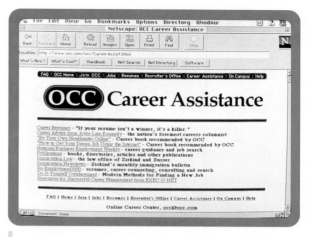

Keywords The Internet is an effective tool for finding jobs. *What keywords might lead you to jobs in your field of interest?*

post your résumé online so that recruiters can access it while searching for qualified applicants. Other sites provide support services such as personal job search agents, career counseling, career networks, chat and message boards, and free newsletters.

If you know of a specific company that you're interested in working for, you may also want to visit that company's official Web site. Some companies opt to post job opportunities directly on their own site.

SECTION 6.1 REVIEW

 Key Concept Checkpoint

Comprehension

1. Explain why networking is one of the most effective means of finding a job.
2. Whom should you include on your contact list? Why?
3. Which source for job leads will you use first in job hunting? Why?
4. What are six keywords you might use in a job search on the Internet?

Critical Thinking

5. What are some advantages and disadvantages of sending your résumé to a company via e-mail?

CAREER FOCUS

Alison Scarratt
Curator of Fishes
National Aquarium in Baltimore

CAREER FACTS

Education or Training Work in the husbandry (animal care) division of an aquarium requires an undergraduate degree in biology, oceanography, aquaculture, or another related field. Most aquariums also like to see a SCUBA certification, experience with keeping animals, and fieldwork. An advanced degree (master's or doctorate) may be required for a research or advanced management position.

Aptitudes, Abilities, and Skills Strong organizational skills, good communication skills, and thorough knowledge of the basics of fish husbandry.

Career Outlook Average job growth is expected through 2008.

Career Path To move into management, experience as an aquarist and training in management are necessary. With management experience, curators can become program directors.

What is your key to success?

"I've always had a clear vision of what I hope to accomplish in my career. This helps me set goals and make good decisions on how to reach those goals. I also attribute my success to my ability to work well with others."

What does your job entail?

"I oversee the administration and management of the Fishes Department at the aquarium, including acquisition, upkeep of the exhibit and quarantine tanks, maintenance of life-support systems, and long-term planning for the department. I supervise a staff of ten aquarists and three departmental managers who share the daily responsibility of caring for our 8,000 animals. I also review and evaluate special programs, projects, and exhibits."

What skills are most important to you?

"Strong skills in communication, organization, and trouble-shooting are essential. The lives of our animals and the safety of our staff depend on clear communication and careful organization. Problems need to be identified and solved before they can have any adverse effect on the animals' health."

What training do you recommend for students?

"It is very helpful to seek hands-on experience as an aquarist, taking care of a wide variety of fish and invertebrates. If you live near a public aquarium, zoo, or science center, become an active volunteer or intern in the husbandry department. While these are often unpaid positions, the experience, as well as the contacts you make, will be invaluable."

> **Critical Thinking** What other types of organizations might require a curator to organize and catalog material or specimens?

Applying for a Job

Think of a personnel director with three piles of applications before him. One pile is labeled "Yes." One is labeled "Maybe." One is labeled "No." Your job is to get your application into the "Yes" pile. How will you do that?

It comes down to how well you present yourself in your phone calls, job application, résumé, and cover letter. Your writing, problem solving, creative thinking, and reasoning skills will show.

Employers are looking for the best person to fill the job. They want to know whether or not you have the ability to do the work. They will be influenced by the way you dress and whether or not you are well-groomed. They will also notice if you use slang or any other language that is not standard English. In fact, they will want to know everything about you that relates to the job.

Be Confident and Be Prepared

You may feel anxious and insecure when applying for a job. That's natural, but don't show it. Project confidence and a positive, businesslike image. Display this image every time you communicate with an employer by phone, in writing, or in person.

WHAT YOU'LL LEARN

- How to prepare for your job search
- Procedures for creating effective résumés and cover letters

WHY IT'S IMPORTANT

Making a good first impression on potential employers is essential to securing employment.

KEY TERMS

- **Social Security number**
- **work permit**
- **standard English**
- **references**
- **résumé**
- **cover letter**

Be Prepared

An employer will require you to have certain documents. If you don't have them when you apply for a job, it shows that you aren't prepared. Get them before you go job hunting.

First, you'll need a **Social Security number**, a number issued by the federal government that is required for all workers. You probably already have one. If not, you can get one at the post office.

If you are under 16, you will also need a work permit. Some states require work permits for workers under 18. A **work permit** shows that you have been advised of laws restricting the hours young people can work and the kinds of jobs they can hold. You should be able to get a work permit at your school's guidance office.

An employer may also request your résumé. A résumé is a great way to list your experience, education, and skills in a professional manner. It is important for your résumé to be free of spelling and grammatical errors. Employers will see your résumé as a reflection of you, so make sure it is well written and polished. Résumés are discussed in greater depth later in this chapter.

Communicating Effectively

The way you speak and write is one of the first and strongest impressions you'll make, so use **standard English**. This is the form of writing and speaking you've learned in school. It is the form used in newspapers and on television news programs. If you have trouble with grammar and usage, now is the time to polish those skills. Be sure to avoid the use of slang and words such as *um* and *like*. You may want to prepare by practicing asking and answering typical interview questions with a friend.

Filling Out the Job Application

A *job application* is one way an employer screens applicants. This form asks questions about your skills, work experience, education, and interests. Always fill out

Job Applications A job application is a type of interview. *What could an employer learn about you from your handwriting?*

a job application completely and accurately. Keep these additional suggestions in mind:

- Read and follow directions exactly.
- Keep the application neat and clean.
- Make your statements positive. If you believe that answering a question might disqualify you, write "Will explain in interview."
- Keep your options open. Do not state the salary you want. Write "Negotiable." If you are asked whether you will work nights, write "Will consider."

- Prepare any lists of information, such as schools attended, in advance.

Applications often request **references.** These are people who will recommend you to an employer. Choose references carefully and be prepared to list them on the application. Employers trust teachers or former employers the most. Make sure you ask permission to use people as references.

Employers don't have a right to ask about your race, religion, sex, children, or marital status. You don't have to tell if you've been arrested, although you are

Creative BUSINESS PRACTICES

CVS
Employing Older Workers

CVS/Pharmacy, based in Woonsocket, Rhode Island, is one of the leading drugstore chains in the U.S. CVS actively recruits older workers to join its team of retail and pharmacy employees.

Workers over age 50 make up 14 percent of the CVS work force. Because many people are continuing to work at least part-time during retirement, CVS hopes to recruit even more seniors for positions in its stores.

Adding seniors to the CVS team is a win-win situation. Seniors have the chance to earn extra money, stay active, and feel connected with the community. At the same time, CVS retains experienced, responsible workers who are good examples for

younger employees, and the pharmacy is able to avoid labor shortages.

Critical Thinking

What are some ways that companies can recruit older workers? How can younger employees benefit from working with seniors?

Link and Learn

For more information about CVS and other companies' commitments to employ older workers, visit the Web site of the National Council on the Aging via the link on the *Succeeding in the World of Work* Web site at **www.careers.glencoe.com**.

required to tell if you've been convicted of a felony. If you are asked for this information on an application form, you might indicate that you'll explain in the interview. To get practice completing job applications, obtain one from a local company for which you would like to work. Fill out the application for an employment opportunity in your career interest area, then prepare a list of the information that you needed to complete the form.

Preparing a Résumé

A **résumé** is a brief summary of your personal information, education, skills, work experience, activities, and interests. You will send it to an employer when applying for a job by mail or via the Internet. A résumé can get you an interview or kill your chance for a job. Don't be shy. Make yourself look good!

You do this by carefully choosing what

you'll include, what you'll emphasize, and how you'll describe your experience. Do not include any negative information. If you don't have work experience, don't mention it. Focus on the skills, education, and training you do have. Don't hesitate to include awards, hobbies, or activities. References can be included, or you can indicate you'll provide them on request.

The best résumés are brief. Keep yours to one page. It must be typed or computer generated. Of course, it must be neat, and there should be no errors in spelling, grammar, or usage. There are two basic forms of résumés.

A *chronological résumé* gives your experience in time order. You list your most recent job first, then your previous job, and so on. You organize your education and other information in the same reverse time order. ***Figure 6.3*** shows an example of a chronological résumé.

The advantage of a chronological résumé is that it shows your growth in experience. It works best for a person with continuous work experience.

A *skills résumé* highlights your skills and accomplishments. It is organized around skills or strengths, such as attention to detail or interpersonal skills. After each heading is a description. The advantage of this résumé is that you can emphasize your strengths. ***Figure 6.4*** on page 124 shows one way to organize a skills résumé.

Résumé Strategies The information you include on a résumé must be accurate and true. What you include and how you state it is up to you. *What can you do to make yourself look good on a résumé?*

FIGURE
6.3

Chronological Résumé Résumés may be organized in different formats. Keep your résumé brief.
An outline form is best because it is easy to read.
Use titles and spacing to identify major categories
of information. Most résumés include the following
information.

1 Name and Address Write your name, full
address, e-mail address, and telephone number
(with area code) at the top of your résumé.

2 Job Objective State the job you are
applying for. Be sure to change this item if you
are using the same résumé when applying for
different jobs.

3 Work Experience List your work
experience, beginning with your most recent job.
Include volunteer work if it relates to the job you
are applying for.

4 Education List the schools you have
attended and diplomas or degrees you have
received. You may also include any subjects or
programs you specialized in.

5 Honors and Activities Include any
honors or awards you have received or activities
you have participated in that relate to the job
you want.

6 Special Skills and Abilities Identify any
business or other skills and abilities that you
have gained in school, on a job, or in other
situations.

7 References If your résumé is short, you
may include references. If not, say "Available
upon request."

Laura Calero
621 Bradley Street
Kirkwood, MO 63122
314-555-8210
lcalero@linknet.com

JOB OBJECTIVE

A position as a junior production editor utilizing my proofreading and computer
skills.

WORK EXPERIENCE

July 2000–present: Production Assistant, Benjamin Publishing Company,
Chesterfield, Missouri. Responsible for a variety of tasks involving
textbook production, including acquiring photos, desktop
publishing, proofreading, and inputting of corrections on computer.

August 1999–   Sales Associate (part-time), J.H. Covington Company, St. Louis,
June 2000:   Missouri. Responsible for customer service, assisted in keeping
and taking inventory.

Summers, 1997   Swimming instructor, Kennedy High School, Webster Groves,
and 1998:   Missouri. Trained intermediate-level students in diving and
lifesaving techniques.

EDUCATION

High School Diploma (college preparatory program), Kennedy High School,
Webster Groves, Missouri

HONORS AND ACTIVITIES

honor roll, student council member, yearbook sports editor, swim team member

SPECIAL SKILLS AND ABILITIES

Solid knowledge of both Macintosh and IBM-compatible computers, Windows,
Microsoft Word, and Quark. General familiarity with textbook publishing production.
Strong math skills. Excellent attendance record.

REFERENCES

Available upon request.

Electronic Résumés

Increasingly, companies *scan* résumés into their computers. That is, they copy and store them electronically in their computers. When companies need to hire someone, they do an electronic search of the résumés. They look for keywords that describe skills or job experiences they're seeking, such as *food service, mathematics,* and *French.*

Here are some tips for making your résumé "scannable":

- Keep the résumé clean.
- Use crisp, dark type.
- Avoid italics, underscores, and other fancy type.
- Use white paper.
- Use keywords in describing your experience.

FIGURE 6.4

SKILLS RÉSUMÉ

Laura Calero
621 Bradley Street
Kirkwood, MO 63122
314-555-8210
lcalero@linknet.com

JOB OBJECTIVE

A position as a junior production editor. Desire position with opportunity for career growth.

SKILLS AND ABILITIES

Computer Skills
Skilled on both Macintosh and IBM-compatible computers. Classes using IBM-compatible computers in middle and high school. On-the-job training on Macintosh with Benjamin Publishing Company. Familiar with Windows, Microsoft Word, and Quark.

Communications Skills
Excellent writing and speaking skills. Good with grammar and usage. Short stories published in high school journal, *The Athenaeum.*

Hardworking
Have worked outside of school since age 16 as a swimming instructor during summer vacation and as a part-time sales associate for J.H. Covington Company. Worked 20 hours per week while going to school.

Consumer Relations
As a sales associate with J.H. Covington, had direct customer contact. Successfully handled both sales and returns. Won "Sales Associate of the Month" award in April 1994.

Attention to Detail
Precise and careful in work. As a production assistant for Benjamin Publishing Company, did proofreading and input corrections on the computer.

EDUCATION

High School Diploma, Kennedy High School, Webster Groves, Missouri. Followed college preparatory program.

ACTIVITIES AND AWARDS

High school activities included member of student council, yearbook sports editor, member of swimming team. Awards included honor roll.

▲ **Skills Résumé** A skills résumé lets you highlight skills, aptitudes, and experience that you have. *What categories would you list under Skills and Abilities?*

Writing Cover Letters

Do not send your résumé by itself. Always include a **cover letter**. A cover letter is a one-page letter telling the employer who you are and why you're sending your résumé. It introduces you and allows you to say why you can do a good job for the company. Your cover letter should reflect your understanding of the company and how you may be able to meet its needs. Emphasize facts that make you especially well qualified for the job. Your cover letter should be divided into three parts (see **Figure 6.5**).

FIGURE 6.5

COVER LETTER

Laura Calero
621 Bradley Street
Kirkwood, MO 63122
November 16, 2001

Mr. David Schweizer
Managing Editor
Premiere Publishing Company, Inc.
St. Louis, MO 63108

Dear Mr. Schweizer:

Ann Leiter, the editorial director for Sunshine Publishing, suggested I contact you about the position of junior production editor that is open with your company. Please consider me as an applicant for this position.

I have been working since July 2000 as a production assistant for Benjamin Publishing Company in Chesterfield, Missouri. I've had an opportunity to develop skills in desktop publishing and to learn about many aspects of textbook publishing. Please review my enclosed résumé. It provides more details about the experience and skills I can bring to your company.

I am especially interested in pursuing a career with Premiere Publishing because of your reputation for creative use of graphics and page design. I hope you agree that my skills and experience would make me a valuable asset to your company.

May I have an interview? I will be glad to call at your convenience. My home telephone number is (314) 555-8210.

Sincerely,

Laura Calero

Laura Calero

▲ **Cover Letter** Make the purpose of your cover letter clear. Let your personality come through. *How has this writer included the key elements of the three parts of the cover letter?*

The opening paragraph of your cover letter should explain why you are writing. Drop names! Say where, or from whom, you learned about the job.

The body of your cover letter should be your sales pitch. In this section, highlight personal qualities, skills, and experiences that make you a good candidate for the job opening.

The closing paragraph should tell how you will follow up. Always include your telephone number in this paragraph so that the employer can contact you.

Put time and effort into producing your cover letter. Like your résumé, it should be free of errors in spelling and punctuation. If possible, ask someone else to proofread your cover letter before sending it to a prospective employer.

It's also a good idea to try to personalize your letter. One woman applied for a job with Playskool. As a child, she had loved the company's toys. She mentioned this fact in her cover letter, and it helped her get the job.

Remember that a business won't hire you just because you need a job. Your cover letter should convince the employer that you have the necessary skills and abilities.

ETHICS *in Action*

Mixed Messages Your uncle's friend owns a music store in the mall, and he needs a part-time sales clerk. Your uncle left a message on your family's answering machine to tell your older sister about the job and to let her know that his friend would be at the store this afternoon to interview her. You are also looking for a job, and you know that your sister is out with her friends and will not be home until tonight.

THINK ABOUT IT
Would you go to see your uncle's friend about the job? Why or why not?

Taking Tests

When you apply for a job, you may have to take one or more tests.

- A performance test evaluates how well you can do a particular task. An example is a typing test.

- A drug test is a blood or urine test for illegal drugs. Most companies in the nuclear power and transportation industries use drug tests.

- A polygraph test is a lie detector test. It may be required if you are applying for a job in law enforcement or government.

SECTION 6.2 REVIEW

✓ **Key Concept Checkpoint**

Comprehension
1. Why should you use standard English throughout the job application process?

2. When is it appropriate to use a skills résumé rather than a chronological résumé?

Critical Thinking
3. Given the fact that all people make mistakes, why would a prospective employer be likely to disregard a résumé with only minor mistakes?

SECTION 6.1

- There are numerous sources for job leads. They include networking, employment agencies, school placement centers, classified ads, and the Internet. (pp. 112–117)

- Networking means talking with people who can help you in your job search. Contact lists provide the foundation of networks. (pp. 112–113)

- You build a network by getting referrals from people you know. (p. 113)

- School counselors and placement centers can help you identify and apply for jobs. (pp. 114–115)

- You can find classified ads in newspapers and a variety of other publications. They should not be the only method for finding job leads. (p. 115)

- Employment agencies match job seekers with businesses seeking new employees. There are public and private employment agencies. (p. 116)

- The Internet has job lists, online career centers, and sites where you can post your résumé. (p. 117)

KEY TERMS
job lead (p. 112)
networking (p. 112)
contact list (p. 113)
referral (p. 113)
school-to-work
  programs (p. 115)
Internet (p. 117)

SECTION 6.2

- Before you apply for a job, you should get a Social Security number, and you may need a work permit. (p. 120)

- When you apply for a job, use standard English, the form of speaking and writing that you learned in school. (p. 120)

- Employers screen applicants through job applications, résumés, and cover letters. You want to project a positive image of yourself in these documents. (pp. 120–126)

- Some employers require tests—such as performance tests, drug tests, or polygraph tests—as part of the application process. (p. 126)

KEY TERMS
Social Security
  number (p. 120)
work permit (p. 120)
standard English (p. 120)
references (p. 121)
résumé (p. 122)
cover letter (p. 125)

Reviewing Key Terms

1. On a separate sheet of paper, write one or two paragraphs describing how you would conduct a job search. Use the terms below in your description.
   - job lead
   - networking
   - contact list
   - referral
   - school-to-work programs
   - Internet
   - Social Security number
   - work permit
   - standard English
   - references
   - résumé
   - cover letter

Recalling Key Concepts

2. Getting a job lead is the first step in ____.
   (a) building a network
   (b) finding a job
   (c) locating a school-to-work program

3. You build your network by asking for ____.
   (a) contact lists (b) job leads
   (c) referrals

4. A fee may be charged by a ____.
   (a) private employment agency
   (b) public employment agency
   (c) school placement center

5. When completing a job application, you should ____.
   (a) make it scannable
   (b) make your statements positive
   (c) ask for referrals

6. A résumé that lists your last job first is a ____.
   (a) skills résumé
   (b) chronological résumé
   (c) electronic résumé

Problem Solving

7. Many employers like to hire people referred to them through a network. Why do you think this is so?

8. If you were an employer, what would you think of an applicant who did not use standard English?

9. List information you would include on your résumé, and explain why.

10. Why would an employer give applicants a skill test before hiring them?

11. If you were an employer, what would you look for in an applicant's cover letter?

Work-Based Learning

Thinking Skills Knowing How to Learn

12. In a paragraph, describe how your school placement office can help you find job leads.

Personal Qualities Integrity/Honesty

13. Jennifer is filling out a job application. She was fired from her last job. She wants to answer no to the question "Have you ever been fired?" What should she do and why?

Resources Allocating Time

14. Imagine you are looking for a job. Prepare a daily schedule for your job search.

School-Based Learning

Mathematics Calculate Contacts

15. Bill has 20 people on his first contact list. If each person on his list refers him to two more people, and each of those people refers him to one more person, how many people will be on his new list?

Social Studies/Language Arts Write a Cover Letter

16. Laura is interested in sending a résumé to a corporation. Choose a corporation she might apply to and research it. Then write a cover letter she might send to the corporation. Use your research in your letter.

Computer Science Find Nursing Jobs

17. Sheila wants to find out about opportunities in nursing in Texas. Use the Internet to find some online job bulletin boards. Find some jobs for Sheila. Contact an online career service to get some advice for her.

Role Play

18. Offering Advice

Situation Your friend Tracey wants to apply for a summer internship. She was absent from school on the days that your class discussed how to write a résumé and she would like you to teach her how to write it.

Activity Teach Tracey how to prepare a résumé. Explain the importance and purpose of the résumé, and then prepare a brief lesson in which you share the key steps involved in writing a résumé. Be sure to present an example of a good résumé so that Tracey will understand exactly what she needs to do to prepare her own.

Evaluation You will be evaluated based on how well you meet the following performance indicators:

- Explain the essential steps relevant to résumé-writing
- Provide and explain the parts of a sample résumé
- Organize your points in a coherent lesson

*inter*NET
CONNECTION

19. Prepare a Résumé

Collaborate with a classmate to research ways to write a résumé. Then write a résumé for an employment opportunity in your career interest area. Exchange résumés with your partner for review and proofreading. Check each other's résumé for standard English.

Connect Find a career Web site that allows people to post their résumés online. Use the information presented on the Web site to write a report on rules for posting résumés online.

Chapter 7

Interviewing

Section 7.1
Before an Interview:
Getting Ready

Section 7.2
During an Interview:
It's Show Time

Section 7.3
After an Interview:
Following Up

CHAPTER OBJECTIVES

After completing this chapter, you will be able to

- Identify methods of preparing for interviews.
- Recognize the factors that create an employer's first impression of a job candidate.
- Anticipate and answer typical and tough interview questions.
- Apply procedures for following up on an interview.
- Recognize proper methods of accepting and rejecting employment.

JOURNAL

Personal Career Plan

In your journal, write four questions you would want to ask a job applicant. Think of questions that would help you understand the applicant as an individual and as a possible employee, regardless of job skills. Now switch roles from interviewer to applicant; record your answers to the questions.

Personal Career Project

Talk to an employer or a manager who has interviewed job applicants. Ask this person about common mistakes that people make during job interviews. What advice would this person give every applicant? Record the key points of your interview in your journal.

Before an Interview: Getting Ready

WHAT YOU'LL LEARN

- How to prepare for an interview by rehearsing and conducting research
- How to dress appropriately for a job interview

WHY IT'S IMPORTANT

Preparing for a job interview will increase your chances of getting the job.

KEY TERM

- interview

Your heart's pounding and your palms are sweaty. You're feeling that mix of confidence and excitement that is part of your first job interview. You prepared well, and you're ready to shine!

The **interview**—a formal meeting between an employer and a job applicant—is the employer's chance to meet you as a person, not just as a name on a résumé. Here's where research and rehearsal pay off.

Know Before You Go

Interviews are usually conducted by a manager or a member of a company's human resources department. Professionals such as these may interview as many as ten candidates a day for any given position. The decision to hire just one person can be very difficult, especially if many of the candidates seem qualified and competent. In such competitive situations, your attention to the small details overlooked by other candidates may prove to be the deciding factor that wins you the job offer.

How can you stand out in a job market packed with qualified people? Cheryl Nickerson of Nike says, "Please do your research. Be able to ask intelligent questions about the company and what's going on in the industry." Employers, Nickerson adds, want people with a "willingness to learn and grow."

Here are some smart ways to research a company before an interview:

- Use the library to find books, magazines, and newspaper articles about the company.
- Use financial magazines or newspapers to research current industry events or market trends that affect the company.
- Research competitors that affect the company's sales.
- Ask the public relations department for the company's annual report or press kit to check out the company's history. Use these resources to find out the names of the company's leaders.
- Visit the company's Web site for up-to-the-minute information.
- Talk to people who work for the company.

Do these techniques work? Absolutely. The more you know about a company, the better you can showcase your ideas. Also, your willingness to conduct research before the interview shows that you're genuinely interested in the company and that you're the sort of person who is willing to go to extra effort to make a good impression.

Conducting research about a company is a detail that's often overlooked by candidates. A person who takes the time to perform such preparation stands out among his or her competition.

Researching a company can also protect you. For instance, your investigation could reveal that the company is not a good place to work, after all. It may be experiencing serious financial trouble or have a history of treating its employees poorly.

Rehearsal Time

Practicing interviewing techniques will improve your performance. Team up with a classmate and role-play appropriate interviewing techniques for an employment opportunity in your career interest area.

- **Practice your telephone skills.** When you request an interview, speak clearly and repeat the appointment time and location. Remember: You make your first impression on the telephone.

- **Interview with a friend.** Have a friend ask you typical questions and comment on your interview style.

- **Use a mirror.** Are you sitting straight? Are you fidgeting? Is your facial expression alert and pleasant?

- **Use a tape recorder.** Are your words clear? Do you sound confident?

- **Prepare answers to typical questions.** For example, "What can you tell me about yourself?" One clever strategy is to prepare a 30-second "commercial" that highlights your unique talents and skills.

Practice Makes Perfect Rehearsing before an interview will make the interview less stressful. *What aspects of the interview should you practice?*

Dress for Success

What does an employer see first when you walk through the door? Not your great personality or your long list of accomplishments. It's your clothes.

Carefully plan what you will wear to your interview. Dress as you would for an actual day on the job, but a little bit better. Match your clothes to the job and, if you can, visit the workplace to see what other workers are wearing.

When in doubt, think conservative. Let your skills stand out, not your tie or dress. Be sure you're neat, clean, and well-groomed, with shined shoes and no fancy jewelry. What would an employer think of the Don'ts in *Figure 7.1?*

CAREER CHECKLIST

On the Day of the Interview...

✔ Arrive on time, well rested from a good night's sleep.

✔ Think through the answers that you have prepared for key questions.

✔ Plan to go to the interview alone—you can call your friends or family after to tell them how it went.

✔ Dress appropriately and with a clean and neat appearance.

✔ Act confident and enthusiastic—it will be obvious to the interviewer if you are comfortable.

✔ Maintain a positive and friendly attitude.

✔ Sell yourself! Let the interviewer know why he or she should hire you.

FIGURE
7.1

DRESSING FOR SUCCESS

Do's	Don'ts
• Make sure hair is clean and combed.	• Use lots of hair spray.
• Shower; use deodorant.	• Use perfume or cologne.
• Shave.	• Use heavy makeup.
• Wear clean shoes.	• Wear sandals.
• Wear conservative and appropriate clothes, neatly pressed.	• Wear clothes that will wrinkle easily.
• Trim fingernails.	• Wear bright nail polish.

▲ **Looking Your Best** Dressing for success means following a certain dress code. *What is the most important message you can send with this dress code?*

From Door to Door

Here's a simple but vital tip: Arrive at the interview alone and on time (maybe even make a trial run the day before). It's the mark of a responsible individual. You may want to arrive a few minutes early to give yourself time to fill out an application.

Bring a pen, a notepad, and two copies of your résumé—even if you've already sent one. Also, make sure that you have your Social Security number, as well as phone numbers and addresses for all your references. You may need to supply this information on an application.

SECTION 7.1 REVIEW

Key Concept Checkpoint

Comprehension

1. How can you research an employer?
2. What methods can you use to rehearse an interview?

3. Why is it important to dress for success at a job interview?

Critical Thinking

4. Why is it important to arrive at an interview alone and on time?

During an Interview: It's Show Time

- How to create the right first impression by displaying a good attitude and communicating effectively
- Effective responses to typical and tough interview questions
- Strategies for managing interview stress

WHY IT'S IMPORTANT

Your ability to project a positive first impression is essential for achieving success in your career and personal life.

KEY TERMS

- **body language**
- **role-playing**
- **problem solving**
- **stress**

By preparing for an interview carefully, you can meet the challenge of the interview itself with confidence. With practice, you will be able to project a positive attitude, communicate effectively, and lessen the level of stress.

At the Top of the List: Attitude

When James Coblin of Nucor Steel interviews applicants for a mill in South Carolina, he doesn't focus on job skills. Coblin knows that he can teach workers how to make steel. What he looks for is the right *attitude*. He wants people who can speak honestly to each other, understand other people's feelings, and pitch in to solve problems together.

Let your smile and enthusiasm project your positive attitude. As Brian Johnson of the Dogwater Cafe, a Florida restaurant chain, puts it, "When I'm interviewing, I'm looking for someone with a lot of energy who wants this job more than anything." What do you think *Figure 7.2* says about attitude?

Body Talk

When you interact with people, you communicate through **body language**—the gestures, posture, and eye contact you use to send messages.

Eye contact, for example, shows that you're paying attention. A firm handshake signals self-confidence. Nodding your head shows that you are thinking, while

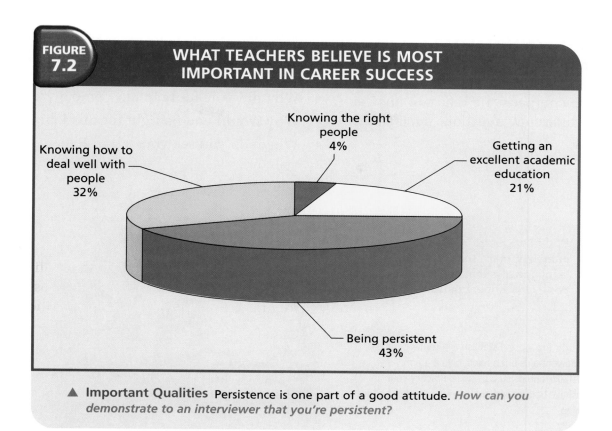

FIGURE 7.2

WHAT TEACHERS BELIEVE IS MOST IMPORTANT IN CAREER SUCCESS

Knowing the right people 4%

Knowing how to deal well with people 32%

Getting an excellent academic education 21%

Being persistent 43%

▲ **Important Qualities** Persistence is one part of a good attitude. *How can you demonstrate to an interviewer that you're persistent?*

biting your nails may suggest that you're too nervous to handle the job. What message is body language sending in *Figure 7.3* on pages 138–139?

Good manners count too. Don't throw your coat or papers on the interviewer's desk, and wait until the interviewer asks you to be seated.

Listen attentively, too. Listening can calm you and keep you focused.

When you speak, use standard English. Don't speak too quickly; and be sure to enunciate. Show the communication skills that employers look for.

Speaking for Success

Interview success depends not only on what you say but also on how you say it. Saying "Hello, it's nice to meet you" in a clear, confident voice creates a positive, mature impression.

Good Attitude A good attitude is crucial in the workplace. *What are some essential components of a good attitude?*

Typical Questions

At an interview, an employer tries to find out who you are and what you can do for the company. Be ready to answer standard interview questions such as the following:

- What goals have you set for yourself?
- What do you think are your greatest strengths? Your greatest weaknesses?
- Why did you apply to our company?
- Why would you be right for this job?
- Where do you see yourself in five years?

FIGURE 7.3 **Body Language** At a job interview, make sure your body language says that you're a positive, confident person.

A **Greeting Protocol** Establish eye contact. If the interviewer holds out a hand, give it a firm handshake, and be sure to smile. Practice your handshake beforehand, making sure it's firm but not crushing.

B **Show Interest** Lean forward slightly in your chair. Look at the interviewer, and listen to the questions. Nod your head, when appropriate, as you listen to the interviewer.

Honesty is the best policy. If you don't understand a question, ask the interviewer to clarify it. Interviewers also prefer specific answers that show you think clearly. Compare these answers:

Question: "Do you enjoy working with others or on your own?"

Answer 1: "I enjoy working with others."

Answer 2: "Well, that depends. Some tasks demand teamwork. Our soccer team, for example, won the city tournament because we worked together to put our strategy into action."

Which answer do you prefer? Why?

C **Use Your Hands** Think about your hands as you speak. Don't clench your fists or bite your nails. Use your hands in a relaxed, confident way.

D **Departure Protocol** Be friendly as the interview closes. Shake the interviewer's hand. Even if you don't get this job, the interviewer may be able to refer you to someone else.

Tough Questions

Sometimes an interviewer may toss a tough question your way. Don't be surprised. The interviewer might want to see how you respond, how you act when you're rattled, or how you think under pressure. You might hear eyebrow raisers such as these:

Staying Cool Don't panic under tough questioning. *How can you prepare for tough questions?*

- How can the company be assured that you'll give us your best effort?
- What qualities do you have that offset your lack of experience?
- Are you going to move to a better job as soon as you gain experience here?
- We're a very competitive company. Why do you want to work here?
- Let's pretend you made a major mistake on the job. What would you do to fix it?
- Don't you feel a little too inexperienced for this position?
- I can only offer you a lower position, so you'll have to work your way up. Can you handle that?
- Why should I hire you?
- Why should I trust you?
- What makes you different from all of the other candidates I've interviewed?
- How would you describe your relationship with your current employer?

You may want to storm out of the office, but stay calm and don't get defensive. Turn the question around to focus on your skills. For example: "You're right. I'm not experienced, but my work on the Smith project proves that I'm a great organizer."

If a panel of several people interview you simultaneously, stay calm and address one question at a time. You may also face think-on-your-feet questions designed to stump you. Remember: There's often no right answer. It's how you react that counts.

Be prepared to ask your own questions too. Asking questions can demonstrate genuine interest.

- What are the employee benefits?
- Does the company pay for training?
- What is the potential for growth in this company?

Standing in the Spotlight

Some interviews include **role-playing**, in which you are asked to play a role in an invented situation and are evaluated on the skills you display. Microtraining Plus in Connecticut, for example, trains people to use computers. Job candidates, however, play the role of teachers and make a presentation on a topic other than computers. David Knise, the company's CEO, says, "We're hiring people for their ability to get up in front of six people they don't know and present material."

You also may face a question that requires **problem solving**, using thinking skills to suggest a solution. For example, "If you faced a deadline you couldn't meet, what would you do?" Remember that the interviewer is evaluating your resourcefulness, creativity, and attitude, not looking for one right answer.

Some interviewers will expect you to do all of the talking. They may not be prepared with specific questions, or they may simply prefer a hands-off style of interviewing. Such an interviewer may pose just a few vague questions such as, "Tell me about yourself." Although this type of interview sounds casual, it can prove very difficult.

Prepare a brief mental outline of what points you will cover if your interview is unstructured. Be sure to highlight your qualifications for the job, including relevant skills, experience, and personal qualities. Also make sure to mention why you would like to work for the company, which is where your company research will come in handy.

Creative BUSINESS PRACTICES

Macy's
Focusing on Employee Retention

San Francisco-based Macy's West realizes that the turnover rate for retail salespersons is among the highest in any industry. Macy's uses a retention program that begins with management to help keep good employees at its department stores.

With its retention strategy, instead of adding extra responsibilities to managers' already full schedules, Macy's restructured all management positions so managers have more time to devote to their employees. The company encourages managers to be flexible and accommodate family schedules whenever possible. It also promotes a family-like atmosphere among the staff.

To keep sales associates interested in their work, Macy's provides opportunities for training and advancement. Associates can work with a mentor, attend career development seminars, receive monthly and yearly awards, and volunteer with other associates to help community groups.

Critical Thinking
If you owned your own business, what would you do to keep employees happy with their jobs? What are some of the reasons that people leave their jobs?

Link and Learn
For more information on Macy's, visit the company's Web site, via the link on the *Succeeding in the World of Work* Web site at **www.careers.glencoe.com**.

Can They Ask You That?

An interviewer does not have the right to ask you about certain matters. For example, you don't have to answer questions about children or child care, age, disabilities, citizenship, lawsuits, or AIDS or HIV status.

If an interviewer asks you a question that isn't job-related, you might say, "I assure you that this area is not a problem. Let me tell you about the skills I have that fit this job."

The Stress Factor

During an interview, you may experience **stress**—mental or physical tension that is the body's natural response to conflict. You may feel stress before you perform in a concert or play in a big game. What should you do?

First of all, tell yourself you're doing well. (You probably are.) Don't worry about saying "the right thing." That can make you more tense. Stop trying so hard—relax and be yourself.

Most important, keep the experience in perspective. The worst thing that can happen is that you don't get the job. There are

other jobs. Besides, if the interviewer does not think you're right for the company, the company may not be right for you.

Wrapping It Up

At the end of the interview, you may be offered the job on the spot. If not, thank the interviewer and ask when he or she hopes to make a decision. You might say, "May I call you next week to hear your decision?"

---

*inter*NET CONNECTION

Know your Potential Employer
You have an interview next week for the position of Running Shoe Brand Manager at a large athletic apparel company. You need to know more about the company and industry before the interview.

Connect
- Visit the Web site of a major athletic apparel company and research its history. Also search the Web sites of business and retail magazines for articles on trends in the industry.
- Write a one-page summary of important facts that may be helpful to know during your interview.

SECTION 7.2 REVIEW

✔ Key Concept Checkpoint

Comprehension
1. Why is a positive attitude essential to succeeding in the workplace?
2. Where in the job market do you see yourself in five years?

3. Why do you think employers ask tough questions?
4. How do you control interview stress?

Critical Thinking
5. Why should you ask questions at the end of an interview?

CAREER FOCUS

Kerry Butler
Actor

CAREER FACTS

Education or Training While formal training in theater, drama, music, or dance is helpful, real-world experience is vital in getting roles. This experience can come from high school, college, local, and regional theater productions.

Aptitudes, Abilities, and Skills Talent, creative ability, and stage presence are necessary to get ahead. Patience and resilience are needed to overcome rejection and to cope with not finding steady work.

Career Outlook While employment of actors is expected to grow faster than the average through 2008, competition remains high.

Career Path Many actors start their careers in local or regional theater, in commercials, or in supporting roles before advancing to bigger roles in large productions.

What is your key to success?

"You have to get good training and then believe in yourself. Go into auditions with confidence, and don't give up even when things aren't going well."

What kind of training did you have?

"I knew this was what I wanted to do since I was 3 years old. I didn't really choose acting; it chose me. I've always been performing. I studied musical theater at Ithaca College, and I continue to study voice and acting in New York City. I performed on Broadway in *Beauty and the Beast*, *Les Misérables*, and *Blood Brothers*, and took on various roles in theater, film, and television."

What do you like most about your work?

"I love being an actress! There are times when I get sick of the auditions and the rejection, but it is still such an exciting career. It's amazing how one minute I may be unemployed and searching for a new role, and then the next minute I'm flying to California for a screen test. I also enjoy the variety of roles that I have had the opportunity to play."

What training do you recommend for students?

"I would recommend taking acting classes, body movement classes, voice classes, even auditioning classes. There is an art to auditioning. Perform in any show you can; it doesn't matter whether or not you get paid. School and community theater programs can give you great experience. You will always learn something, and you never know who will be in the audience."

> **Critical Thinking** Is an actor with great talent but little resilience likely to experience success?

After an Interview: Following Up

The interview process doesn't end when you walk out the door of an employer's office. It's important to consider how you did at the interview. What went well? What skills do you need to sharpen? Another major consideration is how you will follow up on the interview. For example, how will you thank the interviewer? How will you get the interviewer to remember you? Most important, of course, is what you'll do if you're offered a job—or rejected.

Tying Up the Loose Ends

You've gotten through the interview! Now's the time to evaluate your own performance.

- Jot down some notes. Did you speak clearly? Did you use standard English? Show enthusiasm? Forget something important? Can you think of any additional information about yourself that you should have provided? Use the notes to improve your next interview.

- Send a follow-up letter soon—even the same day as the interview—in which you thank the interviewer, reinforce how your skills can benefit the company, and restate your continued interest in the job.

- Don't forget to call back.

FIGURE
7.4

THANK-YOU LETTER

Mark Abbott
5867 South Toland Road
Williamsville, FL 55500

November 29, 2000

Ms. Michelle McDermot
Director of Personnel
Cortland Office Supplies, Inc.
1400 Corporate Park Drive
Barton, FL 55555

Dear Ms. McDermot:

Thank you for the interview regarding your retail sales position. I enjoyed meeting you and discussing the job's responsibilities and rewards.

As I mentioned during the interview, my communication skills are well suited to the job, and I feel confident that I would be able to contribute to Cortland's success in today's challenging market.

I am very interested in the position, and I would be happy to provide you with any additional information that you might need. Feel free to call me at 555-2567 with any questions.

Sincerely,

Mark Abbott

Mark Abbott

▲ **Thank-You Letter** Everyone likes to be thanked, even an interviewer. *What might you mention about the interview in your letter?*

Accepting: See You Monday Morning

You hear those magic words: "The job's yours." Now what do you do? Believe it or not, you don't have to say yes immediately. If you want time to think about it, ask the employer if you can take a day to decide. List the job's pros and cons before calling back to accept the job. Ask for a formal offer letter for your files. Send an acceptance letter, and keep a copy.

Rejecting: Thanks, But No Thanks

Suppose an employer wants to hire you, but the salary is low or the job isn't exactly what you want. Don't say no at the interview. Take a day to think about it, and talk it over with other people. You might change your mind, or you might be able to negotiate the salary. When you call back, thank the interviewer, give a reason for your answer, and keep your options open.

Handling Rejection

If an employer turns you down, consider it a learning experience. Ask why you weren't hired. Do you need more training? How did you come across in your interview? Feedback will help you in future interviews.

Review your notes on how you performed in the interview, and practice again so you'll be better prepared for the next one.

Making Decisions Sometimes it helps to make a pro/con list before deciding whether to take a job. *What are some factors you might consider on a list of pros and cons?*

SECTION 7.3 REVIEW

Key Concept Checkpoint

Comprehension

1. What questions could you ask yourself to evaluate an interview?

2. What are some disadvantages to instantly accepting or rejecting a job?

Critical Thinking

3. Why is it important to follow-up on a job interview with a phone call and letter?

KEY TERM
interview (p. 132)

SECTION 7.1

- Prepare carefully for an interview. Research the company and current events in the industry. (pp. 132–133)
- Rehearse before an interview. Practice with a mirror and a tape recorder, and ask a friend for comments. (pp. 133–134)
- Plan what you will wear at an interview. Dress conservatively and avoid flashy items. Appear neat and well-groomed. (pp. 134–135)
- Arrive on time. (p. 135)

KEY TERMS
body language (p. 136)
role-playing (p. 140)
problem solving (p. 141)
stress (p. 142)

SECTION 7.2

- Employers will be evaluating your attitude and your communication skills. Be positive and enthusiastic. (pp. 136–137)
- You will probably be asked some typical questions at an interview. Be prepared to answer them. (pp. 138–139)
- You may be asked some tough questions designed to rattle you. Be prepared to respond to them with a calm and positive attitude. (p. 140)
- Some questions may involve role-playing or problem solving to evaluate your ability to think on your feet. (pp. 140–141)
- Some questions are illegal for an employer to ask during an interview. You are not required to answer them. (p. 142)

SECTION 7.3

- Evaluate your performance after an interview. Send a follow-up letter. (p. 144)
- Follow standard procedures for accepting or rejecting employment. Don't say no during an interview. Always leave the door open for the future. (pp. 145–146)

Reviewing Key Terms

1. On a separate sheet of paper, write a paragraph describing how you would prepare for an interview. Use the terms below in your paragraph.
   - interview
   - stress
   - body language
   - problem solving
   - role-playing

Recalling Key Concepts

2. Researching a company before an interview enables you to ____.
   (a) ask intelligent questions
   (b) impress your friends
   (c) dress for success

3. Preparing a 30-second "commercial" about yourself is a good way to ____.
   (a) research a company
   (b) negotiate a salary
   (c) rehearse for an interview

4. Which of the following topics is illegal for an employer to ask about? ____
   (a) your skills (b) your goals
   (c) your citizenship

5. Interviewers look for applicants ____.
   (a) wearing fashionable clothes
   (b) demonstrating a positive attitude
   (c) with a sense of humor

6. In a follow-up letter, you should ____.
   (a) restate your continued interest
   (b) invent additional references
   (c) apologize for being nervous

Problem Solving

7. In what ways can you stand out positively at an interview?

8. Summarize the importance of body language at a job interview.

9. Compare rehearsing for an interview alone and rehearsing with a friend. Identify the advantages of each method.

10. What would you infer about a job applicant who asks questions about a job's responsibilities and chances for advancement in the company?

11. Imagine that you are an employer. List the five most important qualities of a great job applicant in order of priority. Give reasons for the order.

Work-Based Learning

Basic Skills Speaking

12. Compose a 30-second "commercial" to summarize your abilities. In it, act as if you were being interviewed.

Thinking Skills Reasoning

13. An interviewer asks Wendy: "Do you plan to have children anytime soon?" How should she answer this question?

Personal Skills Self-Esteem

14. Michael is in the middle of a job interview. Suddenly, he feels very stressed. Write a paragraph telling what he can do to calm down and finish the interview successfully.

Interpersonal Skills Exercising Leadership

15. An interviewer says to you: "You have no experience in this field. Why should I hire you?" Describe how you could answer this question in a way that shows maturity and ability to take charge of a situation.

School-Based Learning

Social Studies Research Industry Trends

16. Ella wants to research trends in the computer industry before her job interview at a software company. Using the library, current magazines, newspapers, or the Internet, find relevant information. Then describe some ways she might use this information in an interview.

Human Relations Understand Cultural Differences

17. Kyle has an interview scheduled with a company that is based in a foreign country. He wants to make sure he understands the body language in this country. Choose a country (such as Japan, Saudi Arabia, Kenya, or Norway), and research its "rules" about body language. What movements and gestures should Kyle be aware of?

Math Calculate Driving Time

18. It is a 20-minute ride to Laura's job interview. However, due to construction, she will have to take a detour that will add 15 minutes. If she wants to arrive 15 minutes early, how much time should she allow for the trip?

Role Play

19. Mock Interviews

Situation You are conducting your first interview for an entry-level sales position at the department store where you work. Your supervisor would like to sit in on the interview. Together, you have reviewed many résumés and have chosen four candidates to interview.

Activity Create a description for your company's job opening and identify the skills it requires. Then role-play interviewing four candidates as your supervisor observes. Decide which person you would like to hire and explain this decision to your supervisor.

Evaluation You will be evaluated on how well you meet the following performance indicators:

- Develop a relevant job description
- Conduct realistic interviews
- Evaluate candidates using appropriate criteria

*inter*NET
CONNECTION

20. Evaluate Your Performance
Create a rubric or self-evaluation sheet that you can use after an interview to "grade" your performance. Rate yourself using key criteria such as personal appearance, enthusiasm, and body language.

Connect Human resources professionals often use standardized scoring systems to evaluate job candidates. Using the Internet, locate examples of such guides.

CAREER LAB

Real-World Workshop

Making a Good First Impression

✓ Overview

Making a good first impression on an interview is essential to getting a job. In this lab, you will practice interviewing in order to learn how to make the best possible impression.

✓ Assignment

Working with a partner, create two role-play situations in which you interview one another. Each partner should serve once as an interviewer and once as an interviewee. With your partner, decide upon two realistic scenarios, which will serve as backdrops for your interviews. Arrange to record both of your interviews. Watch the tapes of your interviews together and critique both interviews. Note things that you did well and things that could be improved. Compile your notes and create a presentation to share with the class. Play the tapes of your interviews during your presentation.

✓ Tools/Resources

To complete this assignment, you will need to research common interview questions and techniques. Public libraries, human resources professionals in your area, and the Internet can provide valuable information. Use a video camera or a tape recorder to record your interviews.

✓ Procedures

Before you and your partner get started, decide on the scenario for the interview. A job interview for a bank teller would be very different from an interview for a position at a fitness center. Follow the steps below to prepare a thorough and realistic presentation.

- Research the types of questions that would be posed in real-life interviews similar to your role-play exercises.
- As an interviewer, decide which questions you will ask. As an interviewee, formulate answers to the likely questions.
- Select suitable clothing for your interviews.
- Before recording your presentation, practice your part independently.

- Choose an appropriate setting for recording your interviews. If you don't have much experience using a camcorder, ask an experienced person to help you.
- Watch your interviews several times to critique them thoroughly. Think about things that you did well and areas that need improvement.
- Combine your notes and observations and prepare a presentation for the class. Create an outline to guide your presentation.
- Practice your presentation before delivering it. Make sure that you and your partner deliver equal portions of the presentation.

✓ Report

Your final product for this lab should include two videotaped interviews and a presentation that highlights and critiques your interviews.

✓ Presentation and Evaluation

Your interviews will be evaluated based on

- Preparation displayed
- Realism
- Evidence of thoroughness

Your presentation will be evaluated based on

- Preparation displayed
- Content and thoughtfulness
- Quality of delivery
- Quality of critique and suggestions offered

✓ Personal Career Portfolio

Include a copy of your presentation outline in your personal career portfolio.

HELPFUL HINTS

Interviewer Tips

- Prepare for the interview by generating a list of questions.
- Don't share your questions with your partner before the interview. You want to see how well your interviewee thinks on his or her feet.
- Make frequent eye contact throughout the interview.
- Listen for a confident tone of voice.

Interviewee Tips

- Pretend that your partner is truly an interviewer. If you treat your interviewer as a friend or classmate, your interview will not be a valid practice exercise.
- Think about common interview questions and prepare solid responses.
- Make frequent eye contact throughout the interview.
- Use a confident tone of voice.

UNIT 4 Joining the Workforce

Portfolio Project

Research Legal Matters Sometimes even well-meaning employees are sued for negligence or other work-related mistakes. Select a career that interests you, and conduct research to find legal cases brought against workers in this field. In an essay, choose one such lawsuit and note steps that you could take to avoid having such charges brought against you.

CAREER LAB PREVIEW

Ensuring a Safe, Healthy Career

As part of this unit, you will investigate safety and health hazards in your chosen career field. You'll pinpoint major problems in your industry and develop solutions to reduce or eliminate these risks. Using presentation software, you'll share your ideas and research with the class in a dynamic presentation.

Chapter 8

Beginning a New Job

Section 8.1
Preparing for Your First
Day on the Job

Section 8.2
What You Can Expect
From Your Employer

CHAPTER OBJECTIVES

After completing this chapter, you will be able to

- Anticipate and manage the anxieties and challenges of a first day of work.

- Understand company policies and payment procedures.

- Explain benefits that employers offer workers.

- Discuss the significance of employee performance reviews.

JOURNAL

Personal Career Plan

The first day on a new job is a time of excitement and anxiety. In your journal, write a list of questions and concerns you might have on your first day of work. Then write a list of things that might give you confidence on your first day.

Personal Career Project

Talk to at least three people who have started a new job within the past six months. Ask them what they did to prepare themselves for their first day. Choose the strategies that you think would help you most on your first day and write out the list in your journal.

Preparing for Your First Day on the Job

Getting a new job is like moving to a different country. Who knows what's waiting for you there? Many unexpected things can happen. What can you do to prepare? What do employers expect from you? How can you deal with first-day anxieties?

Having a Good First Day

Your first day on the job can be exciting. Enjoy it. It will almost certainly be stressful as well. You can't avoid the stress, but you can prepare yourself for it.

Figure out how long it will take you to get ready and to get to work. Then get up even earlier. Don't make yourself more nervous by running late and then hurrying to get to your job on time.

At work, you'll be introduced to your new coworkers. You'll probably forget their names. Don't worry. You can't be expected to remember everyone's name at first. Just ask again. A simple trick that may help you remember is to repeat each person's name out loud as you're introduced. Then use the name again while talking to the person.

Company Culture

As soon as you walk in to work as an employee, you'll become immersed in the **company culture**. This is the behavior, attitudes, values, and habits of the employees and owners that are unique to a particular company.

Learning the company culture will take you a while. Until you understand it, take your time trying

On Time Plan to get to your new job early. *What would your new supervisor think if you were late?*

ETHICS *in Action*

Changing Places You and your friend recently started working at a large corporation. The human resources department conducts random drug testing, and your friend was picked but you were not. Your friend tells you that she has been taking pain pills for her bad back and asks you to take the test for her. She says that because the company is so big, no one will ever know the difference.

THINK ABOUT IT
Will you take the drug test for your friend? Why or why not?

to fit in. You don't have to do a lot of talking your first few days. Concentrate on listening and observing. Watch your coworkers to learn how they work and interact. The skills of listening, knowing how to learn, and sociability will help you.

Dressing for the Job

One anxiety about your first day of work may concern how to dress. What's appropriate? How dressed up should you get? What makes this matter even more confusing is that dress codes keep chang-

ing. Unless your job calls for a uniform, it's hard to know what to wear.

Office workers once wore suits and ties, skirts and high heels. That rule no longer applies in most places. The majority of companies are now moving toward more casual dress. Unfortunately, there's no "norm." What's correct in one office is inappropriate in another. Jeans and a golf shirt might be fine at one place but too casual at another.

To complicate matters further, many companies now have "casual Fridays" and "jeans days." These allow even more casual dress. Even on these days, though, not everything goes.

If you work in a manufacturing plant, in a garage, or on a construction site, your choices may be more predictable. Even dress codes for these jobs have changed in recent years, however.

How do you know what to wear? When you show up for your interview, observe what other people are wearing. Make a point of asking about the dress code. It's also a good idea to ask for examples

Appropriate Dress Office casual means casual "business" clothing, not casual wear. You may need a separate wardrobe of work clothing. *What's wrong with the clothing these people are wearing at the office? What's right?*

*inter*NET
CONNECTION

Company Dress Codes
You want to work for a company that has a relaxed dress code, while your friend thinks that the key to success is dressing professionally.

Connect
• Choose several large companies that you like and visit the employee benefits sections of their Web sites to research company dress codes.
• Make a list of company dress codes. Tell which would suit you and which would better suit your friend. Do you think their corporate images are in line with their dress codes?

because "office casual" means different things in different companies.

Still uncertain? Consider these pointers:

• Err on the side of conservative dress.

• Avoid bright or garish colors and clothes that are faddish.

• Keep jewelry simple and not too large.

• Wear clean clothes, and never wear clothes that are frayed or worn out.

• If you're meeting the public, wear more traditional business clothing. A business suit might be right if you're in sales, for example.

Learning the Ropes

You'll have a lot to prepare for and to think about on your first day. Your employer will also be preparing for you.

Orientation

To help new employees get started, companies provide **orientation**. This is a program that will introduce you to the company's policies, procedures, values, and benefits. You may get a tour of the company, meet coworkers, and be shown where the lunchroom and restrooms are.

At a small company, orientation may be informal. You may simply meet with the office manager to talk about benefits, have lunch with your supervisor, and tour the workplace. Most large companies have more elaborate orientations. You may receive a company manual and have formal presentations. Orientations may last a few hours, all day, or much longer. Some employers even use games such as scavenger hunts to help introduce new employees to the workplace. Employers may also include team-building activities to help new employees develop their abilities to work together. Regardless of the size and type of the orientation, both the employee and employer will reap the benefits.

At some companies, the new employee may be paired with a senior coworker who acts as a mentor. At companies where there is not a formal mentoring process, an inexperienced worker may seek an older worker on his or her own to act as a mentor. **Mentors** are informal teachers or guides who help new employees adjust to their new workplace. They introduce new employees to their coworkers and coach them in the skills and procedures needed

---

Creative BUSINESS PRACTICES

Walt Disney World
Strong Corporate Culture

Walt Disney World, home of the Magic Kingdom, Epcot Center, and Disney-MGM Studios near Orlando, Florida, has a strong corporate culture that is reflected in all of its employees. Disney employs more than 50,000 "cast members," and its human resources department makes sure that all potential employees understand Disney's cultural standards.

New cast members are instructed on how to act in the park and how to be friendly to guests. Disney believes that its trademark friendliness is a key to attracting repeat customers.

Disney's strictly enforced appearance standards emphasize neatness and simplicity: natural looking hair color and nails, groomed facial hair, minimal jewelry, and no visible tattoos. The company feels that straying from these standards would dis-

tract guests and take away from their Disney experience.

Although it is estimated that 10 to 20 percent of applicants are turned off by the Disney culture, many stay on to pursue careers. Employees are regularly rewarded for maintaining the Disney culture with more than 20 employee recognition programs.

Critical Thinking
Why do you think it is important for service-oriented companies to have a corporate culture?

Link and Learn
For information about careers at Disney World, visit the company's Web site via the link on the *Succeeding in the World of Work* Web site at **www.careers.glencoe.com**.

---

for their jobs. Mentors help new employees learn the company culture and company policies. Mentors can also provide valuable guidance and advice to help you advance in your career.

After three months, new employees often meet with their supervisors to talk about their new jobs, the company, and their future. *Figure 8.1* gives you an idea of the scope of some orientation programs.

A **Orientation** In the past, orientation often consisted of filling out insurance forms and reading lengthy company policy manuals. At some companies today, this is what you will still find.

However your company handles orientation, use it to get a clear idea of your responsibilities and the company goals. Get answers to the following questions:

- What is the company's mission, or purpose? How do your job and your department fit into the mission?

- What are your exact job responsibilities? What should you do first? Next?

- How will your performance be evaluated? When?

- What benefits will you receive and when will you receive them?

B **Interactive Training** Many companies now offer interactive training programs. The programs enable new workers to ask questions and to meet each other as they learn about their employer.

C **Reorientation** Orientation does not necessarily stop with new employees. Employers often "reorient" their entire staff to boost morale and to help employees keep up with changes within the company.

Company Policies

Every company has specific policies that spell out what the company expects of you and what you can expect of the company. You will probably be given a company manual or other written statement of official policies. You should learn about these policies right away. By making sure that you understand the company's policies, you will protect yourself and ensure that you fully live up to your employer's expectations. Following are questions about just a few company policies.

- When will you be paid?

- What happens if you're late for work?

- How many sick days will you be paid for each year? What happens if you need more days than you're allowed?

- How much vacation time will you get, and when can you take it?

- What paid holidays does the company grant?

- When will you receive a raise? What will be the basis for it?

SECTION 8.1 REVIEW

✔ Key Concept Checkpoint

Comprehension

1. What worries you about starting a new job? How can you prepare for your first day at work?

2. How will knowing about your new employer's dress code help make your first day on the job successful?

3. Why should you learn about company policies as soon as possible?

Critical Thinking

4. How will understanding company policy protect your rights as an employee?

CAREER FOCUS

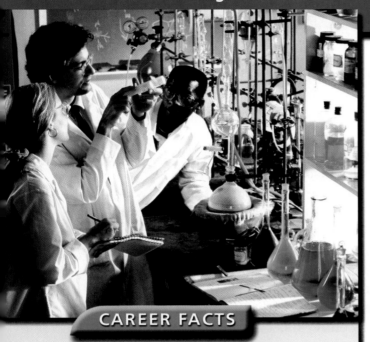

CAREER FACTS

Education or Training For most jobs, a bachelor's degree is adequate, with courses in food chemistry, food analysis, food microbiology, and food processing operations. An understanding of government regulations is also necessary.

Aptitudes, Abilities, and Skills The ability to work both independently and as part of a team is vital; so is the ability to apply knowledge of chemistry, microbiology, and other sciences. Strong written and verbal communication skills are key.

Career Outlook Average employment growth is expected through 2008.

Career Path Food scientists usually begin by researching or teaching, then advance to supervisory or managerial positions in research programs or departments.

What is your key to success?

"My key to success is having a college degree and the ability to work well with a diverse range of people. I also have a passion for my job, helping parents raise happy, healthy babies."

What skills are most important to you?

"My most important skill is the ability to work well with people of diverse backgrounds and in different areas of the company. Technical knowledge in food science is also critical. A third important skill is effectively leading teams and managing projects. To create and improve food products for infants and toddlers, these skills must all come together."

What kind of training did you have?

"I have a bachelor's and a master's degree in food science. I also have a Ph.D. in food science with a focus on food chemistry. Significant on-the-job and company-sponsored training, along with outside seminars on team leadership, project management, and computer and technical training, helped me further develop my job skills."

What kind of training do you recommend for students?

"Students interested in food science should obtain a college degree in food science, biochemistry, engineering, or microbiology. An internship with a food company is great for practical experience and exposure to the field."

> **Critical Thinking** What could happen if food scientists did not stay informed of government regulations in the food industry?

What You Can Expect From Your Employer

WHAT YOU'LL LEARN

- Typical forms of payment
- Common employee benefits
- The importance of employee performance reviews

WHY IT'S IMPORTANT

Understanding company policies and procedures will help you perform your best and protect your rights.

KEY TERMS

- **hourly wages**
- **overtime**
- **nonexempt employees**
- **exempt employees**
- **salary**
- **commission**
- **profit-sharing plan**
- **performance bonuses**
- **pension plan**
- **probation**
- **layoff**

Every employee works for a reason. What's yours? A salary? Health insurance? A pension? The challenge of interesting work? Job security? You may want and expect these and other things from your employer.

The answers keep changing as business moves closer to the global market. Companies must be more efficient and more competitive. The result is a changing relationship between workers and their employers. *Figure 8.2* shows how the relationship has changed in recent years.

Payment

Of course, you expect to get paid for the work you do. This is one aspect of the employer-employee relationship that has not changed. However, your pay may be calculated in any number of ways.

Basic Payment Methods

Most entry-level employees receive **hourly wages**. In other words, the employer pays a fixed amount of money, such as $7, for each hour worked. At the end of each week, pay is calculated by multiplying the number of hours worked times the hourly rate.

Hourly wages may be affected by whether or not workers are paid **overtime** for working more than 40 hours in a week. Usually workers on overtime are paid one and one-half times their normal pay for each hour in excess of 40 hours. For example, if workers are normally paid $10 per hour, they will get $15 when working overtime.

FIGURE
8.2

CHANGING WORKER EXPECTATIONS

	In the Past	Today
Job Security	• Length of time with a company or experience in career field guarantees job security • Workforce consisted mainly of full-time employees • Company responsible for worker's security	• Continued training provides job security • Increasing numbers of temporary workers and independent contractors • Freedom from company ties
Salary	• Based on experience • Based on number of years experience with company	• Based on current value of work • Based on knowledge and skill level

▲ **Worker Expectations** The competitive global and technology-based economy has changed the expectations of the American worker. *What are the advantages and disadvantages for today's worker?*

Not everyone gets paid overtime. Who does? A federal law requires that certain types of workers must be paid overtime. Workers who are covered by this law are called **nonexempt employees**. These workers are normally paid an hourly wage. Workers who are not covered by the law are **exempt employees**. Most exempt employees earn a **salary**. That is, they are paid a fixed amount for a certain period of time, usually a month or a year. Exempt employees do not have to be paid overtime.

Workers in some kinds of jobs—such as sales or telemarketing—may be paid a **commission**. These workers' earnings are based on how much they sell. They might, for example, earn 2 percent of the value of the merchandise they sell. By basing pay directly on their performance, this system aims to motivate salespeople to work harder.

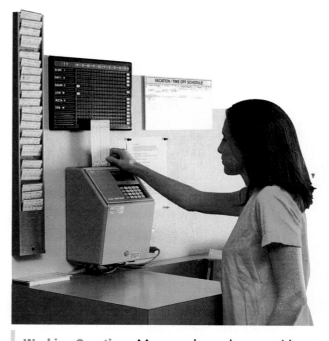

Working Overtime Many workers who are paid an hourly wage must "clock in" at a time clock. This worker normally works seven hours per day, five days per week. This week she has worked eight hours per day for five days. *How many hours of overtime has she worked this week?*

Incentive Plans

One change in how workers are paid is in incentive plans. These plans reward workers for achievement and help to keep them motivated. Incentive plans also ensure that employees know that they are appreciated.

In a **profit-sharing plan**, workers receive a share of the company's profits. The better the company performs, the more the worker receives. One example of this is the rewarding of stock options to hard-working employees.

Performance bonuses reward workers for high levels of performance. Some companies pay bonuses to workers who increase the quantity or quality of their work. These bonuses vary greatly in amounts and how they are awarded. At Dow Brands, for example, employees may receive cash awards of several hundred dollars for doing good work. At Steelcase, factory workers are paid relatively low salaries, but their bonuses can almost double their incomes.

Benefits

The rewards for working are not limited to a paycheck. Various benefits may also come with a job. Benefits are the "extras" that a company provides in addition to pay. They range from health care to child care to gym memberships. Usually there is a waiting period before employees are eligible for these benefits.

The kinds and value of benefits vary dramatically from employer to employer. A recent study showed that benefits average about 40 percent of employers' payrolls. Offering a comprehensive benefits package is one way an employer can attract and retain quality employees in a competetive job market.

Health Benefits

Health insurance is probably the most sought after benefit. It's also the most costly one for employers. Health care costs have risen sharply over the past 20 years, and the trend is likely to continue. As a result, many employers have increased the amount that their employees are required to pay for coverage, as seen in *Figure 8.3*. Companies that are willing to pay the majority of their workers' health care costs are becoming increasingly attractive to potential employees.

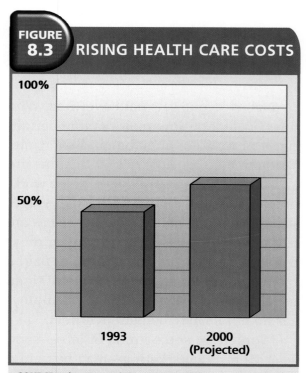

FIGURE 8.3 RISING HEALTH CARE COSTS

1993   2000 (Projected)

SOURCE: Labor Research Association, 1998.

▲ Rising Health Care Costs These graphs show the projected growth of the percentage of premiums paid by employees for family health care plans. *How might this affect the way job-hunters rate potential employers?*

Retirement Plans

Many companies offer a **pension plan** that builds a retirement fund for each worker. Some employers make contributions for each worker. Some plans allow workers to contribute a portion of each paycheck to the fund. Many companies match the amount of each worker's contribution up to a certain percentage of his or her salary.

Convenience Benefits

Some employers also provide *convenience benefits*—services that make workers' lives easier. There is great variety in the types of convenience benefits. They range from flexible work hours and legal counseling services to on-site oil changes for employees' cars. Quad/Graphics, Inc., provides an accredited kindergarten for employees' children, a fitness center, and popcorn carts, where employees can get a

Employee Benefits Some workers receive health-club memberships as an employee benefit. *How does this service benefit employees? How does it benefit employers?*

snack for a quarter. Hallmark Cards provides twice-monthly seminars to help employees handle family issues, such as elder care and parenting. Such benefits are designed to reduce employee stress, improve workers' health, and make workers more productive, loyal, and satisfied.

Cafeteria Plan

A *cafeteria plan* is not a benefit but a policy that lets employees choose the benefits they want. Employers realize that not all employees want or need the same benefits, so they let employees choose those they do want. For example, rather than vacation time, an employee may prefer disability insurance.

Honest and Fair Treatment

You have a right to expect your employer to be honest with you. You should be paid the amount you agreed to. You should receive all the benefits promised when you were hired. If your work situation changes, you should be told as soon as possible.

You also have a right to be treated fairly by your employer, supervisor, and coworkers. If you feel you have been treated unfairly, discuss it with the person involved or with your supervisor. Try to resolve the problem before it gets out of hand. Chapter 12 discusses additional options you have if your rights are violated.

Evaluations

How well are you succeeding at your work? Many companies have formal, scheduled *performance reviews*. These are

Job Security When businesses are forced to lay off workers, they often lay off more recently hired workers before those who have worked for the company longer. *Do you think this is fair? Why or why not?*

meetings between you and your supervisor to evaluate how well you're doing your job.

Reviews are important to you and to your supervisor. Promotions, pay increases, new responsibilities, and your future with the company may be based on these evaluations. If your company does not have regular evaluations, ask for one. You need feedback to improve your performance and build your career.

In some companies, new employees are put on **probation**. This is the period after you are first hired when you are "on trial."

During your probation period, your employer will decide whether you are suited to the job. When you are hired, ask if your company has a probation period policy. If it does, ask what guidelines will be used for the evaluation.

Standard Separation Procedures

Most people, at some time during their careers, will lose their jobs. There are several reasons why a company will *terminate*, or end, a worker's employment.

Employees may be terminated, or fired, for poor job performance. Your employer should have a clear policy for handling these situations.

Sometimes companies have to terminate employees because business is slow. This kind of job loss, which often affects many workers at once, is a **layoff**. Workers who are laid off may be rehired once a company's business improves.

Because you can't always avoid job loss, you should prepare for it. Keep your job-hunting network active and your skills up-to-date. Put aside money to help you through a time of unemployment.

SECTION 8.2 REVIEW

 Key Concept Checkpoint

Comprehension

1. Why does working for a commission offer less financial security than working for a salary?

2. How do benefits improve employee morale?

3. Why are performance reviews as important to workers as to their employers?

Critical Thinking

4. What steps would you take if you received a negative performance review?

KEY TERMS
company culture (p. 156)
orientation (p. 158)
mentors (p. 159)

SECTION 8.1

- Reduce anxiety on the first day of work by giving yourself ample time to get ready and to get to work. (p. 156)
- Learn the company culture by listening and observing how your coworkers work and interact. (pp. 156–157)
- Dress codes are changing, and different companies have different standards. Ask about the dress code at your interview. Observe what other workers are wearing. (pp. 157–158)
- Companies help new employees learn policies and procedures through orientation programs. (pp. 158–161)
- Company policies spell out what the company expects of new employees and what employees can expect from the company. Learn these policies as soon as possible. (p. 162)

KEY TERMS
hourly wages (p. 164)
overtime (p. 164)
nonexempt
   employees (p. 165)
exempt employees (p. 165)
salary (p. 165)
commission (p. 165)
profit-sharing plan (p. 166)
performance
   bonuses (p. 166)
pension plan (p. 167)
probation (p. 168)
layoff (p. 168)

SECTION 8.2

- The basic methods of payment include hourly wages, salary, and commission. (pp. 164–165)
- Incentive programs offer workers a chance to share in their company's success. (p. 166)
- Workers usually receive benefits, such as health insurance and a retirement plan. They may also receive convenience benefits. (pp. 166–167)
- Employees have a right to honest and fair treatment from their employer. (p. 167)
- Employers and employees both benefit from performance reviews. (pp. 167–168)
- Some employers have probation periods for new employees. (p. 168)
- Employee termination may result from poor worker performance or bad business. Companies should have a clear termination policy. (p. 168)
- You can prepare for possible job loss by maintaining your network of contacts, keeping your skills up-to-date, and having some money saved. (p. 168)

Reviewing Key Terms

1. On a separate sheet of paper, write a one- to two-page employee manual. Use the terms listed below to explain the policies of an imaginary employer.

- company culture
- mentors
- overtime
- exempt employees
- commission
- performance bonuses
- pension plan
- orientation
- hourly wages
- nonexempt employees
- salary
- profit-sharing plan
- probation
- layoff

Recalling Key Concepts

Determine whether each statement is true or false. Rewrite any false statements to make them true.

2. Companies are beginning to insist on more formal business clothing.

3. During orientation, new employees are introduced to the company's policies, procedures, values, and benefits.

4. Typically, workers are paid an hourly wage, a salary, or a commission.

5. A cafeteria plan is a convenience benefit that allows workers to eat free meals while at work.

6. If you are on probation, it means that you are being considered for a pay raise.

Problem Solving

7. How can watching other employees help a worker succeed on the job?

8. Why do some companies devote so much time to new-employee orientation?

9. If benefits are so expensive, why do companies provide so many for employees?

10. How does fair and honest treatment contribute to a good workplace?

11. Why do some companies place new employees on probation?

Work-Based Learning

Thinking Skills Knowing How to Learn

12. Working with a partner, role-play your first conversation with your new employer, who has called to congratulate you and answer any questions you may have about your first day at work. What questions will you ask?

Personal Qualities Sociability

13. Brainstorm a list of suggestions for ways to get to know coworkers.

Technology Selecting Technology

14. Your employer plans to link the personal computers in the accounting department. What issues should the employer address in making this change?

School-Based Learning

Math Calculate Earnings

15. Kumar earns $7.00 per hour. If he works an average of 40 hours a week, what does he earn a week? How much does he earn a year if he works 50 weeks? One week he worked 10 hours of overtime, for which he earned time-and-a-half pay. What were his total earnings that week?

Health and Physical Education Create a Survey

16. Your employer has decided to create a company wellness program to improve employee health and fitness. Write a one-page questionnaire for workers to complete that will inform your employer about the habits that affect their health and general well-being.

Foreign Language Give Instructions

17. You work in a company's shipping room. You have been assigned to be a mentor for a new employee whose native language is not English. Her duties include copying order forms, filling out address labels, and wrapping packages. How would you explain these tasks to her?

Role Play

18. Orientation Program

Situation You are part of a four-person human resources team for a large company. You need to develop an orientation program for your company's new employees.

Activity Design an informative presentation to welcome new employees (your classmates) to their new jobs. You can choose to make up the company or choose an existing one. Be prepared to answer questions that would typically be asked by a new employee.

Evaluation Your group will be evaluated on how well it meets the following performance indicators:
- Give an overview of the company's values and mission
- Describe the company's policies and procedures
- Explain the various benefits offered to employees

*inter*NET CONNECTION

19. Conduct Research
Determine the salaries of at least three career choices in your interest area with varying education requirements (for example, no high school diploma, high school diploma, and postsecondary training).

Connect Surf the Web for information about benefits packages and salary payment methods. Determine which career choice matches your salary preferences most closely.

Chapter 9

Workplace Ethics

Section 9.1
Desirable Employee Qualities

Section 9.2
Ethical Behavior

CHAPTER OBJECTIVES

After completing this chapter, you will be able to

- Identify and develop the skills that employers look for in employees.

- Explain why ethics are important to employers.

- Describe ways to behave ethically in the workplace.

JOURNAL

Personal Career Plan

What basic ethics should guide the behavior of a well-known business leader? In what ways—if any—should that leader's ethics differ from those of a part-time worker in that leader's company? How do the leader and the part-time worker affect each other's work ethics? Write a journal entry discussing your ideas.

Personal Career Project

Pick a negative or unethical characteristic that you sometimes see in yourself. For one week concentrate on acting in the opposite manner. At the end of the week, write a short report describing your attempts to change and evaluating your success.

Desirable Employee Qualities

WHAT YOU'LL LEARN

- The personal qualities that employers look for when choosing employees
- Strategies for developing and exhibiting important personal qualities

WHY IT'S IMPORTANT

Your success in the workplace is largely dependent on your ability to develop and project the personal qualities that most employers seek.

KEY TERMS

- **cooperativeness**
- **initiative**
- **responsibility**
- **self-management**

In the past, employers looked for workers with specific skills. They wanted people who excelled at computer keyboarding, bookkeeping, or graphic art, for example. Skills such as these may still get you a job, but the workplace is changing. According to Raymond Brixley, director of human resources for the Quaker Oats Company, employers are beginning to ask for more. "We look for someone capable of doing lots of things well," he says, "and more importantly, someone who 'fits' into the organization's structure."

How do you prepare for doing lots of things well and fitting in? Master a wide range of personal and academic skills. Solid thinking skills, skills in math and communications, and strong personal qualities will help you adapt to the changing needs of today's workplace.

Cooperativeness

One of an employee's most valued qualities is cooperativeness. **Cooperativeness** is a willingness to work well with everyone else on the job to reach a common goal. Cooperativeness is closely linked to several other important personal qualities and skills, including listening skills, responsibility, and self-management.

Be forewarned. Your first job will put your cooperativeness to the test. You may get the worst tasks and little responsibility. If this happens, all you can do is smile, do the job well, and demonstrate a spirit of cooperativeness.

How can you be cooperative?

- Do tasks you don't like without complaining or trying to avoid them.
- Do your fair share of a job when working with others.
- Pitch in to help a coworker who has a tough job or has fallen behind.
- Volunteer to help coworkers meet a deadline or reach a goal.

Willingness to Follow Directions

On the job, you will be asked to complete many tasks. To complete a task, you must first follow directions. This is a vital skill on any job.

Following directions requires many skills. Listening is one of the most important ones. These suggestions may help you follow directions:

- Stop whatever you are doing, and listen to the directions being given.
- Listen carefully, even if you think you already know the procedure. Some details might surprise you.
- Take notes, if possible.
- Identify the goal or purpose of the task. Then try to visualize the steps leading to the goal.
- If you do not understand the directions, don't guess at what is needed. Ask questions!

Cooperation Workers can show cooperation by willingly doing whatever tasks they are assigned. *Why is it important to demonstrate cooperation?*

Speak Up Asking questions is the best way to learn a new job. It's also a good way to avoid making embarrassing mistakes. *What should you do if you ask a question, receive an answer, and your directions are still not clear?*

Willingness to Learn

Think ahead a few months or years. You've completed your education and started your first full-time job. You may think you're done with learning. You're not. You'll have lots to learn about your new job, even if the job is one you've been trained for. You'll have to learn the company's system and how to work with your coworkers.

Because you're a new employee, your employer will not expect you to know everything. So don't pretend to know something you don't. Ask questions.

Be willing to learn any job, no matter how small. When the copier gets jammed, watch how to fix it. Next time, you can take care of it yourself.

Look for opportunities to get more training. Many companies will pay for their employees to attend workshops, training programs, or college. Take advantage of any chance to learn more.

Initiative

You may get by, just by doing what you're told. Employers expect more from you, however. They want employees to show **initiative**. Taking initiative means doing what needs to be done without being told to do it.

Disney World deliberately seeks out employees who have initiative. Robert Sias, a trainer for Disney, gives an example of what it wants. A mother had just bought her son a box of popcorn, he explains. The child, about 4 years old, stumbled and dropped the popcorn, spilling it all over. The little boy burst into tears, and the mother became upset. Just at that moment, a costumed employee who was on his way to another attraction walked by. Without a pause, he scooped up the empty popcorn box, got it refilled by the vendor, handed it to the little boy, and went on his way.

The employee showed initiative. He saw a problem and fixed it. It was no big deal, but it made a customer happy. That's what employers want.

Willingness to Take on More Responsibility

Business today is more competitive than ever. Companies must do more to satisfy customers. Employers know the key is empowered employees. They want employees to take more responsibility. **Responsibility** is the willingness to accept an obligation and to be accountable for an action or situation.

Marriott Hotels has this attitude. One of its employees is Tony Prsyszlak (Prush-lak). If he worked for another hotel, he might be called a doorman. At Marriott, he's called a "guest service associate." The difference is more than the title. Prsyszlak picks up a guest's luggage at the curb and

Take the Initiative
You would like to take more initiative at work, so you have decided to start a recycling program at your office. Copier paper and beverage cans are the main items you would like to start recycling.

Connect
- Visit your local government's Web site to see if there is a drop-off spot or a special collection site for recycling the above items. Also research the benefits of recycling.
- Draw up a brief plan of action for your recycling program. Write a few slogans to convince your coworkers to recycle.

carries it up to the room. He can also check the guest in, obtain theater tickets for a play, reserve a table at a restaurant, or provide other services for the guest.

Showing Initiative Human resource managers look for employees who help customers without being told to do so. *How can workers prepare themselves for showing initiative on their jobs?*

"I'm a bellman, a doorman, a front-desk clerk, and a concierge all rolled into one," Prsyszlak says. "I have more responsibilities. I feel better about my job, and the guest gets better service."

What do you get out of taking on more responsibility? Your job becomes more interesting. You gain experience and a chance at better jobs. You increase your value to the company and earn job security.

Prove to your employer that you can accept greater responsibility. Show that you're not afraid of change. Volunteer for new jobs. Think about where the added responsibility will get you in a year.

Self-Management

Who do you think is going to get you a job, a promotion, a raise? Only you. You've got to take responsibility for the work you do and the career you want. This is called **self-management**. It means doing the things necessary to build a better career. Here are some tips:

- Set career goals, and develop a plan for reaching them. As you achieve goals, or as your situation changes, set new goals.

- Monitor your work habits and performance. For example, you might keep

Creative BUSINESS PRACTICES

Ben & Jerry's
Commitment to Our Planet

Ben & Jerry's Homemade, Inc. manufactures ice cream, frozen yogurt, and sorbet. This Burlington, Vermont, company has made a name for itself with innovative flavors like Chubby Hubby and Chunky Monkey and by its commitment to making the world a better place.

Ben & Jerry's gives 7.5 percent of its pretax earnings to nonprofit organizations. Much of this charitable giving is through the Ben & Jerry's Foundation, which supports grassroots projects that promote awareness and social change.

One of Ben & Jerry's latest initiatives is not a famous new flavor, but rather the containers the company uses for packaging. Because bleached paper is one of the biggest causes of toxic water pollution in

the U.S., Ben & Jerry's started manufacturing containers with unbleached paper to help protect our waterways.

Critical Thinking

Why should companies be concerned with the environment and the community? If you owned a successful company, what would you do to make the world a better place?

Link and Learn

To read more about Ben & Jerry's commitment to our planet, visit the company's Web site via the link on the *Succeeding in the World of Work* Web site at **www.careers.glencoe.com.**

a diary to track how you spend your time. Then you can identify ways to be more time-efficient.

- Ask for feedback on how you're doing your job. Ask coworkers and supervisors. Act on what you learn to improve your work habits and skills.

Loyalty

You know what it means to be loyal to your country and your school. It's also important to be loyal to your company. After all, you, your coworkers, your supervisors, and the owners are all in the business together. You're a team working toward a common goal.

How do you show loyalty at work? Be positive. Look for solutions. Keep critical comments to yourself.

When there's a crisis, pitch in and help the company get through it. This may involve self-sacrifice, some overtime, maybe even unpaid overtime. Remember you're doing it for yourself, too.

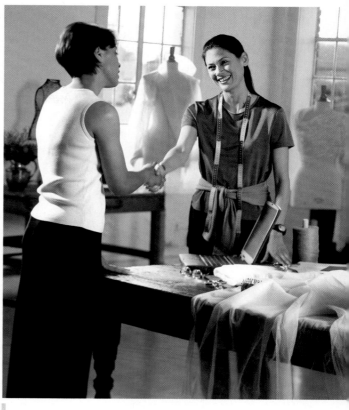

Keeping Customers Happy Business owners today know they must do more to earn customer loyalty. *How does empowering employees with greater responsibility improve customer service?*

SECTION 9.1 REVIEW

✔ Key Concept Checkpoint

Comprehension

1. Consider the qualities employers are seeking in employees. How will employees with these qualities enable companies to do less "managing"?

2. How is self-management good for you and good for your employer?

Critical Thinking

3. What are some qualities that you should look for in an employer?

CAREER FOCUS

CAREER FACTS

Education or Training
A bachelor's degree in accounting is necessary. Advanced degrees, specialized training, and certification increase job opportunities. It is particularly important to be a Certified Public Accountant (CPA).

Aptitudes, Abilities, and Skills
Familiarity with tax laws and legislation and accounting business procedures are necessary. Strong business, math, communication, and computer skills are also necessary.

Career Outlook
Average job growth is expected through 2008.

Career Path
Some accountants pursue certification and go on to be senior accountants or to work for prestigious firms.

What is your key to success?
"Setting goals and working hard to achieve them has been key to my success. I examined various career paths before deciding to become an accountant. While developing my career as an accountant, I have made a point of pursuing outside interests. It's essential to maintain a healthy balance between your personal and professional life."

What skills are most important to you?
"As a tax accountant, I prepare tax returns for both corporate and individual clients. I compile detailed information about clients to provide them with the best service possible. I rely on my communication skills daily to offer solutions, answer questions, and discuss clients' accounts. Communication also helps me keep my clients and coworkers aware of any issues or problems that arise."

What kind of training did you have?
"I majored in accounting in college. The firm I work for provides regular training in our local office as well as intense training sessions once a year on a national level. This helps me develop my skills and learn new concepts"

How does your workload vary?
"Tax accounting is a seasonal profession—certain times of the year are busier than other times. The busy season requires working longer hours and meeting deadlines. The nice part of a seasonal workload is that, for the most part, I know in advance when I'll be busiest at work and can plan accordingly."

> **Critical Thinking** Would you prefer to have a steady workload or a workload that varies by season?

Ethical Behavior

Ethics are the principles of conduct that govern a group or society. How crucial are ethics in the workplace? Is it important for employees to behave ethically toward one another? Toward their company?

Many business people think ethical behavior is critically important to success. Why? *Figure 9.1* on pages 182–183 shows how unethical behavior can have repercussions throughout a company.

Some companies have created programs to promote ethics. Do you think this is a good idea? Write down your answer to this question in your journal. List reasons for your opinion. As you read this section, add other reasons you discover.

Honesty

Employers expect their employees to be honest. Often, they're disappointed. Dishonesty is at the root of most ethics problems in the workplace.

What's the penalty for dishonesty? On a personal level, it can be devastating. One lie can destroy your reputation. How much does your reputation matter? If you were an employer, would you hire someone with a reputation for dishonesty? Be honest with your employer and your company. As an honest worker you will have a much better chance of being successful in a career.

WHAT YOU'LL LEARN

- Why ethics are important in the workplace
- How you can behave ethically in the workplace

WHY IT'S IMPORTANT

Your ability to behave ethically in the workplace will enable you to earn the trust and respect of your employers and coworkers.

KEY TERMS

- **ethics**
- **confidentiality**
- **prejudice**

FIGURE 9.1 Ethics on the Job Having a code of ethics and a personal sense of what is right and wrong will help you choose the right course of action at work. You can serve as a role model for others by acting ethically in five important areas: with customers, coworkers, company property, the community, and the environment.

A Coworkers All coworkers should be treated with fairness and respect. Workers should be hired and promoted based on their talents and achievements. To create a workplace that is safe for everyone, follow safety and health rules and report unsafe conditions. Be a role model—avoid actions that could set an improper example for others. If you are unsure about an ethical decision, seek guidance from your supervisor.

B Customers Your customers deserve safe, high-quality products and services. Always be honest and accurate in marketing your product. Strive to resolve customer complaints, but don't promise more than you can do. Share customers' personal or business information only with those who need to know it.

C **Property** Company property includes both objects, such as computers and office supplies, and information, such as trade secrets and sales figures. Don't share company information with others, and don't use it for your own financial gain. Because organizations rely on accurate records to make responsible decisions, make sure to be as accurate as possible when filling out forms and reports.

D **Community** Is your workplace an asset to the community? Encourage your employer to sponsor a community service program, such as a volunteer program or a school-to-work program. Be sensitive to the concerns of people who live near your business, and remember that you represent your employer to the outside world.

E **Environment** It is everyone's responsibility to protect the environment. Many companies strive to minimize the environmental impact of their operations by using renewable resources, reducing the use of hazardous substances, and recycling wherever possible. If you see environmental laws being broken, notify management immediately. Help to set up a recycling program in your office if there is not one already.

FIGURE 9.2

COMMONLY OBSERVED UNETHICAL BEHAVIOR

1	Lying
2	Withholding Needed Information
3	Abusive or Intimidating Behavior Toward Employees
4	Misreporting Actual Time or Hours Worked
5	Discrimination

SOURCE: Ethics Resource Center (ERC); 2000 National Business Ethics Survey

▲ **Unethical Behavior at Work** A recent study by the Ethics Resource Center revealed that one in three employees observes misconduct at work. This chart shows the most common observations. *Does the information in the chart surprise you? Why or why not?*

Honesty About Time

One of the most common ways in which employees can demonstrate honesty concerns their work hours. This is especially true for employees whose work takes them away from the company, who work at home, or who work on flextime, or flexible schedules. In each case, employees are trusted to work the hours they say they will. What might be the consequence if employees are dishonest about the time they work?

Honesty About Money

Taking money out of the cash drawer is clearly dishonest. In many instances, the issue is more subtle. Consider the following case.

Juanita Benes is a salesperson. On a business trip, she spent more for meals than her expense account allowed. She thought she'd have to pay the difference out of her own pocket. On the other hand, she thought she could make up the difference by adding the amount to two blank taxi receipts. Would this be dishonest?

Benes at first reasoned that it was only a technicality. Other employees probably did it. She wouldn't feel guilty telling her husband. Then she thought about telling her children. She realized that in their eyes, it would be dishonest.

Often you may think there is a thin line between honesty and dishonesty. As you reason through such cases in your career, think how your action might appear to others. Also remember that, like everything else, dishonesty becomes easier with practice. Once you lie about one small matter, it will be that much easier to lie in future situations. *Figure 9.2* shows the types of unethical behavior observed during a one-year period.

Respecting Employers' Property

Another way to risk your reputation and job is to be careless with company property. Don't illegally copy company software for your personal use. Don't take office supplies home for your own use. These items may seem petty, but the small costs do add up. Also, think about it from your supervisor's point of view. If he or she knows you're stealing stamps, will he or she put you in charge of more costly items?

Interacting With Others

Whatever business you enter, you'll be talking and working with others. Occasionally, your interactions may involve ethical issues.

Confidentiality

As an employee, you may have information that would harm the company if others learned about it. This information might have to do with new products, expansion plans, promotions, and so on. Your company will expect you to observe **confidentiality**. In other words, don't tell secrets to people who are not supposed to know them.

Confidentiality is behavior your friends, family, and coworkers also expect from you. They don't want their secrets told either.

ETHICS *in Action*

Sharing Secrets You recently started working at a new software company. Your new supervisor wants you to tell her everything you know about a secret program that you were working on at your old company. You never signed a confidentiality agreement, but you know that the program will be a great accomplishment for your former company once it is released. Your supervisor tells you that you will receive a large bonus and a promotion if you tell her about the program.

THINK ABOUT IT
Would you tell her about the program? Why or why not?

Expense Accounts Business travelers have expense accounts. Their employers will pay for transportation, meals, and other job-related expenses. *Why do employers set limits for travel expenses?*

On the surface, confidentiality seems easy. Sometimes, though, there are conflicting interests. Take the situation involving Sheila Williams.

Williams ran into a former coworker and friend at a seminar. They had dinner together. While talking, Williams learned about a new product her friend's company was developing. It was a product similar to one Williams's own company was working on. Not only that, but her friend's company had solved a problem that Williams's company was stuck on. Her friend didn't know Williams's company was a rival. Should Williams use the information to help her company beat out the rival?

The Ethics Quiz in *Figure 9.3* may help you with such decisions. Use it to resolve Williams's dilemma.

Using Discretion
Coworkers often become good friends. *Why is confidentiality especially important when a coworker who has become a friend moves to a new job?*

FIGURE 9.3

ETHICS QUIZ

Is this action against the law? *If it is, don't do it.*
Do you know the action is wrong? *If so, don't do it.*
Is the action contrary to company values? *Every company has a set of values. Sometimes they are written policy. Sometimes they are not written but are part of an unwritten code of behavior.*
Will you feel bad if you perform this action? *If so, don't do it.*
Are you unsure if the action is wrong? *Ask someone. Check with coworkers, your supervisor, friends, or associates outside of work.*
If this action were reported on the five o'clock news, what would viewers think about it?
If you asked an 8-year-old about the action, what would he or she tell you to do?

▲ **Gray Areas** Questions about ethical issues often do not have definite or clear-cut answers. You must simply use your best judgment. *Why does it help to try to consider the situation without preconception or prejudice?*

Fairness

Virtually every business includes men and women of different races and religions. You'll interact with them as customers, owners, and coworkers. Treat everyone fairly, openly, and honestly.

Prejudice—an unjustifiable negative attitude toward a person or group—is an ethical issue. Prejudice comes in many forms, including racist or sexist comments, stereotyping, name calling, and generalizations. Prejudice in any form, however, is hurtful, offensive, and unacceptable; it cannot be tolerated in today's workplace. Not only can employees be fired for prejudicial comments, but they and their companies can be sued.

Handling Unethical Practices

What if you're the victim of unethical practices? What if you experience prejudice in the workplace? What if you observe unethical business practices?

Consider whether it was an isolated incident or an ongoing practice. Maybe it can be cleared up by a calm, open discussion.

If the offense is deliberate, don't ignore it. Don't act rashly either. First, consider your options. If you're dealing with a customer, you might simply walk away. You don't have to sell a product to an abusive or dishonest customer. Report the incident to your supervisor.

If you're dealing with a coworker, you might tell him or her you will not tolerate his or her prejudiced behavior. If that does not work, talk to your supervisor. Look for solutions, not revenge.

What if your employer is unethical? You can choose to live with the situation. You can keep quiet and find another job. You can report it to the appropriate authority. The choice may not be easy. Remember that in the end, other people's opinion of you will largely reflect how ethically you act. If you decide to take action, these pointers may help:

- Keep a written record as shown in *Figure 9.4*. Describe each incident. Record the date and time.

- Check your observations with others. Maybe they can explain matters. Maybe they will help.

- Get advice from people you trust.

- Check your motives. Are you acting for the right reasons?

- Collect any evidence you can, such as receipts, invoices, or contracts.

- Decide whether you want to remain anonymous or to speak up openly.

- Report only facts or observations. Don't exaggerate or speculate.

FIGURE 9.4 **KEEPING RECORDS**

July 23, 10:45 AM

I saw Mr. Jones meeting with Andrew Mathes, a sales representative for XYZ company. They met in Mr. Jones's office for 25 minutes. When they left, Mr. Jones said, "I'll take care of it. When I get your company's bid, I'll make sure that it's given preferential treatment."

July 27, 3:30 PM

A courier arrived with an envelope for Mr. Jones. I signed for the envelope. It was from Mr. Mathes. Mr. Jones opened the envelope in front of me. It contained two play-off tickets.

▲ **Keeping Records** Accurate, complete records of unethical behavior can serve as partial proof of the events. *Why would it be a good idea to have a coworker keep additional records?*

SECTION 9.2 REVIEW

 Key Concept Checkpoint

Comprehension

1. Imagine that you've observed a coworker lying to a customer. How might this unethical behavior affect you?

2. Of the different kinds of ethical behavior, which do you think will be your biggest challenge? Why?

Critical Thinking

3. Are you born with a set of ethics, or do you acquire ethical beliefs and attitudes through experience?

KEY TERMS
cooperativeness (p. 174)
initiative (p. 176)
responsibility (p. 177)
self-management (p. 178)

SECTION 9.1

- Today's employers want employees who can do many things and who will fit into the company's structure. A key is cooperativeness. This means working well with coworkers and managers. (pp. 174–175)

- Employees must be skilled at listening to and following directions. (p. 175)

- You should be prepared to continue learning throughout your working career. (p. 176)

- Businesses are looking for employees who show initiative. These are people who will step forward and do what needs to be done without having to be told. (pp. 176–177)

- Most employers want workers to take on more responsibility. Taking on additional responsibility will make your work more interesting and make you more valuable to your employer. (pp. 177–178)

- To succeed in the world of work, you must manage your own career. (pp. 178–179)

KEY TERMS
ethics (p. 181)
confidentiality (p. 185)
prejudice (p. 187)

SECTION 9.2

- Ethics are the moral rules of society. Ethics are very important because unethical behavior can have negative repercussions throughout a company. (p. 181)

- As an employee, you should strive to be honest, especially as this relates to time, money, and your employer's property. (pp. 181–185)

- Every career involves interactions with other people. Respecting the confidentiality of your employer and coworkers and acting fairly with everyone are critical to your success. (pp. 185–187)

- You must maintain your own values. When you are the victim or observer of unethical behavior, there are several ways to respond. Choosing the correct response can be a difficult decision. (pp. 187–188)

Reviewing Key Terms

1. On a separate sheet of paper, write a paragraph about the qualities employers seek in employees. Use each of the key terms.
   - cooperativeness
   - responsibility
   - ethics
   - prejudice
   - initiative
   - self-management
   - confidentiality

Recalling Key Concepts

2. A willingness to work with others is ____.
   (a) initiative (b) cooperativeness
   (c) ethics

3. When you are given directions, you should ____.
   (a) listen (b) show initiative
   (c) experiment

4. When you take on unassigned tasks, you are demonstrating ____.
   (a) honesty (b) initiative (c) caution

5. The ethics of your coworkers ____.
   (a) cannot affect a business's success
   (b) should not concern you
   (c) can affect your job security

6. If you observe confidentiality, you ____.
   (a) report a coworker's dishonesty
   (b) work the hours you are expected to work
   (c) don't tell company secrets

Problem Solving

7. Why might you need a strong sense of self-esteem to be cooperative in the workplace?

8. How might learning tasks that are not part of your regular job make you a more valuable employee?

9. What are some positive and some negative consequences that might result from reporting a coworker's unethical behavior?

Work-Based Learning

Information Acquiring and Evaluating Information

10. Employees in retail stores spend time at a variety of tasks, such as helping customers, stocking shelves, taking inventory, and ordering products. To operate efficiently, store managers must know how much time employees spend at each task. Create a chart that might be used to collect and record this information.

Basic Skills Math

11. Because retail stores are busier at certain times of the day, more employees are needed to run the cash registers at different hours. Construct a line graph that presents the following information: one employee at 8:00 A.M., two at 9:00, two at 10:00, three at 11:00, four at 12:00, five at 1:00 P.M., two at 2:00, one at 3:00, one at 4:00, two at 5:00, five at 6:00, six at 7:00, six at 8:00, four at 9:00, two at 10:00.

School-Based Learning

Science Investigate Options

12. Li works for a small manufacturing company in your area. The owner has 50 cans of latex paint stored in the back of his warehouse. The paint is old, and the owner wants to dispose of it. He has asked Li to investigate options for safely disposing of the paint. Find out how old paint can be legally disposed of in your area, and provide two practical options.

Social Studies Research Ethics

13. Conduct interviews with two local employers to determine the importance of work ethics such as dependability, promptness, getting along with others, and honesty. Write a two-page report that details your findings and demonstrates your understanding of productive work habits and attitudes.

Role Play

14. Offering Helpful Advice

Situation You and your friend Don are working at an office as administrative assistants for the summer. At first, Don was very diligent about his job. Lately, though, Don has been receiving a lot of personal calls, taking long lunches, and has even left work early twice without permission. You've noticed that your supervisor has been taking note of Don's behavior.

Activity Role-play a conversation in which you tactfully offer advice to Don. Plan what you'll say in advance and try to avoid making comments that will cause Don to feel defensive or angry. Offer suggestions as to how Don can regain his good standing at work.

Evaluation You will be evaluated based on how well you meet the following performance indicators:

- Choose an appropriate approach for making suggestions to Don
- Offer helpful, realistic advice
- Present suggestions and advice in a tactful and caring manner

15. Record Behavior

Select a day at work or school and record all of the ethical and unethical behavior that you observe. At the end of the day, reflect on the items you've listed. Which type of behavior did you observe most frequently—ethical or unethical? Share your findings and opinions with the class.

Connect Many professional associations, universities, and nonprofit groups have created Web sites and organizations devoted to fostering ethical standards for specific groups or society in general. Visit three such Web sites and write a report about what you discover.

Chapter 10

Developing a Positive Attitude

Section 10.1
Attitudes for Success

Section 10.2
Acting Like a
Professional

CHAPTER OBJECTIVES

After completing this chapter, you will be able to

- Understand how a positive attitude, high self-esteem, and enthusiasm lead to success on the job.

- Describe how to assert yourself at work.

- Handle criticism, workplace pressure, and gossip professionally.

- Control anger on the job.

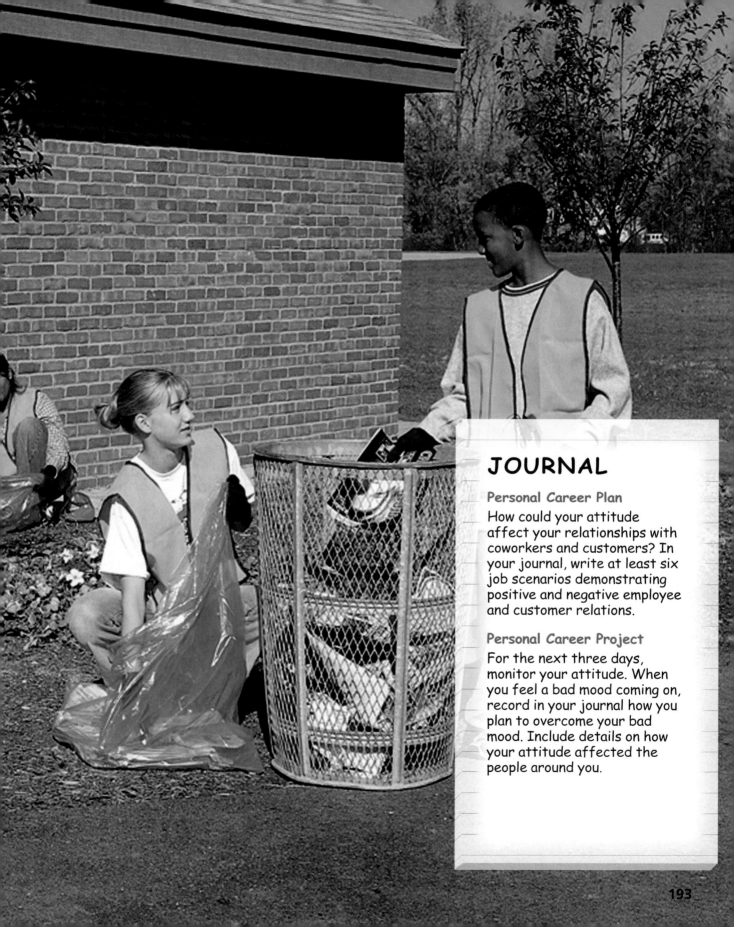

JOURNAL

Personal Career Plan

How could your attitude affect your relationships with coworkers and customers? In your journal, write at least six job scenarios demonstrating positive and negative employee and customer relations.

Personal Career Project

For the next three days, monitor your attitude. When you feel a bad mood coming on, record in your journal how you plan to overcome your bad mood. Include details on how your attitude affected the people around you.

Attitudes for Success

WHAT YOU'LL LEARN

- The importance of a positive attitude, high self-esteem, and enthusiasm in the workplace
- How to assert yourself on the job

WHY IT'S IMPORTANT

Employers value workers who are upbeat, enthusiastic, and confident in their abilities and ideas.

KEY TERMS

- attitude
- self-esteem
- enthusiasm
- assertiveness
- arrogance

School-to-work students Roy Marcus and Gary Sikes have just received some surprising news. Amy Ngo, their coworker at the administrative offices of LaSalle Industries, is moving to another city. She will be leaving in two weeks and will not be replaced. After celebrating with Amy over lunch, Roy and Gary discuss their reactions in private.

Roy thinks the news is great—not only for Amy but also for himself and Gary. Without Amy, they will have the opportunity to learn more about running the business. They will be able to prove themselves to the company. They may even earn permanent positions at LaSalle.

Gary, on the other hand, considers the situation a problem. "What's so great?" he scowls. "All this means is we'll be doing more work for the same pay."

Does this scene sound familiar? If not, be prepared. You may face a similar one at work. While you can't control everything that happens on the job, you can control how you react.

If you are more a "Gary" than a "Roy," pay special attention to this section. Your **attitude,** or basic outlook on life, matters. It determines how you react to certain situations and, often, how you are perceived by others. It is your way of looking at the world and the people in it. How well you get along with your employer and your coworkers will depend on your attitude. If you have a positive attitude, you are already on your way to success on the job.

Positive Attitude Building a positive attitude is like climbing a spiral staircase. *How can positive thinking help you get ahead?*

I'm Positive!

The first step in building a positive attitude is to think positively. When you think positively, you reap many rewards.

What Positive Thinking Can Do for You

Have you ever heard people attribute their success to "the power of positive thinking"? Well, they may be right. Evidence shows that thinking positively can bring you power—in your life and on the job. Think back to Roy and Gary. Whom do you think is more likely to succeed at work? Why?

Here are some ways that positive thinking can lead to positive results:

- *Positive thinkers get along better with others.* When you think positively, you are more receptive, or open, to the people around you.

- *Others feel more comfortable with positive thinkers.* Whom would you rather be around: someone who is optimistic or someone who is negative?

- *Positive thinkers handle problems more effectively.* Consider this "upward spiral": When you think positively, you elevate your mood. When you elevate your mood, you make better decisions. When you make better decisions, you feel even better, and so forth.

- *Positive thinking can help you reach your goals by motivating you to act.* As Les Brown, author of *Live Your Dreams*, explains, "People who expect to achieve their goals don't stand around talking about them. They're engaged in action."

- *Positive thinkers are healthier.* In fact, a study has shown that pessimistic students get sick twice as often as optimistic ones.

FIGURE
10.1

Building a Positive Attitude If you want to build a positive attitude, it helps to practice the four steps shown here.

B Positive Energy Surround yourself with positive thinkers. Positive energy is contagious. Unfortunately, negative energy can be as well. This does not mean you should desert friends in need. However, if many of your friends are negative, and often bring you down, it may be a good idea to seek out new friends.

A Positive Actions Promote positive thoughts by taking positive actions. Instead of wasting time complaining about problems, mobilize and act. Join or form a group or club for a one-time or ongoing project.

C Positive Thinking Turn a negative situation into a positive one by listing its good aspects. Even the worst situations may have some benefits. For example, having to work overtime to catch up on a project may let you feel more in control. It may also mean a larger paycheck or extra vacation time.

D Positive Communication Present your ideas positively, without apologizing. Attending a school-, job-, or community-related meeting offers an excellent opportunity to work on this step. Remember to speak slowly and clearly and to watch your body language.

How to Build a Positive Attitude

OK, you may be thinking, a positive attitude is good. Now how do I go about getting one? The answer is you must build one, step-by-step. *Figure 10.1* shows some of the steps in the process.

Developing Self-Esteem

As *Figure 10.1* shows, when you present your ideas without apologizing, you show **self-esteem**, or a recognition and regard for yourself and your abilities. Self-esteem is essential for a positive attitude.

Here's another "upward spiral": Self-esteem breeds confidence. Confidence generates success. Success boosts self-esteem.

Overcoming Doubt

Do you have a little voice inside your head? Does it sometimes whisper negative messages, such as "You don't deserve to get that new job" or "You're not smart enough to pass that test"? Would you like to get rid of that voice? One technique that works for many people is called positive self-talk.

Positive self-talk means you "outtalk" your negative inner voice. When the voice says, "You can't," you answer, "I can—and I will!" Making a list of positive statements also can help you overcome doubt. Some positive statements might include "I am in charge of my life" and "I can achieve whatever I want with hard work." Try repeating these statements to yourself as often as possible. Eventually your confidence in your abilities will improve.

How to Build Self-Esteem

Once you begin to ignore that negative voice, you allow your self-esteem to grow. Here are some techniques to help you boost your self-esteem:

• Make lists of your abilities and successes. Review them often and remind yourself that you have even more successes ahead.

• Set reachable goals, and work to achieve them.

• Think about how you have had a positive impact on someone else's life, and strive to continue to help other people.

• Work on improving your abilities, both things at which you succeed and things with which you have trouble. When you accomplish something that is challenging, your self-esteem improves significantly.

The Importance of Enthusiasm

What do employers think is the most important quality of their employees? Their experience? Their skills? Their grades? Many employers value a positive attitude most. They look for enthusiastic people who take pride in their work and show initiative.

It's easy to have **enthusiasm**, or eager interest, when you love your work and things are going smoothly. However, even your dream job will have its down moments and frustrating days. How can you ensure that you remain enthusiastic throughout your working experiences?

Sometimes you may have to push yourself to act with enthusiasm. While this may not feel natural, it's worth the effort. An upbeat attitude in difficult situations will help you develop a reputation as a hard and willing worker who can handle a challenge. When you act with enthusiasm, you are more likely to end up really feeling enthusiastic.

Dealing With Mistakes

No one is perfect. Everyone makes mistakes in their personal and professional

lives. In fact, it would be impossible to improve and be successful if we didn't make some errors! The difference between highly successful people and those who feel less successful is not that the successful people make fewer mistakes. It's that they don't give up. Instead of letting mistakes bring them down, they use them as opportunities to learn and grow.

Remember: Whenever you make a mistake, be patient with yourself. You will probably have the opportunity to correct the mistake. Also, you will have other opportunities to succeed.

Once you have accepted that you will make mistakes from time to time, you can prepare yourself to act effectively when you do. When you think you have made a mistake, try following these steps:

1. Make sure it's really a mistake. Because a project didn't turn out the way you planned doesn't mean it's wrong.

2. It's easier to handle a mistake you acknowledge than one you try to hide. Tell your supervisor immediately, and accept responsibility.

3. Offer a way to solve the problem.

4. Find a lesson you can learn from your mistake.

5. Forgive yourself. Don't dwell on your mistake. Learn from it, and move on.

Asserting Yourself

Most people who work hard to do a good job want to be recognized for their efforts. To get the credit you deserve practice **assertiveness**. When you confidently present yourself and your abilities to those around you, you are showing assertiveness.

Representing Yourself

In some cultures, asserting individuality is frowned upon. In the United States, however, confidence is usually admired.

The first step in practicing assertiveness is to be friendly and outgoing. Introduce yourself to new coworkers. Use positive body language and speak with confidence.

Make an effort to get to know your supervisor better too. Offer your opinions or suggestions from time to time. Asking for advice is also an excellent way to let your supervisor know that you care about your job.

Here are some other ways to make yourself better known:

- Volunteer for committees and projects.

- Keep informed. Become an expert on your job or company.

- Keep a journal of your accomplishments. Bring your journal to performance reviews.

Asserting Yourself This woman is offering a suggestion that she thinks will streamline her supervisor's proposal. *Why is it important to voice your ideas?*

Due Credit You and your coworker are both up for a promotion because of a successful project that the two of you recently worked on. What your boss doesn't know is that your coworker was having problems at home and you worked late many nights to pick up her slack. Your coworker has not brought this to your boss's attention, and the decision is scheduled to be made next week.

THINK ABOUT IT
How should you respond to your coworker? What should you say to your boss?

Personal Achievements This woman keeps a record of her accomplishments on the job. *How can keeping a journal help your reputation as a good worker?*

Assertiveness—Not Arrogance

Here's an important distinction to remember: Most employers will accept, and even admire, employees who confidently indicate their real accomplishments and abilities. That is assertiveness. However, no one likes employees who are overbearing and full of self-importance. That is **arrogance**, which you want to avoid. The difference has to do with respecting other people and *their* abilities. It's a question of using the proper attitude and tone.

SECTION 10.1 REVIEW

✓ Key Concept Checkpoint

Comprehension

1. How might having a positive attitude help an employee get a raise or a promotion?
2. On Sheila's second day on her new job at an accounting firm, her supervisor asks her to reorganize the storage closet. Sheila knows this will involve many hours of tedious work. How should she respond to the request? Why?
3. Marco's supervisor is about to prepare her quarterly evaluation of him. He is fairly sure she doesn't realize that he worked much harder than his coworkers on a recent team project. How can Marco get the credit he deserves?

Critical Thinking

4. What steps can you take to show that you are confident and assertive on the job?

CAREER FOCUS

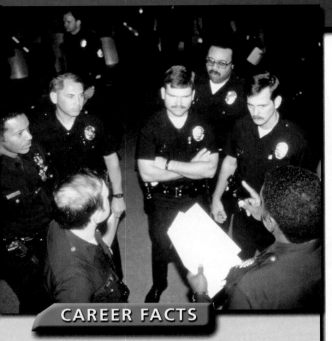

CAREER FACTS

Education and Training College-level courses in criminology and policing are recommended, as are courses in accounting, computer science, and foreign languages. Physical education and sports are helpful as well. Officers undergo training before receiving their first assignment.

Skills, Aptitudes, and Abilities Honesty, integrity, and a sense of responsibility are important, as are strong communication skills and an interest in working with the public. Physical and mental health are vital.

Career Outlook Employment opportunities are expected to increase faster than average.

Career Path Police officers typically become eligible for promotion after a six-month to three-year probationary period. An officer may be promoted to detective or be assigned to specialized police work, such as working with juveniles.

What is your key to success?

"The key to my success is the value I place on giving direction to other officers. Hard work and diligent study have also helped me reach my current position."

What does your job entail?

"I direct a patrol shift of 46 officers and 6 supervisors. My other job duties include supervising major crime scenes, ensuring that officers receive updated training, and handling complaints against officers. When I'm not engaged in administrative duties, I perform routine neighborhood patrols."

What training do you recommend for students?

"I recommend academic studies that develop strong reading, writing, and communication skills. Some states require police academy applicants to take specific college courses. However, all of the training and education in the world will not guarantee you a position as a police officer. You need to maintain a clean criminal record, engage in productive activities such as volunteering or sports, and be mentally stable."

What do you like most about your work?

"I like the variety of my job—new challenges always arise. Emergencies, such as bomb threats, shootings, and serious car accidents, require direct response and quick decisions. I enjoy serving citizens during these times of crisis. I also enjoy lifting the burden of minor issues off patrol officers so they can focus on their daily job functions."

Critical Thinking How could playing on a sports team in high school prepare you for a career as a police officer?

Acting Like a Professional

Think back to a difficult time at school or work. Maybe you had a classmate who challenged you every time you spoke up. Perhaps you were so overworked you felt you would explode if someone told you to do just one more thing.

Now divide a sheet of paper into three columns. In the first column, briefly describe the *situation* you recalled. In the second, list the *feelings* you experienced. In the third, describe the *action* you took. Turn the paper over. Then answer these questions: Was your reaction a mature response to your problem? Was your answer constructive? What could you have done differently?

When you experience difficulties, these will be important questions to ask yourself. Particularly in the workplace, you should question yourself before you react to a problem. At work, you will need to show **professionalism**. That is, you will need to handle problems and criticism gracefully and maturely. Instead of reacting prematurely, think things through before you take any action.

Accepting Criticism

You already know that properly handling criticism can be difficult. However, it is vital to your survival in any job.

WHAT YOU'LL LEARN

- How to react professionally to workplace pressures, criticism, and gossip
- Methods used to control anger on the job

WHY IT'S IMPORTANT

To succeed in the workplace, you must be able to handle difficult situations in a professional manner.

KEY TERMS

- **professionalism**
- **constructive criticism**
- **defensiveness**
- **gossip**

Criticism that is presented in a way that can help you learn and grow is called **constructive criticism**. Your ability to accept this type of criticism will demonstrate that you are a mature and reasonable employee.

Although constructive criticism is often presented formally during a performance review or evaluation, it may also come up in casual conversation or during daily work activities.

Many supervisors try to offset constructive criticism by offering positive comments along with their suggestions for improvement. Such supervisors may even make it a point to offer commendation *before* criticism. This is an effective strategy that allows the supervisor to show his or her regard for the feelings of others. By praising an employee, the supervisor reminds the employee that he or she is valued. As a result, the employee is more

Creative
BUSINESS PRACTICES

Mary Kay Cosmetics
Recognition and Rewards

Have you ever seen a pink Cadillac around town? Chances are you have because there are more than 1,600 pink Mary Kay edition Cadillacs in the United States. Top performers can earn the use of the famous pink Cadillac, the ultimate symbol of success for Mary Kay's independent sales force.

Mary Kay Inc. is a global direct-selling company founded in Dallas in 1963 by Mary Kay Ash, and today has more than 850,000 Independent Beauty Consultants in 37 markets worldwide. The company was founded to give women an unparalleled professional career opportunity that would provide flexibility, unlimited earnings potential and personal growth. Mary Kay created a highly personalized means of selling products, allowing customers to try and learn about the products in their homes before buying them.

Mary Kay strongly believed in praising people to success. She recognized rewarding employees for good work was one of the best ways to enhance their skills and promote personal fulfillment. Other awards include diamond rings, all-expense paid trips around the world and business equipment, as well as the pink Cadillac and several other GM cars.

Critical Thinking
How do you feel when you are recognized for your accomplishments?

Link and Learn
For more information about Mary Kay Cosmetics and its recognition program, visit the company Web site via the link on the *Succeeding in the World of Work* Web site at **www.careers.glencoe.com**.

likely to accept the constructive criticism.

However, not all constructive criticism is offered tactfully. If your supervisor is abrupt when making suggestions, remind yourself to focus on how using the advice will help you grow professionally.

When you see criticism as potentially helpful, it becomes easier to handle. Believe it or not, some employees actually welcome criticism. They have found that it teaches them better ways to succeed at their jobs.

Of course, not all criticism is equally productive. *Figure 10.2* compares constructive criticism to less helpful criticism. You can use the standards in this figure to evaluate criticism you receive. You can also use them if your job requires you to evaluate employees.

Responding to Criticism

What does the term *defensiveness* bring to mind? Consider this situation:

Janet's coworker Paolo has been late many times. Recently, Janet overheard her supervisor tell a colleague that if Paolo continued to be late, he would lose his job. After work, Janet told Paolo what she had heard and suggested he try to get to work on time. Paolo snapped back, "But it's not my fault! My car is always breaking down. Besides, who are you to judge me?" Janet understood why Paolo was upset. However, she wished that he had really listened to what she had to say. After all, she felt the criticism had been for his own good.

Defensiveness means putting up an emotional guard against negative opinions. Remember the upward spirals from Section 10.1? Here's a downward spiral: When Paolo reacts defensively, he becomes closed. When he is closed, he cannot listen. When he cannot listen, he cannot grow. The only way he could have benefited from Janet's criticism was to be receptive and not defensive.

FIGURE 10.2	WHAT MAKES CRITICISM CONSTRUCTIVE?	
Constructive Criticism	**Less Helpful Criticism**	
Addresses behavior	Addresses attitude	
Is specific	Is general	
Is offered immediately	Is not offered immediately	
Makes some mention of positive points	Focuses exclusively on negative points	
Offers specific actions to solve the problem(s)	Offers no solution to the problem(s)	
Is given in private	Is announced in public	

▲ Criticism You can learn to give and accept constructive criticism. *Why is it easier to accept constructive criticism than non-constructive criticism?*

Here are four steps that can help you respond effectively to criticism:

1. Listen to the criticism.
2. Make sure you understand the criticism. If the speaker does not specify the problem, ask him or her to do so.
3. Identify a solution to the problem.
4. Take action to remedy the problem. If the problem is complex, break it down into smaller bits. Then you can take action one step at a time.

Accepting Criticism If you are closed to criticism, you may be following a downward spiral. *How can defensiveness prevent growth?*

FIGURE 10.3

ON-THE-JOB PRESSURES AND HOW TO HANDLE THEM

Meeting Deadlines	Learn to break large tasks into smaller steps. Carefully schedule when you will complete each step. If the deadline seems unrealistic, *ask for help as early as possible.*
Juggling Tasks	A daily "to do" list, where you define and prioritize your duties, can be a lifesaver. As you complete each task, cross it off the list. For example: A. ~~Cal MF and LS about the meeting Wednesday.~~ B. ~~Prepare minutes from last month's meeting.~~ C. Copy fund-raising report for GG. D. Make calls to caterers about May event.
Having More Than One Supervisor	If two supervisors give you assignments due at the same time or if they give you conflicting instructions, speak up! Request a meeting with both supervisors so that they can sort out their priorities together.

▲ **Dealing with Pressure** Every job has pressure. *Why is it important to have a plan for handling the different kinds of on-the-job pressure?*

A final word on responding to criticism: In the end, you must use your own judgment. Even if the rest of the world thinks you've made a poor decision, you may know inside that you did the right thing. This is especially true when you need to stand up for your values.

Handling Pressure

Pressure is everywhere! Supervisors set deadlines. Coworkers make demands. Difficult customers need polite attention. You wonder if you are making the right decisions. You wonder if you will ever be able to get all your work done. You wonder if you are succeeding at your job. You wonder if you are in the right job at all. ...

Does this sound familiar? *Figure 10.3* offers some tips that can help you handle on-the-job pressure.

Handling Gossip

Idle talk that usually consists mostly of rumors is called **gossip**. The problem with such talk is that the information it spreads is often untrue—and hurtful. According to Adele Scheele, a writer for *Working Woman* magazine, people gossip so that they can feel important. "Gossip is a bribe," she says, "a way of enhancing your status at someone else's expense."

In the end, gossip usually hurts the gossiper most. The more an employee gossips, the less coworkers will confide in that person. Eventually, the gossiper develops a reputation as someone who cannot be trusted. Before you join in gossip, ask yourself these questions:

- What is my motivation for gossiping?
- Could my comments damage someone else's reputation unfairly?

Professional Behavior This woman has some gossip about a coworker. *Should she share it with her other coworkers? Why or why not?*

Controlling Anger

Some frustration is inevitable in any job. As you work to develop new skills and advance in your career, things will not always go well. However, you must avoid letting frustration turn to anger and your anger boil over on the job. If you do get angry, here are some tips for "damage control:"

- Count to ten. It gives you a chance to calm down and not say something you will regret later.

- Consider what you are really angry about. Are you angry about a situation at work or with friends?

- Channel your energy into problem solving. Here's a five-step model: (1) define the problem, (2) decide on possible solutions, (3) evaluate those solutions, (4) make a decision, (5) take action.

CAREER CHECKLIST

Developing a Positive Work Attitude...

☑ Accept challenges as opportunities.

☑ Learn to analyze a situation from all angles, even if some of those viewpoints differ from your own.

☑ Always show respect and consideration for other employees, even if you disagree.

☑ Take responsibility for your actions.

☑ Never take on more responsibility than you can handle if you cannot get the job done properly.

☑ Avoid negative talk about work, both in and out of the workplace. Your positive attitude will be infectious.

SECTION 10.2 REVIEW

✓ Key Concept Checkpoint

Comprehension

1. Sean's supervisor wants to speak to him about some problems with the project he just completed. Sean feels that he worked hard on the project and did an excellent job. What should he do when he meets with his supervisor?

2. Jake is overwhelmed by the amount of work he must complete every day. What is one step Jake can take to reduce the pressure he feels?

3. What is the difference between sharing helpful information with your coworkers and gossiping?

4. List three tips for controlling anger on the job.

Critical Thinking

5. Have you always acted with professionalism in the past? What can you do to ensure that you act professionally in the future?

KEY TERMS
attitude (p. 194)
self-esteem (p. 197)
enthusiasm (p. 198)
assertiveness (p. 200)
arrogance (p. 201)

SECTION 10.1

- While employees cannot control everything that happens on the job, they can control how they react. A positive attitude can help workers succeed. (pp. 194–197)

- A positive attitude is based on self-esteem. Self-esteem and confidence in your abilities are closely related. (p. 197)

- To build self-esteem, you can train your positive inner voice to "outtalk" your negative inner voice. (pp. 197–198)

- Employers value an upbeat attitude. You can learn to act with enthusiasm even during your job's down moments. (p. 198)

- Be patient with yourself. It's OK to make mistakes as long as you try to learn from them. (pp. 198–199)

- Being assertive, but not arrogant, can help you get the recognition you deserve on the job. (pp. 200–201)

KEY TERMS
professionalism (p. 203)
constructive
   criticism (p. 204)
defensiveness (p. 205)
gossip (p. 207)

SECTION 10.2

- Employees need to handle criticism gracefully and to react maturely. These are important aspects of professionalism. (pp. 203–207)

- It is best to avoid being defensive when receiving constructive criticism. (pp. 205–206)

- Learning to handle pressure effectively will help you succeed at your work. (p. 207)

- People usually gossip to enhance their status. However, gossipers often end up damaging their own reputations. (p. 207)

- Things at work don't always go the way you want them to. Employees must learn to prevent frustration from becoming anger and anger from boiling over. (p. 208)

Reviewing Key Terms

1. On separate paper, write a short story about a high school graduate's first week of work. Use the terms below in your story.

   - attitude
   - self-esteem
   - enthusiasm
   - assertiveness
   - arrogance
   - professionalism
   - constructive criticism
   - defensiveness
   - gossip

Recalling Key Concepts

Determine whether each statement is true or false. Rewrite any false statements to make them true.

2. Optimists get sick less often than pessimists.

3. When you act with enthusiasm, you are more likely to start feeling enthusiastic.

4. Failure is who you are, not something you did.

5. Assertiveness is assuming you know everything and bragging about your accomplishments.

6. People usually gossip so that they will feel more important.

Problem Solving

7. Why do you think positive "self-talk" can help you build self-esteem and confidence?

8. Do you think it's OK to "push" enthusiasm when you're feeling down on the job? Is this dishonest? Why or why not?

9. When you are angry, counting to ten can help you calm down and think clearly. What other techniques might accomplish the same goal?

Work-Based Learning

Thinking Skills Knowing How to Learn

10. Explain how each of the following skills can help you develop a better attitude on the job: writing, thinking, listening.

Interpersonal Skills Participating as a Team Member

11. Abigail, Dara, and Thomas work as a team as cashiers and baggers at a supermarket. All of them are being considered for one new managerial position. Though the three are good friends, Thomas and Dara tell Abigail that they think she is "playing up" too much to their supervisor by always complimenting him. How should Abigail respond to this criticism? Should she change her behavior? Why or why not?

School-Based Learning

Human Relations Solve Problems

12. Interview the human resource administrator at a local company. Ask what human relations problems are of particular concern at that company and how the administrator works to solve those problems. Report your findings to the class.

Health and Physical Education Research Stress Management

13. Do research in the library or on the Internet to find out what long-term effects a negative job attitude and work-related stress and anger can have on a person's health. What do doctors recommend to prevent these health risks?

Music/Science Evaluate Types of Music

14. Many companies pipe music into certain areas of the workplace in an attempt to improve the working environment and boost worker performance. Contact such employers as supermarkets, mall stores, and doctors' offices to find out what kind of music is used and why.

Role Play

15. Human Resources Seminar

Situation You are part of a human resources team for your company. Recently, several employees have come to you with problems ranging from not enjoying their work environment to fearing that a supervisor is making a number of mistakes on a project. One employee has complained that he puts in long hours to complete his work, but his supervisor receives the credit. Another employee who was assigned a new, complex assignment wonders if she can manage.

Activity Working with a three-person team, prepare and run a seminar for the office. Address the concerns of the employees, explaining to them why they feel as they do, and how they can manage those feelings. In order to avoid office gossip, you must address these concerns without linking any one employee with a particular problem.

Evaluation Your group will be evaluated based on how well it meets the following performance indicators:

- Demonstrate understanding of the problems and their solutions
- Present a clear, well-organized, and animated seminar
- Discuss the problems in a professional and understanding manner

interNET CONNECTION

16. Investigate Your Dream Job
Interview someone who holds a job you would like to have. Ask them if they ever have to cope with any of the attitude difficulties discussed in the chapter. Find out what strategies help them at work.

Connect Look up three different jobs you would enjoy. Find out what you would have to do on a typical day at the job. Would you still enjoy the jobs?

Chapter 11

Workplace Health and Safety

Section 11.1
Becoming a Healthy Worker

Section 11.2
Safety on the Job

CHAPTER OBJECTIVES

After completing this chapter, you will be able to

- Recognize the relationship between good health and career success.

- Describe strategies for coping with stress.

- Identify rules and procedures for maintaining a safe workplace.

- Identify workplace conservation and environmental practices and policies.

- Explain how to respond effectively to various workplace emergencies.

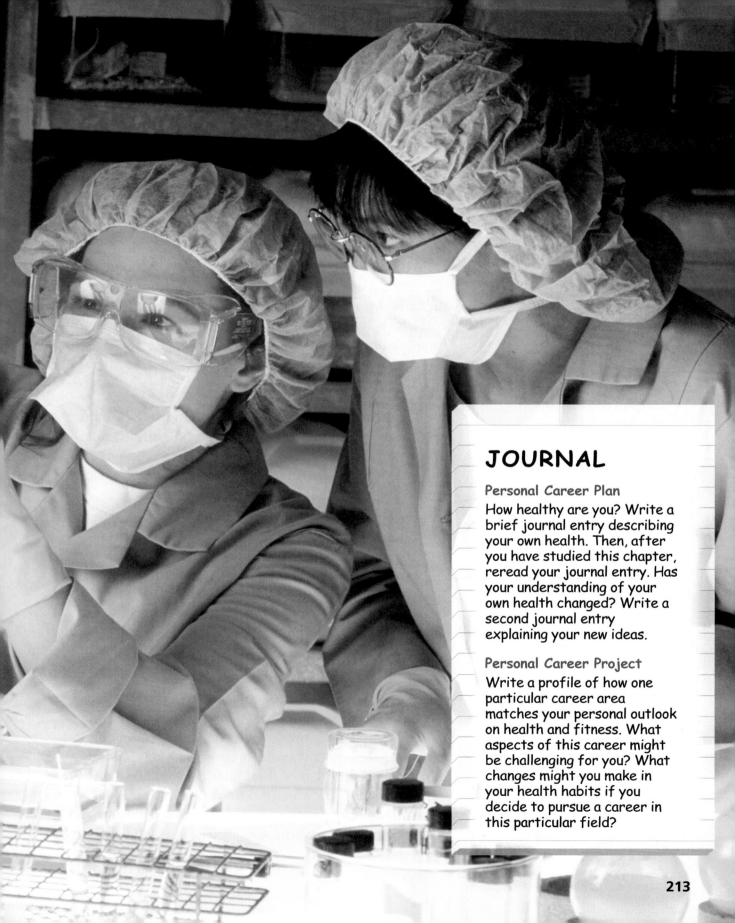

JOURNAL

Personal Career Plan

How healthy are you? Write a brief journal entry describing your own health. Then, after you have studied this chapter, reread your journal entry. Has your understanding of your own health changed? Write a second journal entry explaining your new ideas.

Personal Career Project

Write a profile of how one particular career area matches your personal outlook on health and fitness. What aspects of this career might be challenging for you? What changes might you make in your health habits if you decide to pursue a career in this particular field?

Becoming a Healthy Worker

Athletes know that good health makes success possible. Without it, there are no touchdown passes, no 20-foot jump shots. To score the kinds of goals you want in whatever career you choose, you, too, need to pay attention to your health.

What It Takes to Be Healthy

Good health means more than being free of pain and illness. It means having the mental and physical energy to do what you need and want to do. You can't have total control over your health, but you can influence these major health factors:

- diet
- exercise
- rest

You can also stay on guard against disease and addiction. This advice will help you build a solid foundation for career success.

Eating Wisely

Maria Cisneros, a telemarketer, assumed she was healthy. Yet after a busy day at work, all she wanted to do was pick up a pizza, collapse on the couch, and watch television. "I was really tired, and I blamed my job," she recalls. "I gave it all I had." Then her doctor explained that she was tired because she wasn't getting enough **nutrients**—the substances in food that the body needs to produce energy and stay healthy.

Check for the nutrients you need in *Figure 11.1* on page 216, which shows the **Food Guide Pyramid**. This is a guideline created by the U.S. Department of Health and Human Services to show you the nutrients you need each day.

Exercising for Fitness

Exercise takes energy, but it also gives *back* energy. Exercise helps you do the following:

- build strength and endurance
- feel mentally alert
- reduce tension and anxiety

Employees who exercise are productive and don't get ill as often as employees who don't exercise. Exercise is particularly important if you have a **sedentary** job—one in which you spend much of your time sitting. Think you're too busy to

At-Work Workouts

You work in a busy office, often sitting at your desk for nine hours a day. You're usually too tired to exercise after work. You need to develop an exercise program to boost your health and productivity.

Connect

- Visit the Web sites of health and fitness magazines. Research ways you can do mini-workouts throughout the day, including techniques for doing stretches and strength training right at your desk.
- Write up a list of the exercises that you can do when you can't get in a full workout.

Balanced Diet Eating wisely does not necessarily mean eating less. It means eating foods that nourish you. *What foods would make up another nutritious breakfast?*

FIGURE
11.1

FOOD GUIDE PYRAMID

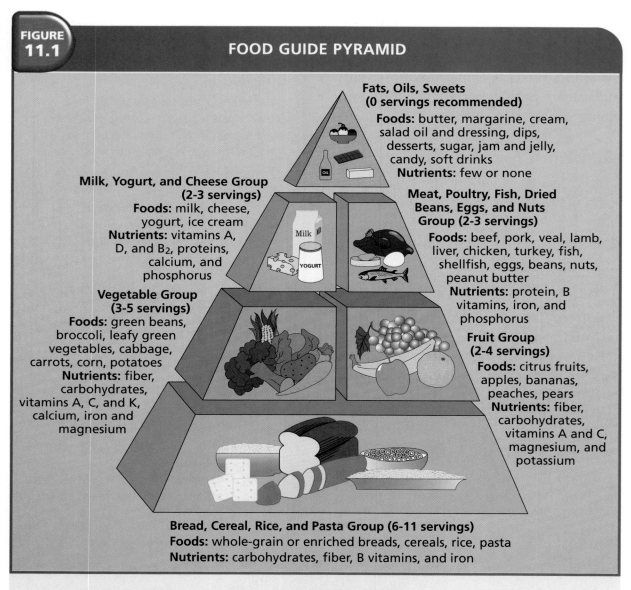

**Fats, Oils, Sweets
(0 servings recommended)**
Foods: butter, margarine, cream,
salad oil and dressing, dips,
desserts, sugar, jam and jelly,
candy, soft drinks
Nutrients: few or none

**Milk, Yogurt, and Cheese Group
(2-3 servings)**
Foods: milk, cheese,
yogurt, ice cream
Nutrients: vitamins A,
D, and B_2, proteins,
calcium, and
phosphorus

**Meat, Poultry, Fish, Dried
Beans, Eggs, and Nuts
Group (2-3 servings)**
Foods: beef, pork, veal, lamb,
liver, chicken, turkey, fish,
shellfish, eggs, beans, nuts,
peanut butter
Nutrients: protein, B
vitamins, iron, and
phosphorus

**Vegetable Group
(3-5 servings)**
Foods: green beans,
broccoli, leafy green
vegetables, cabbage,
carrots, corn, potatoes
Nutrients: fiber,
carbohydrates,
vitamins A, C, and K,
calcium, iron and
magnesium

**Fruit Group
(2-4 servings)**
Foods: citrus fruits,
apples, bananas,
peaches, pears
Nutrients: fiber,
carbohydrates,
vitamins A and C,
magnesium, and
potassium

Bread, Cereal, Rice, and Pasta Group (6-11 servings)
Foods: whole-grain or enriched breads, cereals, rice, pasta
Nutrients: carbohydrates, fiber, B vitamins, and iron

▲ **Suggested Servings** Foods are usually grouped according to the nutrients they provide. This pyramid shows you how many daily servings from each food group you need. *Why doesn't the Food Guide Pyramid recommend any servings of fats, oils, and sweets?*

exercise? Think again. Health profession-als say you need only 20 minutes of exer-cise three times a week to reap the benefits. So what do you like? Aerobics? Dancing? Basketball? Go for it! You'll build strength and endurance and feel better!

Recharging Yourself—Sleep

There's a lot happening in Laurie McBride's life. Three nights a week, she has a class at the community college. At other times, she goes out with friends. Most nights, after taking care of household

Staying Fit The secret of a successful exercise program is doing something you enjoy. *If you exercise regularly, what are some of the health benefits you experience?*

Staying on Guard

Beyond maintaining a balanced diet and getting the right amounts of exercise and rest, you need to stay on guard to stay healthy. That means following rules of hygiene, getting regular checkups, and guarding against drug and alcohol addiction.

Addiction is a physical or psychological need for a substance. Addictive substances can include alcohol and prescription drugs, as well as illegal substances such as marijuana and cocaine. Addiction can lead to devastating physical and mental effects, including depression, heart attack, liver disease, and even death.

Addiction can have a drastic impact on business, causing injuries, absenteeism, and poor productivity. That is why many

chores and winding down in front of the television set, she usually gets about six hours of sleep. What's the result? Laurie struggles to stay alert at work.

Almost everyone needs about eight hours of sleep a night. Too little sleep can cause difficulty concentrating and make a person more prone to accidents.

Sleep restores the body and recharges the brain. To get a good night's sleep, try to go to bed about the same time every night. Avoid caffeine-rich foods and drinks, such as chocolate and caffeinated sodas, before bed.

Sleeping Aids Eating or drinking certain foods, such as milk, before bedtime helps some people sleep well. *What other nighttime routines might help this person get a good night's rest?*

companies have established *drug-testing programs*, programs designed to detect illegal drug use. Some companies might test you when you apply for a job; others have a policy of testing employees periodically. Companies are not likely to hire job applicants who test positive for drugs. Employees with positive drug tests face possible job termination or may be referred to counseling and treatment.

Managing Stress

Another vital factor in staying healthy is learning to manage stress. Sam Burnett, a real estate agent, faced a hectic daily schedule. An economic downturn in his region made selling homes a difficult task. Although some amount of stress is natural, Sam found that the pressure gave him severe headaches. The stress—which is one's physical and emotional reaction to change or conflict—was getting to him.

According to a recent study by the American Institute of Stress, close to half of American workers say that they suffer from symptoms of burnout, a reaction to stress on the job. An estimated 1 million workers are absent on an average workday due to stress-related complaints. Stress on the job is estimated to cost U.S. industry $300 billion per year, due to stress-related accidents, absenteeism, diminished productivity, etc.

Stress—Positive and Negative

Stress is a natural reaction to conflict. When you are challenged, your heart rate and breathing accelerate, your muscles tighten, and your blood pressure climbs. In the short term, these effects can be positive because they help you focus more clearly and act more decisively. When the challenge is over, your body returns to normal.

Stress becomes negative, however, when your body doesn't return to normal but stays in an unnecessary state of alertness. This state can wear you out and produce such effects as headaches, chest pain, irritability, and depression.

Coping with Stress

Health experts say that one of the most effective ways of dealing with stress is to identify the cause of the stress and then to

Headache Stress often causes physical symptoms such as headaches and chest pain. *What are some relaxation techniques that you can use to relieve stress?*

FIGURE
11.2

COPING WITH STRESS

Recognizing the Problem	Finding Solutions
Major changes, such as marriage, a new job, or the death of a family member	Try to limit changes in other areas of your life. If you've just started a new job, for example, you might want to delay other changes (such as getting married).
Conflict or uncertainty caused by disagreements with coworkers or unclear instructions about what is expected of you	Talk the problem out with a trusted coworker, human relations worker, or company counselor. If the problem persists, consider getting someone to mediate—to listen to what you both have to say—and negotiate.
Prolonged overwork or pressure when you have to pick up the work of employees who have been laid off or when you have to work additional hours during seasonal deadlines	Review your responsibilities with a coworker or mentor. Can one person do them all? Are there ways to do them more efficiently? If the workload is too great, discuss getting help from your supervisor. Until help comes, set priorities, and take one step at a time.
Environmental stresses, such as noise, uncomfortable temperatures, crowding	Brainstorm with coworkers. Bring comforts from home, such as headphones, a small fan or heater, or a desk lamp. Use visualization to move to a calmer, quieter place.

▲ **Reducing Stress** You can use your problem-solving skills to manage stress on the job. *What positive aspects of a workplace might relieve stress?*

address the problem directly. **Figure 11.2** identifies some problems and their possible solutions. In addition, you can develop your own relaxation techniques. Here are three widely used methods:

- *Deep breathing.* Slowly fill your lungs with air. Hold it. Release. Deep breathing has a calming effect on your mind and body.

- *Visualization.* Close your eyes and picture yourself in a calm place—for example, resting on a beach or under a tree.

- *Taking a time-out.* Get away from a pressure-packed situation for a few minutes—for example, take a walk outside. When you return, you may see solutions you didn't see before.

Being able to handle job stress will make you a valuable employee who can be depended on by your supervisor.

The benefits of reducing stress can be increased productivity, greater job satisfaction, and better self-management. Handling stress is also a leadership skill: Only people who can manage themselves can lead others effectively.

ETHICS *in Action*

Handling Stress Lately, a coworker has been rude to customers and other employees at the grocery store where you work. She often leaves early and always has excuses as to why she doesn't do her share of the work. You have been handling the work she leaves behind, and the situation has caused you to have a poor attitude about your job. When you approach your boss about your coworker's behavior, he says that she is stressed out from problems at home and that she should get better soon.

THINK ABOUT IT
How do you respond to your boss's reaction to the situation?

Managing Stress Cathy, the character in this cartoon, is overwhelmed by her work. *What advice would you give Cathy?*

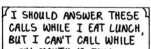

by Cathy Guisewite

SECTION 11.1 REVIEW

✔ Key Concept Checkpoint

Comprehension

1. In what ways can being healthy help your career?

2. Name three obstacles that keep people from regularly managing their diet, exercise schedule, and rest schedule.

3. What negative effects could stress have on your work?

4. Why is it important to prepare yourself to cope effectively with stress on the job?

Critical Thinking

5. What are some "high-stress" jobs? Why do some people opt to work at jobs that are very stressful?

CAREER FACTS

Education or Training Most production managers must have extensive experience working on the production floor. An increasing number of manufacturing firms prefer to hire production managers who have some postsecondary education, such as an associate or bachelor's degree.

Aptitudes, Abilities, and Skills Production managers must have excellent people, math, communication, and problem-solving skills. A sense of responsibility and the ability to simultaneously manage many different types of tasks are also important.

Career Outlook Employment is expected to grow more slowly than average through 2008.

Career Path Most production managers start out as machine operators and are promoted to team leaders or shift managers. When candidates prove themselves as lower-level managers, they are promoted to higher-level positions.

What is your key to success?

"I feel that the key to my success is my good people skills. I try to convey a willingness to listen. I also stay open-minded, maintain a positive attitude, and show equal respect for everyone. When managing other people, I must set a good example. Actions usually speak louder than words."

What does your job entail?

"I spend the majority of my time dealing with people. I conduct interviews and employee performance reviews and attend weekly production and distribution meetings. I also spend a lot of time dealing with employees one-on-one, discussing issues such as company policies and work problems. Some of my other responsibilities include analyzing production reports, creating production schedules, and managing employees' hours."

What skills are most important to you?

"The skills and abilities that matter most to me are maintaining a positive attitude, working well with others, paying attention to detail, solving problems, and having overall knowledge and experience with our product and the manufacturing production process."

What do you like most about your work?

"I like the fact that I'm never stuck doing the same thing all day long. In one workday, I might deal with personnel issues, troubleshoot equipment, write procedures, train employees, and even operate machines."

Critical Thinking Why is it especially important for a production manager to have experience working on the production floor?

Safety on the Job

Workplace accidents cost businesses billions of dollars annually in lost wages, medical expenses, and insurance claims. Nearly 6 million people are injured on the job every year. Part of your job is to make sure you're not one of them.

Rules and Regulations

Government, employers, and workers all have a stake in preventing accidents. Therefore, they cooperate to make workplaces safer.

The Government's Role

The federal government protects American workers by setting workplace safety standards and by making sure that accident victims receive care. The **Occupational Safety and Health Administration (OSHA)** is the branch of the U.S. Department of Labor that sets job safety standards and inspects job sites. If a company fails to meet OSHA's standards, it can face fines and other penalties. OSHA keeps pace with the world of work by revising standards when work conditions change or new technology, such as the use of lasers, is developed.

The government also makes sure that workers are compensated, or paid, if they have an accident and can't work. **Workers' compensation** laws guarantee that if you are hurt on the job, you will receive financial help to cover lost wages and medical expenses.

Employers' Roles

Safety regulations for employers can be very complex. In a nutshell, employers must do the following:

- provide a workplace free from recognized health and accident hazards,
- provide equipment and materials needed to do the work safely and teach employees how to use them,
- inform employees when materials or conditions are hazardous, and
- keep records of job-related illnesses and injuries.

In addition, employers establish policies and procedures for conservation and environmental protection. These procedures—such as those for recycling glass and safely disposing of hazardous waste—may vary from company to company. As more and more work, education, and recreation involves computers, everyone needs to be aware of the hazard of **repetitive stress injuries**, ailments that develop after the same motions are performed over and over. To address this problem and other similar injuries, industrial engineers are engaged in a new field of applied science called **ergonomics**, in which they redesign workstations to make them safer, more comfortable, and more efficient.

Workers' Responsibilities

Workplace safety is also the responsibility of individual employees. In addition to following regulations for environmental protection, workers must learn and follow safety regulations set down by OSHA. These include the following:

- learn to perform a job safely,
- know how to operate, maintain, and troubleshoot tools and equipment safely, and
- report unsafe conditions or practices immediately.

Figure 11.3 shows other ways businesses can reduce workplace accidents.

Taking Action Employers and employees are responsible for protecting the environment. *What is one step you can take to do this?*

ADOPT A HIGHWAY
LITTER CONTROL
NEXT 2 MILES

ASHLAND CHEMICAL, INC

FIGURE
11.3

Workplace Safety A major concern for businesses is trying to reduce workplace accidents. This can be done by following OSHA guidelines, training employees through company newsletters and safety meetings, and offering employees incentives such as safety awards.

A **Safety Meetings** A company should hold several safety meetings each year. Employee attendance at such meetings should be required.

B **Safety Awards** Safety awards can be an important part of a safety program. These awards can be anything from a sticker to a fancy plaque to cash awards.

C **Safety Through Empowerment** Perhaps the most beneficial way for a company to reduce workplace accidents is by empowering the employees. Empowerment occurs when employees are granted the authority to improve safety in the workplace. Employees who have a say in their own safety will take safety more seriously.

Responding to Emergencies

Your own safety and the safety of other employees can depend upon your awareness of what to do in an emergency. Knowing **first aid**—what to do *first*, before help arrives—may mean the difference between life and death.

Juwon Taylor, a student driving home in a heavy windstorm, watched helplessly as a giant tree limb came crashing down on the car in front of him. Stopping his own car, Juwon started toward the dam-aged vehicle to see if anyone was injured. Quickly taking in the scene as he approached, Juwon spotted an exposed power line draped across the car's hood. By looking around before touching the car, Juwon saved his own life and was able to get help for the injured motorist.

Always survey an accident scene before you do anything. Figure out what has already happened, and try to determine what may happen next. If someone is injured and you are nearby, follow the easy-to-remember American Red Cross guidelines in the following sections.

Provide A-I-D

The letters of the word *AID* help you remember what to do.

- **A**sk for help. If someone is seriously injured, call the Emergency Medical Service immediately.
- **I**ntervene, but ask the victim first.
- **D**o no further harm. Do not move a victim whose back or neck may be broken.

Know Your ABCs

The ABCs are another easy way to remember priorities in an emergency.

- **Airway.** If necessary, clear the victim's airway (the passage that allows the person to breathe). Do this by placing one hand on the person's forehead and two fingers of the other hand under the person's chin. Tilt the head back by pushing on the forehead and lifting the chin.
- **Breathing.** Check to see if the victim is breathing.
- **Circulation.** Check to see if the victim has a pulse and whether he or she is bleeding severely. If so, press a clean cloth on the wound, and hold firmly with your palm.

Always follow the ABCs. If necessary, administer rescue breathing.

When the Elements Strike

Nature's fury can cause emergencies too. You need to know what to do to protect yourself and those you live and work with in case of fire or weather emergencies.

Preventing Accidents Workers can take steps to ensure a safe working environment. *What are three of them?*

Fire

Your best protection against fire is to be prepared. Learn the location of fire exits at your workplace, and know your escape routes. If a fire breaks out, take these precautions:

- Leave the building immediately. Take the stairs or go out a window; do not use an elevator.
- If you cannot leave, stay close to the floor to avoid smoke.
- Before opening a door, put your hand on it. If the door is hot, don't open it. Find another way out or wait for help.
- If your clothes catch fire, stop, drop to the floor, and roll to put the fire out.
- Leave fire fighting to the experts. Don't try to put out the flames yourself.

Earthquakes

The most common danger in an earthquake comes from collapsing structures, falling objects, and glass. When an earthquake strikes, follow these precautions:

- If you are inside, stay inside. Move to a doorway or under a table or desk.

- If you are outdoors, stand in the open, away from tumbling trees, utility poles, and buildings.

Hurricanes

A hurricane is a tropical cyclone with winds of 74 miles per hour or greater. These powerful storms can pack raging winds and driving rains. When a hurricane threatens, take these precautions:

- Listen to bulletins from the National Weather Service. Be prepared with candles and matches, a flashlight, and a battery-operated radio.

Creative BUSINESS PRACTICES

Northwestern Mutual Life Insurance Company
Encouraging Healthy Employees

Northwestern Mutual Life Insurance Company focuses on the health and well-being of not only its policy holders, but also its employees. By providing wellness programs and exercise facilities, Northwestern Mutual encourages employees to make positive health choices.

Northwestern Mutual's commitment to employee health started more than 20 years ago, when it began reimbursing employees for their YMCA memberships. The Milwaukee, Wisconsin-based headquarters building now houses a fitness center complete with aerobic exercise machines and weight-training equipment. Almost half of Northwestern Mutual's 3,300 employees work out at the center, and others still take advantage of the outside gym membership reimbursements.

Northwestern Mutual also regularly offers medical screenings for blood pressure and cholesterol, as well as weight reduction, smoking cessation, and stress management programs.

Critical Thinking

How do you think a healthy worker benefits an employer? What can employers do to help their employees stay healthy?

Link and Learn

To learn more about Northwestern Mutual Life Insurance Company, visit their Web site via the link on the *Succeeding in the World of Work* Web site at **www.careers.glencoe.com**

Preparation Be prepared to handle emergency situations. *What should you do if a fire breaks out at work?*

- At home, board up windows and doors. Tie down or remove loose objects or furniture.
- If evacuation is ordered, follow police instructions.

Tornadoes

These unpredictable funnel-shaped windstorms have enough power to pick up entire buildings and smash them down miles away. If a tornado threatens, take these precautions:

- Go indoors and stay away from windows. (Hallways and basements are safest.) Cover yourself with a mattress or blanket.

- If you cannot get inside, dive into a ditch or another low ground area, and stay down.

SECTION 11.2 REVIEW

Key Concept Checkpoint

Comprehension

1. What does the acronym OSHA stand for, and how does OSHA help workers?

2. How might you protect the environment at work?

3. How can clear thinking skills help you in an emergency situation?

Critical Thinking

4. Why must the government play such an active role in ensuring safety in the workplace?

KEY TERMS
nutrients (p. 214)
Food Guide Pyramid
    (p. 215)
sedentary (p. 215)
addiction (p. 217)

SECTION 11.1

- Being healthy means having the mental and physical energy to pursue your goals. (p. 214)

- Nutrients are the substances in food that your body needs to produce energy and stay healthy. The Food Guide Pyramid shows how you can achieve a balanced diet. (pp. 215–216)

- Everyone needs to exercise regularly and get enough rest. (pp. 215–217)

- Addiction is a physical or emotional dependence on alcohol, illegal substances, or prescription drugs. It can cause devastating effects. (pp. 217–218)

- Stress—a natural reaction to change or conflict—needs to be managed. People can cope with stress by identifying the causes of stress and by taking action to minimize its harmful effects. (pp. 218–220)

KEY TERMS
Occupational Safety and
    Health Administration
    (OSHA) (p. 222)
workers' compensation
    (p. 222)
repetitive stress injuries
    (p. 223)
ergonomics (p. 223)
first aid (p. 225)

SECTION 11.2

- Government, employers, and employees share responsibility for creating and maintaining safe workplaces. (p. 222)

- The government sets and enforces safety standards. (p. 222)

- Employers must provide hazard-free workplaces, safe equipment, and health and safety information. (p. 223)

- Employees should know and follow safety rules. (pp. 223–224)

- When an emergency occurs, you should follow American Red Cross guidelines: first survey the scene, then follow AID and ABC guidelines. (pp. 225–226)

- To respond safely to fire and weather emergencies, be prepared and know what to do in each emergency. (pp. 226–228)

Reviewing Key Terms

1. On separate paper, write a company newsletter describing proper health and safety practices to be used on the job. Use the terms below in your newsletter.
   - nutrients
   - Food Guide Pyramid
   - sedentary
   - addiction
   - first aid
   - OSHA
   - workers' compensation
   - ergonomics
   - repetitive stress injuries

Recalling Key Concepts

2. The main purpose of following the Food Guide Pyramid is to ____.
   (a) lose weight (b) save money
   (c) get the nutrients your body needs

3. In order to cope with stress, ____.
   (a) take a deep breath
   (b) take a brief break
   (c) do both a and b

4. Workers' compensation is ____.
   (a) pay for working overtime
   (b) medical coverage and partial pay for an injury
   (c) time off without pay

5. In order to help protect the environment, businesses often ask employees to ____.
   (a) wash their hands
   (b) avoid repetitive stress
   (c) recycle paper

6. The first thing you should do in an emergency is ____.
   (a) survey the scene
   (b) check the victim's breathing
   (c) call for help

Problem Solving

7. Why would a prospective employer be interested in your health?

8. Compare the effects of positive and negative stress.

9. Describe how government, employers, and employees—working together—create a comprehensive system to ensure workplace safety.

10. Explain how the ABCs of first aid help you deal with emergencies effectively.

11. What are the advantages and disadvantages of workplace fire drills? What would you do to make them more useful?

Work-Based Learning

Thinking Skills Problem Solving

12. Mark and Keisha work on an assembly line in a toy factory. Lately, they are both feeling negative stress because their workload has increased and their boss is pressuring them to perform more efficiently. Describe in writing a strategy for solving their problem and reducing their symptoms of stress. Explain the benefits of learning to handle stress effectively.

Technology Skills Maintaining and Troubleshooting Technology

13. Research employee manuals or interview a supervisor in a company to find out how one company ensures safe operation and maintenance of its equipment. Prepare a report that identifies three pieces of equipment and the training and maintenance procedures that lead to a safe workplace.

School-Based Learning

Art Design a Poster

14. Tom, a teacher's aide at your school, says he doesn't have time to do the shopping and cooking it takes to eat wisely. Design a Food Guide Pyramid poster for people such as Tom, including foods that are easy to buy and prepare. Use paints or a collage to make the poster as appealing as possible.

Role Play

15. Emergency Planning

Situation You are part of the emergency planning team for a large company. Your group has been asked to design a plan for dealing with a specific weather emergency that could occur in your area.

Activity Within your group, select a specific weather emergency: hurricane, flood, tornado, blizzard, or other severe condition. Identify the specific procedures for workers to follow in such an emergency. Include as many details as you can, and present your plan to the class.

Evaluation You will be evaluated on how well you meet the following performance indicators:
- Identify specific emergency preparations
- Present clear instructions for protection and evacuation
- Answer any questions that your classmates may have

*inter*NET
CONNECTION

16. Learn about Environmental Procedures Interview someone in an industry you are interested in to learn about conservation and environmental practices followed in that person's workplace. Find out how the company works with local government to conserve resources and how the company attempts to protect the environment. Prepare a report that describes your findings.

Connect Conduct research on the Internet to find additional ways that the company could improve its conservation and environmental procedures. Add those recommendations to your report.

Chapter 12

Workplace Legal Matters

Section 12.1
Laws About the Workplace

Section 12.2
You and the Legal System

CHAPTER OBJECTIVES

After completing this chapter, you will be able to

- Identify how laws and labor unions affect the workplace.

- Describe discrimination in the workplace and identify some of the laws that address it.

- Recognize sexual harassment and identify actions to take against it.

- Identify types of civil law cases and explain how they get resolved.

- Understand the difference between civil and criminal law.

- Identify and evaluate legal services that can help you solve problems.

JOURNAL

Personal Career Plan

In your journal, list five words or phrases that each of these terms brings to mind: police officer, lawyer, and judge. What do you think your responses say about your understanding of—and attitude toward—our legal system?

Personal Career Project

The law states that all new employees must fill out an I-9 form to prove their eligibility to work. When you fill out this form, you will be asked for three forms of identification. Research what identification is required, and gather the cards and papers you could present. The Immigration and Naturalization Service can provide information.

233

Laws About the Workplace

You're standing at a major intersection, and cars are whizzing by as you wait to cross. Then the light facing you turns green. You take a quick glance to either side before you step into the street. Still, you assume that drivers will obey the law and stop so that you can cross. This everyday event reminds us that the life of our society—from crossing the street to electing a leader—depends on laws.

Labor Laws

Just like traffic laws, labor laws set some ground rules. The difference is these laws are designed to protect you from unfair treatment on the job. They strive to ensure that all Americans have an equal opportunity to get and to keep a job, to be paid a just wage, to be considered fairly for promotion, and to be protected in times of personal and economic change. It is important that you understand your rights and responsibilities concerning labor laws.

Laws About Work and Pay

In 1938, the federal government passed the Fair Labor Standards Act (FLSA). This important law requires employers to pay a **minimum wage**—the lowest hourly wage that an employer can legally pay

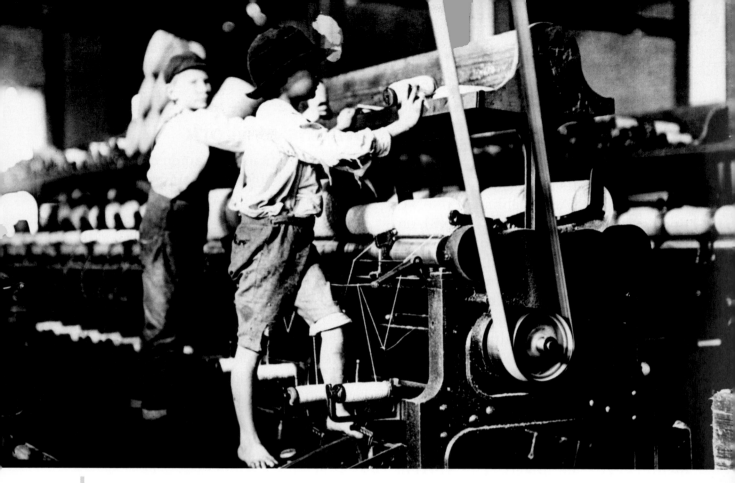

Child Labor Laws This photo, taken in the early 1900s, shows the inside of a cotton mill. *How would you describe this work environment? Does it strike you as unfair?*

for a worker's services. Believe it or not, the first minimum wage was set at 40¢ per hour, although it has risen to more than $5 over the years. The FLSA also set the 40-hour workweek and created the practice of *overtime* for hourly workers who work more than 40 hours a week. You read about this practice in Chapter 8. In addition, employees may receive **compensatory time,** paid time off from work rather than cash in exchange for working overtime. Employees, however, must agree in advance to this arrangement.

Child labor laws are another product of the FLSA. Imagine a 10-year-old working 60 hours a week in a factory! Sad to say, children worked under terrible conditions in this country less than 100 years ago. To put an end to a practice that robbed children of their childhood—and often of their good health as well—the FLSA set the minimum age for factory jobs at 16.

The Organization of Labor Unions

In another effort to protect people who work, the Wagner Act of 1935 (also called the National Labor Relations Act) made it legal to organize labor unions and engage in union activities. Before this act was established, labor unions existed, but they had very little power. As early as 1773, workers began uniting to fight for fair treatment and pay. Throughout the 19th century, skilled workers formed unions, and by 1886 the American Federation of Labor (AFL) was established.

The Wagner Act established the National Labor Relations Board (NLRB), an independent judicial agency of the United States government. The NLRB is responsible for determining whether workers wish to be unionized, and investigating charges of unfair labor practices. These unfair practices include interfering with, restraining, or coercing employees who wish to form or join a legally sanctioned union.

Representing Workers

Labor unions represent workers in their dealings with employers. The workers elect union leaders, who negotiate for better wages, increased benefits, better working conditions, and other job improvements through **collective bargaining**. In other words, unions use the power of their numbers (the workers in the union) to bargain with company management. If an agreement is not reached, the union may use its most powerful tool—a strike. A *strike* occurs when workers stop working in an effort to force an employer to agree to the union's terms. In most cases, unions maintain *strike funds*, which provide partial salaries to workers on strike.

When an agreement is reached between the union and company management, the company signs a *labor contract*, which is a legal agreement specifying wages, work hours, working conditions, benefits, and grievance procedures. The union members must approve the contract before it goes into effect.

Unions at Work

There are 16 million union members in the United States, in all kinds of professions, from janitors and electricians, to teachers and professional baseball players. If you join a union, you will be asked to pay an initiation fee and pay regular dues. This money supports the work of the union and the strike fund.

If you are thinking about joining a union, consider these factors:

- *Membership Cost*, including dues and initiation fee
- *Track Record* What has the union accomplished on behalf of these workers in the past?
- *Membership Benefits*, such as health care and pension plans

Unemployment Insurance

State laws provide for unemployment insurance to help workers cope with the loss of a job. For example, Ben Dyal worked for five years selling athletic gear to department stores. The competition was fierce, and when his company suddenly went out of business, Ben had trouble landing a new job right away. "I had to eat," he said. "I had to pay the rent. So I went down to the local government office and filed for unemployment." Soon he received an unemployment check each week. "It allowed me to pay my basic living expenses until I found a new job. The temporary funds gave me a chance to get back on my feet."

Sometimes accidents and illness throw lives out of balance as well. Workers need to know that if they get sick, their jobs won't be given away to other workers. Some people need to take time off from work to care for relatives. To meet these needs, Congress passed the Family and Medical Leave Act in 1993. This law guarantees employees at companies with more than 50 employees up to 12 weeks of leave for family or personal medical care or for the birth or adoption of a child.

Drawing the Line

The law goes a long way toward protecting workers, but it draws the line at people who are working illegally. The Immigration Reform and Control Act of 1990 makes it very difficult for illegal immigrants (noncitizens living in our country without authorization from our government) to find work. Employers should make sure that *all* new employees have proper working papers and identification. Businesses can face huge fines if they break this law.

Discrimination

Under laws passed by Congress, it is illegal for employers to engage in **discrimination**—unequal treatment based on such factors as race, religion, nationality, *gender* (being male or female), age, or physical appearance.

Creative BUSINESS PRACTICES

Atlanta Braves
Training Players in Diversity

Even though their office is a ballpark, baseball players still need human resources instruction. During spring training, the Atlanta Braves organization includes a full-day training seminar in diversity.

Because of the many racial differences among American athletes, as well as the increasing number of international ball players, diversity training is necessary to help players better understand each other and their managers and coaches. The key to the success of the Atlanta Braves' diversity training is that it is specifically tailored to the needs and real-life situations of the athletes.

Players are encouraged to share their personal experiences with racial discrimination and stereotypes, especially within the organization. Hearing each others' problems and concerns helps players relate on a personal level, and to be more accommodating to other cultures.

Critical Thinking
How can employees benefit from diversity training?

Link and Learn
To learn more about the Atlanta Braves baseball team, visit its Web site via the link on the *Succeeding in the World of Work* Web site at **www.careers.glencoe.com**.

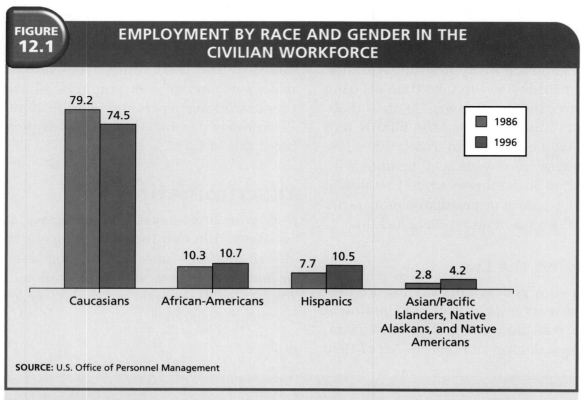

FIGURE
12.1

EMPLOYMENT BY RACE AND GENDER IN THE CIVILIAN WORKFORCE

- 1986
- 1996

79.2 74.5
Caucasians

10.3 10.7
African-Americans

7.7 10.5
Hispanics

2.8 4.2
Asian/Pacific Islanders, Native Alaskans, and Native Americans

SOURCE: U.S. Office of Personnel Management

▲ **A Changing Demographic** Minorities make up a growing percentage of the civilian workforce. *How do you think these percentages will change over the next two decades?*

Major Antidiscrimination Laws

Every employee has a legal right to fair treatment under one of a number of state and federal laws.

- The **Civil Rights Act of 1964** bans discrimination in employment based on race, color, religion, or gender. As *Figure 12.1* shows the number of minorities in the workforce is steadily increasing.

- The **Age Discrimination Act of 1967** makes it illegal to discriminate against people over 40 in hiring, promoting, or discharging employees.

- The **Rehabilitation Act of 1973** and the **Americans with Disabilities Act of**

1990 protect the rights of individuals with *disabilities*—conditions that include blindness, visual or hearing impairment, mental illness, or paralysis. For example, the law requires businesses to provide aids such as wheelchair ramps and other special equipment for disabled workers.

Courts have recognized some exceptions to the fundamental discrimination laws. Some employers are allowed to hire only people with certain qualifications if those qualifications are necessary to do a particular job. Models and actors, for example, may need to be a particular age or gender to do a particular job.

The government also created **affirmative action** plans that aim to provide access to jobs for those who suffered discrimination in the past and to give everyone a fair chance to compete in the working world. These plans, which continue to be the subject of intense debate, sometimes set numerical goals for the hiring of groups such as ethnic minorities, females, or people with disabilities.

Equal Rights on the Job

Look at *Figure 12.2,* which shows how the percentage of women in the workforce has grown. Before 1960, few women worked full-time, and those who did worked in positions not usually held by men. Now men and women often compete for the same jobs and aim for the same

raises and promotions. Have you ever wondered how being a male or a female might affect your career?

Hilary Frye worked as a laborer with a landscaping company. One day she had lunch with a male coworker who casually mentioned his salary. Hilary was surprised to find that he was getting paid $3 an hour more than she was—for doing the same job with the same amount of experience for the same amount of time. Hilary was a victim of discrimination. **The Equal Pay Act of 1963** requires equal pay for equal work.

Sexual Harassment

Another gender-related problem in the workplace is **sexual harassment**—any unwelcome behavior of a sexual nature. Such behavior may include jokes, gestures,

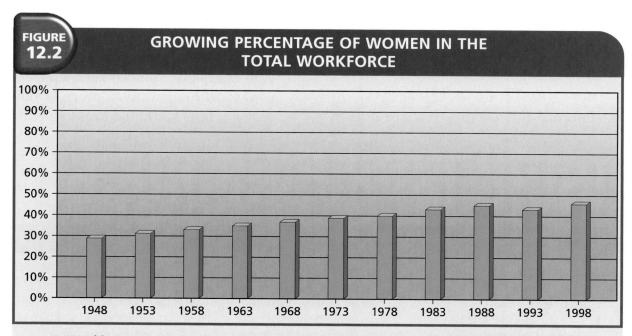

FIGURE 12.2

GROWING PERCENTAGE OF WOMEN IN THE TOTAL WORKFORCE

▲ **Working Women** Women have steadily taken their places in the world of work since World War II. *What do you predict will happen in terms of the percentage of women in the total workforce in the 21st century? Base your prediction on the pattern shown in this graph.*

repeated or threatening requests for dates, and unwanted touching. Although most reported victims are female, males have also been the victims of sexual harassment.

Would you consider the following two examples cases of sexual harassment? Courts have declared that they are.

- A male worker's female boss told him that he could keep his job only if he started to date her.

- Female employees were "rated" by male employees, who also made comments about their physical appearance, as the women walked past the male employees' desks.

What if you feel you are the victim of sexual harassment? Here are some practical suggestions:

- Immediately tell the person to stop. Be clear and direct; don't assume the harassment will stop if you ignore it.

- Write down what happened, noting the date, time, and place. Include the names of any witnesses and your own comments about how the harassment directly affected your work.

- Inform a trusted supervisor or human resource officer of the incident.

CAREER CHECKLIST

When Protecting Your Legal Interests...

- ✔ Know your rights.
- ✔ Voice any legal concerns immediately to protect yourself.
- ✔ Support others who are fighting legal battles, but don't take on their battle as your own.
- ✔ Investigate all of your options before threatening legal action.
- ✔ Avoid denial—if an uncomfortable situation seems to violate your rights, it probably does!

- If the issue is not resolved within your company, you can get help from your local human rights office or the office of the U.S. Equal Employment Opportunity Commission.

SECTION 12.1 REVIEW

✔ Key Concept Checkpoint

Comprehension
1. Describe one law that is designed to establish and maintain fairness in the workplace.

2. How do employers benefit from hiring people over 40?
3. How does sexual harassment create problems in the workplace?

Critical Thinking
4. What actions would you take if you felt you were being discriminated against on the job?

CAREER FOCUS

CAREER CLUSTER: Education and Training

Kristin Dolan
Adult Technology Teacher

CAREER FACTS

Education or Training   Adult education teachers need a bachelor's degree, and in some cases a master's degree. They also need professional experience in their field.

Aptitudes, Abilities, and Skills Patience, solid teaching and organizational skills, and the ability to motivate and encourage adult students are necessary.

Career Outlook   Employment growth for adult education teachers is expected to be average.

Career Path   Adult education teachers, or corporate trainers, may go on to management positions or to form their own companies.

What is your key to success?

"The key to my success is a combination of three abilities: the ability to teach groups of people from diverse educational backgrounds, the ability to quickly learn and update my knowledge of a variety of software applications; and the ability to write."

What does your job entail?

"The company I work for provides computer trainers to large investment and law firms. My job involves teaching classes on software such as Microsoft Office (Word, Excel, and PowerPoint), Visio, and CorelDRAW to classrooms of six to ten adults. Students in my classes may go on to become software trainers or designers of books and slide presentations. Occasionally, I also write reference manuals and practice books for students and teaching manuals for companies who want to start their own training programs."

What skills are most important to you?

"Before one of my first classes another trainer said to me, 'If you don't know something, be honest about it. Open it up to your students and figure to out together. You'll be surprised how much you learn from your students' questions.' I've always followed that advice, it has helped me do my job with ease and learn a large amount about the software I teach."

Why do you like most about your work?

"I enjoy a flexible, well-paying job that allows me extra time to pursue other interests and be with my family. I also like the fact that I help people gain the skills they need to find a job or make a career change."

> **Critical Thinking**   What challenges might you face as an adult education teacher?

You and the Legal System

Most of us have recited the Pledge of Allegiance, which ends: "with liberty and justice for all." You have seen how labor laws strive to make these noble words a reality in the workplace, protecting workers and serving as a ballast in times of personal and social change. Many job-related situations, however, are not clear-cut or easily resolved. Therefore, one responsibility of the legal system is to provide a set of procedures for resolving conflicts. In court, lawyers, judges, and sometimes jurors make decisions about *disputes,* or disagreements, between employers and employees. It is important that you learn some basic facts about the law and how it affects you.

The Legal Battlefield

Many court cases involve **civil law,** which applies to conflicts between private parties, concerning rights and obligations. Divorce, custody battles, and personal injury cases all fall into this category. Companies may also become involved in civil law disputes. Here are a few examples of civil law cases:

- Tracy worked as a bank teller, and her employment contract stated that the company provided paid maternity leave. When she became pregnant, the bank fired her, claiming that it couldn't afford to pay for her benefits. According to civil law, the bank broke the contract and was *liable,* or responsible, for doing what it had originally promised.

Setting Precedents When a high court makes a decision about a labor law, it sets the standard for future cases. *How do you think this process helps laws keep up with changes in society?*

- John, an accountant, sued his employer because he developed chronic bronchitis as a result of being placed in an office with several heavy smokers. The employer was found guilty of *negligence,* or disregard, of John's right to a smoke-free environment.

- Michael, an autoworker, was physically searched by his company's security guards, who suspected him of stealing. The guards found no stolen goods, and Michael's shoulder was bruised during the search, when he was shoved against a wall. A court found the company guilty of *deliberate* (purposeful) injury.

How do cases such as these move from the workplace to the courtroom? The process starts when a person files an official complaint with the court. The court clerk delivers a **summons,** or an order to appear in court, to the accused party. This person (or company) then files an answer.

For some business problems, small-claims court is an effective low-cost solution. *Small-claims court* is designed to handle minor disputes and small claims on debts. It does not require lawyers. Rules vary from state to state, but in general, small-claims court procedures and paperwork are less complicated than those in other courts.

Most people resolve their civil cases before they get to court. Opponents often come to a mutual agreement, or *settlement,* that does not state that either party is right or wrong. A settlement often takes the form of a cash award or a correction of the situation that caused the complaint. Many states require that both sides in a civil case first try to settle out of court, thus avoiding trial. *Figure 12.3* explains still other ways to resolve civil disputes and avoid trials.

FIGURE 12.3 **Avoiding a Trial** The court system is overcrowded with cases. Taking advantage of other methods of settling disputes can save you time and money.

A **File a Formal Complaint** Many states require workers to file a formal complaint with the Equal Employment Opportunity Commission or a similar agency. Sometimes these labor agencies can settle labor-management disputes.

B **Follow Complaint Procedures** You may be able to settle a dispute by discussing it with your employer. Some companies have complaint procedures in place to handle legal problems between workers.

C **Go to Court** If your dispute involves less than $5,000, you may be able to go to small-claims court and argue your own case for a fee as low as $25. The judge's decision carries just as much weight as a state or federal court decision.

D **Consider Compromising** *Mediation* is a process in which you and your opponent present the case to a neutral third person, who helps you both talk to each other and reach a compromise, or a settlement.

E **Arbitrate** Union disputes are often resolved through *arbitration*. Both sides present evidence and witnesses to an arbitrator, who issues a written decision, just as a judge or a jury would do.

Legal Action The employer and employee shown here with the employee's lawyer have just settled a dispute out of court. *Why might a company agree to pay an employee for damages rather than take the dispute before a judge and jury?*

Civil laws cover most workplace disputes, but sometimes incidents will occur on the job site that fall under criminal law. Under **criminal law,** the government brings an *indictment,* or list of criminal charges, such as assault or fraud, against a person or a business. A serious crime punishable by imprisonment or death, such as murder or rape, is called a **felony.** A less serious crime is called a **misdemeanor** and could be anything from shoplifting to striking another worker during a dispute.

Using Legal Services

If you have tried to solve a problem too big for small-claims court and feel that other legal action is the only answer, then your best bet is to contact a lawyer. Laws are very complex, and legal procedures are often confusing. It usually takes an expert to argue a case in court. Although hiring a lawyer can be expensive, having a knowledgeable lawyer may produce better results.

Finding a Lawyer

If you had a cavity, you wouldn't dream of going to an eye doctor to get it taken care of. One doctor isn't the same as another. Similarly, you'll want to take your legal problem to a lawyer with just the right specialty. To start your search, try the following:

- Use your phone book to find legal referral services. The local bar association and your state's chapter of the Association of Trial Lawyers of America are possible sources of help.

- Ask friends and family members if they know any lawyers. These contacts may lead you to others.

- If you are a member of a group or prepaid legal plan through your job or other organization, you can contact this service for a lawyer referral. Often, these services will also assist with legal costs if you do not have enough money to hire a lawyer on your own.

It is important that you choose a lawyer who is right for your situation. Here is a list of questions to ask a potential lawyer that will help you to decide:

1. What type of experience do you have?

2. What is your specialty?

3. What will it cost?

4. What references can you provide?

5. What is your policy on returning phone calls?

6. How long will my matter take to reach a conclusion?

7. Will I be regularly updated?

8. Who will handle my matter?

9. Would handling my case involve a potential conflict with another client?

10. Do you have malpractice insurance?

You may also want to ask for references, other clients who have hired this lawyer and who could tell you whether they were satisfied with the lawyer's work.

While some of these questions can be answered over the phone, it is best to arrange an initial face-to-face consultation with a lawyer before making your final decision.

Many lawyers will have an initial meeting with you before charging you a fee. Use this opportunity to interview a lawyer carefully. Is the lawyer efficient and organized? Does he or she have the kind of experience you need? Do you feel you can trust this person?

Lawyers' Fees

Lawyers generally charge an hourly rate or set a flat fee based on how much work they expect to do for you. Some lawyers work for a **contingency fee**. This means that they take as payment a percentage of any money that you win in the lawsuit. Make sure you understand the fee system and projected costs before you agree to anything. Legal advice can be expensive.

Low-cost legal assistance in civil cases may be available from the Legal Aid Society. If you are charged in a criminal case, the office of the public defender can provide free legal representation.

No matter where you go for legal advice, be prepared for the meeting: bring documents, records, and names of witnesses. Do not expect your lawyer to do all the work, particularly if you are receiving help from a Legal Aid Society. Ask how you can be involved and what you can and should do to help your case. There

Unions

You work in an automobile manufacturing plant and you are represented by the United Auto Workers (UAW), a union that negotiates wages and benefits for its members.

Connect

- Visit the UAW Web site and find out more about the union. Read about some of the latest benefits that the union has negotiated for members.
- Write a one-paragraph summary of the advantages of being a member of this union.

may be ways that you can help your lawyer prepare your case. Remember, too, that legal proceedings can take a very long time—months or even years.

SECTION 12.2 REVIEW

 ### Key Concept Checkpoint

Comprehension

1. Why might you want to resolve a civil case out of court rather than through a trial?

2. Describe a workplace situation that could lead to a civil case and one that could lead to a criminal case.

3. Do you think it is a good idea to defend your own case in court? Why or why not?

Critical Thinking

4. What qualities would you look for when hiring a lawyer?

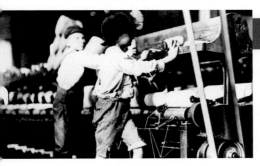

SECTION 12.1

- Labor laws set basic rules for fair treatment in the workplace. (pp. 234–235)
- Labor unions organize workers and bargain with employers to protect workers' rights. (pp. 235–236)
- Labor and employment laws help employees deal with medical and financial emergencies. (pp. 236–237)
- Antidiscrimination laws protect workers from job discrimination based on factors such as race, religion, age, gender, and disability. (pp. 237–239)
- The government creates programs to help employers put antidiscrimination laws into action. (pp. 238–239)
- Sexual harassment is unwelcome behavior of a sexual nature. If you experience harassment, you should take immediate steps to deal with it. (pp. 239–240)

KEY TERMS
minimum wage (p. 234)
compensatory time (p. 235)
collective bargaining (p. 236)
discrimination (p. 237)
affirmative action (p. 239)
sexual harassment (p. 239)

SECTION 12.2

- The legal system—with its courts, judges, and lawyers—provides a set of procedures for resolving conflicts. (p. 242)
- Civil law applies to conflicts between private parties, such as an employee and a company, concerning rights and obligations. (pp. 242–243)
- There are several ways to resolve a civil dispute without going to trial, including mediation and arbitration. (pp. 244–245)
- Criminal law involves cases in which the government charges a person or a business with committing a crime. More serious offenses are called felonies, and less serious offenses are called misdemeanors. (p. 246)
- If you need to take legal action, consider going to small-claims court or hire a lawyer. Before you hire a lawyer, search carefully for the best person, make sure you understand what the fees will be, and provide all pertinent information to the lawyer you choose. (pp. 246–248)

KEY TERMS
civil law (p. 242)
summons (p. 243)
criminal law (p. 246)
felony (p. 246)
misdemeanor (p. 246)
contingency fee (p. 248)

Reviewing Key Terms

1. You are interviewing a lawyer who specializes in labor and employment law. On a separate sheet of paper, write out a list of questions, using each of the following terms.
   - minimum wage
   - compensatory time
   - collective bargaining
   - discrimination
   - affirmative action
   - sexual harassment
   - civil law
   - criminal law
   - summons
   - felony
   - misdemeanor
   - contingency fee

Recalling Key Concepts

Determine whether each statement is true or false. Rewrite any false statements to make them true.

2. The minimum wage has remained the same since it was first created.

3. Antidiscrimination laws protect certain groups of citizens from unfair employment practices.

4. Sexual harassment is any unwelcome behavior of a sexual nature.

5. Civil law refers to charges the government brings against a person.

6. You do not need to hire a lawyer if you are taking a case to a court other than small-claims court.

Problem Solving

7. Why are antidiscrimination laws important?

8. How could effective communication skills help you defend yourself against an unfair situation at work?

9. How might sexual harassment interfere with a person's career advancement?

10. Explain the difference between criminal law and civil law.

11. Give an example of a case that you might take to small-claims court.

Work-Based Learning

Basic Skills Reading and Writing

12. Working in a team of three, locate and read several articles on sexual harassment in the workplace. Together, create a list of do's and don'ts for a fair and comfortable business environment.

Thinking Skills Problem Solving

13. Working in a group of three, come up with an imaginary dispute that requires arbitration. Decide who will be the arbitrator, and have the other two group members defend their side of the dispute. After listening to both arguments, the arbitrator should make a judgment in favor of one side, explaining his or her reasons. Then switch roles until all group members have had a chance to play arbitrator.

School-Based Learning

Social Studies Research Societal Change

14. It is important to understand the effect change has on society and career opportunities. Compose a report citing at least three examples of change in our society. In your report, explain the positive and negative aspects of one of the examples of societal change.

Social Studies Research Labor Laws

15. Labor laws have played a major role in American history and culture. Choose one aspect of the world of work—such as hours, wages, child labor, minorities, unions, safety, benefits, or pollution—and research one federal or state law that has affected that aspect. Report to the class on what conditions were like before the law existed and how conditions changed after the law was passed.

Role Play

16. Mediation

Situation You are to assume the role of mediator in a dispute between an employer and an employee. While on an errand for the company, the employee was in an accident that destroyed his/her car; the employee feels that the company is financially responsible for the damages. The employer refuses to pay.

Activity Listen as both sides explain their positions. Remember that you are to remain neutral as you help the parties talk to each other and reach a compromise.

Evaluation You will be evaluated on how well you meet the following performance indicators:

- Listen attentively to both people
- Ask questions and lead the discussion objectively
- Help the parties reach a settlement that they both agree upon

interNET CONNECTION

17. Investigate Careers in the Legal Field

Arrange a visit to a state or federal courthouse, and sit in on a trial. You can do this by writing a letter to the court clerk or by calling the courthouse. Take notes on the court process, indicating at least four career opportunities in the court system.

Connect On the Internet, research the four career opportunities you listed above. Investigate the type and level of education required, as well as any necessary experience, such as internships. Report your findings to the class.

Strategies for Success
Ensuring a Safe, Healthy Career

✓ Overview

You want to make sure that the career you've chosen is safe and healthy. You've decided to gather specific data to find out more about the hazards associated with your career. You understand that all jobs pose some risks, and you're willing to stick with your career choice despite its pros and cons.

✓ Assignment

Conduct research on the health risks that affect workers in your desired field. As part of your research, consult a wide variety of sources, including the Internet, employers and employees in your field, the Occupational Safety and Health Administration (OSHA), and library resources. Choose three significant risks. Locate current statistics about these risks and propose solutions to these problems. If you can't think of a solution that will solve a problem, create an action plan that will reduce that health or safety risk. Use presentation software to demonstrate your research and suggestions.

✓ Tools/Resources

To complete this assignment, you must have access to presentation software.

✓ Procedures

Follow the steps listed below to compose a solid presentation.

- Before you begin to write, conduct sufficient research. Use current sources, and a variety of resources. Contact people who work in your chosen field; their comments will add a valuable human perspective.
- Create a "Works Cited" section of your presentation to explain where you found the data.

- Develop a general outline for your presentation. Devote special attention to key elements, including the introduction and conclusion.

✓ Report

Your final product for this lab should include a presentation with at least 15 slides that identify three current health and safety risks in your chosen field, as well as strategies for reducing or overcoming these hazards. Your presentation should also include a section on "Works Cited."

✓ Presentation and Evaluation

Your performance will be evaluated based on

- Depth of research
- Quality of sources and "Works Cited"
- Quality of delivery and slides
- Creativity of solutions proposed

✓ Personal Career Portfolio

Print out copies of your slides and presentation outline. Include these items in your personal career portfolio.

HELPFUL HINTS

Preparing Your Presentation
- Pay special attention to your introduction. Start with interesting information or comments to get the attention of your audience. You can use shocking statistics, humor, testimonials, or a vibrant slide to pique your audience's attention.
- When writing and delivering your speech, follow an organized outline. Don't ramble or skip from topic to topic.
- Memorize enough of your presentation so that you can work from an outline. Don't shuffle through papers or note-cards in front of your audience.

- Design slides that summarize key information or points. Don't type your entire presentation on slides; you'll end up "reading" your speech.
- Don't "clutter" your slides. Limit yourself to a few basic colors and fonts.
- Make sure you're comfortable using presentation software.
- Practice your speech at home to gain confidence and poise.
- Maintain eye contact and speak slowly and clearly.
- Write your presentation so that it concludes smoothly. Don't say "I'm done" or "thank you" when you're finished.

UNIT 5
Professional Development

Portfolio Project

Career Scrapbook Conduct research to find out the names of several journals, newsletters, or magazines that report exclusively on a career or industry that interests you. Read as many of these resources as possible. Look for information on job trends, job opportunities, and other aspects of your industry. Assemble a scrapbook with at least 20 articles, job descriptions, and other items that you find important. Write your thoughts and ideas regarding each item. At the end of your scrapbook, include a two-page reflective piece explaining what you've learned about your chosen industry.

CAREER LAB PREVIEW

Technology Training for Your Field

As part of this unit, you will investigate how technology impacts a career field that interests you. You'll begin by researching and preparing a report that outlines the technological programs and resources used in your industry. Then you'll choose a technological program or resource essential to this field and gain experience using this tool. You'll design a product using your new skills, and share this item with your classmates.

Interpersonal Relationships at Work

Section 13.1
Your Personal Traits at Work

Section 13.2
Applying Interpersonal Skills

CHAPTER OBJECTIVES

After completing this chapter, you will be able to

● Work effectively with a variety of coworkers by recognizing and developing positive and respectful personal traits.

● Understand and practice effective methods of conflict resolution.

● Appreciate and increase sensitivity to diversity in the workplace.

JOURNAL

Personal Career Plan

Imagine yourself in the career of your choice. In your journal, write a list of traits you hope to find in the people you work with. Which of those traits do you have? Which should you try to develop?

Personal Career Project

Many companies use team-building strategies to help employees bond outside of work. These activities give coworkers opportunities to develop personal relationships and boost morale. Devise a team-building exercise that would be appropriate for workers in a career that interests you, and explain why it would be beneficial.

Your Personal Traits at Work

WHAT YOU'LL LEARN

- How to recognize and develop personal traits that will enable you to get along with others in the workplace
- Methods for developing behaviors that will make you a more effective coworker

WHY IT'S IMPORTANT

Your ability to demonstrate the personal traits and behaviors that employers and employees desire will greatly affect your success in the workplace.

KEY TERMS

- **tact**
- **empathize**

What do you think is the most important workplace skill? According to a recent survey, many employees believe it is "getting along with others at work." Whether you're working already or beginning to plan your career, you need to think about your relationships with coworkers.

If you develop good interpersonal relationships with your coworkers, you'll enjoy your time at work more. After all, think of all the hours you'll be spending together. In addition, you'll be able to do your job more successfully. By showing a willingness to cooperate with your coworkers, you'll probably receive their cooperation in return.

What can you do to develop good relationships with your coworkers? Begin by assessing your own traits. (Look back at the work you did in Chapter 2 on getting to know yourself.) What traits do you already have that help you work well with other people? What traits do you need to develop?

Important Personal Traits

The personal traits that help you get along with others at your job are the same ones that help you at school or in social situations. As you learned in Chapters 9 and 10, the following skills are important personal qualities for the workplace:

- *Responsibility*, including dependability and positive motivation;
- *Self-esteem*, including confidence;

- *Sociability*, including friendliness, enthusiasm, adaptability, and respect for other workers;
- *Self-management*, including self-control and **tact**, the ability to say and do things in a way that will not offend other people; and
- *Integrity/Honesty*, including loyalty and trustworthiness.

How do you rate when it comes to these personal traits? If you're like most people, you probably have strengths and weaknesses. For instance, you may be very honest and dependable, but lack self-esteem or self-management. Now is the ideal time to work on developing any personal traits that need attention.

Your personal traits have been developing since you were born and have probably become habits by now. Habits can be difficult to change. The longer you wait to adjust certain behaviors, the harder the task becomes. Likewise, the younger you are, the greater your chances are for affecting change.

Always keep in mind that you're striving to improve because you want to enjoy a happy life. Your success at work will likely be an important factor in your sense of overall well-being, and success isn't attainable without the right personal qualities.

How should you go about getting started? The first step is to carefully contemplate your current status.

Self-Awareness on the Job

Self-awareness is your knowledge of your personality and individuality. Understanding your own unique blend of qualities can help you adjust to new work situations and get along well with others. If you are self-aware, you know not only your strengths but also the traits you need to improve.

Tracy Kagan of Miami, Florida, learned a great deal about her personal traits when she changed jobs at the same restaurant. After working for two years as a server, Tracy was promoted to assistant manager. While she had been well liked as a server, Tracy was not popular when she first became an assistant manager.

"I wasn't confident that I could handle my responsibilities," she explains. In her nervousness, she yelled at the cooks and criticized servers in front of customers. Fortunately, Tracy's supervisor recognized the problem. She spoke with Tracy about her need to control her emotions and to be tactful. Still, changing was not easy.

"Whenever I felt pressured, I had to remind myself to be polite," Tracy says.

Constructive Criticism Tracy needed help from her supervisor to improve her personal traits at work. *Why is it important to be able to listen to constructive criticism?*

"I made it a habit to take a deep breath when I felt myself getting upset. Then I'd smile."

In time, Tracy developed her self-management skills. Now she enjoys her job and has won back the respect of her coworkers.

Improving Your Personal Traits

Can you improve yourself? Of course you can. One of the most successful people in American history—Benjamin Franklin—used a notebook to keep track of how effectively he practiced the personal qualities he wanted to improve. Each day he'd write notes for himself about such traits as justice, diligence, and sincerity.

FIGURE 13.1 **Four Steps to Self-Improvement** Self-improvement takes time and effort. The process involves a series of clearly defined steps.

Step 1 **Zero in on one trait at a time** Kenny is confident that he is sociable and honest. He's decided that he needs to focus on becoming more responsible.

Step 2 **Draw up a plan and stick to it** Kenny makes a list of several things he can do on a regular basis to help out around the house. He makes sure he takes responsibility for at least one chore each day.

Look back at the list of important personal traits on pages 258–259. In your journal, write down which traits you think are your strong points and which you would like to improve. *Figure 13.1* shows four steps to self-improvement and how one person put them into action.

Becoming an Effective Coworker

Remember the "upward spirals" you read about in Chapter 10? Here's another

one: By developing your positive traits, you will be better able to get along with your coworkers. By getting along with your coworkers, you will be more effective at your job. By being more effective at your job, you will be more likely to advance in your career.

Being effective—that is, getting a job done quickly and well—seldom happens in isolation. Within the workplace, you'll find that effectiveness comes about when workers cooperate with one another. Four interpersonal behaviors are essential for being an effective coworker: respect, understanding, communication, and good humor.

Step 3 Keep track of your progress Kenny checks his progress each night by keeping a record of every responsibility he's fulfilled that day. He also writes notes to himself about areas in which he might do better. Once a week he asks his family, "How am I doing?"

Step 4 Move on Once Kenny feels that he has made progress in becoming more responsible, he starts to work on improving another trait. He has decided to work on boosting his self-esteem by reading to students in a local elementary school.

Respecting Others

Without mutual respect, there can be little cooperation in the workplace. Which two negative traits do you think do the most to prevent respect? One is an "I'm-better-than-you" attitude. The other negative trait is jealousy.

An "I'm-better-than-you" attitude is simply the idea that you are superior to someone else. Remember that each worker—no matter what his or her job may be—has something important to contribute. Regardless of your job title, all your coworkers deserve respect.

Jealousy can act like a poison in the workplace. Workers who become jealous of their coworkers view them as rivals. They withhold respect, and cooperation becomes more difficult—a downward spiral. A jealous worker refuses to admit that coworkers may have worked more effectively and deserve raises or promotions.

Remember that respect is a two-way street. In most cases, the more you give, the more you'll gain in return.

Understanding Others

You don't have to have a deep understanding of your coworkers in order to work well together. Instead, you can develop understanding by being an interested observer.

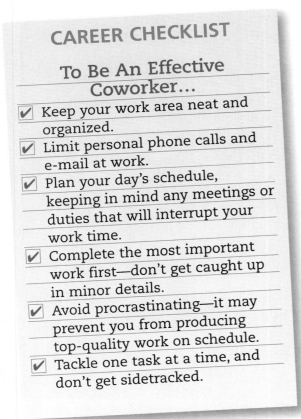

CAREER CHECKLIST

To Be An Effective Coworker...

- ✔ Keep your work area neat and organized.
- ✔ Limit personal phone calls and e-mail at work.
- ✔ Plan your day's schedule, keeping in mind any meetings or duties that will interrupt your work time.
- ✔ Complete the most important work first—don't get caught up in minor details.
- ✔ Avoid procrastinating—it may prevent you from producing top-quality work on schedule.
- ✔ Tackle one task at a time, and don't get sidetracked.

Body Language People show their feelings through body language, whether they mean to or not. *How do you know that one of the women below is angry?*

- Notice the personal traits of your coworkers.
- Ask your coworkers about their short-term and long-term career goals.
- Try to **empathize** with your coworkers—that is, try to see things from their point of view and to gain an understanding of their situation.
- Pay attention to your coworkers' body language—how their physical actions express emotions. Be alert to facial expressions, which very often give clues to a person's inner feelings.

Diversity
A man from Spain recently came to work in your office. He has only been in the United States for a short time, and his English is sometimes broken. Because your coworkers cannot communicate that well with him, they tend to leave him out.

Connect
- Do some research about Spain on travel and cultural Web sites to learn about its culture and language.
- Develop a one-page plan of how you and your coworkers can make your Spanish friend feel comfortable. Include things like learning a new Spanish word each day or bringing in ethnic dishes for a potluck lunch.

Creative BUSINESS PRACTICES

First USA Bank
Career Management

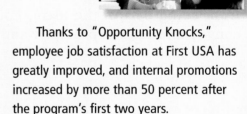

After a job satisfaction survey, First USA Bank found that many of its employees weren't satisfied with their jobs at the Wilmington, Delaware-based company. First USA developed "Opportunity Knocks," a program that helps employees zero in on their career goals and achieve these goals within the organization.

"Opportunity Knocks" provides career development workshops, skills training, and professional career counselors. At each First USA facility, there is a career resource center where employees can spend several paid hours a week reading career management literature and creating or updating their résumés.

Thanks to "Opportunity Knocks," employee job satisfaction at First USA has greatly improved, and internal promotions increased by more than 50 percent after the program's first two years.

Critical Thinking
What steps would you take if you weren't happy with your job?

Link and Learn
To learn more about First USA's career programs, visit the company's Web site via the link on the *Succeeding in the World of Work* Web site at **www.careers.glencoe.com**.

Communicating with Others

Communication, like respect, is a two-way street. How you listen is as important as what you say. Both listening and speaking well are especially important when you are working as part of a team. If you don't listen well, you won't benefit from being part of the team. Failure to convey information promptly and clearly can disrupt a project. It can make everyone on the team look bad.

Don't be reluctant to speak up and ask a coworker or supervisor for help if you need it. Remember that being effective means producing results. A coworker can often provide the guidance you'll need to overcome problems and get the job done.

Communicating, however, does not mean talking about your private life. You can be warm and friendly without revealing personal secrets. As you get to know your coworkers, it can be tempting to talk about personal matters. Don't. Your best route is to leave personal issues at home. In the workplace, it's better to spend time discussing work-related matters.

Keep Smiling!

Your sense of humor can carry you—and your coworkers—through times of stress. It can also help unite a team and make people feel better about themselves. You don't have to be a comedian. Just try to find ways to see the light side of a situation.

SECTION 13.1 REVIEW

 Key Concept Checkpoint

Comprehension
1. Describe a situation in which you effectively applied one of the skills listed on pages 258–259. What did you learn from this experience?

2. Which of the four interpersonal behaviors discussed in this section do you think is the most important? Why?

Critical Thinking
3. What type of body language can you use to show that you're a caring and respectful coworker?

CAREER FOCUS

CAREER FACTS

Education or Training   A college education is important, with courses in accounting, business administration, economics, and finance. Depending on occupational specialty, various licenses and certifications may be required.

Aptitudes, Abilities, and Skills Good interpersonal and communication skills, self-confidence, and the ability to explain financial concepts to investors are all essential.

Career Outlook   Employment is expected to grow much faster than average through 2008.

Career Path   Investment advisors and financial planners may go on to work for large firms or move into management positions.

What is you key to success?

"The key to being a successful investment advisor is to aggressively search out new public information before it reaches the masses. The only way to find this information this on a continual basis is to perform extensive research."

What does you job entail?

"My job is to figure out what an investor is trying to achieve, the amount of time he or she has to invest to achieve this goal, and how much risk the investor wishes to take. Once I answer these questions, I offer them financial guidance. I also recruit new business for my company by conducting educational seminars, participating in trade shows, and offering corporate training sessions."

What kind of training did you have?

"In order to participate in this industry, I was required to pass several licensing exams as mandated by the National Association of Securities Dealers (NASD) and the Securities and Exchange Commission (SEC). My company also required an intensive ten-week class that covered every aspect of investing. I am also required to attend continuing education seminars to keep my registrations current."

What do you like most about your work?

"My job enables me to help others achieve their goals. Devising an investment strategy that helps people turn their dreams into a reality is very rewarding."

> **Critical Thinking**   How can continuing your education help you succeed on the job?

Applying Interpersonal Skills

Etiquette may sound more like something you need to have at a wedding than at the workplace. However, **etiquette** really just means having good manners in your dealings with people.

How do you identify the right behavior for your workplace? First, use common sense. Treat people as you would want them to treat you. When in doubt, observe experienced and well-liked workers who are successful in their jobs. How do they conduct themselves at work? What do they do to get along with other people? What kinds of actions or responses do they avoid?

Workplace Etiquette

Here are a few basic do's and don'ts of etiquette that apply to all workplaces:

- *Be courteous* Greet your coworkers when you come to work, and address people by name whenever you can. Don't interrupt private conversations, and don't talk so loudly that you disturb other people, especially those working near you. Avoid tying up equipment that other people may need to use.

- *Dress appropriately* Whether your job has a dress code or not, you should wear neat, clean clothes. As a new employee, don't use your wardrobe or hairstyle to attract attention. Let your on-the-job performance speak for itself.

- *Be punctual* Be at work on time, arrive at meetings promptly, and meet your deadlines. If you promise someone that you'll call at a certain time, be sure to keep your word.

- *Avoid workplace gossip* Gossiping wastes valuable work time and can result in the spread of false or hurtful rumors. Gossiping is just plain unprofessional.

Respecting Privacy

Workplace etiquette also involves respecting your coworkers' privacy. This concerns more than not listening in on telephone calls and private conversations.

- *Faxes, e-mail, and voice mail* Treat these means of electronic communication as you would treat private mail. Don't read or listen to them unless they are addressed to you.

- *Computers* Sharing a computer with a coworker does not give you the right to examine or alter files that you have not created—unless you have permission.

Privacy Many companies have access to employees' e-mail accounts. *How should this affect your e-mail correspondence at work?*

- *Shared office space* Respect your coworkers' private spaces. Never look in a locker, file cabinet, or desk that is not your own.

Working with Your Supervisor

If you treat your supervisor with the same proper respect and courtesy that you do your coworkers, you should get along well. Naturally, however, you face the added element of wanting—and needing—your supervisor's approval. Here are some things you can do to develop and maintain a good working relationship with your supervisor:

- Deal with any criticism from your supervisor in an objective and professional manner. Do not get defensive.

- Practice initiative instead of bothering your supervisor with details that do not need his or her approval.

- Whenever you can, offer to help your supervisor.

- If you have a work-related complaint, discuss it with your supervisor. Be prepared, however, to suggest your own solution.

Conflict Resolution

Even when coworkers practice mutual courtesy and respect, it is a rare workplace that does not experience tension from time to time. When conflicts arise in the workplace, you will have to decide how to deal with them.

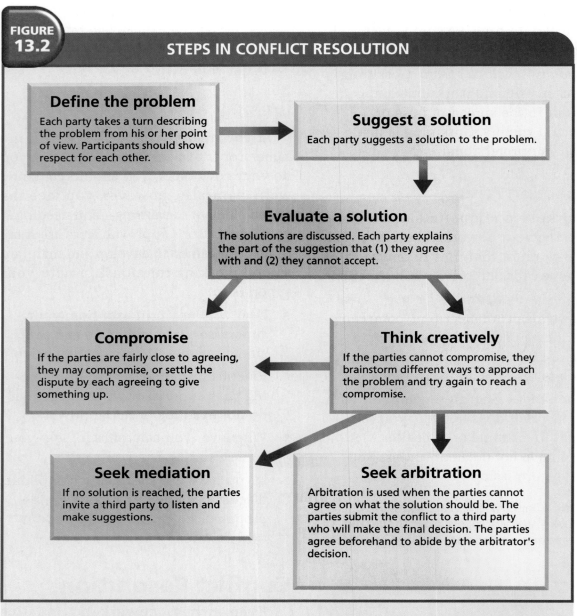

FIGURE
13.2
STEPS IN CONFLICT RESOLUTION

Define the problem

Each party takes a turn describing the problem from his or her point of view. Participants should show respect for each other.

Suggest a solution

Each party suggests a solution to the problem.

Evaluate a solution

The solutions are discussed. Each party explains the part of the suggestion that (1) they agree with and (2) they cannot accept.

Compromise

If the parties are fairly close to agreeing, they may compromise, or settle the dispute by each agreeing to give something up.

Think creatively

If the parties cannot compromise, they brainstorm different ways to approach the problem and try again to reach a compromise.

Seek mediation

If no solution is reached, the parties invite a third party to listen and make suggestions.

Seek arbitration

Arbitration is used when the parties cannot agree on what the solution should be. The parties submit the conflict to a third party who will make the final decision. The parties agree beforehand to abide by the arbitrator's decision.

▲ **Finding Solutions** Conflict resolution is a way for the people involved in a dispute to work out a solution to their problem. They try to work together to bring the conflict to an end. *Why do you think this diagram shows a choice of steps for finding a resolution?*

As a worker, you may find yourself involved in a process called **conflict resolution**, a problem-solving strategy for settling disputes and finding solutions that will allow each side to "save face" and leave the least amount of ill-feeling. *Figure 13.2* illustrates this strategy.

Remember that conflict resolution focuses on the issues, not on the personalities of the people involved. You can best prepare yourself for conflict resolution by practicing your communication and problem-solving skills in school and in the disputes you may have with friends.

Diversity in the Workplace

The United States has always been a nation of **diversity**, or variety, where each group contributes something special. In most workplaces in this country, many different kinds of people come together for a common purpose—to get a job done and to earn a living. *Figure 13.3* shows how the U.S. population is expected to continue to become more diverse.

Embracing this diversity is one way to discourage conflict at work. How can you accomplish this? Begin by showing respect for cultural differences as well as for differences in religion, age, gender, and viewpoint. This shows that you are part of a community of workers with common needs and goals. It's also a way to broaden your understanding—and perhaps make some exciting discoveries as well.

Overcoming Stereotypes

To succeed in a diverse workplace, workers need to look beyond stereotypes of groups of people. A **stereotype** is an oversimplified and distorted belief about a person or group. The danger of thinking in stereotypes is that it does not allow for individuality. In addition, it encourages an "us versus them" mentality.

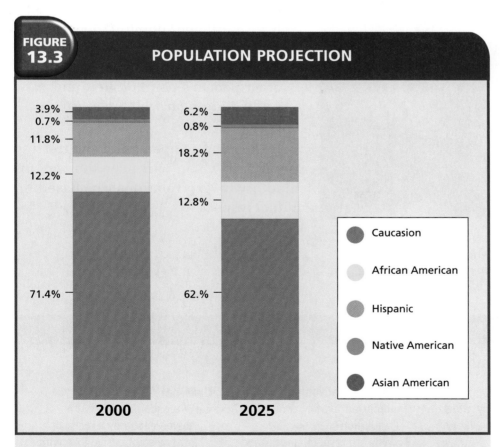

FIGURE 13.3

POPULATION PROJECTION

2000:
- 3.9%
- 0.7%
- 11.8%
- 12.2%
- 71.4%

2025:
- 6.2%
- 0.8%
- 18.2%
- 12.8%
- 62.%

Legend:
- Caucasion
- African American
- Hispanic
- Native American
- Asian American

▲ **Census 2000** The United States conducts a census every ten years to determine the characteristics of the population. *How will the workplace be affected by projected population trends?*

To get along with a diverse group of people the four behaviors of respect, understanding, sensitivity, and communication are important. Many businesses today sponsor diversity training programs to help employees overcome stereotyping in the following areas.

- *Cultural distinctions* People from different ethnic backgrounds have different customs. What's polite in one society may be rude in another, such as certain gestures or forms of address. It's important to remember, however, that cultural blunders happen even among the best-intentioned people. Learn by reading and observing, and apologize if you are unintentionally impolite.

- *Gender distinctions* Effective coworkers have mutual respect for members of the other sex. It is not sexist to acknowledge that women and men may have different styles of working and interacting. It is wrong—and illegal—however, to harass anyone because of gender.

- *Generational distinctions* People of one age group sometimes feel they have little in common with other age groups. As a young person, you may have a different point of view from your elders. You can bridge the difference by listening carefully to the other person's point of view and finding ideas on which you can agree.

By keeping an open mind and treating people fairly, you will pave the way for smooth working relationships based on mutual respect.

Diversity Overcoming stereotypes can lead to good working relationships. *How can getting along with different people at work affect other aspects of your life?*

SECTION 13.2 REVIEW

✓ Key Concept Checkpoint

Comprehension

1. How does technology affect etiquette in the workplace? Give an example.

2. Why is creative thinking an important part of conflict resolution?

3. Why are respect, understanding, and communication especially important in a diverse workplace?

Critical Thinking

4. What should you do if a coworker shares a racist or otherwise offensive joke with you?

KEY TERMS

tact (p. 259)
empathize (p. 263)

SECTION 13.1

- Getting along with your coworkers means you will have greater job satisfaction and enjoy your time at work more. (p. 258)

- Personal traits you need to develop to get along with your coworkers include responsibility, self-esteem, sociability, self-management, and integrity/honesty. (pp. 258–259)

- To improve your personal qualities, work on one trait at a time, devise a plan for working on the trait, check your progress, and then proceed to work on other traits. (pp. 260–261)

- To be an effective coworker, you need to respect others, try to understand them, communicate well, and maintain a sense of humor. (pp. 261–264)

KEY TERMS

etiquette (p. 266)
conflict resolution (p. 268)
diversity (p. 269)
stereotype (p. 269)

SECTION 13.2

- Basic etiquette in the workplace includes being courteous, dressing appropriately, being punctual, and avoiding gossip. Etiquette also includes respecting your coworkers' privacy. (pp. 266–267)

- You can develop and maintain a good working relationship with your supervisor by dealing with criticism objectively, practicing initiative, offering your help, and suggesting solutions to problems. (p. 267)

- When trying to resolve a conflict, discuss issues, not people. When compromise is not possible, creative thinking may lead to a solution. Mediation and arbitration are other possible ways to arrive at solutions. (pp. 267–268)

- The U.S. workplace is diverse, and workers need to be sensitive to cultural, gender, and generational differences. (pp. 269–270)

Chapter 13 Review

Reviewing Key Terms

1. Write one or two paragraphs on getting along with coworkers. Use the terms below in your paragraph(s).
   - tact
   - empathize
   - etiquette
   - conflict resolution
   - diversity
   - stereotype

Recalling Key Concepts

Determine whether each statement is true or false. Rewrite any false statements to make them true.

2. The personal traits that help you get along with others at your job are different from the ones that help you in school or in social situations.

3. Effective coworkers display respect, understanding, and good communication skills.

4. It is acceptable to read a fax that arrives for a coworker because the fax machine is there for everyone to use.

5. When you compromise to resolve a conflict, you let the other person have his or her way.

6. Being sensitive to diversity helps overcome stereotyping.

Problem Solving

7. How are the personal traits of responsibility and self-management related to each other?

8. Identify two sources of praise you might receive in the workplace and two sources of criticism. Tell how you would respond to each.

9. When trying to improve yourself, why should you work on one trait at a time?

10. Why does conflict resolution focus on the problem rather than the personality of the opposing person?

11. Describe how you might broaden your perspectives by communicating with others in a diverse workplace.

Work-Based Learning

Personal Qualities Self-Management

12. Write a one-page paper on why it is important to control emotions in the workplace. Discuss ways that emotions can be channeled properly to allow people to work together effectively. Within the paper, note possible consequences of lack of emotional control.

Interpersonal Skills Working with Diversity

13. Research some of the cultural differences between your culture and that of another country. Focus on differences that affect the workplace. Summarize your findings for the class.

School-Based Learning

Computer Science Design Training Program

14. Imagine that you work in an office that has just acquired new word-processing software. It's a program you are familiar with. Describe steps you would take to teach a coworker to use it. Keep in mind that this coworker is much older than you and has limited knowledge of computers.

Human Relations Create a Checklist

15. Brittany is an administrative assistant in a human resources department. Her supervisor wants to develop a checklist of positive attitudes for the workplace. He has asked Brittany to submit a list of her own. Draw up a list that Brittany could submit to her supervisor. In addition, make a list of attitudes to avoid.

Math Estimate Figures

16. Stephen works in a busy music store at a mall. Part of his job is to check the addition on purchase orders before they are sent to the distributor. Stephen's coworker, Max, suggests that he make a rough estimate before adding the prices on a calculator. Stephen thinks estimating is a waste of time. Imagine that you are Max, and explain to Stephen why estimating helps accuracy.

Role Play

17. Managing Workplace Distractions

Situation You work in a large corporate office. Because your desk is located near the coffee pot, your coworkers have formed the habit of congregating in front of your work area and they often try to draw you into their conversations. You'd like to be free of the disruption.

Activity With a group of friends, create a skit that models a tactful approach for dealing with the described situation. At the end of the skit, explain why the approach would be likely to work in a real-life setting.

Evaluation You will be evaluated on how well you meet the following performance indicators:

- Present your skit in a mature, convincing manner
- Model appropriate office etiquette
- Explain why your approach would be effective in a real-life setting

18. Research Affirmative Action

Affirmative action is a controversial policy that seeks to redress past discrimination.

Connect Research affirmative action on the Web. Prepare a one-page essay explaining your opinion on affirmative action.

Chapter 14

Teamwork and Leadership

CHAPTER OBJECTIVES

After completing this chapter, you will be able to

- Explain how teamwork benefits both team members and businesses.

- Describe the procedures necessary for organizing and maintaining an effective team.

- Define *total quality management* and explain its effect on workers.

- Discuss the characteristics of effective leaders and supervisors.

- Describe procedures for leading meetings.

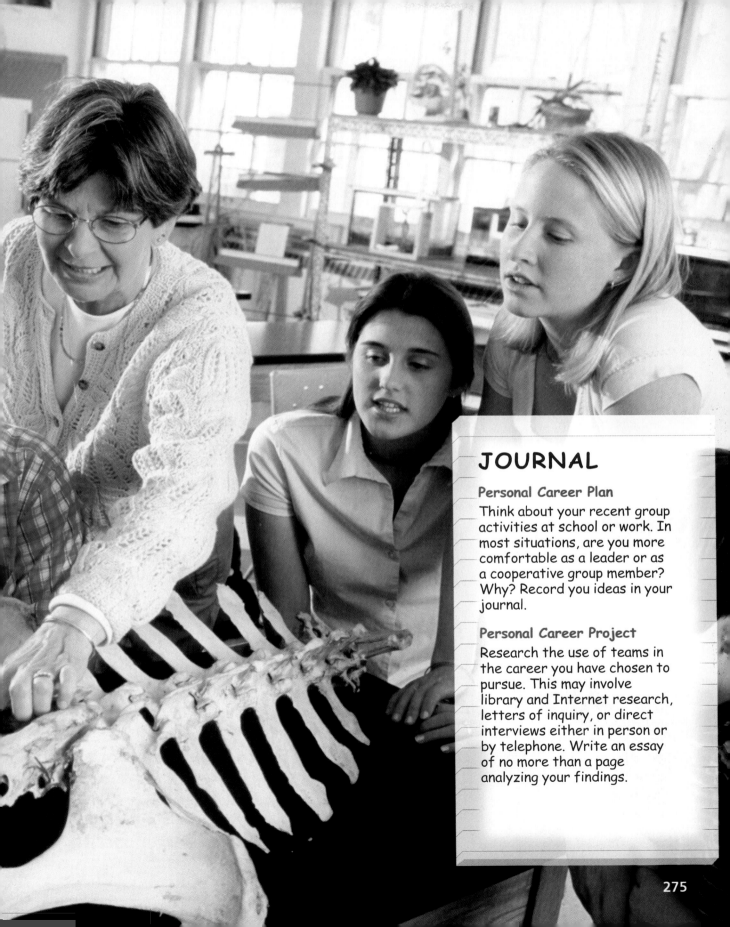

JOURNAL

Personal Career Plan

Think about your recent group activities at school or work. In most situations, are you more comfortable as a leader or as a cooperative group member? Why? Record you ideas in your journal.

Personal Career Project

Research the use of teams in the career you have chosen to pursue. This may involve library and Internet research, letters of inquiry, or direct interviews either in person or by telephone. Write an essay of no more than a page analyzing your findings.

Teamwork

Have you ever worked in a cooperative learning group at school? A learning group is one type of team, a group of people who work together to reach a common goal. Working as a team member in school will prepare you for today's business world.

Teamwork in Business

Today, businesses rely more and more on teams of workers to get jobs done. Once, such teamwork was rare. For example, in the past, automobile assembly-line workers did just one task. They might attach a radiator or put on a door. They would perform the same job over and over again. Today, workers are more likely to be part of a team. Teams work together to complete an entire phase of production. Members of such teams share the responsibilities and the rewards of their efforts.

Some teams are supervised by managers. Others are **self-directed,** or responsible for choosing their own methods for reaching their goals. Self-directed teams work without supervision. If you were a member of such a team, you might work without a manager from the start to the finish of a lengthy project.

Why Businesses Encourage Teamwork

Companies have found that teamwork pays off. It's good for team members and for businesses. Why? Teams tend to be more productive than the same number of employees working separately. Greater productivity means greater profits. Other business benefits include:

- improved quality and customer service,
- increased employee morale, and
- fewer layers of management.

Individual workers also benefit from being part of a team. Workers report the following rewards:

- *Greater job satisfaction.* Teams often rotate tasks among members. This variety reduces boredom and allows each team member to develop an array of skills.

- *Improved self-esteem.* As a rule, each team member is given the authority to help make and carry out decisions. Many team members report that the most satisfying part of their jobs is feeling in charge of their own work. Of course, team members must be *self-starters.* They have to work without always being told what to do.

- *Better communication.* Here's an extra bonus. When people work in a team, they've got to talk. As a result, they get to know each other better.

Workers learn about each other's behavior, attitudes, and ways of thinking. They get along better and are not so quick to judge one another. Tension and conflict among workers are reduced.

> ## CAREER CHECKLIST
>
> ### To Become a Strong Leader...
>
> ☑ Expand your boundaries beyond your job description.
> ☑ Earn the respect of your peers first; respect from higher-ups will follow.
> ☑ Take risks.
> ☑ Be ready to make mistakes.
> ☑ Use intuition and creativity when solving problems and developing new ideas.

Collaboration These students are working on a group project. *Why do you think their teacher requires them to work in teams?*

Working Together The members of this team are from a variety of national and ethnic backgrounds. *How might their working on a team benefit their company?*

Types of Teams

On a business team, you may work with as many as nine or ten other people. As *Figure 14.1* shows, your team will be either a **cross-functional team** or a **functional team**.

Team Planning

Imagine that you and your friends have decided to throw a surprise birthday party. If each of you goes ahead and does what you think should be done, the result may be chaos. If, however, you plan who will send invitations, set up decorations, be in

charge of music, and buy the food, the result will probably be a great party.

The same goes for running a successful team project at work. Before you start, make a plan. Since you will be working as a team, plan as a team. **Team planning** involves setting goals, assigning roles, and communicating regularly.

Setting Goals

Do you remember the personal career goals you set in Chapter 5? When you work in a team, think about group goals. Your company's overall goal, or *mission,* is a place to start.

FIGURE 14.1

TYPES OF BUSINESS TEAMS

Type	Definition	Examples
Functional Team	A group of people from one company department or area of expertise, working together to reach a common business goal.	• Six architects designing a building complex for an architectural firm • Seven chemists developing a cold medicine for a medical laboratory
Cross-Functional Team	A group of people from two or more departments or areas of expertise, working together to reach a common business goal.	• A building maintenance supervisor, two bricklayers, a landscaper, and a financial officer planning the gardens around a company's new headquarters

▲ **Types of Teams** Cross-functional teams are becoming more and more common in the business world. *What is an advantage of a cross-functional team?*

A company's mission statement expresses its purpose and values. A great deal of thought goes into creating a mission statement. Some mission statements are very brief. For example, Volkswagen's mission statement is "to provide an economical means of private transportation." On the other hand, Ben & Jerry's mission statement is much more detailed. The maker of ice cream and frozen yogurt "is dedicated to the creation and demonstration of a new corporate concept of linked prosperity. Our mission consists of three related parts." The mission statement then goes on to explain, in several paragraphs, how Ben & Jerry's mission involves its product as well as economic and social concerns.

Considering your company's mission will give you a clear picture of the unique culture that exists at your workplace. Obviously, each company values different things and sets its own priorities. Keep your company's mission in mind when you begin a project. Then set short-, medium-, and long-term project goals. Imagine that you are working on a team for a sportswear company. Your goals might include the following:

- **Short-Term Goal** Analyze the team's procedure for assembling jackets.
- **Medium-Term Goal** Figure out more efficient procedures.
- **Long-Term Goal** Produce more jackets in less time.

As you know from reading Chapter 5, the best way to approach a large project is to use "stepping-stone goals." First, break the project into smaller tasks. Then assign a start date and an end date for each task. A useful tool for teams is a *tracking schedule.* Such a schedule identifies the people who will be working on each part of a project. It tells when they will start and when they will finish.

Assigning Roles and Duties

Remember the party you planned? You could have chosen one friend to oversee the process. Then the tasks might have been done even more efficiently. Likewise, team projects often work more smoothly if the team appoints a **facilitator,** or leader. This is especially true for self-directed teams. The facilitator coordinates the tasks so that the team works efficiently.

When assigning roles in the workplace, it is important to match tasks to abilities. For example, Jason Sedrick works on the landscaping crew at a community zoo. Recently, he was assigned to a self-directed functional team to work on a new zoo entrance. The team chose a facilitator who had experience in landscape design. Jason knew about stonework. He agreed to handle this part of the job. Other members were assigned roles based on their skills.

Jason explains: "I felt uncomfortable at first. I wasn't used to working without a supervisor to report to. I thought, 'What if we do something wrong? What if no one finds out until it's too late?' I got used to taking responsibility, though. Now it feels good to be trusted. I like relying on the team and making our own decisions."

Communicating Effectively When you are part of a team, you need to take time-outs occasionally to communicate about strategy. *How can asking and answering questions help a team succeed?*

Regular Assessment

If a project doesn't get assessed regularly, small problems can become major obstacles. Communication is the key to assessment. Jason's team, for example, meets daily for quick updates. They meet weekly to evaluate overall progress. Sometimes the team has to rethink its goals.

Potential Obstacles

Can there be trouble in "team paradise"? Of course. These are some common team problems:

- unclear goals,
- misunderstandings about how much authority the team has and how much authority individuals have,
- confusion about how to assess the performance of individuals,
- competitiveness among team members,
- resentment at a lack of individual recognition, and
- reduced effort by individuals on the team, especially as the size of the team increases.

Creative
BUSINESS PRACTICES

U.S. Postal Service
Using Mediators to Resolve Conflicts

The United States Postal Service uses professional mediators to resolve conflicts in the workplace. Mediators are neutral third parties who are trained to fairly manage the problem-solving process. Most of the conflicts brought to mediation deal with claims of discrimination and civil rights violations, although less serious issues have also been handled.

The Postal Service uses mediators when a problem is first recognized to resolve conflicts before they reach the court system. All employees have the option to use mediation to resolve any conflict that is part of a civil rights complaint. Mediations occur within two weeks of the filing of the complaint.

The mediators are not employed by the Postal Service, nor have they been previously involved in the dispute. Their role is to let both sides be heard in the discussion and to encourage the conflicting parties to come to an agreement on their own.

Mediation has been very successful for the Postal Service, saving both time and money, and creating a better working environment for the staff.

Critical Thinking
Why do you think companies use mediators to resolve workplace conflicts?

Link and Learn
To learn more about the U.S. Postal Service, visit its Web site via the link on the *Succeeding in the World of Work* Web site at **www.careers.glencoe.com**.

Most obstacles can be overcome if teams define goals clearly, take action promptly, and—above all—keep communicating. Poor communication can create serious obstacles to success—from a single missed deadline to repeated personality clashes. Talking with the team leader or calling a team meeting is a good way to start to solve problems.

Being an Effective Team Member

What makes a person an effective team player? The following list describes valuable attitudes and actions. How can these help you overcome the obstacles you just read about?

- Make the team's goals your top priority.
- In meetings, listen actively and offer suggestions. Continue to communicate with team members outside meetings.
- Follow up on what you've been assigned to do.
- Work to resolve conflicts among team members. Respect the other members of your team.
- Try to inspire other employees to get involved.

Total Quality Management

Total quality management (TQM) is a theory of management that seeks to continually improve product quality and customer satisfaction. TQM is sometimes referred to as the "quality movement."

According to TQM, quality comes first at every stage of the business process. It begins with planning and design and carries through to production and distribution. Every worker at every stage is challenged to find ways to improve the quality of the product. The goal? To maximize customer satisfaction.

Here's a twist, however: TQM defines a *customer* as anyone who receives the results of your work. That can mean either a coworker within the company or an outside consumer. This way of defining customers means that the responsibility for providing quality isn't limited to the salespeople. It involves each employee all the way down the line. Each person, in fact, is encouraged to determine how his or her own job might be done better. *Figure 14.2* shows the upward spiral that can result when TQM is put to work.

FIGURE 14.2

TOTAL QUALITY MANAGEMENT: A CHAIN REACTION

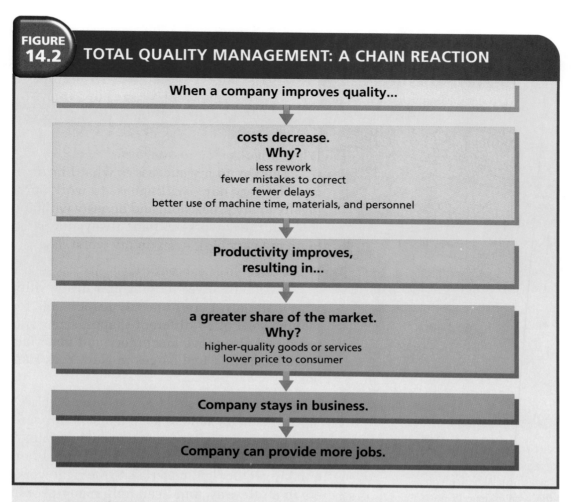

When a company improves quality...

costs decrease.
Why?
less rework
fewer mistakes to correct
fewer delays
better use of machine time, materials, and personnel

Productivity improves,
resulting in...

a greater share of the market.
Why?
higher-quality goods or services
lower price to consumer

Company stays in business.

Company can provide more jobs.

▲ **TQM Philosophy** An important part of the TQM philosophy is that providing high-quality goods or services actually costs less than providing low-quality ones. *Why do you suppose this is true?*

SECTION 14.1 REVIEW

Key Concept Checkpoint

Comprehension

1. What might be the consequences of employees not working as a team?
2. The salespeople in an appliance store are planning a campaign to improve sales. Identify short-, medium-, and long-range team goals.
3. Choose two obstacles to team success, and provide suggestions for dealing with them.
4. Your company has decided to change to a TQM style of management. Describe two ways that this might affect you as an employee.

Critical Thinking

5. What types of people might find teamwork especially difficult?

CAREER CLUSTER: Architecture and Construction

Bill Murray
Crane Operator

CAREER FACTS

Education and Training Most heavy equipment operators receive on-the-job training. Employers usually prefer high school graduates with training in automobile or diesel mechanics. A diploma from a technical school and completion of an apprenticeship is recommended.

Aptitudes, Abilities, and Skills Operators must be in good physical condition and have good balance, depth perception, and coordination. Keeping records requires good organizational skills.

Career Outlook Employment is expected to increase slower than average. Employment for operators in manufacturing will decline, while employment in construction will grow faster than average.

Career Path Heavy equipment operators often begin as apprentices or in jobs handling smaller equipment, then move on to operating larger equipment.

What is your key to success?

"The key to my success is what I bring to my job every day—willingness to work hard, loyalty to my profession, and honesty with myself and my coworkers. I am always prepared to do my very best, even on my worst day."

What does your job entail?

"My job involves moving and lifting shipyard materials. I am primarily responsible for moving steel of all different shapes, sizes, and weights. I also move machinery and materials for tugboats and fuel barges in New York Harbor."

What do you like most about your work?

"I like being able to keep a major shipyard repair job moving along. As a crane operator, I have a great sense of responsibility. I can quickly get the right materials to the right workers in a safe way, and I can help many people complete strenuous jobs. Being in this position of trust gives me satisfaction."

What kind of training did you have?

"I received formal training for my job through the Operating Engineers Apprenticeship Program. This program taught me the basics of the job and how to operate the machinery and equipment I work with today. I have also had lots of on-the-job training, which has helped me succeed and grow in my career. In this field, strong communication skills and dexterity are of great importance. I work on developing these skills on-site every day."

Critical Thinking Why would employment for heavy equipment operators decrease in manufacturing but increase in construction?

Leadership

What do your favorite teacher, a coach, and the president of the United States have in common? All are leaders. Consider what it takes to be a leader. Then write a list of qualities in your journal. As you read this section, revise and add to your list.

What Makes a Leader?

Whether you are a supervisor, a team facilitator, or simply the person in charge of training a new intern, you are a leader. Leaders are necessary if workers are to achieve their maximum potential. People have different ideas about what makes a good leader, but most agree on certain qualities.

Personal Qualities: A Leadership Checklist

Do you have the makings of a good leader? Learning the attributes of leadership and honing your leadership skills are the first steps toward becoming the leader you want to be. For a list of leadership qualities, see *Figure 14.3* on page 286.

Of course, no one is born with every quality. If you want to be a leader, you must work at developing those qualities that are most useful to you. How do you know which ones those are? Both your career choices and your personal values will be a guide.

WHAT YOU'LL LEARN

- The qualities, characteristics, and leadership styles of effective leaders and supervisors
- The procedures involved in leading a formal meeting

WHY IT'S IMPORTANT

To be an effective leader, you must possess certain essential skills and knowledge.

KEY TERMS

- leadership style
- parliamentary procedure

Leadership Styles

How you behave when you are in charge of other employees is called your **leadership style**. A successful leader is someone who mixes management styles according to the situation. Here are the four basic styles:

1. *directing*, or giving others specific instructions and closely supervising tasks;

2. *coaching*, or closely supervising but also explaining decisions and asking for suggestions;

3. *supporting*, or sharing decision-making responsibility and encouraging independent completion of tasks; and

4. *delegating*, or turning over responsibility for decision making and completion of tasks.

The most effective leaders combine these styles. The challenge is to decide which style will work best in a given situation. Whatever style you use, your success as a leader will depend on your ability to communicate well.

FIGURE 14.3

LEADERSHIP QUALITIES

Quality	Definition	Quality	Definition
Accountability	Willingness to take both the credit and the blame for one's actions	Integrity	Soundness of moral character, sticking to one's values
Anticipation	Ability to predict, on the basis of experience, what is likely to happen	Loyalty	Faithful commitment, fidelity
Competitiveness	Drive to succeed or to be the best	Physical strength	Good health, vigor, energy
Courage	Ability and willingness to face difficulties and take risks	Positive attitude	Optimistic outlook on life
Credibility	Trustworthiness	Responsibility	Reliability, accountability
Decisiveness	Clarity of purpose, determination	Self-confidence	Belief in oneself and one's ability to succeed
Dependability	Stability, consistency	Sense of humor	Ability and readiness to see the comic side of things
Emotional strength	Mental alertness, evenness of temper, ability to recover from disappointment	Stewardship	Ability to take care of resources, including human resources
Empathy	Identification with and understanding of others	Tenacity	Unyielding drive to accomplish one's goals
Enthusiasm	Eagerness, passion, excitement	Timing	Ability to judge the best moment for action
Honesty	Truthfulness, sincerity	Vision	Clear idea of where one wants to go
Imagination	Creativity, ingenuity, resourcefulness		

▲ **Leadership Qualities** No one could be expected to have *all* these leadership qualities! *Which ones do you strive to develop? Why?*

Leading a Meeting: Parliamentary Procedure

As a team leader or supervisor, you will probably find yourself leading meetings. Most business meetings are casual. However, some are formal, especially when many people are involved. To keep meetings running smoothly, many companies follow a formal process with strict rules of order that is known as **parliamentary procedure**. This way of running meetings was developed in 16th-century England to keep order in Parliament, England's governing body.

The best way to learn parliamentary procedure is to observe it in action. You might try, for example, sitting in on meetings of your school board or community government. *Figure 14.4* lists some of the parliamentary terminology that you'll hear used at such meetings. You can further develop your skills with the help of groups such as the Future Business Leaders of America, which hold conferences and competitions on leadership skills.

FIGURE 14.4

PARLIAMENTARY TERMINOLOGY

adjourn motion to close a meeting	**majority** number greater than one-half of the voting members at a meeting
agenda list of items to be addressed at a meeting	**minority** number less than one-half of the voting members at a meeting
amend change a motion	**minutes** written record of what is said and done during a meeting; kept by the secretary
aye formal way of saying yes (pronounced eye)	**motion** official request for a group to take action or reach a decision
bylaws rules and regulations that govern an organization's operation, including such matters as the election of officers, membership qualifications, and meeting times	**nay** formal way of saying no
call to question statement made by a member when he or she believes it is time to vote on a motion	**new business** topic brought before the group for the first time
chair chairperson; one who is in charge of a meeting	**quorum** minimum number of members who must be present at a meeting for the group to conduct official business
constitution document stating an organization's official name, objectives, and purposes and describing how it is organized	**second** statement made to show approval of a motion made by another member of the group; at least one member must second a motion before it can be discussed
convene gather for a meeting; call a meeting to order	**table** postpone making a decision on an issue under discussion
gavel mallet used by the chair to bring a meeting to order	**unfinished business** topic brought before the members for at least the second time

▲ **Formal Terminology** The terms used in parliamentary procedure have evolved over several centuries. *How do you think formal terminology and an established procedure help large meetings?*

When you attend a formal meeting, you'll find that it follows an *agenda*. This is a list of topics drawn up beforehand that will be discussed at the meeting. An agenda usually includes a reading of the minutes. The *minutes* are a written summary of the last meeting. The agenda will usually include *unfinished business,* or topics from the last meeting that need more discussion. It will also include *new business. **Figure 14.5*** shows how parliamentary procedure can be followed in a meeting.

Parliamentary procedure may seem complicated. Remember, however, that it has a simple aim: to make sure that meetings are run efficiently and fairly. Using parliamentary procedure to run a meeting is a skill every business leader should master.

FIGURE 14.5 **Parliamentary Procedure** Following parliamentary procedure can be an effective way for leaders to make sure meetings are orderly and productive. A quick formal meeting might look something like this. (Refer to **Figure 14.4** for definitions of any terms you do not understand.)

A **Coming to Order** A meeting begins when the chair taps her gavel and announces: "The meeting will now come to order." The first item on the agenda is usually for the secretary to read the minutes of the last meeting. The second item is often the reading of brief reports from officers of the company or organization, such as the treasurer or the chair of the fundraising committee.

B **Discussing New Business** Unfinished business from the previous meeting is discussed and decided. Then new business is introduced. For example, a member might make a motion to create a trial cross-functional team. For the motion to be considered, another member must second it.

D **Adjourning** If there is no additional business, a member moves to adjourn. The motion is seconded, voted on, and passed. The meeting is now over.

C **Voting on a Motion** After a motion is introduced and seconded, it is discussed. The chair recognizes each member who wishes to comment. After all have spoken, she calls for a vote. If a majority votes "aye," the motion is carried, or approved.

Communicating as a Leader

You already know how important communication is for team members. It's twice as important for a team leader. No matter how clear your vision of a business goal, if you cannot communicate it, your team will never reach it. Effective communication requires the skills of speaking and writing. In Chapter 15, you'll read more about how to develop these skills.

Some Tips for Supervisors

In Chapter 13, you learned some tips for working with your supervisor. Now consider the other side of the coin. How can *you* be a good supervisor? Here are some do's and don'ts for being in charge:

- Provide enough training, and be a patient teacher.
- Give clear direction.
- Know when to intervene.
- Don't be afraid to admit when you have made a mistake.
- Be consistent in what you say and do.
- Treat workers fairly and equally.

- Be firm when necessary.
- Recognize effort and initiative.
- Congratulate in public; reprimand in private.
- Make sure workers understand what you expect from them.

Most importantly when you are in a supervisory role, treat workers the way you want to be treated.

ETHICS *in Action*

Decisions, Decisions You work at a restaurant, and just as you are about to punch out, the owner asks you and several coworkers to stick around and help get ready for a last-minute catering job. You know that if you help out, the work will get done sooner and everyone will be able to leave earlier. The problem is, you have a date tonight and want to go home to get ready.

THINK ABOUT IT
Should you stay later to help with the catering job? Why or why not?

SECTION 14.2 REVIEW

✓ Key Concept Checkpoint

Comprehension
1. Name a leadership quality that is important for each of the four leadership styles.
2. Which elements of a formal meeting might also help an informal meeting run more smoothly?
3. Why do supervisors need good communication skills?

Critical Thinking
4. In what type of scenario would it be most effective to use the *directing* style of leadership?

KEY TERMS
self-directed (p. 276)
cross-functional
    team (p. 278)
functional team (p. 278)
team planning (p. 278)
facilitator (p. 280)
total quality management
    (TQM) (p. 282)

SECTION 14.1

- A team is a group of people who work together to reach a common goal. Businesses today rely more and more on teamwork. (p. 276)

- Teamwork benefits both team members and the companies they work for. Companies find that teams are more productive than individuals working alone. Team members experience greater job satisfaction and improved self-esteem. (pp. 276–277)

- The two basic types of teams are cross-functional and functional. (pp. 278–279)

- Team planning involves setting goals, assigning roles, and conducting regular assessment. (pp. 278–281)

- Obstacles to teamwork include unclear goals, competitiveness among team members, and teams that are too large. Most obstacles can be overcome by clear goal definition, prompt action, and good communication. (pp. 281–282)

- Total quality management (TQM) is a management process that tries to continually improve product quality and maximize customer satisfaction at every stage of the process. (pp. 282–283)

KEY TERMS
leadership style (p. 286)
parliamentary
    procedure (p. 287)

SECTION 14.2

- To act effectively as a leader, you must develop qualities such as decisiveness, enthusiasm, and vision. (pp. 285–286)

- Leadership styles include directing, coaching, supporting, and delegating. Most leaders use a combination of these styles. (p. 286)

- To lead or participate in a formal meeting, you need to know the basics of parliamentary procedure. This procedure is a process that helps meetings run smoothly. (p. 287)

- When following parliamentary procedure, a meeting begins with the reading of the minutes. It continues with unfinished business and then with new business. Motions are made, seconded, discussed, and then voted on. The meeting ends with adjournment. (pp. 288–289)

- Strong communication skills are essential for a leader. (p. 290)

Reviewing Key Terms

1. Write several paragraphs telling what you might learn at a teamwork and leadership seminar. Use the following key terms in your description.
   - self-directed
   - cross-functional team
   - functional team
   - team planning
   - facilitator
   - total quality management (TQM)
   - leadership style
   - parliamentary procedure

Recalling Key Concepts

2. Which of the following is *not* a benefit of teamwork?

   (a) improved worker self-esteem

   (b) TQM (c) improved productivity

3. Potential obstacles to team success include _____.

   (a) unclear goals (b) regular assessment

   (c) conflict resolution

4. Maximizing customer satisfaction through constant quality improvement is the goal of _____.

   (a) every leadership style (b) TQM

   (c) parliamentary procedure

5. The four leadership styles are directing, coaching, supporting, and _____.

   (a) convening (b) tracking

   (c) delegating

6. A(n) _____ is a request at a formal meeting.

   (a) motion (b) agenda (c) gavel

Problem Solving

7. Why do you think teams that are too large run into problems?

8. You've been asked to train a new intern in sales at your office. Which leadership style will you use? Why?

9. Imagine that you are running a company according to the principles of total quality management. Will you use teams? Why or why not?

Work-Based Learning

Basic Skills Writing

10. Write a paper that compares the four leadership styles. Discuss at least two advantages and two disadvantages of each style.

Interpersonal Skills Exercising Leadership

11. Valia is a department manager. She is concerned about the attitude of her staff. Employees are often late, show little enthusiasm, and rarely make suggestions or show initiative. What questions should she ask herself as a leader about her own role in her department's problems?

School-Based Learning

Math Calculate Supply and Labor Force

12. Imagine that you supervise the delivery team at a dairy that owns two trucks and employs two drivers. Each truck can deliver up to 45 crates of milk a day. Right now, the dairy delivers 80 crates a day. As the result of a successful advertising campaign, however, orders for the next month increase by 275 percent. How many trucks (and drivers) will you need to make your new deliveries? How many additional crates will you be able to carry before needing another new truck?

Social Studies Research Japanese Business

13. Your company is preparing a report on total quality management throughout the world. Use the library or Internet to learn how TQM has been applied in Japan.

Human Relations Find New Talent

14. Suppose you are on a personnel development team at a computer software company. Your company wants to improve employees' teamwork skills. Create a list of the characteristics of an effective team member.

Role Play

15. Collaborate and Plan

Situation You and three of your classmates are working as a team to plan your school's prom. Your team must adhere to the budget suggested by the student council.

Activity Collaborate with your team members to plan the prom and prepare a proposal to submit to the student council. Then work as a team to create a list of characteristics of an effective team member. Use the list to complete an "effective team member" profile, which you will place in your personal career portfolio. Share your proposal and effective team member profile with the class.

Evaluation You will be evaluated on how well you meet the following performance indicators:

- Set appropriate goals
- Utilize effective strategies for conducting teamwork
- Create an "effective team member" profile.
- Present a viable and complete proposal

*inter*NET CONNECTION

16. Contact Local Businesses

Find out which companies in your area rely on teamwork to accomplish tasks. Arrange to talk to a supervisor or team leader about what types of activities are performed by teams.

Connect Search the Internet for information on the use of teams in the workplace. Look for specific data that links teamwork to job satisfaction and employee retention. Share your discoveries with the class.

Chapter 15

Professional Communication Skills

Section 15.1
Speaking and Listening

Section 15.2
Writing and Reading

CHAPTER OBJECTIVES

After completing this chapter, you will be able to

- Identify ways of planning and organizing oral messages.

- Describe the importance of effective speaking and listening skills in customer relations.

- Identify and describe basic writing skills.

- Explain the importance of writing and reading skills in customer relations.

JOURNAL

Personal Career Plan

At a large state convention, your vocational club is unexpectedly invited to present a five-minute speech. You and the other club members will have only half an hour to prepare. Which task would you choose—to write the speech or to deliver the speech? Why? Write a journal entry describing your responses.

Personal Career Project

Identify instances in which you have used your communication skills. Assess how you performed in these situations. How can you improve? In your journal, record strategies that you can use to improve your communication skills.

Speaking and Listening

WHAT YOU'LL LEARN

- How to improve your communication skills by considering your purpose, audience, and subject before speaking
- Strategies for improving your listening and note-taking skills

WHY IT'S IMPORTANT

Strong communication skills will help you reach your personal and professional goals.

KEY TERMS

- **communication**
- **customer relations**
- **purpose**
- **audience**
- **subject**
- **inflection**
- **pronunciation**
- **enunciation**
- **active listening**

If a tree falls in a forest and no one is there, does it make a sound? If you have a great idea at work but don't share it with others, does it have an effect? What's missing in both cases?

For a sound or an idea to have an effect, it needs a receiver as well as a sender. The exchange of information between senders and receivers is called **communication**. Regardless of your task at work, you'll spend much of your time communicating: speaking, listening, writing, and reading.

Speaking, listening, writing, and reading are important basic skills. You'll use them as tools to gain information, solve problems, and share ideas. Most important of all, you'll use them in customer relations. **Customer relations** is the use of communication skills to meet the needs of customers.

Consumers are more sophisticated and demanding than ever. Your success on the job will depend a great deal upon your ability to communicate effectively with customers. *Figure 15.1* shows the different ways you communicate, through verbal and nonverbal signals.

Speaking: What's Your Point?

Whether you're speaking to an audience of one or one hundred, you'll want your listeners to get your point. This means that you'll need to be clear about your purpose, your audience, and your subject.

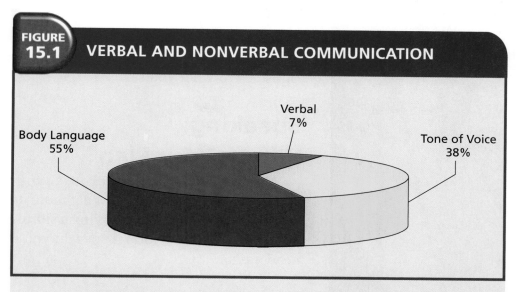

FIGURE 15.1 VERBAL AND NONVERBAL COMMUNICATION

Verbal
7%

Body Language
55%

Tone of Voice
38%

▲ **Sending the Right Signals** Body language can account for over half of what you communicate when you are talking to someone. *When dealing with an angry customer, what are some gestures or facial expressions that you should avoid using?*

Know Your Purpose

Who was the last person you spoke to? What was your reason for speaking? A speaker's **purpose** is his or her overall goal or reason for speaking. Purposes for speaking may include the following:

- greeting clients or customers,
- informing employees of a new policy,
- giving directions to a coworker,
- requesting help or information,
- persuading a supervisor to make a change, and
- proposing a new idea.

Without a clear purpose, you cannot communicate effectively. Sometimes you may have overlapping purposes. What examples can you give?

Know Your Audience

When you think of an audience, do you imagine people seated at a theater or a stadium? In fact, an **audience** is anyone who receives information. Once you know your purpose in speaking, you need to know your audience. You might ask yourself questions such as these:

- Who are my listeners? Am I speaking to coworkers or supervisors?
- What are my listeners' beliefs, values, and interests?
- What do they already know about my subject? What do they need to know?
- What do they expect to learn from me? Do they expect to be entertained, informed, or persuaded?

Effective Communication Elicia is explaining a new company insurance program to her coworkers. *Why is it important for her to know her audience?*

Your answers to these questions can help you develop a clear idea of your subject and purpose. In addition, when you know your listeners, you're better able to reach them with your words and ideas.

Know Your Subject

The **subject** in speaking is the main topic or key idea. Compare these statements: "Rain forests are important," or "Rain forests house three-fourths of the plant and animal species on Earth." The first statement is a *generality*, or broad statement. The second is a specific fact. Generalities are easy to make, but most people are convinced by hard facts.

Knowing your subject may require research. It's well worth the time, though. Using specific facts and examples will give "muscle" to what you say.

Speaking: What's Your Plan?

Now you know your purpose, your audience, and your subject. What more do you need? Whether you're giving a simple phone message or a formal speech, you'll need a plan.

Organizing What You Want to Say

As you plan your message, ask yourself:

- How does my subject relate to my listeners' needs?
- What's my most important point?
- How can I make this point clearly?
- What facts and examples can I use?

No matter what technique you use, the best approach is to be clear, brief, and direct.

ETHICS *in Action*

Respecting E-Mail You work as an assistant in a small advertising agency. One day, you go into your boss's office to leave a report on her desk. With a quick glance at her computer monitor, you notice that her e-mail program is up and that your name is in the subject line of an unopened e-mail from the owner of the company. You know your boss is in a meeting at a client's office, so there is no chance she will see you at her computer.

THINK ABOUT IT
What will you do about the e-mail?

Move logically from point to point as you speak. Reinforce main ideas. Look for signs from your listeners that your message is getting through. *Figure 15.2* shows various techniques for organizing your message.

Using Good Speaking Habits

Which is more important: *what* you say or *how* you say it? Your delivery, style, and attitude are as important as your message.

Say this sentence aloud: "I didn't say you were late for work." Now say it a different way, emphasizing a different word.

How many different messages can you send by changing the **inflection**, or the pitch or loudness of your voice?

Keep these suggestions in mind as you think about your spoken messages:

- Make emotional contact with listeners. "Communicating is a contact sport," advises communications consultant Bert Decker. Address people by name. Make eye contact with your listeners.

- Use posture and body language that match your message.

- Avoid nonwords such as *uh* and *um* and "empty" words such as *sort of*,

---

FIGURE 15.2 TECHNIQUES FOR ORGANIZING SPOKEN MESSAGES

Technique	Description	Example
Enumeration	Listing key points	"As part of our lawn service contract, we'll cut your grass, weed your flower beds, and trim your shrubs once a week."
Generalization, followed by examples	Stating a general law, condition, or principle, backed up by specific facts or examples	"The parking situation at work is getting worse. Last week, my car was blocked by another car. Yesterday, I couldn't even find a parking space."
Cause and Effect	Telling what happened and why it happened	"Flight 473 will be delayed. The airport in Chicago has ice on the runways, and planes are unable to leave the ground."
Comparison and Contrast	Pointing out similarities and differences	"Our cheesecakes contain fresh ingredients, as do our competitor's. However, ours are much lower in fat."

▲ **Speaking Sccessfully** Successful speaking means being organized. *Could you use more than one of these organizing techniques in the same message? If so, give an example.*

well, and *OK* that clutter your message and make you seem uncertain.

- Use inflection to stress key ideas.
- Pay attention to volume and speed.
- Pronounce words correctly and enunciate clearly. **Pronunciation** is how you say the sounds and stresses of a word. **Enunciation** is the speaking of each syllable clearly and separately.
- Project enthusiasm and a positive attitude, or outlook. Be courteous and attentive when speaking to customers. If you show that you really care, customers are more likely to do business with your company. When speaking in a group, be responsive to others and avoid interrupting them.

Telephone Tips

When you place calls in today's world, you may find yourself speaking to machines as often as to people. Either way, good speaking habits still apply. Keep these additional tips in mind when placing calls and leaving voice mail or answering machine messages:

- Be aware of differences in time zones when placing calls.
- Always identify yourself. Give your first and last name.
- Speak clearly and directly into the mouthpiece.
- "Smile" with your voice by using a pleasant tone.

Sometimes you'll need to take or leave a message. If you answer a call for another person, ask, "May I take a message?" Then write a brief, clear message with the date

Handling Phone Calls Michael answers the phone for his department. *Why is effective speaking especially important when answering the phone?*

and time, the full name of the caller, his or her phone number, and the purpose of the call. When you leave a message, the same rules apply. Briefly and clearly state the key information as to why you are calling.

Active Listening

Is there a difference between hearing and listening? Suppose a friend is talking to you in a noisy hallway. You may hear the noise, but you're listening to your friend. Hearing is an automatic response. Listening is a conscious action. You use your brain to *interpret*, or make sense of, what you hear.

Active listening is listening and responding with full attention to what's being said. In the world of work, active listening can be your most powerful communication tool. It involves the following steps:

- identifying the speaker's purpose,
- listening for main ideas,
- distinguishing between fact and opinion,
- noting the speaker's inflection, speed, and volume, as well as body language,
- using your own body language and facial expressions to respond to the speaker—for example, sitting up straight or leaning toward the speaker to show that you're interested, and
- reacting to the speaker with comments or questions.

Taking Notes

What are some ways that taking notes in class helps you succeed in school? Note taking can help you succeed in the world of work too. It helps you remember facts and keeps your attention focused. When you take notes, both your mind and your hands are involved in listening.

"I always take notes when a client makes a special request," says caterer Janna Hyde. "That way, I always get the order right." Practice these skills as you take notes in class or on the job:

- Don't try to write down everything a speaker says. Instead, focus on key words and main ideas. Jot down summaries in your own words.
- Note actions you need to take.
- Used bulleted lists, asterisks, and arrows to show relationships among ideas.

CAREER CHECKLIST

To Exhibit a Professional Attitude...

- ☑ Listen attentively.
- ☑ Take accurate notes during meetings and conference calls.
- ☑ Write succinct and direct e-mails and memos, always remembering to check for errors before sending.
- ☑ Avoid office gossip that can harm others and hurt your reputation.
- ☑ Never blame someone else for your mistakes.
- ☑ Treat all coworkers as skilled, competent associates.

- Review your notes to make sure you understand concepts and instructions.
- Write quickly, but make sure that your handwriting is legible.
- If you need the speaker to repeat an important point, don't hesitate to speak up.
- If necessary, make additions and clarifications to your notes immediately after you finish taking them.
- If you can't take written notes, make mental notes of the main points.

Figure 15.3 on pages 302–303 shows how speaking and listening skills can be used when you handle customer complaints.

FIGURE
15.3

Handling Customer Complaints
Handling customer complaints skillfully is important to a company's success. People don't always remember when things go right, but they do remember when things go wrong. Make sure to follow your company's established policies and procedures for handling customer complaints.

A **Listening** When a customer has a complaint, it's important to give him or her your full attention. Here's where active listening skills are helpful. Listening carefully will help you identify problems and find solutions. Always use courtesy and good manners with customers.

B **Taking Notes** Taking notes shows a customer that you're doing your best to understand his or her needs. It also helps establish a written record of the problem and the steps you have taken toward a solution.

Showing Initiative When speaking to a customer who has a complaint, be polite, clear, and brief. Let the customer know that you understand the problem and will do all you can to solve it.

D **Reaping the Rewards** Your skill in handling complaints can make the difference between losing existing customers and gaining new ones.

SECTION 15.1 REVIEW

✔ Key Concept Checkpoint

Comprehension

1. Your supervisor wants you to give your division's progress report to company executives at their fall meeting. Should you use the opportunity to complain about the company vacation policy? Explain.

2. Why might you choose to vary your speed when making a long speech?

3. Why do people "get better at telling you things" when you listen well?

4. Why is note taking a good idea when a customer is making a complaint?

Critical Thinking

5. What types of jobs require especially strong communication skills?

CAREER FOCUS

CAREER FACTS

Education or Training Each state requires admission to the bar, which is an organization of lawyers. Lawyers must earn a bachelor's degree and a juris doctor (JD) degree and pass the bar exam. Undergraduate college courses should focus on political science, history, English, social science, and economics.

Aptitudes, Abilities, and Skills Thorough understanding of law, solid research skills, and technological skills are necessary for preparing cases. Reasoning ability, creativity, strong communication skills, and persistence are also necessary.

Career Outlook Average job growth is expected through 2008, with competition remaining keen.

Career Path Most lawyers begin as associates in a law firm and go on to become partners or to start their own firms. An experienced lawyer may become a judge or run for district attorney.

What is your key to success?

"My keys to success are listening and focusing. When I'm at work, I have to be there 100 percent."

What skills are most important to you?

"My negotiating skills are essential to my success as a lawyer. On a case, I have to negotiate with other lawyers, judges, and clients to ensure that the outcome is just and fair. Good listening skills and analytical skills are also important."

What does your job entail?

"My workload varies. Some days I hold conferences about cases and perform case management tasks in the courtroom. Other days are dedicated to research and writing. A typical attorney has an extremely heavy caseload, and many attorneys, especially recent graduates, often work long hours and weekends."

What training do you recommend for students?

"Before entering law school, students should intern in an area of law that interests them. Internships are available in environmental law firms, district attorney's offices, family law firms, and in the public interest sector. Students should take high school courses that will help them develop persuasive writing skills. A speech class or participating in the debate or mock trial team can develop good public speaking skills."

> **Critical Thinking** What kind of research would a lawyer have to do when preparing a case?

Writing and Reading

Can you name a job that doesn't involve writing and reading? Vast amounts of written information are exchanged every business day. Increasingly, a company's success depends on employees who have strong skills in writing and reading.

Basic Writing Skills

Much of the advice for speaking well applies to writing well: define your audience, purpose, and subject; be clear, direct, and organized. Here are some additional tips to keep in mind:

- Organize your writing. Use a logical order, such as chronological, or time order, or order of importance. Use headings and subheadings when writing reports.

- Pay close attention to spelling and grammar. Use a dictionary and stylebook to check words and rules you are unsure of.

- Be aware of your *tone*, or manner, when you write. In a letter responding to a customer's request, you would write in a tone that is respectful and polite.

- If you're unsure of your proofreading skills, ask a colleague or friend to read important documents you've composed.

- Once you have finished, read your product aloud to make sure there are no awkward words or phrases.

WHAT YOU'LL LEARN

- How to write appropriately for a variety of formats, including e-mail, business letters, and memos
- How to use reading strategies such as previewing and skimming

WHY IT'S IMPORTANT

In order to succeed at work, you must be able to read and write effectively.

KEY TERMS

- **e-mail**
- **modem**
- **previewing**
- **skimming**

FIGURE 15.4

STYLE DO'S AND DON'TS

Do...	Don't...	Examples
use language everyone can understand	use slang or jargon. *Jargon* is vocabulary specific to your area of work	Instead of "Let's run over the specs on this computer," write: "Let's discuss the features of this computer."
use your own language	use clichés, or overused phrases and expressions	Instead of "This is way over my head," write: "This is complicated, and I don't understand it completely."
use gender-neutral language	use sexist language	Instead of "Each man will make his own choice," write: "Each person will make his or her own choice."
use the active voice	use the passive voice	Instead of "The report was written by Zach," write: "Zach wrote the report."
use simple, natural words and phrases	use complicated words or phrases	Instead of "My home is in proximity to hers," write: "My home is near hers."
use short, simple sentences	use long, complicated sentences	Instead of "I am requesting that you write to the client, after which you should contact her by telephone," write: "Please write to the client, and then call her."

▲ **Developing Your Style** This chart shows ways to develop your own style. *Why is developing your own style important in writing?*

- Be mindful of wordiness, and always say things in the simplest way possible. Although you want your writing to be interesting, using too many words detracts from the point you want to make.

- Present your writing in an appropriate, professional manner. For instance, don't make copies of your work using a photocopier that needs toner.

- When you think you are done, go back one more time and edit your work. Keep revising until your message is clear.

- Carefully proofread your work before sending it out.

Writing Style

Writer E. B. White defined *style* as "the sound [a writer's] words make on paper." Style isn't something you "add" to your writing, as a top hat or glittery necklace; it's what shines through when you write in a clear and straightforward way.

The trend in business writing is toward a direct conversational style. See *Figure 15.4* for some basics on developing style.

At some point in your career, you will probably need to write business correspondence. When that time arrives, you'll need to be well acquainted with the standard formats for business memos, e-mail, and letters. *Figures 15.5* below, and *15.6*, and *15.7* on page 308 compare business memos, letters and e-mail.

Using E-Mail and Fax Machines

E-mail, or electronic mail, is a fast, efficient way to communicate. E-mail is sent using a **modem**, which translates data from your computer into digital signals that travel over an ordinary telephone line. Dial-up modems "dial up" like a telephone and are common in residential use. Businesses typically use *broadband access,* which is faster than dial-up access. Cable modems, which use the same wires as cable television, and DSL modems, which use telephone lines but have a constant connection, are examples of broadband access.

Many companies also communicate by *fax*, short for *facsimile*, which means a copy or a replica. A fax machine scans written messages and transmits them via telephone lines.

When sending business e-mail and faxes, you should keep messages short and to the point. E-mail messages are generally less formal than other forms of business communication.

FIGURE 15.5 MEMORANDUM

OFFICE MEMORANDUM

TO: Accounting Department
cc: Brenda Gold
From: Margaret Sterling
Date: November 2, 2001
Subject: Departmental Meeting

There will be a departmental meeting, led by Human Resources Director Brenda Gold, on Thursday, November 8, in the main conference room to discuss our new policy regarding e-mail and Internet use. This policy will take effect on Monday, November 12.

Each employee will be required to sign a notice stating that he/she has read the policy and agrees to abide by it. The text of the new policy will be e-mailed to each employee for review.

▲ **Using Memos** The use of the memo is declining in many business settings. *What form of communication can be an effective alternative to the memo?*

FIGURE
15.6

BUSINESS LETTER

Java Joe's Coffee Supply, Inc.

420 Market Street • Suite 236 • Chicago, Illinois 60647 • (312) 555-0244

August 24, 2002

Ms. Sarah Severson
Timbuktu Coffee Emporium
1700 Park Boulevard
Indianapolis, IN 46223

Dear Ms. Severson,

Today we received your written order for ten (10) pounds of whole-bean
Mocha Java coffee and five (5) pounds of whole-bean Columbia Supreme
coffee. We have contacted our distributors, and the projected date of delivery is
in four (4) days, on August 28. We will contact you with any changes in the
status of your order.

Java Joe's Coffee Supply appreciates your business. We look forward to
meeting your coffee supply needs, and hope to do more business with
Timbuktu Coffee Emporium in the future.

Sincerely,

Natalie M. Brown

Natalie M. Brown, Manager

◀ **Business Correspondence**
The business letter is still an
important form of communication in the business world.
*Why might an individual
choose to send a business letter rather than an e-mail message?*

FIGURE
15.7

BUSINESS E-MAIL

From: Natalie M. Brown <n.brown@javajoes.com>
To: Sarah Severson <smseverson@timbuktucoffee.net>
Date: Friday, August 24, 2002, 2:34 PM
Subject: Your Order

Dear Ms. Severson,

Today we received your online order for ten (10) pounds of whole-bean Mocha Java
coffee and five (5) pounds of whole-bean Columbia Supreme coffee. We have
contacted our distributors, and the projected delivery time is in four (4) days. We will
contact you with any changes in the status of your order.

Java Joe's Coffee Supply appreciates your business. We look forward to meeting your
coffee supply needs, and hope to do more business with Timbuktu Coffee Emporium
in the future.

Natalie M. Brown

– – – – – – –

Natalie M. Brown
Manager
Java Joe's Coffee Supply
n.brown@javajoes.com
Phone: (312) 555-0244
Fax: (312) 555-0200

▲ **Business E-mail** Today, most written business communication is sent by e-mail. E-mail is faster and usually
more informal than traditional mail. *Which method of
communicating is the most advantageous?*

Reading Skills

You're likely to spend as much time reading as writing on the job. Name or list in your journal some of the reading skills you've used in social studies, science, and English classes. You'll find yourself using many of these skills in your job as you acquire, evaluate, and interpret information.

You'll use them to get a job: reading help-wanted ads and job applications. You'll use them on the job: reading memos, bulletins, letters, directions, and reports. Sometimes you'll want to read quickly for general information. At other times, you'll want to read carefully for specific facts.

Previewing

Do you enjoy movie previews? What information can you get from them? When you're **previewing**, you read only those parts of a written work that outline or summarize its content. These parts may include book titles, chapter titles, or headings. Previewing saves time when you need a general idea of what is in a work.

Creative BUSINESS PRACTICES

American Airlines
Getting Staff Online

American Airlines believes that it is important for all of its employees to have convenient access to the Internet. The airline is investing more than $55 million over three years in its "On-time On-line Home Computer Program" to help its employees purchase home computers and Internet access.

Because American Airlines is a large company, it can buy large quantities of machines at a discounted rate. For a small monthly fee, each of the 100,000 American Airlines employees worldwide can get a home computer system with Internet access. After three years, the employees own the computers outright. More than half of the airline's employees have already participated in the program.

By getting online, the airline employees have the opportunity to advance their education, enhance their computer skills, and handle personal business such as paying bills and corresponding with friends and family. American Airlines also plans to make payroll accounts, benefits updates, and other important information available on the Internet, making it easier for employees to be more informed about their jobs.

Critical Thinking

In what ways can employees who have home computers benefit their employers?

Link and Learn

To learn more about American Airlines and its employee programs, visit the company's Web site via the link on the *Succeeding in the World of Work* Web site at **www.careers.glencoe.com**.

Reading Strategies Skimming can be very helpful, especially when you're researching a great deal of material. *How do you decide when to skim a book or document and when to read it more carefully?*

Skimming

Another timesaving reading skill is skimming. In **skimming**, you read through a book or a document quickly, picking out key points. To skim, you look at the first sentences of paragraphs, as well as key words and phrases.

*inter***NET**
C O N N E C T I O N

E-Mail Accounts
You want to apply for jobs on the Internet, and you need an e-mail address to receive responses from potential employers.

Connect
• Search the Internet for companies that offer free e-mail accounts. Compare the different companies and see which one is right for you.
• Set up a free e-mail account and write a one-paragraph summary explaining how your account works and why you chose that particular service.

Taking Notes

Taking notes is important as a reading skill as well as a listening skill. Jotting down main ideas, useful quotes, new vocabulary, and your own summaries of information helps you understand and recall what you read. Note taking can be especially helpful when you're reading technical information.

SECTION 15.2 REVIEW

 Key Concept Checkpoint

Comprehension
1. What are some ways in which you might organize the information in a report that describes your company's activities this past year?
2. Which of these business forms would you use to respond to a customer complaint: memo, business letter, e-mail, fax? Explain why.

3. Which skill—previewing or skimming—would you use to find your weekly schedule in a company memo that shows all employee schedules? Explain your answer.
4. Give a specific example of the usefulness of good reading skills in customer relations.

Critical Thinking
5. Why is it a bad idea to skim important documents, such as memos from your boss or your employee manual?

KEY TERMS

communication (p. 296)
customer relations (p. 296)
purpose (p. 297)
audience (p. 297)
subject (p. 298)
inflection (p. 299)
pronunciation (p. 301)
enunciation (p. 301)
active listening (p. 301)

SECTION 15.1

- Communication is the process of exchanging information. (p. 296)
- Communication skills include speaking, listening, writing, and reading. (p. 296)
- Before you speak, you need to consider your purpose, audience, and subject. You also need to organize what you plan to say. (pp. 296–299)
- There is more to speaking than what you say. How you say things matters too, whether in person or on the telephone. (pp. 299–300)
- Active listening is especially important in customer relations. It involves body language and verbal responses. (pp. 300–301)
- Taking notes can help you remember what you hear. (p. 301)

KEY TERMS

e-mail (p. 307)
modem (p. 307)
previewing (p. 309)
skimming (p. 310)

SECTION 15.2

- Writing requires some of the same skills as speaking. You need to know your audience, purpose, and subject. You must also be clear, direct, and organized. (pp. 305–306)
- When you write, you must consider your style, tone, spelling, and grammar. You must also remember to revise and proofread. (p. 306)
- The most common business forms are memos, e-mail, and letters. (pp. 307–308)
- In today's business world, e-mail and faxes are important communication tools. (p. 307)
- Good reading skills, including previewing, skimming, and note taking, are necessary for any type of job. (pp. 309–310)

Reviewing Key Terms

1. Write one or two paragraphs about the importance of communication skills in the world of work. Use the terms below.
   - communication ✓
   - customer relations
   - purpose ✓
   - audience
   - subject ✓
   - inflection
   - pronunciation ✓
   - enunciation ✓
   - active listening ✓
   - e-mail ✓
   - modem
   - previewing
   - skimming

Recalling Key Concepts

2. Before speaking to an audience, you should ____.
   (a) speak clearly
   (b) know who your audience is
   (c) use eye contact

3. "Our cleaning service costs less than others in town" is an example of ____.
   (a) enumeration
   (b) cause and effect
   (c) comparison and contrast

4. Taking notes when customers place orders is a type of ____ skill.
   (a) speaking (b) reading (c) listening

5. After writing a business letter to a customer, you should ____.
   (a) proofread it for errors
   (b) send it via e-mail
   (c) send it as a fax

6. To determine whether or not to buy a book for one of your projects, you should ____.
   (a) read the book carefully
   (b) skim it for the main ideas
   (c) preview it by looking at the table of contents, headings, and illustrations

Problem Solving

7. Why is knowing your audience's values and expectations important in speaking?

8. When listening to a customer, what are some ways to show that your attention is focused on the customer?

9. Why would you want to avoid jargon when talking to people outside your department or company?

10. As an employer, how would you help employees strengthen communication skills in the workplace?

Work-Based Learning

Basic Skills Writing

11. You are the office manager of an accounting firm. Write a memo to inform staff members that the office will close at 2:00 P.M. on the Wednesday before Thanksgiving and to remind supervisors to submit weekly reports before the holiday closing.

Interpersonal Skills Teaching Others

12. Using only your voice, explain to classmates how to fold a letter on paper that measures 8½ x 11 inches so that it will fit into an envelope that measures 4¼ x 9½ inches.

School-Based Learning

Social Studies Plan a Delivery Route

13. Aaron is a truck driver for a moving company in your state. As Aaron's supervisor, you need to give him written directions for his next assignment. Using your state map, plan a route that begins at one point in the state and ends at another point. Write the directions on a sheet of paper. Provide at least three steps in the directions. Then exchange your written directions with another student. Use a pencil to map Aaron's route on a road map of your state.

Language Arts Write a Message

14. Toni is checking her supervisor's voice-mail messages. There is one call, recorded at 2:10 P.M. on February 7: "Hi, John. Sam Jennings here. I need to know if you want me to order that special card stock we talked about. If you let me know by the end of the day, I can still get you the discount rate. I'll be here 'til six o'clock. I'm at 555-6636. Thanks. So long." Using this information, write a professional phone message for Toni's supervisor.

Role Play

15. Give a Presentation

Situation You have been chosen by your supervisor to give a presentation to the rest of the department regarding a new computer program. You have already mastered the program and must give a presentation in which you teach your colleagues how it works.

Activity Prepare a presentation that will help your coworkers understand the new program. Then create a role-playing exercise in which you give the presentation to a small group, including your supervisor. Use visual aids and clear instructions to help your audience understand the new program.

Evaluation You will be evaluated based on how well you meet the following performance indicators:

- Organization of ideas
- Preparation of presentation
- Quality of delivery, including the pace, tone, enunciation, and eye contact

*inter*NET CONNECTION

16. Improve Your Writing

Ask your English teacher to review a few of your writing samples. Then ask your teacher to identify weaknesses in your overall writing style as well as specific errors. Using this analysis, complete relevant exercises in a grammar book that will help you improve your writing.

Connect Search the Internet for grammar Web sites published by reliable sources. Using the information on these sites, correct the grammatical errors identified by your teacher on a recent writing assignment.

Chapter 16

Thinking Skills on the Job

Section 16.1
Making Decisions on the Job

Section 16.2
Solving Workplace Problems

CHAPTER OBJECTIVES

After completing this chapter, you will be able to

- Make appropriate decisions using the seven steps in the decision-making process.

- Consider a variety of factors in making decisions at work, including personal values and purposes, and the alternatives and consequences of decisions.

- Prioritize your work.

- Identify and clarify problems using the six basic steps in the problem-solving process.

- Generate alternative solutions to problems.

- Implement solutions and evaluate their results.

JOURNAL

Personal Career Plan

Think of a difficult situation you faced recently, either at school or at work. What was the problem? How did you solve it? If you could go back now and deal with the situation again, what would you do this time? Write your experiences and ideas in your journal.

Personal Career Project

Interview someone who works in a career area that interests you. Ask about the usual methods for solving problems in that career area. If possible, obtain a specific example of a successful solution to a problem. Present your findings to the class.

Making Decisions on the Job

- How to use the decision-making process to streamline, clarify, and prioritize decisions
- How to evaluate the alternatives and the consequences of decisions

WHY IT'S IMPORTANT

Responsible and effective decision making is an indispensable skill that will help you in your personal and professional life.

KEY TERMS

- **resources**
- **criteria**
- **consequence**
- **procrastinate**
- **prioritize**

You make hundreds of decisions every day, some trivial, some important. Do you turn left here? What do you want for lunch? What career do you choose? In the world of work, you will want to make the best decisions possible, both everyday decisions and significant long-term ones.

Reviewing the Decision-Making Process

As you learned in Chapter 2, decision making is following a logical series of steps to identify and evaluate possibilities and arrive at a workable choice. Whether you're buying new shoes or facing a big on-the-job decision, the steps are basically the same. What decisions have you made lately that followed this process?

1. Define your needs or wants.
2. Analyze your resources.
3. Identify your choices.
4. Gather information.
5. Evaluate your choices.
6. Make a decision.
7. Plan how to reach your goal.

Analyzing Your Resources The second step of the decision-making process involves analyzing your resources. *What resources in addition to the blueprint are being used here to make a decision?*

Step 1. Figuring Out What You Need and Want

Once you know what you need or want in order to meet your job responsibilities, you have completed the first step of the decision-making process. Having a strong grasp of your purpose will help you clarify the decision you need to make.

Maria Delfino works at SuperSounds, a large music store. Her duties include making sure that the display racks are kept filled with the latest CDs. When she discovers an empty rack, she faces a decision. First she identifies her needs and wants.

She needs to keep the rack filled, and she needs a new supply of CDs. She wants to fulfill her responsibility and to do a good job too.

Step 2. Checking Out Resources

Can you make something out of nothing? Of course not—you need resources. In the world of work, the most basic **resources** are time, money, material, information, facilities, and people.

At SuperSounds, Maria moves to the second step of the decision-making process by finding out what resources she has. She checks back in the stockroom, and she finds that the CD she needs is out of stock. She knows, however, that new supplies—additional resources—are available from a distributor.

Step 3. Identifying the Best and the Rest

What do you do when different choices all seem like good ones? Smart decision makers use **criteria**—standards of judgment—for comparing and evaluating choices.

As you learn more about a workplace, you'll learn not only *how* but also *why* certain decisions are made—in other words, what criteria are important, including product quality, customer satisfaction, safety, efficiency, and economic factors.

Maria knows that SuperSounds values keeping its display racks filled. However, another criterion—the chain of command—is also important. Maria identifies her three choices. She can (a) order the CDs immediately, (b) inform her supervisor of the situation, or (c) do nothing about the CDs and wait for someone else to notice the situation.

Creative BUSINESS PRACTICES

L.L. Bean
Total Quality Management

Meeting customers' needs is key for L.L. Bean, the clothing, furniture, and outdoor sporting gear retailer and manufacturer based in Freeport, Maine. L.L. Bean's employees learned that to maximize customer satisfaction, everyone in the company needed to be involved in improving processes. This led to the development of a total quality management program.

The human resources department set up mandatory training for all L.L. Bean employees. A survey was created to evaluate managers' efforts to improve the workplace. Individuals traded jobs with people in other departments to find ways to improve how departments work together.

Since L.L. Bean implemented its total quality management program, return on sales has greatly increased, as has job satisfaction.

Critical Thinking

What can employees get out of trading jobs with coworkers in other departments?

Link and Learn

Visit L.L. Bean's Web site via the link on the *Succeeding in the World of Work* Web site at **www.careers.glencoe.com**.

Asking Questions No one knows everything. If you have a question, ask it. *What might a supervisor think of a worker who never asks questions?*

Step 4. Collecting More Info

Sometimes you simply don't have enough information to make a good decision. What's the solution? Don't act in the dark—ask questions. Get the information you need. If you don't ask, no one will know you need information.

Maria has taken a SuperSounds training program in how to place orders. However, she does not have the authority to do so or even know the number of new CDs to order. Her next move is to ask a coworker for more *information.* Steven, an assistant who has been on the job for about six months, recommends that Maria inform her supervisor of the situation.

Step 5. Assuming the Role of Judge

Every decision you make will have a **consequence**—an effect or outcome. Evaluating alternatives usually means understanding and predicting possible consequences:

- What are the risks involved in this decision? Are the rewards worth it?
- How does this decision directly affect me? How will I be judged?
- What effect will this decision have on my team or department?
- What effect will this decision have on my company?

FIGURE
16.1

Prioritizing On any job, a worker must often decide what to do first, second, third, and so on. When deciding what to tackle first, take these four factors into account: logic, importance, feasibility, and time.

A **Logic** Sometimes it's only logical to complete one task before going on to the next one. For example, a house-painter starts painting a room with the ceiling, because any paint splatters that get on the walls will be covered when the walls are painted.

B **Importance** Which job absolutely, positively has to get done today? The sooner you start an important task, the more likely you'll be to complete it on time. For example, if a customer is coming to pick up his car at the end of the day, don't procrastinate—get started on his car first before getting distracted by other tasks.

Maria thinks about the consequences of the three choices she faces. If she orders the CDs herself, she may be praised for her initiative. However, she may also be reprimanded for breaking the chain of command. If she informs the supervisor, she will be following the store's standard procedure. If she waits and does nothing, she may be accused of not doing her job properly.

C **Feasibility** If two tasks are equally important, start with the one that you're sure you can actually get done right. It's better to wait until you can do a task correctly than to jump in unprepared. For example, if you need to take inventory but the product scanner isn't working properly, its better to do something else rather than risk doing the work incorrectly.

D **Time** Sometimes it's best to finish short tasks first before embarking on longer ones. For example, it might be easiest to answer several e-mails before returning a call to a customer who needs extensive advice.

Step 6. Making Up Your Mind

After you've considered your options and evaluated the possible consequences, there's no need to **procrastinate,** or put off deciding, unless you still need more information. Have you ever decided not to decide? That's a decision too. Just don't procrastinate out of fear.

Maria doesn't procrastinate. She decides to follow the store's standard procedure—to inform her supervisor.

Step 7. Drawing Up Your Plan of Action

Once you've made a decision, put it into action. **Prioritize** the tasks to be done; that is, order them from first to last or from most to least important. *Figure 16.1* shows how a worker prioritizes tasks.

Maria prioritizes her tasks. She first informs her supervisor, who praises her attentiveness and places the order. Second, she rearranges the display to make it look appealing until the new supply arrives. Third, she checks the other new titles to make sure the situation doesn't happen again. Maria will reach both her short-term goal (to fill the display) and her long-term goal (to be responsible).

Working in Order These employees are completing their work by prioritizing. *Why is it important to prioritize tasks?*

SECTION 16.1 REVIEW

✔ Key Concept Checkpoint

Comprehension
1. In your own words, describe the seven steps of the decision-making process.
2. Why do you think having a clear purpose can make a decision easier?
3. What do you predict will happen to a business that does not have a strong chain of command?

4. In what way is customer satisfaction a criterion for decision making?
5. What do you think is the value of prioritizing your job responsibilities?

Critical Thinking
6. Should you ever make a decision based on your "gut" feelings?

CAREER FOCUS

CAREER CLUSTER: Scientific Research and Engineering

Jamie Guidry
Scientific Research Associate II
BBI Biotech Research Labs, Inc.

CAREER FACTS

Education of Training Some jobs require an associate degree and practical experience, but others call for a bachelor's degree and college math and science courses.

Aptitudes, Abilities, and Skills Research workers and technicians must be familiar with how to use laboratory equipment. An understanding of lab procedures also helps workers achieve reliable results in research.

Career Outlook Employment is expected to increase more slowly than average through 2008, although jobs will continue to be available for qualified applicants.

Career Path Many research technicians begin as trainees. Some technicians choose to become scientists, and some are promoted to supervisory positions.

What is your key to success?

"The key to my success is persistence and old-fashioned hard work. Expressing my goals to my superiors, taking on additional responsibilities, and showing a willingness to learn have also helped me succeed."

What does your job entail?

"I work as a biotechnology research assistant, focusing on AIDS and cancer research. I write scientific papers for publication, prepare presentations based on my data and conclusions, and keep an organized laboratory notebook of the research protocols, tools, and data from my experiments. I also order supplies and keep the laboratory functioning safely and efficiently."

What training do you recommend?

"I recommend a strong background in biology. Basic lab skills, such as knowing how to operate pipettes, scales, centrifuges, and other biological and chemical equipment, are crucial. Undergraduate research is also helpful. Students should get an early start with internships and a diverse range of laboratory courses."

What do you like most about work?

"Biotechnology involves life-changing research, which is rewarding and fulfilling. While the day-to-day routine can be repetitive at times, the rewards that come from assisting in research that may find a vaccine for AIDS or a cure for cancer are indescribable."

Critical Thinking What kind of classes could you take in high school to prepare you for a career as a scientific researcher?

Solving Workplace Problems

"Houston, we have a problem," crackled the voice of astronaut Jim Lovell as the damaged *Apollo 13* capsule hurtled through space. That statement set in motion a heroic group effort in problem solving—resolving a difficulty through creative thinking and reasoning.

Understanding the Problem-Solving Process

Your workplace problems may not be as dramatic as those of *Apollo 13,* but your approach to solving them should be the same. Follow these six steps:

1. Identify and clarify the problem.
2. Generate alternative solutions, using creative thinking and logical reasoning.
3. Evaluate the probable consequences of the solutions.
4. Decide on the best solution.
5. Implement the solution.
6. Evaluate the results.

Step 1. Identify and Clarify the Problem

When an obstacle stands between you and something you need or want, you've got a problem. You

Solving Problems Whether problems are simple or complex, they can ususally be solved with creative thinking and logical reasoning. *What kinds of problems have you already solved during your experience as a student?*

could try the ostrich approach: Stick your head in the sand and hope the problem goes away. Chances are, it won't. The wise move is to see the problem clearly for what it is—not a mystery, not a catastrophe, but just a situation that needs a solution.

First things first. Gather the facts—assemble all the information you can about the problem. Ask specific questions, and stay as objective as possible. Think about your sources too. Are they reliable? Are they giving you facts or opinions?

Lewis Iverson is a part-time assistant at Avery's, a small local hardware store.

One day, Mr. Avery, the owner, tells Lewis that business has been very slow lately. He asks Lewis to think about possible solutions to the problem of the sales slump. To clarify the problem, Lewis makes this list of questions:

- Are fewer people coming in?

- Are customers spending less money?

- Do people want a different selection of goods?

- Do people expect lower prices?

- What products do other local hardware stores offer?

By asking their regular customers these questions, Lewis and Mr. Avery clarify the problem: People are buying less of certain kinds of items, especially tools, because the selection is better at a big new home supply store.

To attack a problem, come up with as many solutions as possible, no matter how crazy some might seem. **Brainstorm** alone or with a group, coming up with as many ideas as you can, but not evaluating or judging those ideas right away. If you judge your ideas as you create them, you'll disturb your flow of thoughts and hinder your mind from thinking creatively. There's no disadvantage to creating a long list of possible solutions. After all, multiple solutions increase your chances of success.

When you plan to participate in a group brainstorming session, it's a good idea to get organized before you start. Clearly state the problem that you want to solve, and select a group member to be in charge of writing down all of the ideas produced in the session. Make sure that everyone in the group feels comfortable sharing his or her ideas. If some members of the group are new or shy, an ice-breaking activity might help to promote a friendly atmosphere in the group.

Step 2. Generate Alternative Solutions

One of the world's great problem solvers, physicist Albert Einstein, once said, "Imagination is more important than knowledge." Do you agree? Think of the problems you've solved by changing your way of thinking, by looking at something from a new angle, by being creative.

When you're working alone to solve a problem, you should also strive to think creatively. For instance, change your point of view. Putting yourself in someone else's shoes can make a problem look quite different.

Here are a few strategies for creative thinking that you can try:

- If an idea comes to you at an odd or inconvenient time, try to jot it down right away—even if it means writing the idea on a piece of scrap paper.

- Use spider maps and clustering (techniques you've probably already used in school) to associate groups of ideas. **Figure 16.2** shows an example of a cluster diagram.

- Invent a model, picture, or symbol to represent the problem. Revealing the "shape" of a problem can open a solution.

Group Creativity Group brainstorming can result in a variety of creative solutions to a problem. *Why do you think the word* brainstorm *is a good one to describe this problem-solving strategy?*

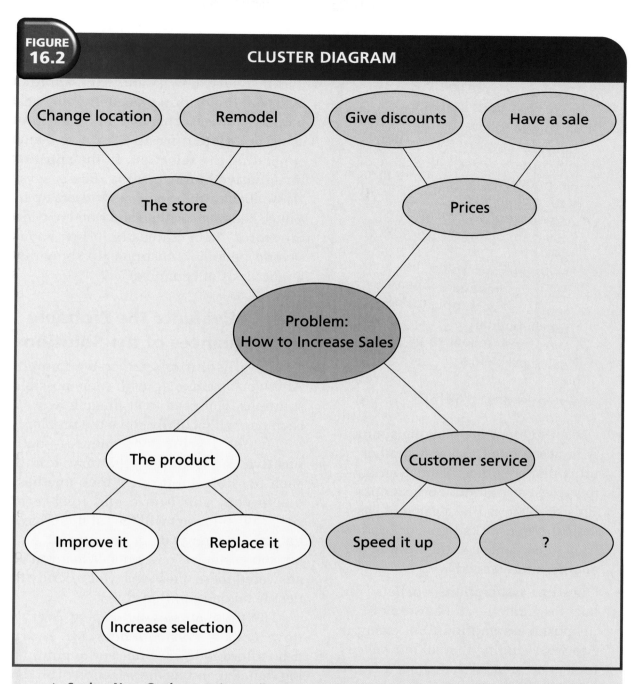

FIGURE 16.2

CLUSTER DIAGRAM

- Change location
- Remodel
- Give discounts
- Have a sale
- The store
- Prices
- Problem: How to Increase Sales
- The product
- Customer service
- Improve it
- Replace it
- Speed it up
- ?
- Increase selection

▲ **Seeing New Options** A cluster diagram can help you associate a variety of ideas and see new connections. *If you were using this cluster, what might you put in the oval with a question mark?*

- Use an **analogy**—a seeming similarity between one thing and another thing that are otherwise dissimilar—to suggest a solution. For example: This problem is like a game of basketball. We need to pass our product from one member of the team to another more quickly.

- Question **assumptions**—beliefs you take for granted—and beware of unspoken assumptions. For example: Are we assuming that all our customers are men? What about advertising aimed at women?

Remember that, in problem solving, more heads are often better than one simply because different people bring different experiences to the table. Participate as a team member to help identify alternative solutions, and ask other people for help when you can. Involving others—making your boss aware of a problem, for example—is often the right move.

Mr. Avery, Lewis, and Kim, another assistant, brainstorm one afternoon. Each proposes ideas, such as having a sale, lowering prices, putting up a new sign, and expanding the selection. In the spirit of imaginative brainstorming, Lewis says, "How about hiring someone to dress up in a huge hammer costume and stand outside the store?" Kim chimes in, "How about several people in costumes to show different kinds of hammers?"

Step 3. Evaluate the Probable Consequences of the Solutions

Not all solutions are created equal. After you've come up with some possible solutions, you need to evaluate how well each one will actually solve the problem.

List the specific consequences—both positive and negative—that may follow each possible solution. Which one best meets your short-term and long-term goals? What impact will the solutions have on you, on your team or department, and on your customers or clients? When you've answered these questions, you're ready to decide on one solution.

The problem-solving team at Avery's now looks at *consequences*. Mr. Avery can't afford to lower prices or to put up a big sign. Expanding the selection of all the items in the store is impractical because Avery's just doesn't have the space. The hammer-costume idea would get people's attention—a short-term goal—but it might also make people think the store was silly—missing a long-term goal of maintaining customers' respect.

Step 4. Decide on the Best Solution

When you choose a solution, remember that you're choosing the best one under the circumstances. Few solutions are perfect, and occasionally time forces you to choose when you're not quite ready. Time pressure is a reality that everyone has to deal with. Just stay calm, focus on the problem, and decide.

When you're choosing a solution, you'll probably still feel some misgivings, even if you've used the problem-solving process to the best of your ability. However, using the problem-solving process should allow you to feel confident that you have addressed the matter at hand in a mature, responsible manner.

Gain reassurance by reminding yourself or your team members that you have approached the problem objectively and from all angles. Keep in mind, too, that everyone experiences some level of doubt when confronted with making an important decision. It's natural to feel apprehensive; feeling this way shows that you care and that you're probably not the sort of person who would make a rash decision in the first place.

There's an advantage to pushing yourself beyond your comfort level. Making decisions and solving tough problems will empower you. Most employees enjoy the rewarding feeling they experience when they've made a challenging decision, even though the problem may have caused them some periods of emotional distress.

Lewis, Kim, and Mr. Avery decide that the best solution is a variation of what Kim said about "different kinds of hammers." They'll increase the selection of certain items—such as hammers—and specialize in tools.

Although the team at Avery's is not completely sure that they've made the best decision, they know that they've weighed the evidence carefully. Now they're ready to move on to the next step of the problem-solving process.

Step 5. Implement the Solution

You may need to explain your solution to coworkers in order to put it into action. Identify the exact steps you need to follow and prioritize them. Following the chain of command, obtain the necessary permission and move ahead.

Covering the Bases Prioritizing your steps and communicating your plan to others are keys to making a solution work. *What do you think are the advantages of presenting all the steps of a plan at a group meeting?*

Mr. Avery takes action. He stops carrying certain items, such as house paint, to make room for a greater selection of tools. He orders and stocks the new items, sets up new displays, and advertises in the local newspaper.

Step 6. Evaluate the Results

To evaluate a solution, look at both its benefits and its drawbacks. Be as objective in evaluating a solution as you were in identifying the problem. If your solution is working, you should be able to cite benefits for yourself, your team or department, and your customers or clients.

If the solution has drawbacks or if it creates new problems, identify them and correct them as well. On-the-job problem solving is a continuous process.

Finally, ask yourself what you learned. An old saying holds true: "The only really bad decisions are the ones you don't learn from." Apply what you learn to new situations to prevent similar problems from happening again.

Online Travel Plans

You and your boss are going on a business trip next week. She has asked you to make the travel arrangements.

Connect
- Choose a city in another state as your destination. Visit travel and airline Web sites to research flights leaving from your city on Tuesday morning and returning Friday afternoon. Compare flight times and airfare, and decide which flights would be the best options.
- List the flights you chose, and write a one-paragraph summary explaining how you reached this decision.

At Avery's, the greatest drawback is eliminating house paint—a moneymaker—to make room for new tools. However, tool sales are increasing dramatically, so the benefits outweigh the drawbacks, as customers are impressed with the new selection and spend more money.

SECTION 16.2 REVIEW

✔ Key Concept Checkpoint

Comprehension

1. In your own words, describe the six basic steps of problem solving.
2. In an on-the-job situation, how can you identify good sources of information?
3. Why is creating alternative solutions better than relying on only one solution?

4. What do you think are the advantages of group problem solving?
5. Describe how you and another person solved a similar problem, and compare the consequences of each solution.

Critical Thinking

6. How can your personality affect your problem-solving and decision-making skills?

KEY TERMS
resources (p. 317)
criteria (p. 318)
consequence (p. 319)
procrastinate (p. 321)
prioritize (p. 321)

SECTION 16.1

- The seven steps in the decision-making process are to define your needs or wants, analyze your resources, identify your choices, gather information, evaluate your choices, make a decision, and plan how to reach your goal. (p. 316)

- To determine which decisions are yours to make, follow the chain of command, and know your responsibilities. (p. 317)

- Use criteria for comparing and evaluating possible choices. (p. 318)

- If you need additional information, be sure to get it. (p. 319)

- Evaluate the possible consequences of alternative decisions. (pp. 319–321)

- When you're ready to decide, don't procrastinate. (p. 321)

- Prioritize tasks to be performed in order to create a plan of action. (pp. 321–322)

KEY TERMS
brainstorm (p. 326)
analogy (p. 328)
assumptions (p. 328)

SECTION 16.2

- The six basic steps in problem solving are to identify and clarify the problem, generate alternative solutions, evaluate probable consequences, decide on the best solution, implement the solution, and evaluate the results. (p. 324)

- Gather and evaluate information, distinguishing between reliable and unreliable sources. (pp. 325–326)

- Generate alternative solutions with creative thinking strategies such as brainstorming, clustering, modeling, and using analogies. (pp. 326–328)

- Evaluate consequences of solutions by judging how well they meet long-term and short-term goals. (p. 328)

- Choose the best solution under the circumstances, and prioritize the steps needed to implement it. (pp. 329–330)

- Be objective in evaluating benefits and drawbacks of a solution. (p. 330)

Reviewing Key Terms

1. Write a description of one typical day at a job of your choice. Use the following key terms in your description.
   - resources
   - criteria
   - consequence
   - procrastinate
   - brainstorm
   - analogy
   - assumptions
   - prioritize

Recalling Key Concepts

Determine whether each statement is true or false. Rewrite any false statements to make them true.

2. The final step in the decision-making process is to evaluate your choices.

3. A criterion is a standard of judgment.

4. The first step to solving a problem is to consider analogies.

5. Brainstorming to generate alternative solutions can only be done alone.

6. Evaluating a solution objectively means taking your personal feelings into consideration.

Prolem Solving

7. Most organizations have a chain of command—a system of authority and responsibility. Describe the chain of command in one of the following: your school system, a professional sports team, your state government.

8. Explain in your own words what the following statement says about procrastination: Don't put off until tomorrow what you can do today.

9. Identify a job or work-related goal, such as repairing a bicycle, or building a house. Prioritize at least five tasks that would lead to that goal.

10. If you were trying to solve a problem, how would you separate useful, relevant information from distracting, irrelevant information?

11. Identify a serious world problem, such as poverty or war. Brainstorm at least three creative solutions to the problem—no matter how unusual or "crazy."

Work-Based Learning

Basic Skills Writing/Speaking

12. Choose a problem facing your school or community, and present a solution to the class. Use a written form—such as an advertisement, poster, or song lyric—to accompany your spoken presentation.

Information Acquire and Evaluate Information

13. Imagine that you plan to open an ice-cream shop, video arcade, or other business in your community. Create a questionnaire designed to gather the information you need about the products and services that would attract your classmates. Make your questions as specific as possible, and distribute the questionnaire to at least 20 students. Evaluate the responses, and write a report describing how your shop will meet customers' demands.

School-Based Learning

Human Relations **Boost Morale**

14. In most jobs, productivity increases when morale is high. Workers who feel good about themselves and their work usually perform well. In a group of three, choose a type of company, identify a morale problem, and brainstorm at least five possible solutions. Then evaluate the possible solutions by asking yourself what their practical consequences are. Finally, decide on one solution, and create a presentation in which you cite the benefits of that solution.

Language Arts **Analyze a Character's Actions**

15. Choose a short story, novel, movie, or television show in which a character makes a job-related decision or solves a problem at work. Apply the steps of decision making or problem solving to the character's actions. Then explain whether you think the character should have arrived at a different decision or solution and why.

Role Play

16. Brainstorm Fundraising Ideas

Situation Your soccer team has been invited to play in a week-long tournament in Europe. You and your teammates really want to go on the trip; however, your school doesn't have enough money. Your principal says that the team will have to raise all of the funds necessary to finance the trip. Your coach has estimated that the team will need about $25,000 to pay for travel expenses, accommodations, and tournament registration. The team has only six months to raise the money.

Activity In groups of four, brainstorm to create an extensive list of fundraising ideas to present to the principal. Then choose the best ideas, and design a plan for raising the necessary amount of money. When you've finished, present your ideas to the class.

Evaluation You will be evaluated based on how well you meet the following performance indicators:
- Conduct a productive brainstorming session
- Choose realistic and creative ideas to formulate a fundraising plan
- Present your plan effectively

*inter*NET CONNECTION

17. Assess Critical Thinking Skills

Many psychologists have designed tests to measure critical thinking skills. Do research to locate examples of such tests. Take one of the tests that you find, and contemplate your results. In your journal, record your strengths and weaknesses in terms of critical thinking.

Connect On the Internet, search for Web sites that suggest methods for improving critical thinking skills. Pay special attention to any advice that addresses your weaknesses. Summarize the advice you find and present it in an essay.

Chapter 17

Technology in the Workplace

Section 17.1
Changing Technology in Everyday Living

Section 17.2
Computer Software and Its Applications

CHAPTER OBJECTIVES

After completing this chapter, you will be able to

- Explain how technological advancements transform the workplace.

- Describe ways workers can become technologically literate.

- Explain how businesses use the Internet and various programs such as databases, spreadsheets, and desktop publishing.

- Identify basic copyright law protections.

JOURNAL

Personal Career Plan

Talk with an older adult about how computers and their uses have changed during that person's lifetime. Then think about further changes that may occur during your lifetime. Write a journal entry discussing your findings and ideas.

Personal Career Project

Select one work activity involving computers that appeals to you. In a career reference book, find a job related to this area of interest. In a brief essay, explain your interest and the job you have chosen, describing potential job opportunities.

Changing Technology in Everyday Living

Can you imagine a world not linked by telephone lines and satellite communications? Can you picture schools without computers or business offices without fax machines? You probably can't. Computer technology has become a part of everyday life.

People use a computer when they get money from an automated teller machine (ATM). At the supermarket and the department store, bar codes on purchases are computer-scanned. At school, you may use computers for doing research or writing and revising reports. You can count on the fact that no matter where you choose to work, you will use some type of computer technology in your job.

Technological Change and the Workplace

Technological change isn't new. Technology has been advancing for thousands of years, from simple stone tools to the waterwheel, to the printing press, and to the automobile. The difference today is in the pace of change. Technology seems to be advancing at ever greater speed.

In just a couple of decades, businesses large and small have come to depend on computers and fax machines. Today more companies use devices such as cellular phones, voice mail, electronic schedules, and document scanners. Many experts expect this trend toward greater use of technology to continue. How will this trend affect the workplace—and you?

High-tech Computers are used extensively in engineering. *How might computer simulations be used in designing new automobiles or aircraft?*

A High-Tech Global Village

One effect of changing technology is the globalization of the workplace. **Globalization** refers to the establishment of worldwide communication links between people and groups. These links are made possible through modern technology. Globalization is at work when a business owner in Chicago, Illinois, instantly communicates an investment decision to her partner in Sydney, Australia.

Globalization is at work when the two individuals meet through teleconferencing to discuss that decision. **Teleconferencing** involves simultaneous discussion among people in different locations, by electronic means. Teleconferencing is faster and less expensive than setting up a face-to-face meeting.

The move toward globalization has greatly affected the job market in the U.S. Now that employees can work effectively from nearly any location in the world, an increasing number of large corporations have decided to close American headquarters and move facilities to foreign countries. Such corporations often choose to set up offices in developing countries. The cost of overhead and labor is significantly lower in such countries, and workers are eager to prosper from the new opportunities afforded by globalization.

When an employer can choose from a wide pool of job applicants in countries across the globe, competition for jobs increases. Today's worker must have stronger technological and basic skills to secure top employment opportunities.

Globalization doesn't just impact the job market. This trend is already affecting the world-view of millions of people.

Through technology, the world becomes smaller—a global village. In the workplace, globalization means that you will have contact with people who are living in other cultures. You will need to know and understand what happens in other parts of the world. Those events may directly affect you and your workplace.

New Ways to Work

Technology has also brought about other changes in the workplace, redefining what it means to be an employee, and even what "office" means.

- *Workers are redefining their ties to employers.* In the past, many workers spent their entire career working for just one or two employers. Today's information culture, however, has caused a dramatic shift in the way the people view the employer-employee relationship. For example, many companies now choose to hire workers on a temporary or contractual basis. This trend allows workers to constantly update and reapply their job skills in new situations, while companies are able to periodically adjust their workforce to accommodate varying workloads.

- *Businesses are moving toward a "distributed" workforce.* In other words, employees no longer work just at a company's place of business.

Laptop Computers Business travelers often use laptop computers to make the most of their travel time. *How else might laptops be used in today's workplace?*

Instead, they are distributed, or spread about, in many places. Many employees, for example, work at home.

Chapter 1 introduced you to the concept of telecommuting. During the year 2000, some 21 million people telecommuted. Millions more workers are expected to add to this number, working from home, foreign offices, and even vacation destinations.

The smaller, briefcase-size **laptop** computer is a major contributor to this new workforce trend. Laptops enable workers to take their offices with them when they travel. Thanks to laptop computers, cellular phones, and other technology such as personal digital assistants that provide limited Internet and e-mail access, the workforce will continue to distribute itself over wide geographic areas.

- *Companies will need more "knowledge workers."* In the next decade, an emerging group of workers will be "knowledge workers." These workers will not produce products but will manage information. They will be responsible for finding, organizing, and delivering data. Today's medical technologists and computer installers are knowledge workers. Think about common computer programs in use today. (You will read about them in Section 17.2.) These programs transformed many office jobs.

To succeed and meet the needs of the progressive workforce, nearly all employ-

Knowledge Workers Laboratory technicians are knowledge workers. *What skills would be especially valuable for someone who wants to be a lab technician?*

ees will need to participate in ongoing education throughout their careers. Right now, you can take action to ensure that you're one of the workers who moves forward with the technological advances our society is expected to enjoy.

To further understand the constantly changing nature of technology, develop a timeline covering the last ten years depicting change in a selected career choice.

Technological Literacy

How can you prepare for the technological workplace? First, you need to be comfortable with computer technology. Important skills to master include the following:

- using computers to process information,
- selecting technology,
- applying technology to task, and
- maintaining and troubleshooting technology.

All of these skills are a part of *technological literacy*, which is knowing about and being able to use technology effectively. Technologically literate people understand the nature and role of technology as well as how technological systems are designed, used, and controlled. They also are able to value the benefits and assess the risks associated with technology and are able to respond rationally to ethical dilemmas caused by technology. What skills will you need in a high-tech workplace? *Figure 17.1* gives a few suggestions.

FIGURE 17.1 **Skills for a Technological Workplace** Changes in technology often require new workplace skills. Skills that have become essential in the workplace are communication, reasoning, creative thinking, and decision making.

A **Communication** All workers, especially managers, need specialized communication skills. Communicating by electronic means does not provide the same type of feedback that is available in face-to-face meetings. New skills are needed to make communication effective.

B **Reasoning and Creative Thinking** Because electronic communication is so rapid, people need to respond more swiftly to decisions and events. Reasoning and creative thinking have become increasingly important.

C **Decision Making** Decision making is becoming more important in the 21st century workplace. More people are participating in the decision-making process due to electronic bulletin boards, intra-office computer networks, and e-mail. Managers are faced with the extra challenge of managing this greater flow of ideas.

New Skills for a New Workplace

Technological literacy is basic to workplace success. Fortunately, you probably already know quite a lot about computers. Continue to build your skills, however. At your job, don't just learn enough of a program to get by. Read books or take courses. Ask questions to learn more about equipment you are using. Keep up-to-date with the latest workplace technology. The more you know, the more valuable you will be to your company.

Marissa Kovak, an office manager for a construction company, was asked to provide monthly project status reports in memo form. She took the assignment a step further and learned how to link her memos to detailed budget tables kept for all projects. Her method saved a time-consuming updating step. When Marissa showed her discovery to her boss, he was grateful enough to offer Marissa a bonus—and eventually a promotion.

CAREER CHECKLIST

Using Technology in the Workplace...

✔ Don't be afraid of the latest technological equipment.

✔ Participate in training sessions or ask for guidance when learning a new program or system.

✔ Ask for assistance when equipment is not working properly—don't try to fix it yourself.

✔ Learn your company's policy on using technological equipment for personal matters.

✔ Always look for new opportunities to update your technological skills.

SECTION 17.1 REVIEW

Key Concept Checkpoint

Comprehension

1. How could globalization create a more diverse workplace?

2. What can you do now while in school to increase your technological literacy?

Critical Thinking

3. What are some possible negative consequences of globalization?

CAREER FOCUS

CAREER FACTS

Education or Training A bachelor's degree in computer or electrical engineering, computer science, or information science is necessary.

Aptitudes, Abilities, and Skills Strong knowledge of computer programs and systems, good problem-solving skills, ability to work under pressure, ability to think logically, and good interpersonal skills are all important.

Career Outlook Employment is expected to grow much faster than average.

Career Path Computer engineers may move into project management or leadership positions or gain certification in another area of technology.

What is your key to success?

"My key to success is not to get stressed out and overloaded. I focus on the most important task at hand and prioritize problems. Most importantly, I try to be friendly and personable with everyone I deal with—although computers may seem simple, many people do not feel as comfortable solving technological problems as I do."

What kind of training did you have?

"My training started when I got my first computer at 14 years old. I wanted to understand how things worked and continuously asked questions of both teachers and other kids who had computers. After high school, I went to a 14-week evening course for my A+ and MCSE certifications. I am planning to go back to college to get my degree soon."

What do you like most about your job?

"I enjoy the feeling of accomplishment that comes from completing a project and solving problems. I am never bored at work—there is always something new and exciting to learn. I also love that I don't sit in a cubicle all day—I am constantly talking with coworkers and meeting new people."

What kind of training would you recommend for students?

"I recommend a bachelor's degree in computer science as well as current industry certifications in specific programs published by Microsoft and Cisco Systems. Students also should be familiar with the World Wide Web."

> **Critical Thinking** Why do you think that employment for systems engineers is expected to grow faster than average?

Computer Software and Its Applications

WHAT YOU'LL LEARN

- The uses of common computer programs used in the business world
- How businesses use the Internet
- Basic copyright law protections

WHY IT'S IMPORTANT

Knowledge of the uses of common business technology will help you succeed at work.

KEY TERMS

- **word processing**
- **presentation software**
- **database**
- **spreadsheet**
- **desktop publishing**
- **copyright**

It's easy to think that computers are limitless tools. However, they're only as helpful as the software they run and the software you know how to use. Today, software packages exist to help you do everything from creating professional documents to creating music videos. Learning about the right software will keep you marketable in your chosen field.

Using Computer Software

There are many different types of business software. Types of software commonly used in business include word processing, presentation software, databases, spreadsheets, and desktop publishing programs.

Word-Procesing Software

Using any software that creates text-based documents is called **word processing**. Word processing software allows you to easily add, move, and format text, as well as check spelling and grammar.

Presentation Software

Presentation software allows you to combine visual aids, outlines, graphics, statistics, and data in an interactive slide show. Your slide show can be presented directly on your computer, or projected onto a wall or screen. Presentation software also enables you to create slides that feature links to relevant Web sites.

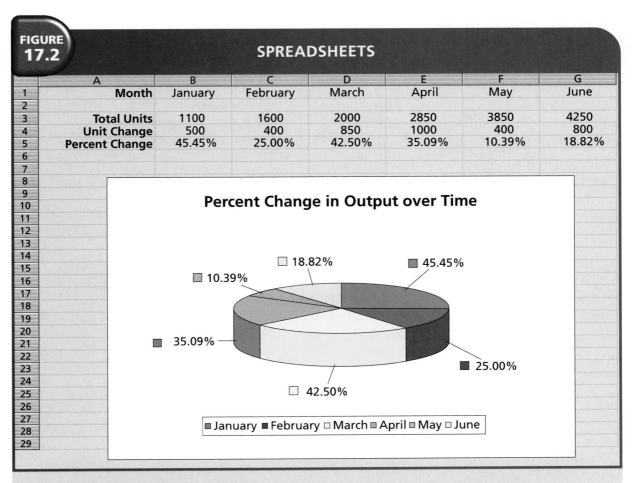

FIGURE 17.2 — SPREADSHEETS

	A	B	C	D	E	F	G
1	Month	January	February	March	April	May	June
2							
3	Total Units	1100	1600	2000	2850	3850	4250
4	Unit Change	500	400	850	1000	400	800
5	Percent Change	45.45%	25.00%	42.50%	35.09%	10.39%	18.82%

Percent Change in Output over Time

- 18.82%
- 10.39%
- 45.45%
- 35.09%
- 25.00%
- 42.50%

■ January ■ February □ March ■ April ■ May □ June

▲ **Facts and Figures** Spreadsheets are useful for accounting, budgeting, and scheduling. Each box on the spreadsheet is called a cell. Changing a number in one cell automatically causes adjustments in other cells. *How might this be used for making up or changing a schedule?*

Database Programs

Organizing business records is made easy with database programs. In a **database**, information is stored in a number of different formats, or tables. The program allows you to search through, sort, and recombine the stored data. A retail store owner, for example, may use a database program to record day-to-day inventory and sales information. Data can be recombined, however, to produce a sales report. Data might also be sorted to show fastest- or slowest-selling items.

Spreadsheet Programs

Data can be viewed and manipulated with a **spreadsheet** (see Figure 17.2). This is a computer program that arranges or "spreads" data, usually numbers, into rows and columns. Spreadsheet programs also perform calculations. Businesspeople can try various calculations to see what would happen if different business decisions were made. Calculations help them make decisions. Spreadsheets are useful for organizing data, making graphs, charts and tables, and doing complex calculations.

Desktop Publishing

Many people now have their own publishing facilities—on their desks. This is the origin of the term *desktop publishing*. **Desktop publishing** involves using computers and special software to create documents that look as if they were printed by professional printers. You can produce just about anything using desktop publishing, including reports, brochures, newsletters, invitations, logos, business cards, greeting cards, and calendars.

Desktop publishing technology enables you to scan and manipulate photos, experiment with different fonts, and much more. There are many different desktop publishing programs on the market, and you can take classes or read books on how to use most of this software. Before designing a product that you plan to use in a professional setting, it's a good idea to seek some training. Some novice designers tend to go overboard when creating their first pieces, using too many fonts, colors, or graphics.

Despite the pitfalls of desktop publishing, many business owners still prefer to design their own promotional materials. Doing so saves time and money, and provides greater control over the finished product.

inter**NET** CONNECTION

Career in Graphic Design
You would like to enhance your desktop publishing skills and eventually become a graphic designer. Besides learning new software programs at your job, you would like to earn a degree in graphic design.

Connect
- Perform an Internet search for colleges in your area that offer degrees or concentrations in graphic design.
- Choose one college, and write a short description of the major. List some of the courses offered that interest you.

Desktop Publishing Desktop publishing is especially useful for people who are in business for themselves. *Why do you think this is true?*

Maintenance and Troubleshooting

Have you ever heard of Murphy's Law? Basically, it says that if something can go wrong, it will. Here's a positive twist to Murphy's Law: If you are prepared for something to go wrong, you may be able to prevent it. The following tips will help you maintain and troubleshoot software at work.

- Attend training sessions and workshops whenever possible.
- Read operating manuals.
- Use the program's "Help" feature.
- Pay attention to what the machine is telling you. Copiers and fax machines, for example, often have a display that flashes a numerical code to indicate a specific problem.
- Know whom to call for help. Most commercial software programs have telephone help lines.
- Save your work frequently. Use the computer's autosave features, but don't rely on them.

Creative BUSINESS PRACTICES

Krispy Kreme Doughnut Corporation
E-training

When Winston-Salem, North Carolina-based Krispy Kreme Doughnut Corporation decided to expand, the company had to make sure that its new managers were trained quickly and consistently. Because many of the new hires were thousands of miles away, Krispy Kreme needed to adopt a portable training program.

Krispy Kreme hired a local technology firm to develop an e-training program. The program's objective is to teach managers how to make doughnuts the Krispy Kreme way and to familiarize them with the company's corporate culture.

The program uses interactive technology to cover Krispy Kreme cultural lessons, such as where to place its different types of doughnuts in the display case.

Krispy Kreme's e-training program launched on the company's intranet and later expanded to the Internet. Krispy Kreme headquarters is also connected to the program so it can track a manager's progress and keep the training updated.

Critical Thinking

What can employers do to complement e-training?

Link and Learn

To read more about Krispy Kreme doughnuts, visit the company's Web site via the link on the *Succeeding in the World of Work* Web site at **www.careers.glencoe.com.**

FIGURE 17.3

INTERNET TERMINOLOGY

Browser	The program you use to visit sites on the Internet
Download	Transfer a file from an Internet site to your computer's hard drive
Upload	Transfer a file from your computer's hard drive onto the Internet
FAQ	Abbreviation for Frequently Asked Questions; a document that displays answers to common questions about a particular topic
Freeware	Software provided by its creator at no charge
Hyperlink	A highlighted word, phrase, or image in a document; by clicking on it you can jump to a document about that subject
Search Engine	Software that finds and retrieves data on the Internet
Shareware	Software you may download free to test; if you decide to use it, you must send payment to the creator or vendor
Cookies	Files stored on your hard drive by your Web browser that hold information about your browsing habits, such as what sites you have visited, which newsgroups you have read, etc.
Site	A location on the Internet
URL	Abbreviation for Uniform Resource Locator; an Internet address
IP Address	A unique number that every computer has that allows a particular computer to be identified over the Internet
Domain	The Internet is divided into domains, including .com (business), .org (organization, nonprofit), .edu (educational), and others.
Domain Name	The name of a Web site, such as Yahoo!, that acts in place of its actual name, which is a numbered IP address

▲ **Know the Lingo** This Internet terminology is important for new users to know. *What would you look at first on a site if you wanted to know more about it?*

The Internet

You can hardly turn on the television or look through a magazine today without encountering a reference to the Internet. The Internet, which millions of people navigate, is a vast network of computer networks. In reality, however, the Internet is people, their computers, the connections between them, and the software used to run the computers. **Figure 17.3** provides a list of Internet terms and their definitions.

Uses of the Internet

The popularity of the Internet has increased dramatically in recent years. Internet use in the early 2000s is increasing at a pace similar to that of television 50 years ago. In 2000, about 100 million computers were connected to the Internet, and there were about 300 million users. The number continues to grow about 40 to 50 percent each year. As it exists today, the Internet has become a business tool, an advertising medium, a distribution channel, a source of entertainment, and a "virtual" meeting place for people with similar interests. Businesses use the Internet in a variety of ways:

- *To communicate* The Internet provides a low-cost, speedy alternative to faxing lengthy documents. The Internet has also reduced the amount of money many companies spend on mail services.

- *To advertise* Many companies take advantage of the worldwide audience that is at their disposal via the Internet. They advertise their products and services by maintaining their own Web sites and by purchasing advertisements on other sites.

- *To provide information and assistance to customers* An increasing number of companies provide customer service to patrons by way of the Internet. For instance, clients of many investment firms can check the status of their mutual fund accounts by entering their account information on specially designed Web sites.

- *To conduct research* The endless amount of information available on the Internet enables workers to conduct extensive research without leaving their workstations.

- *To recruit new employees* Employers often forego placing ads in newspapers in favor of posting job openings on their own Web site or on popular career Web sites. In doing so, companies are able to gather résumés quickly and efficiently via e-mail. E-mail also allows human resources professionals to communicate easily with job candidates.

E-Commerce

The growing popularity of the Internet has also fueled the development of e-commerce. **E-commerce**, also known as e-business, is the buying and selling of goods and services on the Internet, especially the World Wide Web.

Many traditional businesses sell goods and services on the Internet, but the 1990s also saw an explosion in businesses that exist solely on the World Wide Web. These "dot-com" businesses have no "brick and mortar" stores. Many of these Internet-only businesses failed to become profitable and went out of business within a few years.

Even with the number of business failures on the Internet, e-commerce remains an important source of revenue for many companies. Virtually every kind of good and service is available for purchase online, from books and music, to stock trading and accounting services.

Legal and Ethical Technology Issues

In earlier chapters, you learned about ethical issues such as honesty and confidentiality. In business, one form of honesty involves giving credit to others when you make use of something they have created. This applies whether you are using an article from a magazine or a file you've downloaded from the Internet. Newer forms of technology don't change basic ethics.

Copyright law has been developed to help people protect what they create. **Copyright** is the legal right of authors or other creators of works to control the reproduction and use of their works. Permission is usually required to use copyrighted material. Works covered by copyright law include:

- literary and dramatic works, such as poetry, novels, short stories, and plays;
- computer software and databases;
- photographs, videos, and film;
- musical and artistic works; and
- recordings.

Copyright protection means that the copyright owner has the sole right to do the following, or to authorize others to do so:

- make copies,
- distribute copies for sale or lease,
- perform (as with a play) or display (as with a movie or photo), and
- prepare translations or adaptations.

Copyright law protects all written works, whether or not they have been formally published. A file from the Internet and even information you've created on your computer is protected. It is ethical to give credit to the source of any facts you use. Copying text or software that someone else wrote, without permission, is a violation of copyright law.

Get to know enough about copyright laws to protect yourself. There are many books and courses available on copyright protection. If you are not sure whether or not you need to ask permission, always do so—just to be safe.

SECTION 17.2 REVIEW

 Key Concept Checkpoint

Comprehension

1. Why do you think word processing has replaced typewriting in the workplace?
2. What do you think is one of the most important uses of the Internet for businesses? Explain your answer.
3. Do you think having copyright laws is important? Why or why not?

Critical Thinking

4. Does the Internet pose any disadvantages for businesses?

KEY TERMS

globalization (p. 337)
teleconferencing (p. 337)
laptop (p. 339)

SECTION 17.1

- Changes in every aspect of life have resulted from computer technology. Businesses are likely to continue to increase their use of technology. (p. 336)

- New technology has helped bring about globalization, or worldwide communication links. Teleconferencing is one example of globalization. (pp. 337–338)

- Computers and telecommuting technology are making today's workforce more distributed (rather than centralized). Knowledge workers, who find and process information, are becoming increasingly important. (pp. 338–339)

- Technological literacy involves knowing about and being able to use technology effectively. (pp. 340–341)

- Workers should learn as much as they can about the technology they are using. Technology requires new communication and decision-making skills as well as quicker response times. (pp. 340–342)

KEY TERMS

word processing (p. 344)
presentation
    software (p. 344)
database (p. 345)
spreadsheet (p. 345)
desktop publishing (p. 346)
e-commerce (p. 349)
copyright (p. 350)

SECTION 17.2

- Word processing software creates text-based documents easily. (p. 344)

- Presentation software creates computer "slide-shows" that can be projected at high resolution. (p. 344)

- Database programs store data and allow workers to sort and combine them in various forms. (p. 345)

- Spreadsheet programs allow data to be viewed and manipulated in a table format. (p. 345)

- Desktop publishing, which is the use of computers and special software for creating professional-looking documents, saves businesses and individuals time and money. (p. 346)

- Ways to prevent software problems include attending training sessions and workshops, reading operating manuals, and saving work frequently. (pp. 346–347)

- The Internet is a network of computer networks. For business, it offers low-cost, speedy communication and access to information, as well as e-commerce capabilities. (pp. 347–349)

- Copyright laws protect the interests of authors and other creators. (p. 350)

Reviewing Key Terms

1. Write a dialogue between two friends talking about technology in the workplace. Use the terms below.
   - globalization
   - teleconferencing
   - laptop
   - word processing
   - database
   - presentation software
   - spreadsheet
   - desktop publishing
   - copyright
   - e-commerce

Recalling Key Concepts

Determine whether each item below is true or false. Rewrite false statements to make them true.

2. Teleconferencing is not an example of globalization.

3. Technological literacy involves knowing about and using technology effectively.

4. Spreadsheet programs are designed to create, edit, and format text.

5. The Internet has few business uses.

6. Permission is usually required to use copyrighted material.

Problem Solving

7. Why would it be wise for you to learn computer skills before entering the workforce?

8. Does technology always make life easier and draw people together? Explain your answer.

9. What might be one advantage and one disadvantage of a distributed workforce?

10. Discuss at least two ways that using the Internet to locate information could save time and money.

Work-Based Learning

Personal Qualities Integrity/Honesty

11. A friend and coworker in your office is preparing to use her desktop-publishing capabilities to publish and distribute an essay about environmental hazards in industry. She plans to state that the work is her own. You know, however, that the essay appeared recently in a magazine. What should you say to your friend about copyright violation? Write a paragraph explaining and justifying your advice.

Technology Selecting Technology

12. Purchasing a computer can be challenging. How do you research models, prices, and features? What resources would you use to answer these questions?

School-Based Learning

Computer Science Write a Report

13. Charles has just begun working for a public relations company that does a lot of desktop publishing. His supervisor tells him that he will be expected to use a document scanner in his work. Do research to find out what a document scanner is and how it is used. Write a short report that would help Charles use this device.

Business and Office Education **Research Telecommuting**

14. You are employed by an advertising agency. Your firm needs to hire five temporary workers, but no office space is available. Your supervisor has asked you to research the advantages of having these workers telecommute. List the advantages to your company. Then suggest three ways to help the workers adjust to the agency.

Write a Job Forecast

15. Use labor market information, knowledge of technology, and societal and/or economic trends to write a forecast of a job profile for a career in your interest area ten years from now. Include a detailed list of your sources. Present your findings to your class and add your written profile to your personal career portfolio.

Role Play

16. Asking for Help

Situation You were recently hired to work as a marketing assistant at a large, busy corporation. Even though you were honest about your lack of technological expertise during the interview process, your supervisor has been assigning you tasks that are far beyond your skill level. You're afraid that you'll be perceived as incompetent if you speak up, but, at the same time, you feel overwhelmed by some of the assignments you've been given.

Activity Role-play a situation in which you express your concerns to your new supervisor. Carefully plan how you will present your side of the situation, and make sure to present a reasonable solution to the problem at hand.

Evaluation You will be evaluated based on how well you meet the following performance indicators:

- Present workplace problems in a mature, cooperative manner
- Pose reasonable solutions to improve your work situation

*inter*NET
CONNECTION

17. **Interview a Freelancer**
Arrange an interview with a person who works as a freelancer or contractor who telecommutes. Ask this person about advantages and disadvantages of this type of work. Share your findings with the class.

Connect Search the Internet for freelance or contractual job opportunities in a field that interests you. In your journal, record three jobs that you find especially appealing.

Chapter 18

Time and Information Management

Section 18.1
Using Time Effectively

Section 18.2
Organizing Your Work

CHAPTER OBJECTIVES

After completing this chapter, you will be able to

- Prepare a schedule that will enable you to accomplish your most important tasks.

- Employ common techniques to use time effectively.

- Organize your work area, paperwork, tasks, and computer files.

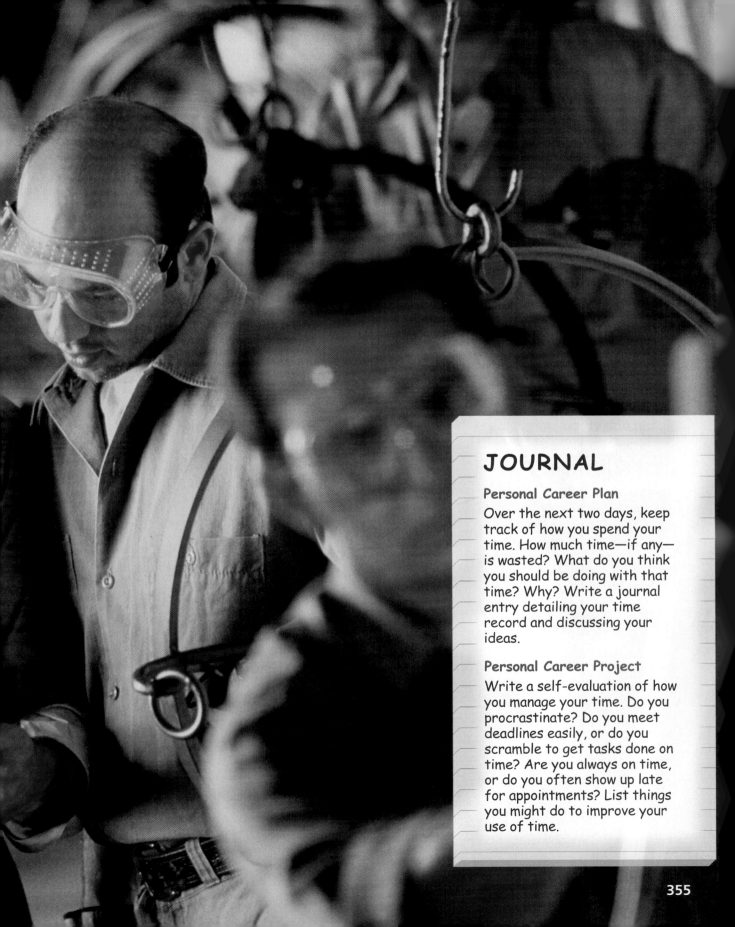

JOURNAL

Personal Career Plan

Over the next two days, keep track of how you spend your time. How much time—if any—is wasted? What do you think you should be doing with that time? Why? Write a journal entry detailing your time record and discussing your ideas.

Personal Career Project

Write a self-evaluation of how you manage your time. Do you procrastinate? Do you meet deadlines easily, or do you scramble to get tasks done on time? Are you always on time, or do you often show up late for appointments? List things you might do to improve your use of time.

Using Time Effectively

WHAT YOU'LL LEARN

- How to prepare a schedule that will help you accomplish your most important tasks
- Strategies and techniques for using time effectively

WHY IT'S IMPORTANT

To meet deadlines and manage your workload, you need to know how to prioritize tasks and budget your time accordingly.

KEY TERMS

- **time line**
- **schedule**
- **downtime**
- **delegating**

Does time sometimes get away from you? Have you found yourself staying up late to finish a report or to prepare for an exam? When you move into the work world, time can get away just as fast. The consequences, however, can be even worse. In school, it's usually just you who suffers when you don't manage your time well. On the job, other people suffer as well—your coworkers, supervisor, and employer.

So what's the solution? Stay on top of your work by using your self-management skills and learning how to manage your time.

To Do or Not to Do

Think of time management as making choices. You can spend your time doing this task or that task. You've got to decide which one to do *now*. If you have just a few choices, the decision may be easy. If you have lots of tasks, though, you may need some tools to help you make the right decisions. The following process can help you manage your time.

1. List all your projects, appointments, and other tasks.
2. Rate the tasks by their importance.
3. Break large, complex projects into small steps.
4. Estimate the time needed to complete each task.
5. Set up a schedule for your tasks.

Teamwork In the business world, your work will always be connected to the work done by others. *What would happen to your coworkers if your assignments were always late?*

Make a List

How can you make good choices? First, you have to know what your choices are, so make a task list. Write down every project, appointment, or meeting you have. List those you must do today plus all those you must complete in the days and weeks ahead. Include the meeting next Saturday, and the training session in December. Next to each task, write the date or time by which you must complete it.

What's Most Important?

If your task list is long, you may be thinking you'll never get it all done. It's okay if you don't. Successful time management doesn't mean always finding time to get *everything* done. It means getting the *most important things* done. You've got to prioritize, or decide the order of importance of completing all the different tasks.

Go back to your task list and analyze the tasks. Label them A, B, or C, according to order of importance. In deciding your priorities, consider the following:

- What were you hired to do? If you're a salesperson, your most important job is to sell. If you're a production worker, your most important job is to produce.

- Are you working alone or with others on a project? If you're working with others, you must coordinate your schedules to get the job done.

- What must you do to fulfill your obligations to the company? Are you expected to do paperwork or file reports? You must fulfill your obligations, even if they don't seem important to you.

Break Big Projects into Small Steps

Now take a second look at the major projects on your list. These large or long-term projects are often the most difficult to manage. People tend to focus on what has to be done today and tomorrow and to overlook things that are further off. Moreover, long-term projects are often complex and require more work. It's hard to get a grip on what needs to be done today on a long-term project to ensure that it will be completed two months from now.

How can you deal with major projects? The best way is to break them into manageable steps. Then you can treat each part as a separate task.

*inter*NET CONNECTION

Saving Time

You are a busy executive and have a problem managing your time wisely. Your tech-savvy friend tells you that you can save time by running errands using the Internet.

Connect

- Search the Internet for companies that offer services such as grocery shopping, banking, and selecting and buying gifts. See how many everyday tasks you can accomplish online without leaving your desk.
- Write a one-page report on how you can use the Internet to better manage your time.

When Walter Sanchez became assistant manager in an auto parts store, he was given several new responsibilities. One task was to find three new employees. Sanchez broke the job down into the following steps:

1. Compose and place a classified ad in the newspaper.

2. Review job applications and choose candidates for interviews.

3. Schedule and conduct interviews.

4. Select the best candidates and schedule them for interviews with the store manager.

5. Meet with the manager to make hiring decisions.

This process of identifying the steps in a project is essential. You have to know what you're facing so you can know

Managing Responsibilities Walter Sanchez has three weeks to hire three new employees. *Why must Walter get started right away? What will happen if he puts the search off until the last week?*

how you're going to get it done. The skill of seeing things in the mind's eye will help you figure out the steps in a complex project. This is the skill of visualization. You'll use it to envision how to break down a project into manageable parts.

Estimate Time Needed to Do Tasks

You now know what jobs you have to do. How long will it take you to do each one?

- If you've done the job before, base your estimate on past experience.
- If the job is new to you, ask someone with experience how long it took him or her.
- If you've been assigned the job, ask your supervisor how long it should take.
- Be wary of underestimating how long a job will take.
- If a job depends on other people, allow for their time.

For large projects, such as Walter Sanchez's, you'll want to set deadlines for completing each step in the project. One way to figure out a timetable for long-term projects is to create a time line. A **time line** is a type of chart that shows the order in which events occur in time. It will help you visualize an entire project so that you can see when to work on each step.

Set Up a Schedule

Now it's time to pull all the steps in this process together. How? By making a schedule. A **schedule** is a list or chart showing when tasks must be completed. If

Time-Management Tools People choose different types of planners because they have different work needs, work habits, and lifestyles. *Compare the advantages and disadvantages of the planner shown here.*

a task must be completed today and you know that it will take an hour, write the time you'll start the task on your schedule. You will then know that an hour of time is set aside for one purpose, getting that task completed. Fill in your schedule hour by hour.

You now have a daily schedule that shows everything to be done today. Your daily schedule will be part of a long-term schedule that shows tasks well into the future. Many people use a calendar or day planner for scheduling. They can enter tasks on the schedule as soon as they know about them. That way, they always know what's coming up.

Here are some more suggestions for making up your schedule:

- Think about your work habits. Are you a morning person or an afternoon person? Schedule difficult tasks for times when you perform at your peak.

- Consider color coding your schedule. Use different colors for deadlines, meetings, travel, and so on.

- Transfer your priorities from your task list to your schedule. If you run out of time, you can see at a glance which tasks you can postpone.

- Check off tasks as you complete them. The accumulating check marks will give you a boost.

Building a schedule is an ongoing process. *Figure 18.1* shows the process Walter Sanchez might follow to put together his schedule. Look at his task list and time line. How do they appear on his schedule?

Creating a Schedule Managing time effectively is a process involving several steps.

A **Make a Task List** Making a task list is the first step in using time wisely. List everything that's coming up, such as meetings, projects, and luncheons. Include personal and business appointments. That way you won't mistakenly schedule two things for the same time. Prioritize tasks by labeling them A, B, or C.

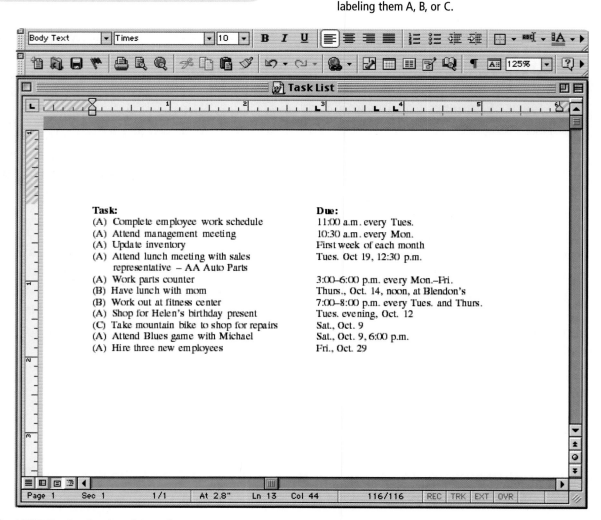

Body Text | Times | 10 | **B** *I* U

Task List

Page 1   Sec 1   1/1   At 2.8"   Ln 13   Col 44   116/116   REC TRK EXT OVR

Task:
(A) Complete employee work schedule
(A) Attend management meeting
(A) Update inventory
(A) Attend lunch meeting with sales
    representative – AA Auto Parts
(A) Work parts counter
(B) Have lunch with mom
(B) Work out at fitness center
(A) Shop for Helen's birthday present
(C) Take mountain bike to shop for repairs
(A) Attend Blues game with Michael
(A) Hire three new employees

Due:
11:00 a.m. every Tues.
10:30 a.m. every Mon.
First week of each month
Tues. Oct 19, 12:30 p.m.

3:00–6:00 p.m. every Mon.–Fri.
Thurs., Oct. 14, noon, at Blendon's
7:00–8:00 p.m. every Tues. and Thurs.
Tues. evening, Oct. 12
Sat., Oct. 9
Sat., Oct. 9, 6:00 p.m.
Fri., Oct. 29

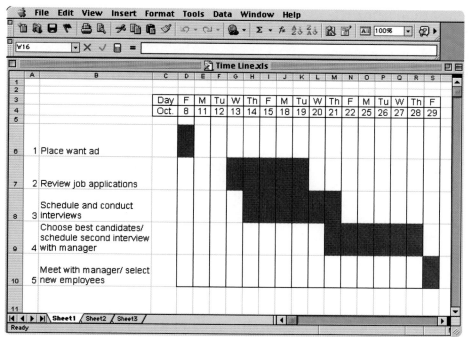

B Make a Time Line
A time line can help you visualize the stages in a complex or long-term project. It will show how one stage must be completed before the next begins. This will give you a better grasp of when parts of the project have to be completed. The time line will also show when stages of the project overlap. Reviewing the time line during the project will help keep you aware of your progress and short-term deadlines.

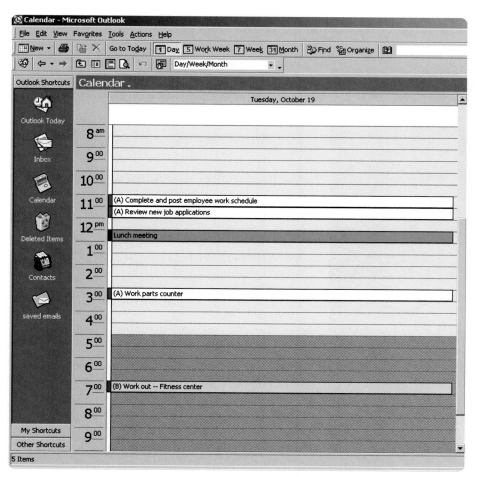

C Keep a Schedule
A calendar or day planner provides for a good schedule as long as there's room to write in all your tasks and appointments. Show the priorities from your task list on your schedule. You might want to color code tasks as well. You might write or highlight personal tasks in blue and meetings in red, for example.

A schedule is a helpful tool for managing your time. You must keep it current, however. Take a few minutes every morning to look at it, update it, and plan. As necessary, make a new task list and go through the scheduling process again.

Timely Tips

A schedule is one part of efficient time management. There's more you can do to use your time and other people's time wisely.

Using Your Time Wisely

Everyone has occasional periods when nothing is on his or her schedule. This is called **downtime**. Don't waste it! Downtime is a good time to get ahead or to improve your skills. You might read an

equipment service manual or learn a new computer program.

Avoid procrastination. As you read in Chapter 16, procrastination is the putting off of work you should be doing. If a job has to be done, do it.

Be flexible. Everything won't work out just as you plan it. The copier may break down, or a client may postpone an appointment. Shift gears and go on to something else on your schedule.

Don't let the telephone control your time. The checklist shown in *Figure 18.2* suggests how to make better use of the telephone.

Look for ways to combine tasks. For example, if you take public transportation to work, read while you're riding. If you drive to work, consider listening to instructional tapes.

Using Downtime Effectively Downtime isn't off time. These medical employees are using downtime to learn more about keeping accurate charts. *How will learning something new about your job help you better manage your time on the next project?*

Always be prepared to get work done. Carry a pen and paper with you all the time. You can write notes when stuck in traffic or waiting in line somewhere.

Using Other People's Time Wisely

When you work with other people, be aware of how you use their time. Your coworkers are probably busy and will find distractions stressful. If you're experiencing downtime, don't occupy your time by starting personal conversations with your colleagues. Doing so will only make your coworkers resent your intrusion. Furthermore, you probably don't appreciate distractions at times when you're especially busy.

If you must communicate with coworkers at busy times, keep your conversations focused. Limit your discussions to matters that are important and work-related. Before you speak with a busy colleague, write down the issues that you need to address so that you don't forget anything when you're talking.

If you need to update coworkers about a work-related matter, give them only the important information. Don't bother them with nonessential details. You may even want to send your coworkers e-mail to update them on projects or other matters.

Meetings are another way that many workers waste valuable time. When attending a meeting, be considerate. Don't try to start personal conversations, and don't ask individual questions that aren't relevant to the entire group. You can pose such questions on your own time.

Be especially mindful of your supervisor's time. When you are assigned a task, listen carefully to the details. Ask questions if you don't understand something. Then you won't have to go back later and interrupt your supervisor with more questions.

FIGURE 18.2 GETTING THE MOST FROM YOUR TELEPHONE

- Plan your use of the phone. Before calling, list questions you want answered. List information you want to pass along.

- Have any information you need to discuss in front of you.

- Set a time limit for your phone calls, and stick to business.

- Cluster your phone calls. Set aside one or two periods a day to call people. Limit phone calls at other times.

- Avoid phone tag when leaving voice mail or a message with a secretary or receptionist. Give a time when you'll call back.

- E-mail messages to people who are hard to reach.

- E-mail relevant information to people before calling. You'll save time explaining subjects you want to discuss.

▲ **Telephone Guidelines** The telephone can take a great deal of your time. This checklist can help you use the phone more efficiently. *How can you use the telephone to save time?*

Timesaving Strategies There's no reason to just sit while waiting for the bus. Get something done. The work you do may give you more time later for an activity you enjoy. *What kinds of work might you do while riding a bus or waiting in traffic?*

Give complete instructions when delegating work to others. **Delegating** means assigning tasks to other people. Make sure they understand what you're asking them to do. Take time to answer questions. How will spending more time answering questions initially save you time later?

SECTION 18.1 REVIEW

 Key Concept Checkpoint

Comprehension

1. How can a schedule help you use your time more efficiently?

2. Why is it important to use your coworkers' time wisely?

Critical Thinking

3. What can you do to overcome the urge to procrastinate?

CAREER FOCUS

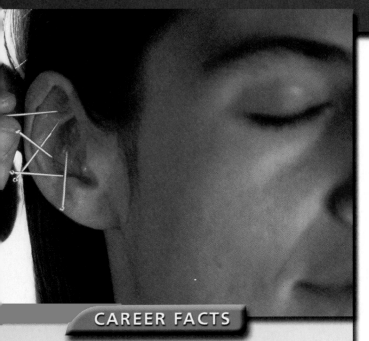

CAREER FACTS

Education or Training The National Certification Commission for Acupuncture and Oriental Medicine (NCCAOM) sets standards for licensing. There are schools around the world for the study of acupuncture.

Aptitudes, Abilities, and Skills A knowledge of Western medicine and biology is necessary, as well as good people skills, dexterity with needles, and good listening skills.

Career Outlook Employment for professionals in alternative medicine, such as chiropractors and acupuncturists, is expected to grow faster than average through 2008.

Career Path Doctors who practice alternative medicine may first work for an organization before going into private practice.

What is the key to your success?

"The key to my success is very simple—I truly enjoy what I do."

What does your job entail?

"I practice acupuncture, herbal medicine, and tui na (Chinese Massage). Followers of traditional Chinese medicine (TCM) believe that there are 14 channels of energy flowing through our bodies along specific paths. This energy is needed to breathe, feel, think, and move blood. Practitioners of TCM believe that when a person is sick, it is because there is an obstruction or deficiency of energy. Using acupuncture therapy, I insert small stainless steel needles into predefined points to release the obstruction or magnetically draw forth a new supply of energy from the body."

What skills are most important to you?

"The most important skills for any healthcare practitioner are the ability to listen to patients and to be sensitive to their needs."

What kind of training did you have?

"I have a bachelor's degree in sociology and a master's degree in education. I studied TCM first informally and then formally. I became a national board certified acupuncturist in 1992 and completed my postgraduate studies in Chinese herbal medicine in 1996."

What do you like most about your work?

"I enjoy the feeling of fulfillment I experience when I help patients heal."

> **Critical Thinking** Why do you think the job outlook for practitioners of alternative medicine is expected to increase through 2008?

Organizing Your Work

WHAT YOU'LL LEARN

- How to organize yourself and your tasks
- How to develop and maintain systems for organizing paperwork and computer files

WHY IT'S IMPORTANT

Strong organizational skills will enable you to manage your personal and professional life more effectively.

KEY TERMS

- **access**
- **directory**
- **subdirectories**

You've learned strategies for using your time more effectively. What else can you do to get your work done faster and better? First, you can organize the things around you in your work area. Second, you can organize the information you use to do your work.

Organizing Your Work Area

You may be very skilled at your job. However, if you can't quickly find the tools or materials you need to do your job, your skill won't matter. Think about your work area. Find a place for everything.

Everything in Its Place

The first rule for organizing a work area might be called the near-far rule. What things do you use most often? They should be near you. What things do you use less frequently? These things can be placed farther away.

Plumbers, for example, carry a toolbox with them when they make a house call. The toolbox contains the most frequently used tools of their trade. Plumbers keep these tools close at hand. Tools used less frequently are kept in the truck.

A second guideline is to put similar things together. Files, supplies, and tools used for one project or type of job should be kept together. Those used for another project or job might be kept in a separate area.

If you store things in boxes, drawers, or files, label them. You won't have to open every box to find the one item you need. If you have lots of boxes or files, alphabetize them, group them by content, or organize them in some other logical order.

Making Neatness Count

Did you ever hear the phrase "neatness counts"? Did you know that neatness also saves time? Take time occasionally to put your work area back in order. Return tools to their correct places. Straighten and re-organize your desk. Keeping things orderly will save you time later. You'll know where everything is.

Organizing Information

Do you have to handle lots of information? Then you've got to be able to organize it. Otherwise, it loses its usefulness. Think about a library. A good library contains vast amounts of information. It's only useful, however, if the information is organized so that you can **access**, or find and use it. Organizing and maintaining information is one key to success.

Is It Important?

The first step in managing information is to decide whether it is important. Ask yourself whether the information is something you need to know or act on. Is it information someone else needs? Is it something you may need to refer to later? If you answer no to these questions, your best management choice may be to discard it. Information you don't need blocks access to the information you do need.

If the information is necessary, try to do something with it the first time you look at it. If you put it in a *pending*, or holding file, you'll have to look at it again later. Then you will have spent time on it

FIGURE
18.3
MANAGING INFORMATION

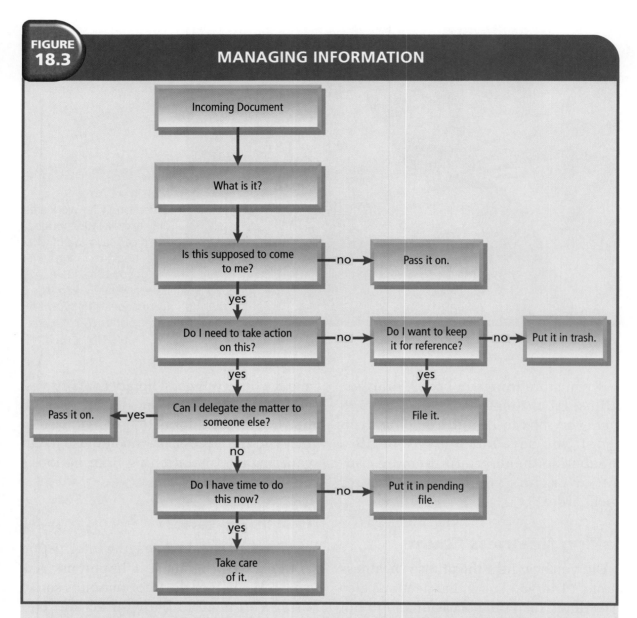

▲ **Putting Paper in Its Place** This chart shows the decision-making process used for incoming paperwork. *Would this process work for information received via e-mail or other electronic means? Why or why not?*

twice. ***Figure 18.3*** charts the basic decision-making process for dealing with information.

Paper Chase

If you think you'll need to refer back to a paper document later, file it. Put your

documents in file folders. Then group the folders in hanging files. These hints will help you set up a system:

- Categorize information. You might organize documents by customers, projects, or dates of receipt.

- Label each file and hanging folder.

- Avoid putting each document in a separate file. Group documents by type.

- Avoid massive files with many documents. Divide them by subtopics.

- Color-code folders or labels to help identify categories or subcategories. For example, green folders might indicate one project, blue another.

- File on a regular basis.

- Periodically sort through your files to see if there are any papers that you can discard. Saving unnecessary papers will only make it harder to stay organized.

- If you're wary of discarding files, ask if your office has a storage area where you can place older files.

- At the end of each day, try to leave your desk free of stray papers. Resolve to file all papers that you receive. Otherwise, it's easy to start accumulating large, disorderly stacks of paper.

- Whenever possible, try to store documents on your computer. Doing so will enable you to cut back on traditional filing. However, never file important documents on your computer without backing-up the files on disks.

Creative BUSINESS PRACTICES

Ernst & Young
Flexible Work Arrangements

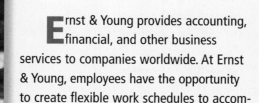

Ernst & Young provides accounting, financial, and other business services to companies worldwide. At Ernst & Young, employees have the opportunity to create flexible work schedules to accommodate their personal lives.

Ernst & Young employees can take advantage of flexible hours, reduced schedules, seasonal schedules, and telecommuting. Approximately 1,600 of Ernst & Young's 23,000 employees are in the flexible work program.

As long as they can make a solid case for joining the flextime program, all Ernst & Young employees are eligible to participate.

The company provides flextime guidelines in two databases that can be accessed by all employees. Potential flextimers can log on for help in planning how they will do their required work, handle customers, and collaborate with coworkers. Supervisors use the database to learn how to handle flextime's challenges and opportunities.

Critical Thinking

Do you think it is important for employers to try to accommodate an employee's personal life?

Link and Learn

For information about Ernst & Young's policies, visit their Web site via the link on the *Succeeding in the World of Work* Web site at **www.careers.glencoe.com**.

Managing Computer Information

If you look around most offices, you'll see desks covered with paper. Despite appearances, more and more information is entering offices as computer files and e-mail. Managing electronic information has become as great a challenge as managing paper documents.

Many of the rules for managing paper documents also apply to managing electronic files. Don't clutter your files with information you don't need. Make a separate **directory**, or computer file, for each category of information. A directory is like a filing cabinet that contains many files on a large topic, such as a project.

Don't let directories get too full; create new **subdirectories**. These are smaller groupings of files. For example, you may have a directory for XYZ Company. As business improves, you might create subdirectories for invoices, orders, letters, and so on.

Choose names for computer files carefully. Select logical, descriptive names, ones you'll remember six months from now. It's also helpful to keep a written record of file names.

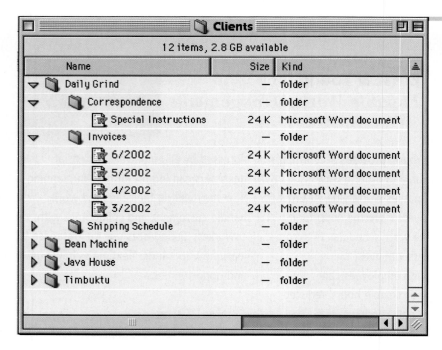

Keeping a Clutter-Free Computer Directories and subdirectories should be given logical, brief names. Use abbreviations that are easy to recognize. *What might you name a directory for Succeeding in the World of Work?*

SECTION 18.2 REVIEW

Key Concept Checkpoint

Comprehension

1. How can organizing your work space make you more efficient?

2. Why should you avoid creating very large files with many documents?

3. Why is it important to choose names for computer files carefully?

Critical Thinking

4. How can disorganization make your job more stressful?

KEY TERMS
time line (p. 359)
schedule (p. 359)
downtime (p. 362)
delegating (p. 364)

SECTION 18.1

- The effective use of time requires knowledge of the skill of self-management and competency in time management. (p. 356)

- Time management is a process of deciding how to use your time wisely. The first step is to identify all your tasks by making a task list. Then prioritize each task. (pp. 356–358)

- Manage long-term projects best by breaking them into smaller, more manageable parts. Then treat the parts as separate tasks. (pp. 358–359)

- Decide how long each task will take to complete. Make a time line to help you figure out how long larger projects will take. (p. 359)

- There are many forms for schedules. Choose the form that fits your style and individual needs. (pp. 359–362)

- Keep your schedule current. Review it daily. (p. 362)

- Make use of downtime, avoid procrastination, and be flexible when plans don't work out. Use the telephone wisely, and combine tasks. (pp. 362–363)

- Use other people's time wisely. Keep conversations brief, listen to assignments carefully, and give complete directions when delegating tasks. (pp. 363–364)

KEY TERMS
access (p. 367)
directory (p. 370)
subdirectories (p. 370)

SECTION 18.2

- Organizing your work area helps you work efficiently. (pp. 366–367)

- Organize information so that it is accessible. Discard information you do not and will not need. (pp. 367–368)

- File paper documents in file folders. Place the folders in hanging files. Categorize information. Avoid creating files with either too many or too few documents. Label files, and consider using color coding to identify information. (pp. 368–369)

- Many of the rules for managing paper documents also apply to managing computer information. (p. 370)

Reviewing Key Terms

1. Write one or two paragraphs explaining how you can better manage your time and information. Use each term below.
   - time line
   - schedule
   - downtime
   - delegating
   - access
   - directory
   - subdirectories

Recalling Key Concepts

Determine whether each statement is true or false. Rewrite any false statements to make them true.

2. A schedule should include only tasks of the highest priority.

3. A time line helps you visualize how the parts of a large project fit together.

4. If you organize your work space by the near-far rule, the materials you use most often will be within easy reach.

5. If you don't need the information in a document and won't need it in the future, you should file it.

6. When setting up computer files, create subdirectories to prevent directories from becoming too large.

Problem Solving

7. In managing your time, why should your emphasis be on getting the most important things done rather than on getting everything done?

8. How does breaking a large task into smaller parts help you manage the work?

9. Should you make a time line for every task? Why or why not?

10. How does a disorganized work area waste your time?

11. Is managing information a greater challenge if the information is on paper or in electronic files? Explain your answer.

Work-Based Learning

Thinking Skills Seeing Things in the Mind's Eye

12. You've been asked to plan your company's annual employee picnic. You must take care of all details. Break down the assignment into manageable parts. List the smaller tasks.

Information Organizing and Maintaining Information

13. Documents on the following topics have arrived on your desk: revised employee insurance policy, company holidays for 2002, winter hours for the child-care facility, vacation policy, flu shots covered under your health plan, how to file for health insurance coverage, New Year's Day work schedule, and child-care policy for children who are ill. Make a list to show how you would organize the topics in files and folders. Name each file and folder.

School-Based Learning

Social Studies Delegate Tasks

14. Jeffrey manages a small electronics store. He has three salespeople and an office assistant. The owner has come to town unexpectedly and has called an all-afternoon meeting. Jeffrey cannot finish the following tasks that remain on his schedule. What should he do about them?

Meet with distributor of new products—2:00 P.M.

Complete inventory of computer software.

Select items for next week's sale.

Read and deal with mail, e-mail, and faxes.

Lunch with sister at noon.

Train new salesperson in how to demonstrate camcorders.

Computer Science Research Software

15. Do research to learn about computer software that will create personal schedules. Compare and contrast the software available, and determine the pros and cons of each. Summarize your findings in a 250-word report.

Role Play

16. Maximize Productivity

Situation At work, you frequently communicate with business clients across the country. To save time and travel expenses, you often participate in conference calls. These calls are essential, but they consume a large part of your day. You need to make your conference calls more efficient so that you have more time to work on other tasks.

Activity Role-play a conference call in which you efficiently address a matter of concern with a business client. Make the conference call as productive as possible by using creative before-, during-, and after-strategies.

Evaluation You will be evaluated based on how well you meet the following performance indicators:

- Utilize creative and appropriate before-, during-, and after-strategies to make a conference call efficient
- Effectively and politely handle matters with client(s)
- Present a realistic, well-developed conference call

*inter*NET CONNECTION

17. Create a Schedule

Brainstorm to create a list of all of your obligations, social events, and school assignments for the next month. Record your schedule on a typical calendar. At the end of the month, decide whether your schedule was helpful.

Connect Based on your own needs and the schedule you've devised, choose an organizational tool, such as a day planner, that would help you manage your time. Conduct research on the Internet to find out the prices and options of this aid.

CAREER LAB
Real-World Workshop

Training to Use Technology in Your Field

✓ Overview

Technology plays an essential role in most fields. Even as a candidate for entry-level positions, you may need technological skills to enter your chosen career. You want to ensure that you have those skills. You're going to conduct research to find out what technology is used in your field and to assess the skills that you need to develop. Then you'll choose a software program or other technological resource and learn how to use it. You'll share your knowledge with the class by presenting a product you've designed using your new skills. You'll also present a brief report that summarizes how technology is used in your field.

✓ Assignment

Find out how technology is used in a career that interests you. Contact real-life employers and employees and consult the Internet and traditional library resources; this information will form the basis for your written report. Profile the software programs or other technological resources relevant to your career choice, and assess your knowledge of these tools. Choose one program or resource that you know little about and seek appropriate training. Then create a product using that technology.

✓ Tools/Resources

To complete this assignment, you'll need access to training materials and a computer program that is used in your field.

✓ Procedures

There are many ways to go about researching the technology that is used in your chosen career field. You can learn about a program, for example, by volunteering at a company or consulting training manuals. When you've developed solid skills in the program, create a product using it. For example, if you know little about databases, learn about a database program and then create your own database.

✓ Report

Your final project for this lab should include a typed two-page report explaining the technology used in your desired career and an original product that you have designed using that technology.

✓ Presentation and Evaluation

Your report will be evaluated based on

- Depth of research
- Presentation of report
- Grammar and mechanics

Your product will be evaluated based on

- Evidence of mastery of program
- Choice of technology
- Presentation of product
- Relevance of product to industry

✓ Personal Career Portfolio

Print out a copy of your report and place it in your personal career portfolio.

HELPFUL HINTS

Technology Tips

- When researching technology used in your desired field, use only the most current resources.
- When choosing a program, select a program that will likely be in use for some time.
- Consider your access to training and technology when choosing your program.

- If possible, design something that you can present to a prospective employer as part of a portfolio.
- When you've finished your project, identify other programs that you would like to learn. Set goals for learning how to use all of the technology relevant to your field.

Portfolio Project

Choosing Where to Live Where you choose to live requires a great deal of thought because it helps determine your lifestyle. Where would you like to live as an adult? Will you move to an area that boasts a large number of jobs in your chosen field? Do you think it's more important to live near friends and family members? List some possible cities or towns in which you would enjoy living. Conduct research to find out the pros and cons of each area. Write a two-page report explaining where you want to live as an adult, and why you have chosen this particular location.

CAREER LAB PREVIEW

Budgeting Time and Money in Your Career

As part of this unit, you'll estimate how you'll spend time and money during your adult life. You'll conduct research to determine the specifics of your monthly budget and plan how to live on an entry-level salary. You will also develop a plan for meeting work, family, and lifestyle demands. You'll present your plans to your classmates and write a report.

Economics and the Consumer

CHAPTER OBJECTIVES

After completing this chapter, you will be able to

- Define a free-enterprise system and identify producers and consumers.

- Describe the marketplace and explain why prices go up and down.

- Explain three factors to consider when measuring the economy's health.

- Identify ways to make wise shopping decisions.

- Describe common types of fraud, and identify ways to protect yourself as a consumer.

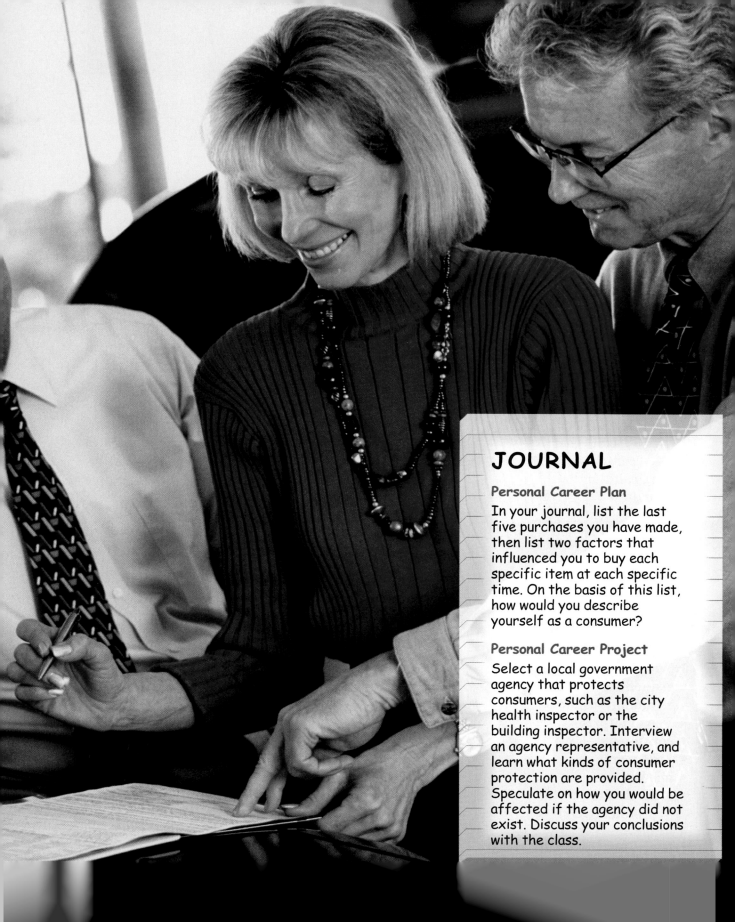

JOURNAL

Personal Career Plan

In your journal, list the last five purchases you have made, then list two factors that influenced you to buy each specific item at each specific time. On the basis of this list, how would you describe yourself as a consumer?

Personal Career Project

Select a local government agency that protects consumers, such as the city health inspector or the building inspector. Interview an agency representative, and learn what kinds of consumer protection are provided. Speculate on how you would be affected if the agency did not exist. Discuss your conclusions with the class.

Economics and the Consumer

WHAT YOU'LL LEARN

- How to define a free-enterprise system and identify producers and consumers
- Why prices go up and down, and what the marketplace is
- Three factors that are used to assess the health of the economy

WHY IT'S IMPORTANT

Understanding the U.S. economy will make you a savvy consumer and producer.

KEY TERMS

- economics
- economic system
- free enterprise
- consumers
- producers
- marketplace
- gross domestic product (GDP)
- inflation

You buy goods and services all the time. It may seem like a simple process, but is it? What do you know about why businesses make and sell the goods they do? How are prices set? What causes prices to drop, or rise? How does this system of buying and selling goods and services work? How does it affect you?

You'll find answers to these questions by studying **economics**, the field of study that tries to explain how people produce, distribute, and use goods and services. The way people participate in these activities depends on the economic system of the country where they live.

An **economic system** is a country's way of using resources to provide goods and services that its people want and need. *Producing* means creating goods or services. *Distributing* means making goods and services available—through selling or delivering, for example—to the people who need them. What kind of economic system does the United States have? What other economic systems are there in the international job market?

As you learn about how our economic system works, you will also learn why conditions change so rapidly. With a basic understanding of the system, you will be able to prepare yourself for the challenges such a system presents. You will also be able to compare and contrast employment opportunities of our free enterprise system with those of the international job market.

The Free-Enterprise System

The economic system used in the United States is known as the free-enterprise system. **Free enterprise** means that individuals or businesses may buy and sell and set prices with little government interference. The government does have a role in our economic system, however. Laws set safety standards, regulate some prices and wages, and protect **consumers**. These are the people who buy and use goods and services.

Producers and Consumers

The companies or individuals who make or provide goods and services are known as **producers.** If you make specialty T-shirts, you are a producer of goods. If you baby-sit, you are a producer of a service. Have you ever been a producer?

What happens once goods and services are produced? People or other businesses *consume,* or buy and use, them. The people who buy your T-shirts and the people for whom you baby-sit are consumers. You become a consumer when you buy lunch, have clothes cleaned, or ride the subway.

Changing Roles Most people are both consumers and producers, although usually not at the same time. *Who are the consumers in this photograph? Who are the producers? How do you know?*

Producers and consumers are like two sides of a coin. Although they're opposites, one can't exist without the other. **Figure 19.1** shows the flow of economic activity between producers and consumers. While you may be both a producer and a consumer, your goals are different in each role.

Producers try to make goods or provide services that consumers will buy. A producer's main purpose is to make a net profit. As you know, net profit is the money left after operating costs and the cost of the goods or services have been paid.

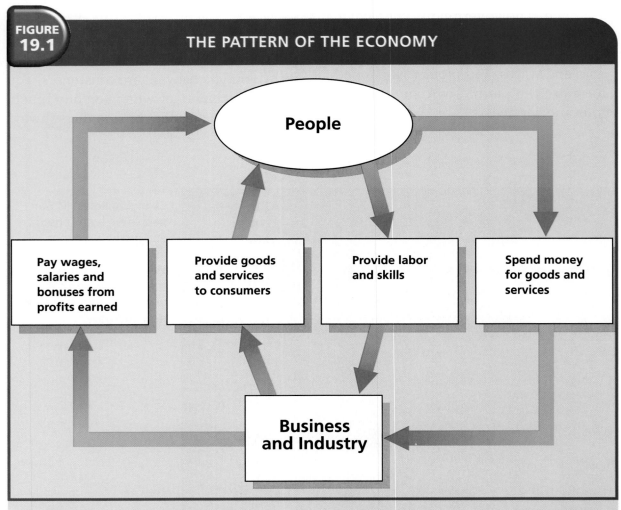

FIGURE
19.1

THE PATTERN OF THE ECONOMY

▲ **Free Enterprise** You are a participant in the free-enterprise system. You will work to help produce goods and services (if you don't already), and you consume goods and services. The outer arrows of this illustration show how consumer spending goes into businesses and comes back to you as a worker. The inner arrows show how your skills help produce goods and services, which consumers such as you need and want. *How does the freedom of choice of a free-enterprise system affect these arrows?*

Consumers try to get what they need and want within the limits of how much money they have. Consumers influence what is made by what they buy.

How do producers and consumers accomplish their aims? They go to the marketplace!

What Is the Marketplace?

The **marketplace** is where buying and selling occur. This term really covers the whole realm of trade and business. Sometimes the producer and consumer are actually in the same place, as when you get your hair cut. Producers and consumers can also be geographically far apart. For example, you might buy a computer that was produced in another country or buy a magazine that was published in another state.

To reach consumers and to promote buying, producers practice marketing. *Marketing* is the process of getting products to consumers. It includes packaging, shipping, advertising, and selling goods and services. Because our economy is based on buying and selling, our free-enterprise system is called a market system.

Price Fluctuations

Have you noticed how the prices of CDs, jeans, haircuts, and other goods and services keep changing? This is normal in a free-enterprise system. Why? Prices *fluctuate,* or go up and down, as a result of three main factors.

- *Supply and demand* Supply is the amount of goods and services available for sale. Demand is the amount of goods and services that consumers

Marketplace Diversity This photo shows a traditional vegetable market, but markets do not have to be physical locations. *What are some examples of the marketplace you've "visited" recently?*

want to buy. When supply is greater than demand, prices lower. When demand is greater than supply, prices rise.

- *Production costs* The more it costs to make a good or provide a service, the higher its price will be. Because businesses must make a profit, they must sell their goods or services for more than it costs to produce them.

- *Competition* When two similar products are offered for sale, they are in competition. When competition is great, prices tend to be lower. When there is little or no competition, prices are higher.

In addition to prices going up and down, the economy itself fluctuates. This movement from good times to bad and back to good is known as the *business cycle.* *Figure 19.2* on page 384 illustrates the four parts of this cycle.

FIGURE 19.2

The Business Cycle The economy normally goes up and down. However, no one can really be sure when each period of the business cycle will occur or how long it will last. For this reason, many economists prefer to talk about business fluctuations rather than the business cycle.

C **Depression** Depression is a long, deep recession. During a depression, consumer spending is very low, unemployment is very high, and production of goods and services goes down significantly. Poverty results, because so many people are out of work and cannot afford to buy food, clothing, or shelter. The Great Depression of the 1930s best illustrates this phase of the business cycle.

A **Prosperity** Prosperity is a period of economic growth and expansion. There is low unemployment, greater output of goods and services, and high consumer spending.

D **Recovery** Recovery is a period of renewed economic growth following a recession or depression. Recovery is characterized by less unemployment, more consumer spending, and moderate expansion by businesses. Periods of recovery differ in length and strength.

B **Recession** Recession is a period of economic slowdown. Unemployment begins to rise, fewer goods and services are produced, and consumer spending goes down. Recessions can be short or long.

Measuring the Economy

The condition of the economy can determine how much you make at a job and what you can afford to buy. Economic indicators measure the performance of the economy each year.

Gross Domestic Product

The total dollar value of all goods and services produced in the United States during a year is known as the **gross domestic product,** or **GDP.** This is the main indicator of the condition of the economy. It enables one to compare this year's economy with last year's.

Consumer Price Index

The consumer price index, or CPI, measures changes in the prices of consumer goods and services. It is based on a monthly survey conducted by the Bureau of Labor Statistics. The survey tracks prices for a specific group of household goods and services, including food, clothing, shelter, fuel, and medical services.

By showing increases or decreases in the cost of living, the CPI also measures inflation. **Inflation** occurs when the average prices of goods and services rise sharply. If prices rise sharply but your wages don't, you cannot buy as much as you used to.

Creative BUSINESS PRACTICES

Popeyes Chicken & Biscuits
Operating Overseas Restaurants from the U.S.

Popeyes Chicken & Biscuits restaurants are located in 21 countries around the world. The overwhelming majority of Popeyes managers, however, live in the United States, handling operations of overseas restaurants from Popeyes' corporate office in Atlanta, Georgia.

Atlanta-based managers direct and assist the foreign units with day-to-day operations, new restaurant openings, store redesign, and the occasional crisis. By answering questions and dealing with problems via e-mail, phone, fax, and video-conferencing, these "virtual managers" are almost always accessible to the foreign staff. Popeyes has found that the foreign employees interact well with off-site

management and tend to work harder in a less-structured environment.

U.S.-based management benefits Popeyes by reducing travel and relocation costs.

Critical Thinking
What problems do you think managers face when overseeing operations in a foreign country?

Link and Learn
For more information on Popeyes Chicken & Biscuits, visit the company's Web site via the link on the *Succeeding in the World of Work* Web site at **www.careers.glencoe.com**.

Your *standard of living,* a measure of your quality of life based on the amount of goods and services you can buy, declines. Inflation affects the business cycle and can lead to higher unemployment.

Controlling inflation is one of a government's major goals. When inflation starts to go up, many governments raise interest rates to reduce everyone's ability to borrow money. The result is a slow-down in economic growth, which helps to bring inflation down.

Unemployment

A third economic indicator is the unemployment rate. It identifies the percentage of the labor force that is without work but is actively seeking employment. Low employment is a sign the economy is doing well because most people are working, earning wages, and consuming. High unemployment, on the other hand, indicates problems in the economy because many people are out of work. The result is a lower standard of living and personal difficulties for the families involved.

The higher the rate of unemployment, the greater the chances of an economic slowdown. Not only does consumer spending decrease when unemployment rises, but the government and businesses are forced to pay out more money. Businesses must pay more for unemployment insurance, which provides assistance for unemployed workers. The government must also spend more money to finance unemployment wages and other social services for those without jobs.

interNET CONNECTION

Unemployment Rate
You are doing a report for one of your classes and need to include information about the current unemployment rate.

Connect
- Search for recent articles about unemployment on business Web sites; the business pages of online newspapers and magazines are good sources.
- Write a one-page report summarizing your findings. Include the current unemployment rate, how it compares to last year's rate at this time, and what the rate says about our economy.

SECTION 19.1 REVIEW

 Key Concept Checkpoint

Comprehension

1. Why do you think the government exercises some control over producers in our free-enterprise system?

2. Why do you think the government keeps track of fluctuations in the economy?

3. What could you infer if the gross domestic product was higher each year for three years in a row?

Critical Thinking

4. How does the release of government figures, such as the unemployment rate, affect the stock market?

CAREER FACTS

Education or Training
Veterinarians must have a doctor of veterinary medicine degree from an accredited college of veterinary medicine. A license is also required to practice.

Aptitudes, Abilities, and Skills
Veterinarians must have scientific knowledge, good decision-making skills in emergency situations, a compassionate and caring attitude, and the ability to get along well with animals and their owners.

Career Outlook   Demand is expected to grow faster than average through 2008.

Career Path   Veterinarians may begin in a large practice working with a wide variety of animals and move on to a specialized private practice.

What is your key to success?
"My key to success was finding out what veterinary services were missing in my area. Emergency work and horse work were missing in my area, so concentrating my efforts in these fields enabled me to build a successful practice."

What does your job entail?
"The first thing I do each day is examine every animal in the hospital and discuss its condition with one of my associate veterinarians. Then I start with appointments, treating sick animals and those in need of vaccinations or checkups. My workday often includes late-night treatments. I usually have at least three emergencies a night."

How does your workload vary?
"My workload varies depending on how many animals are in need of care and on the extent of their injuries. Sometimes there are as many as 30 sick animals in the hospital. Sometimes an emergency takes up a lot of time. My work also varies from day to day because I treat a variety of animals, including cats, dogs, birds, horses, pigs, and goats."

What kind of training did you have?
"I received a bachelor's degree in general science. Then I earned my doctor of veterinary medicine degree (DVM) at the University of Milan in Italy. I still go to lectures, and I'm a very active member of my local veterinary association."

> **Critical Thinking**   Why is it necessary for veterinarians to have good people skills, in addition to working well with animals?

You, the Consumer

WHAT YOU'LL LEARN

- How to make wise shopping decisions
- Strategies for identifying common types of consumer fraud and how to protect yourself against such tactics

WHY IT'S IMPORTANT

Wise consumer habits will enable you to save money and protect yourself from deceptive practices.

KEY TERMS

- **consumer fraud**
- **bait and switch**
- **warranty**

In our free-enterprise system, individuals as well as businesses make choices about earning and spending money. These individual choices are not always easy to make. How can you know the right goods and services to buy? How can you get the best price? You have only so much money to spend, so making the right choice is very important.

Smart Shopping

Making good choices takes competencies such as allocating time, allocating money, and acquiring and evaluating information. Consider how these competencies apply to each of these practical tips:

- *Pay attention to quality.* You'll save money in the long run by buying well-made items, especially when you expect to keep your purchases for a long time. Does a high price mean an item has higher quality than a less costly one? Not necessarily. *Generic products*, or products without brand names, usually have plain packaging and are relatively inexpensive.

  Buying generic products can be a smart move. When the quality of such products is high, you save because you are not paying for fancy packaging or expensive advertising.

- *When possible, plan the timing of your purchases.* You will find more bargains at certain times of the year. January and August are good sale months because many stores try to sell as much as possible to make room for the next season's goods.

You can also use the law of supply and demand. Instead of rushing out to buy a new videotape or CD, wait a few months. By then, the price may have been marked down because demand has lessened.

- *Take advantage of discount stores.* Discount and "warehouse" stores can offer excellent buys. Do your homework, however, *before* you get to the store because customer service may not be a high priority.

- *Consider buying used or second-hand goods.* You can often save money when purchasing major items, such as cars, exercise equipment, or electronics, if you're willing to shop around.

  As with all purchases, it's important to be careful. Used or second-hand products are usually non-returnable, and rarely have a warrantee. If you're thinking of buying a used car, have a trusted mechanic check it out before you decide. Make sure used electronics and appliances work properly by trying them out before you buy them.

- *Explore online options.* Online prices can be surprisingly low, and you may find electronic shopping very convenient. In addition, product information is often available on the Internet. To protect yourself, how-

A Friendly Reminder It's easy to be influenced by your friends when you are buying clothes. *In what ways can your friends help you be a responsible consumer?*

ever, read about online shopping in consumer magazines first. You cannot assume that all the information you get and all the companies you encounter online will be trustworthy.

Buyer Beware!

Be a smart consumer. Learn to protect yourself from **consumer fraud,** or dishonest business practices used by people who are trying to trick or cheat you.

Kathleen Coventry of Illinois learned about fraud the hard way. She responded to a telephone work-at-home offer. She sent a salesperson a check for $153.95, trusting the salesperson's assurance that her money would be refunded if she were unhappy. Kathleen soon received a large envelope full of useless materials that provided only general suggestions such as "Start a home typing business." Kathleen said, "There was no way that any person could read this stuff and actually use the information [to start a home business]."

Kathleen promptly returned the envelope and requested a refund. More than a year later and after follow-up calls and letters, she still had gotten nothing back.

How can you avoid fraud? First, be aware that scams exist. Here are some common tricks of the fraud trade:

- *Fraudulent advertising* Using a tactic known as **bait and switch,** a retailer advertises a bargain—the bait—to lure people into the store. When the customers arrive, the store is "out" of the item. A salesperson tries to sell a similar product at a much higher price. This is the switch.

- *Auto repair fraud* Dishonest mechanics may try to charge you much more than the estimated cost of a repair. They may replace parts that are not defective. To protect yourself, ask for written estimates and request that mechanics keep the old parts and show them to you.

Avoid the Hustle Automobile repairs can be expensive. Make sure anyone working on your car explains the recommended repair to your satisfaction. *Why do you think some auto repair shops get away with fraudulent practices?*

- *Phony prize notifications* "Congratulations! You've just won our grand prize!" This great news may come by mail or phone. To get your prize, all you have to do is send in some money or make a small purchase. Some companies ask you to provide a credit card or checking account number for identification. Beware. Even cautious consumers can fall for this scam.

Most consumer frauds succeed by taking advantage of the consumer's search for a good deal. If an offer sounds too good to be true, it probably is. These tips may save you from becoming a victim: First, *never* give your credit card number over the phone if you didn't place the call. Second, don't send money to any unknown business or organization without checking first to be sure it is legitimate. For information, check with your state or local consumer office or the Better Business Bureau.

Groups That Protect Consumers

Suppose you buy something that breaks the first time you use it. What should you do? First, try to solve the problem by visiting the store where you bought it or by calling the company that produced it. If this doesn't work, you might write a letter of complaint. In your letter, be polite but firm. Be sure to save store receipts, and keep records of your communications with the business. As a last resort, you may need to take legal action. However, help is also available from several other sources.

Government Agencies

Government agencies, specialized organizations within the government, enforce consumer protection laws. They act as watchdogs over certain areas of the marketplace.

- The Federal Trade Commission (FTC) enforces rules about labeling, advertising, and warranties. Thanks to the FTC, the labels in your clothes provide care instructions. This agency also regulates the descriptions of products in ads and commercials to

CAREER CHECKLIST

To Be an Informed Consumer...

- ✔ Know your rights, and keep up with government rules that affect these rights.
- ✔ Save for large purchases instead of relying on credit cards, especially if you don't have the money to pay your balance immediately.
- ✔ Always compare prices—don't just buy the first item you see.
- ✔ Find out the store's policy on refunds and warranties.
- ✔ Avoid buying on impulse or buying items simply because of a low price.
- ✔ Know your needs, and don't allow a sales associate to talk you into a purchase you don't want or can't afford.

make sure they are accurate.
A **warranty** is a guarantee that a product meets certain standards of quality. By FTC standards, a warranty must be clearly worded and conveniently placed.

- The Consumer Product Safety Commission (CPSC) helps protect the public against dangerous products. It sets safety standards for equipment and makes sure these standards are met.

- The Food and Drug Administration (FDA) enforces laws about the quality and labeling of food, drugs, and medical devices. It inspects workplaces that produce food and drugs.

Government agencies at the state and local levels also work to protect consumers.

Consumer Groups

Many private groups investigate consumer complaints, educate the public on consumer issues, and try to get consumer legislation passed. Examples of such groups are consumer action panels (CAPs) formed by trade associations, such as MACAP for major appliance manufacturers. A well-known consumer group is Consumers Union, which publishes *Consumer Reports.*

Taking Precautions Companies are not required by law to offer a warranty, but if they do, they must honor it. *Why would you prefer to buy an appliance that comes with a warranty?*

SECTION 19.2 REVIEW

 Key Concept Checkpoint

Comprehension
1. What benefits will you obtain from being a wise shopper?

2. Where might you find information about new types of consumer fraud?

3. How does protecting yourself against consumer fraud help other consumers as well?

Critical Thinking
4. Why are consumer advocacy groups important? What would the market be like without them?

KEY TERMS
economics (p. 380)
economic system (p. 380)
free enterprise (p. 381)
consumers (p. 381)
producers (p. 381)
marketplace (p. 383)
gross domestic product
    (GDP) (p. 385)
inflation (p. 385)

SECTION 19.1

- The United States has a free-enterprise economic system, in which there is limited governmental intervention in the production, buying, and selling of goods and services. (p. 381)

- The marketplace is the arena where producers and consumers "meet" for buying and selling, even though producers and consumers may be geographically far apart. (p. 383)

- Prices may go up or down, depending on supply and demand, production costs, and competition. (p. 383)

- The economy moves from good times to bad and back to good again. These fluctuations are called the business cycle. (p. 384)

- The condition of the economy can be measured by the gross domestic product, the consumer price index, and the unemployment rate. (pp. 385–386)

KEY TERMS
consumer fraud (p. 389)
bait and switch (p. 390)
warranty (p. 392)

SECTION 19.2

- Smart shopping involves paying attention to quality, timing purchases, taking advantage of discount stores, considering second-hand goods, and exploring online options when possible. (pp. 388–389)

- There are a number of methods of consumer fraud, including fraudulent advertising, auto repair fraud, and phony prize notifications. Consumers need to be aware of fraud schemes and to be on guard against getting cheated. (pp. 389–391)

- Government agencies and private consumer groups protect and educate the consumer as well as handle consumer complaints. (pp. 391–392)

Reviewing Key Terms

1. Write a series of questions and answers that use the following key terms.
   - economics
   - economic system
   - free enterprise
   - consumers
   - producers
   - marketplace
   - gross domestic product
   - inflation
   - consumer fraud
   - bait and switch
   - warranty

Recalling Key Concepts

Determine whether each of the following statements is true or false. Rewrite any false statements to make them true.

2. In a free-enterprise system, prices and wages are strictly controlled by government regulations.

3. The presence or absence of competition has no effect on prices.

4. The consumer price index and the unemployment rate are two yardsticks for measuring the economy.

5. Buying generic products when their quality is comparable to brand-name products is one way to save money.

6. The Consumer Product Safety Commission enforces rules about advertising, labeling, and warranties.

Problem Solving

7. How would life in the United States be different if our economy had much stricter controls?

8. Describe a situation in which your friends might have a negative influence on your shopping choices.

9. How would you deal with a bait-and-switch scam?

10. List three features not mentioned in the text that you think would be important in an effective letter of complaint.

Work-Based Learning

Thinking Skills Creative Thinking

11. You have taken a job with a consumer protection agency. Your first task is to create a poster that provides consumer tips expressed in eye-catching and imaginative ways. Conduct research to come up with ten tips. Then illustrate each one with drawings or magazine photos. Present your poster to the class.

Information Skills Acquiring and Evaluating Information

12. The Consumer Information Center of the U.S. General Services Administration publishes a booklet called the *Consumer Information Catalog.* Find out the number to call to obtain it, how much the booklet costs, and what information it provides. Prepare a report of your findings.

School-Based Learning

Language Arts Write a Letter

13. Adena recently bought an electronic pocket organizer to replace her address book. To her disappointment, the phone numbers keep getting lost. When she tries to recall a name, the number is garbled or has disappeared. Write a letter from Adena to the manufacturer explaining the defect. Tell the manufacturer what kind of action she would like it to take.

Math Calculate Profits

14. Allen rents a cart in the business district to sell coffee to people on their way to work. In one week, he spends $17 on coffee, $7 on milk, and $3 on sugar. The rent for the cart is $105 per week. If each cup of coffee is 65¢, how many cups must Allen sell in a week before he begins to make a profit? What would his profit be if he sold 500 cups in one week?

Role Play

15. Stick to Your Budget

Situation You are a customer at a car dealership, and you are interested in purchasing a new car. You have a limited budget, but the sales representative is determined to sell you an expensive car.

Activity Role-play a situation in which you adhere to your budget when shopping for a new car, despite various persuasive attempts used by the sales representative. Create firm, yet polite responses to address the common sales techniques that you expect to encounter in such a situation. Be sure to explain your budget—and the rationale behind it—to the sales representative.

Evaluation You will be evaluated on how well you meet the following performance indicators:

- Use appropriate responses to manage the situation without resorting to anger, frustration, or giving up
- Demonstrate an understanding of the budgeting concepts presented in the chapter

*inter*NET CONNECTION

16. Compare Economic Systems

Now that you have a basic understanding of the workings of and employment opportunities available in our free enterprise system, research the economic system and job opportunities of a foreign country where you would like to work.

Connect Conduct research on the internet to find information about the economic system and job opportunities of a foreign country. Create a Venn diagram comparing and contrasting the two economic systems and the job opportunities available in each.

Chapter 20

Managing Your Money

Section 20.1
Budgeting

Section 20.2
Coping With Financial
Responsibility

CHAPTER OBJECTIVES

After completing this chapter, you will be able to

● Identify the steps involved in planning a budget.

● Explain how to keep records effectively.

● Describe strategies for staying within your budget.

● Identify personal changes that might affect your finances.

● Discuss ways to adjust to economic change.

● List several sources of help for financial problems.

JOURNAL

Personal Career Plan

In your journal, write your first responses to these questions:

- Should the government stick to a budget? Why or why not?
- Should a small business stick to a budget? Why or why not?
- Should you stick to a budget? Why or why not?

Personal Career Project

Conduct research about saving for retirement. When should you start saving? How much money should you set aside per year? What types of investments are suitable for retirement savings? Write a two-page essay, then share it with the class.

Budgeting

Imagine driving a car with a broken fuel gauge. You wouldn't know how far you could go. You couldn't be sure when your car might sputter and roll to a stop. A fuel gauge enables you to operate for a planned distance. It allows you to balance what you have with how far you want to go. A fuel gauge is a kind of reality check.

Now think about your economic life. To act effectively, you need enough fuel (income) to get where you need to go (to cover your expenses). Your economic fuel gauge is your budget. A **budget** is a plan for saving and spending money based on your income and your expenses. A well-planned budget can give you the same feeling of confidence that a fuel gauge that shows full does. With careful budgeting, you'll be able to handle everyday needs as well as achieve your dreams for your future lifestyle.

Planning Your Budget

Why take the time to plan a budget? There are many valid reasons. After all, the stakes are pretty high. When you work, you trade valuable assets—your time, knowledge, skills, and effort—for money. You'll want to spend this money on things that are worth the time and effort you've put into earning it.

Begin your planning by asking yourself a few questions.

Making it Work Many young couples dream of owning their own home. *What types of costs, other than the actual cost of buying the home, will this couple have to think about as they consider purchasing it?*

- What are your lifestyle goals?
- What's really important to you?
- What do you have, and what do you need?

You'll use your answers to develop a budget plan. You'll also use the competencies of allocating time, money, material, and human resources.

Defining Goals

The first step in getting anywhere is to decide on your goals. To begin budget planning, make two lists. On one list, write the things you need or want to spend money on now or within the next six months. Perhaps you need new glasses or want to buy a new bicycle. On the other list, put the things you need or want to spend money on in the future. Paying for an education, buying a home, and saving for retirement might go on this list.

The lists identify your financial objectives—at least right now. You aren't locked in to them. You can add or cut out some at any time. Writing down your objectives, however, helps you make plans to achieve them.

Making Choices

You probably have more items on the lists than you have money for. That's why the next step is to prioritize—that is, to put your goals in order of importance. Prioritizing helps you clarify what is most important to you and distinguish between your financial needs and your financial wants. As you prioritize, note a target date for each goal. This will help you keep track of how well you're doing.

When making choices, remember to be creative. If you need to trim your budget, you may be able to do so without giving up the items that you really want. How can you shrink your financial needs without giving up too much? Be a "smart" shopper. For instance, the right cell phone plan could be cheaper than paying for long distance calls. With the money that you save from eliminating long-distance expenses, you might be able to afford more clothing or other goods.

Estimating Income and Expenses

The next step in planning your budget is to find out how much money you expect to have coming in *(income)* and how much you think will be going out *(expenses)*. Try to estimate these amounts as accurately as you can.

If you have a job, your main source of income is likely to be your earnings. When you are figuring your earnings income, count only *net earnings*, the amount left after taxes and other amounts are taken out. Income also, however, includes tips, gifts of money, and interest on bank accounts.

Your expenses include costs for food, housing, and so on. Sometimes people divide expenses into two types. One type is *fixed expenses*, expenses you have already agreed to pay and that must be paid by a particular date. Rent and car payments are examples of fixed expenses. *Flexible expenses* are the other type. These are expenses that come irregularly or that you may be able to adjust more easily. Medical costs and costs of clothing are examples of flexible expenses.

Invest in Yourself Funding your education is a valuable financial goal. *How is money that you put into education an investment?*

FIGURE
20.1

ESTIMATING INCOME AND EXPENSES

Average Monthly Income

Net earnings	$1,188
Interest on savings	5
Gifts	20
	$1,213

Average Monthly Expenses

Rent (my share)	$350
Car loan	220
Car insurance	70
Gasoline	60
Medical and dental care	50
Food	160
Entertainment	235
Miscellaneous	50
	$1,195

▲ **Setting a Budget** Here is one person's estimate of her average monthly income and expenses. *Which of the expenses listed here vary most from month to month?*

Preparing and Following Your Budget

You've identified and prioritized your goals and estimated your income and expenses. Now it's time to get down to preparing your budget. Your budget will be your financial plan of action for the next month or year.

As you draw up your budget, remember to be realistic. Just like a diet that's too strict, a budget that's too strict will be impossible to fulfill. You'll end up feeling resentful. Having a budget doesn't mean doing without all the pleasures in your life. It may mean cutting back, however, and it always requires thinking before you spend.

Examine your income and expenses for at least a month at a time. Many expenses (such as car or insurance payments) are paid monthly. Some will be paid even less often. For planning purposes, divide these kinds of payments into monthly chunks. For example, if you pay a life insurance premium every three months, or quarterly, divide the payment amount by three and place that number in your expense record as a monthly expense. *Figure 20.1* shows a sample income and expenses worksheet for a single person in her 20s who has a full-time job and shares an apartment with a friend.

Buying a Home
You are thinking about buying your first home. Since graduating from college a few years ago, you have worked steadily and have managed to save some money.

Connect
- Several organizations, such as Fannie Mae, help first-time homebuyers acquire affordable housing. Find the Web sites of such organizations, and get more information about buying a house for the first time.
- Write a one-paragraph summary of some of the things you need to consider before you buy a house.

Keeping Effective Records

You'll need to get into the habit of **record keeping**, that is, organizing and maintaining records of your income and spending. Records will be useful in many different ways. To estimate income and expenses, for example, you would use records such as a check register, bank account statements, and bill receipts.

A handy and inexpensive way to organize your records is with an accordion folder. If you have a filing cabinet available, that's even better. Record-keeping software allows you to keep records on disk as well in hard copy. Even so, you'll need file folders or an accordion folder to keep your records. Remember, however, that records are useful only if they're kept up-to-date.

Here are some tips for good record keeping:

Maintaining Control
Keeping organized records allows you to find important information when you need it. *How could this person have made this situation easier on himself?*

- Keep files where you can get to them easily.
- File bills and records.
- Keep a calendar to record when bills are due and when they were paid.
- Buy a fireproof box—or rent a safe-deposit box at a bank—for important documents such as insurance papers, birth certificates, and car titles.

Getting Started

Use a standard form to plan your budget. The form shown in **Figure 20.2** is a good place to start. First, transfer the information from your income and expense estimate into your budget. Your income should be equal to or more than your total expenses. To make this happen, you may need to adjust various categories.

FIGURE 20.2 — A BUDGET FORM

Categories	Budgeted Monthly Expenses	Actual Monthly Expenses
Savings		
Emergency fund	_____	_____
Savings account	_____	_____
Fixed Expenses		
Rent or mortgage payment	_____	_____
Installment payments	_____	_____
Car loan	_____	_____
Car insurance	_____	_____
Health insurance	_____	_____
Life insurance	_____	_____
Credit card interest	_____	_____
Flexible Expenses		
Food	_____	_____
Utilities	_____	_____
Household supplies	_____	_____
Medical and dental	_____	_____
Clothing	_____	_____
Entertainment	_____	_____
Miscellaneous	_____	_____
Total Spent	_____	_____
Total Income	_____	_____

▲ **Planning** This form is a typical one for planning a budget. *How would you use the column at the far right?*

Notice that there is a category for savings. This should *not* be an afterthought. Get in the habit of considering savings as a type of projected expense. If you establish a plan to save the same way you formulate a plan to pay your bills and make necessary purchases, you'll be more likely to do it. Chapter 21 will explain different savings options.

Your savings plan is your ticket to achieving your goals. There is also another reason to save regularly. Savings can help you create an emergency fund. An *emergency fund* is money you put aside for needs you can't anticipate. Everyone should have an emergency fund. A major illness or the loss of a job can be devastating if you do not have some money put away in an emergency fund.

Fine-Tuning Your Budget

You've prepared a budget, and you're using it as a guide. Is your job done? Of course it isn't. You will always need to make adjustments.

At the end of each month, check to see how you did at staying within your

---

Creative
BUSINESS PRACTICES

General Motors
Offering Online Education

General Motors (GM), based in Detroit, Michigan, encourages its management staff to take online business courses such as marketing, finance, and e-business. The classes, tailored to GM's corporate culture, are offered to its more than 88,000 salaried employees worldwide.

Internet-based learning gives employees more flexibility with their education, allowing them to learn at their own pace, set their own class schedules, and even earn an MBA degree—all without leaving their desks. Managers simply log on to GM's intranet to access the coursework. Because the courses focus on real-world business situations, students can immediately apply the techniques and tools they learn.

Many of the online classes are adapted from on-campus classes at GM University in Detroit. To provide some of the benefits of a traditional classroom, students use online discussions and e-mail to share ideas and use team problem solving.

GM estimates that it will save $4 million annually on travel and campus expenses by offering its courses online.

Critical Thinking
How can a manager benefit from taking courses online?

Link and Learn
For more information on General Motors' online business courses, visit the company's Web site via the link on the *Succeeding in the World of Work* Web site at www.careers.glencoe.com.

---

budget. If your income doesn't cover your expenses or barely does, what can you do? You really have only two choices.

- *You can cut back on your expenses.* You may be able to fine-tune your budget by cutting flexible expenses. For example, pack your lunch every day instead of buying it. Save money on gas and parking by carpooling with a coworker.

- *You can increase your income.* You may be able to increase your income by working more hours or getting a better-paying job.

Trimming Down Cooking meals at home rather than eating out is one way to cut your expenses. *What is another way you could cut expenses at this point in your life?*

Keep fine-tuning your budget until it fits your needs. Your budget should serve as a guide, but it's not set in concrete. It can be adjusted as your income, expenses, needs, and wants change.

It will probably take a few months to get your budget on the right track. If you're just starting out on your own, many one-time set-up costs for services such as electricity and water, or a security deposit for an apartment, will throw off your monthly expenditures at first. You might have a short waiting period before getting your first paycheck at a new job, or you might need to make several one-time purchases for household necessities. These things add up quickly and need to be taken into account.

If you haven't found a job yet, you might be living on your savings, or getting help from your parents. That money needs to be carefully budgeted, too. When you start receiving a regular paycheck, keep track of your average expenditures on things such as groceries, utility bills, entertainment, and transportation. You may want to keep a running total for each category to refer to at the end of the month, so you can see where you need to trim excess spending or where you have room to spend more.

Following Your Budget

Your budget can help you only if you follow it. Use your self-management skills to keep spending within the limits you have set. You'll find some practical hints for staying within the limits of your budget in *Figure 20.3* on page 406.

FIGURE 20.3

Staying Within Your Budget
Following a few simple spending rules can help you stay within your budget.

A **Keep Track of Your Spending** Carry a small notebook with you at all times. Get in the habit of making a note of every penny you spend. It will help your record keeping, and you will never have to ask yourself where your money went.

B **Don't Carry Cash** Don't carry around a large amount of cash. You'll be too tempted to spend it on impulse. Just take what you'll need for your trip, along with a little extra for an emergency. Leave your ATM card at home too. This will force you to think before making a purchase.

 Shop Smart Always think before you spend. Examine fliers you receive in the mail or that are posted at store entrances. Try to shop at discount stores whenever you can.

D **Pay With Cash** Whenever possible, pay for what you buy with cash. Credit cards can be dangerous. They make overspending too easy.

SECTION 20.1 REVIEW

✔ Key Concept Checkpoint

Comprehension

1. Why do you need to examine your financial goals before you create a budget?

2. How might accurate records be useful for tasks other than drawing up a budget?

3. How could you apply skills used in sticking to a budget in your workplace?

Critical Thinking

4. Do you think it is better to learn about budgets now, or through life experiences? Why?

CAREER FOCUS

CAREER CLUSTER: Business and Administration

Suzanne Aquilone
Administrative Assistant

CAREER FACTS

Education or Training Some companies will hire high school graduates with basic office skills. Other companies require a degree from a community college or certification from the International Association of Administrative Professionals.

Aptitudes, Abilities, and Skills Good interpersonal skills, organizational ability, initiative, adaptability, and knowledge of technology and procedures are necessary.

Career Outlook Little or no change is expected in employment of administrative assistants through 2008.

Career Path Administrative assistants may move on to supervisory, management, or executive positions.

What is your key to success?

"My key to success is my ability to conduct myself in a professional manner. When visitors come to the office, I am the first person they see. When clients call the office, I am the first voice they hear. I have a chance to make a positive first impression. I have to always be polite, professional, and courteous. I also make it a point to arrive at work on time, and I am very organized."

What does your job entail?

"My workload varies a lot. I manage agendas and take care of billing, purchase orders, and check deposits. I answer the phone and handle client requests and issues. I spend a large part of the day working on the computer, typing reports and inputting data. When a lot of people are out of the office, I spend time organizing files and updating the phone systems."

What skills are important to you?

"I am always polite, and I try not to be negative. This is important because my attitude affects our clients. It is also necessary for me to have good typing, computer, and spelling skills to ensure that my work is error-free."

What training do you recommend for students?

"I stongly recommend computer training. Knowledge of word processing, spreadsheet, and database programs is very important when working in an office environment. I recommend learning how to operate office equipment, such as fax and copy machines. It is also important to develop sound interpersonal skills."

> **Critical Thinking** What do you think is the most essential skill for administrative assistants?

Coping With Financial Reponsibility

Ellie was feeling good. She'd landed the job she wanted and her salary was fine. She'd had to move and to buy a car, but with her salary, she thought she'd have no trouble making the payments. Unfortunately, several months into her job, Ellie found out that her employers had overextended themselves. They couldn't afford all the new people they had taken on. Laid off, Ellie was faced with high monthly bills and no way to pay them.

What could she have done differently? After all, no one can be expected to see into the future. Should people go through life expecting the worst to happen? Neither option is a good one. There is a middle ground, however, in which you are willing to take some risks but are also prepared for unexpected problems. The key is responsible financial planning.

Adjusting to Personal Change

As you move toward adulthood, your accountability in money matters, or **financial responsibility**, increases. When you were a child, someone else paid for your food and clothing as well as your wants. When you started getting an allowance or began a part-time job, your financial responsibility may have increased. Perhaps you were expected to pay for some family purchases. In the future, as you move out on your own, your level of financial responsibility will increase even more.

WHAT YOU'LL LEARN

- How to identify personal changes that might affect your finances
- Ways to adjust to economic change
- Several sources of help for financial problems

WHY IT'S IMPORTANT

Information and strategies that you learn now will enable you to successfully manage your finances in the future.

KEY TERM

- financial responsibility

FIGURE 20.4 — PERSONAL LIFE CHANGES

Family	Occupation	Health
Marriage	Starting a career	Becoming disabled
Birth or adoption of children	Changing jobs	Growing older
Family member in need of financial help	Starting your own business	Experiencing chronic illness
Aging parents in need of care	Becoming unemployed	Being diagnosed with terminal illness
Death of a spouse or other close family member		
Receipt of an inheritance		
Separation or divorce		

▲ **Making Choices** This list shows life changes that might require you to alter your financial plans. *How could you prepare yourself for some of these changes ahead of time?*

Increasing independence is one type of personal change that requires financial planning skills. You will experience other types as well. Take a look at *Figure 20.4.* It lists life events—some positive, some not—that will require changes in your financial plans. By recognizing these possibilities, you'll be better able to cope with the changes they will bring.

Adjusting to Economic Change

It's not just personal events that can change your financial outlook. Events throughout the nation and the world also can affect your finances.

Inflation and Recession

You may have to refigure your budget during a time of inflation, or a general increase in prices. As long as economic conditions are good, prices tend to edge upward over time, as do wages. What hurts is rapid inflation, when prices go up but wages don't.

During times of inflation, your dollars will buy less than they did before. Some tips for coping with inflation include:

- Cut back on unnecessary expenses.
- Look for a second job to increase income.
- Be a wise shopper. Take advantage of sales, for example, and buy food in bulk whenever possible.

During a recession, when the economy does not grow for six months or more, your finances may also be affected. Recessions may be local—as when a major employer in the area closes down or moves away—or national. During a recession, some employers lay off workers. Because of widespread unemployment, workers often find it difficult to land new jobs.

As you read in Chapter 19, a recession is a normal part of the business cycle. A recession occurs when businesses produce more goods than consumers can purchase. The loss of income forces the businesses to lay off workers, creating unemployment. If the situation worsens, as more people become unemployed, the recession could become a depression. This rarely occurs, however. Normally, consumers are able to resume their purchasing habits, and the economy slowly picks up again.

The tips you just read for times of inflation will also be helpful in a recession. In addition, you can do the following:

- Save as much money as possible.
- If you are laid off, accept job placement help if your former employer offers it.
- Talk to a loan officer at your bank to see whether you can refinance any debt to make lower payments.
- Talk to your creditors about your financial situation if you are having difficulty making payments. Most financial institutions have programs to help during periods of financial difficulty.

Inflations and recessions are two examples of unexpected occurrences that could drastically alter your financial situation. The budgeting skills you learned in Section 20.1 can help you manage them successfully.

Using Available Resources Most banks are willing to help with financial planning when a job loss occurs. *How could a bank help you if you lost your job?*

Finding Help for Money Management Problems

If you run into trouble managing your finances, help is available. The list that follows highlights sources of help. Remember that many of these sources are good suppliers of financial information even if you aren't having problems.

- *Published Sources* Newspapers often have money management columns that offer timely advice. You can also examine magazines devoted to money matters, such as *Kiplinger's Personal Finance* and *Money*. In addition, most family magazines regularly provide useful tips on money issues. Bookstores carry a comprehensive selection of books on managing your money.

- *Online Sources* Don't forget the Internet. Financial Web sites may provide informational articles, useful statistics, and practical advice.

- *Schools* Many continuing education institutions and community colleges offer money management classes. Teachers and counselors may also be available to give you one-on-one advice.

- *Government Agencies* Free or inexpensive booklets providing consumer financial information are available from government agencies. You can find these at local libraries and at federal and county offices.

- *Banks* Many banks offer free financial advice to their customers. Some even hold seminars on money management.

- *Professionals* Lawyers, accountants, and financial planners will also provide financial advice. You will have to pay for their services, however.

- *Nongovernment Organizations* There are many NGOs that will give financial assistance. Most of these are topic-specific. For instance, an NGO that focuses on health care for people with financial difficulties could advise about health care options.

SECTION 20.2 REVIEW

 Key Concept Checkpoint

Comprehension

1. How will having a budget help you cope with personal changes?

2. What could you do to keep yourself informed about possible economic change?

3. Describe how you might use two of the sources listed in the text to help you manage your money now.

Critical Thinking

4. What are some ways to build a safety net for financial emergencies into your budget?

KEY TERMS
budget (p. 398)
record keeping (p. 402)

SECTION 20.1

- Begin planning your budget by defining your financial goals, prioritizing those goals, and estimating current income and expenses. (pp. 398–401)

- Make your budget realistic. Otherwise, you probably won't follow it. (p. 401)

- Record keeping—organizing and maintaining records of all of your income and spending—is important. Your files should be up-to-date and accessible. Store important documents in a fireproof box or in a safe-deposit box at a bank. (pp. 402–403)

- Your budget will be based on your estimated income and expenses. Be sure to include savings in your budget. You may need to fine-tune your plan by decreasing expenses or increasing income. (pp. 403–405)

- Effective strategies for staying within your budget include paying cash for purchases, shopping wisely, and thinking before spending. (pp. 406–407)

KEY TERM
financial responsibility
(p. 409)

SECTION 20.2

- Financial responsibility, or accountability in money matters, increases during a person's lifetime. Over time, personal changes also occur that require adjustments to budgets and goals. (pp. 409–410)

- Economic changes such as price increases during times of inflation and economic downturns, or recessions, require effective money management skills. Economic changes also may mean cutting down on expenses, increasing income, and accepting help from others. (pp. 410–411)

- Help for money management problems can come from publications, online sources, educational institutions, government agencies, banks, various types of professionals and nongovernment organizations. (p. 412)

Reviewing Key Terms

1. Write a paragraph about managing your own money. Use the terms below in your paragraph.
   - budget
   - record keeping
   - financial responsibility

Recalling Key Concepts

2. The first step in planning your budget is to ____.
   (a) cut expenses
   (b) obtain budget software
   (c) identify your financial goals

3. You should file your bills ____.
   (a) once a year
   (b) as you receive or pay them
   (c) only after you prepare your taxes

4. One way to help yourself stay within your budget is to ____.
   (a) track your spending
   (b) use credit cards for most purchases
   (c) carry your ATM card at all times

5. Personal changes that affect your finances include ____.
   (a) inflation (b) adopting a child
   (c) recession

6. Inflation, recession, and unemployment are all examples of ____.
   (a) economic change
   (b) flexible expenses
   (c) fixed expenses

7. You can usually receive free or low-cost help for financial problems from ____.
   (a) lawyers (b) accountants
   (c) government publications

Problem Solving

8. When you are preparing a budget, why is honesty with yourself important in estimating income and expenses?

9. How are the effects of inflation and a recession similar, and how are they different?

10. Why do you think that many people avoid seeking help with financial problems until the problems become serious?

Work-Based Learning

Thinking Skills Problem Solving

11. Miranda hopes to have her own pottery shop some day. She currently makes and sells planters. This supplements her salary from the grocery store where she works full-time. She is having trouble staying within her budget. List at least three factors that Miranda will have to consider as she seeks to solve her budgeting problem.

Information Organizing and Maintaining Information

12. Assume that you live at home and go to school, have a part-time job, make payments on a car, pay for your own phone, and volunteer at a hospital. How will you organize and label your record-keeping files?

School-Based Learning

Math Evaluate Your Budget

13. Prepare a personal budget reflecting your ideal lifestyle desires. Plan your budget, defining and prioritizing your goals and estimating your income and expenses. How much money would you need to earn to satisfy your lifestyle desires? Select a career that most closely matches your personal lifestyle budget.

Human Relations Financial Counseling

14. Tim works for a company that has plans to cut all salaries by 5 percent. To help employees adjust, the company wants to offer financial counseling. Research resources that could be used in such a program.

Role Play

15. Financial Responsibility

Situation You've just graduated from college, and you want to rent an apartment. However, you haven't established any credit, and so few landlords are willing to rent to you. You need to convince a landlord that you're financially responsible.

Activity Role-play a conversation in which you convince a landlord to rent an apartment to you. Offer specific reasons why you are a good prospective tenant by describing your monthly budget, and previous situations in which you've demonstrated financial responsibility.

Evaluation You will be evaluated based on how well you meet the following performance indicators:

- Offer sound and appropriate evidence of financial responsibility
- Demonstrate preparation and poise

16. **Financial Planning** Working with a partner, contact a bank or other organization that helps people with financial planning. Set up an interview to speak with a representative about financial tips for graduating high school students. Present this information to the class.

Connect Search the Internet for sites that offer advice for those new to financial planning. Choose a site and take notes on the advice given. In a one-page essay, compare your notes with the information you received from the bank representative.

Chapter 21

Banking and Credit

Section 21.1
Saving Money

Section 21.2
Checking Accounts and
Other Banking Services

Section 21.3
Using Credit Wisely

CHAPTER OBJECTIVES

After completing this chapter, you will be able to

- Compare common methods for saving money.
- Explain the characteristics of different savings plans.
- Select, use, and manage a checking account.
- Describe different types of credit.
- Explain the advantages and disadvantages of using credit.
- Explain how to compare credit costs.

JOURNAL

Personal Career Plan

Even though you don't yet have a full-time job, your first credit card—pre-approved— has just arrived in the mail. Will you keep the card? Why or why not? If so, how will you use it? Record your responses in your journal?

Personal Career Project

Select a career in the banking and credit industry that interests you, such as a loan officer or investment counselor. Conduct research to find out specific information about the career you've chosen. Explain your findings in a one-page report.

Saving Money

WHAT YOU'LL LEARN

- How to compare common methods for saving money
- How to explain the characteristics of different retirement plans

WHY IT'S IMPORTANT

Saving and investing money effectively will help you achieve financial security.

KEY TERMS

- **dividend**
- **certificate of deposit (CD)**
- **401(k) plan**
- **individual retirement account (IRA)**
- **Keogh plan**
- **simplified employee pension (SEP)**

It's been termed *moolah, bread, dough, bucks,* and *greenbacks*. In plain language, it's money. Chapter 20 explained how a budget allows you to keep track of money you've worked for. This chapter will give you guidance on how your money can work for you.

Ways to Save

Saving and investing are the way to put your money to work. Most people begin by opening a savings account at a bank, savings and loan association, or credit union. A *credit union* is a not-for-profit financial institution similar to a bank. People who belong to a credit union, however, share a common bond, such as working at the same company.

There are two basic types of savings accounts. With a *passbook account*, you receive a booklet in which transactions are recorded. With a *statement account*, you receive a computerized statement, usually monthly, of transactions.

With either type of account, you deposit money and the institution pays interest. *Interest* is the money that banks pay depositors for the use of their money. Usually, interest is a percentage of the amount deposited.

Normally, interest paid on a savings account is *compounded*. That is, the interest is figured on the amount of money you have deposited *plus* the interest that has accrued on your initial deposit. The effects of compounding are shown in *Figure 21.1*.

FIGURE
21.1

HOW COMPOUNDING MAKES $1,000 GROW

Month	Beginning Balance	Monthly Interest at 5%	Ending Balance
January	$1,000.00	$4.17	$1,004.17
February	$1,004.17	$4.18	$1,008.35
March	$1,008.35	$4.20	$1,012.55
April	$1,012.55	$4.22	$1,016.77
May	$1,016.77	$4.24	$1,021.01
June	$1,021.01	$4.25	$1,025.26

▲ **Calculating Interest** This table shows how much interest is paid on a $1,000 deposit when the interest rate is 5 percent, compounded monthly. The beginning balance is multiplied by 5 percent and then divided by 12 (because a month is 1/12 of a year). *Why does the interest increase from month to month?*

The following are a few other ways of putting your money to work for you. Use your decision-making skills to choose the best ones for you.

- *Savings bonds* When you buy a U.S. savings bond, you are lending money to the government. You buy a bond for half the "face value," which is the amount printed on the bond. Each year the bond grows in value until it has matured, or become payable. You can then *redeem*, or cash it in, for the full face value.

- *Money market deposit accounts or money market mutual funds* Money market accounts are savings accounts offered by banks and require a high minimum balance. With a money market account or fund, you deposit money that is pooled with money from other savers and then invested. You are paid a **dividend**, or share of the fund's profits.

- *Certificates of deposit* With a **certificate of deposit (CD)**, you deposit an amount of money for a fixed amount of time at a stated interest rate. Choosing a longer investment period often ensures you a higher interest rate.

Look at *Figure 21.2* on page 420 for a comparison of these different savings strategies.

Retirement Plans

According to many experts, you should begin putting aside money for retirement when you receive your first paycheck. Social Security, even combined with retirement plans offered by employers, rarely provides sufficient income for the retirement years. The following are some retirement plan options. Use your ability to acquire and interpret information as you examine them.

FIGURE
21.2

COMPARING WAYS TO SAVE

Type of Savings	Characteristics	Advantages	Disadvantages
Savings Passbook or Statement Account	• Money deposited in a savings account at a bank, credit union, or savings and loan association • Interest paid on the money in the account	• Can open an account with only a few dollars • Easy access • Savings of up to $100,000 often protected by Federal Deposit Insurance Corporation (FDIC)	• Low interest rate • Interest rate not fixed
Certificate of Deposit (CD)	• Purchased at banks and other financial institutions • Money invested for a fixed time, usually six months to several years • Interest paid on money in the account • Traditionally, the longer the term of investment, the higher the interest rate	• Fixed rate of interest guaranteed for the term of the deposit • Better interest than regular savings account • Savings of up to $100,000 often protected by FDIC	• Money tied up for a fixed period of time • Penalty for early withdrawal • Must invest larger amounts of money, usually $500 or more
Money Market Deposit Account/Money Market Mutual Fund	• Money market deposit accounts purchased at banks; money market mutual funds sold by mutual funds or insurance companies (a fund is made up of many investors)	• Usually pays higher interest than a regular savings account. • Money can be withdrawn at any time • Checks usually can be written on the account • Savings in money market accounts often insured by FDIC	• Interest rate varies • Requires minimum deposit, which varies with type of account • Bank may not pay interest if balance drops below a minimum amount
U.S. Savings Bond	• Purchased at banks or other financial institutions or directly from the government • Available in set amounts from $50 to $30,000 (face value) • Purchased for half the face value • Grows in value each year; worth face value at maturity	• Can be purchased for as little as $25 • Interest not subject to state or local taxes • Very safe; value guaranteed by the U.S. Treasury	• Money tied up for a period of time • If money is withdrawn early, owner gets less than face value

▲ **Saving Effectively** All of these savings plans are relatively safe investments. Savings bonds, which are guaranteed by the U. S. Treasury, along with plans protected by the FDIC, are extremely safe. *Why might someone invest in a plan that is not insured?*

Pension Plans

A pension plan is a retirement plan funded, at least in part, by an employer or union. The pension builds up throughout a worker's career. The amount of the pension is based on the employee's salary and the length of service with the company. Here are three common types of pension plans:

- In a *defined-benefit plan*, your company pays you a fixed amount at retirement. You know before you retire what amount you will receive.

- In a *defined-contribution plan*, sometimes called a profit-sharing plan, your employer contributes a set amount to the plan each year. The amount you receive at retirement depends on how much money has built up in the fund.

- In a **401(k) plan**, you put a specific portion of your salary into the plan. Employers often match this contribution, up to a specific amount or salary percentage.

The funds in 401(k) plans are invested in stocks, bonds, and mutual funds. As a result, you can accumulate a significant amount of money in this type of account if you begin contributing to it early. The money that accumulates in your 401(k) plan is tax-deferred. You don't have to pay taxes on it until you withdraw it.

Planning Ahead People today are living longer, healthier lives than past generations. *What does this mean for individuals just starting out in their careers?*

Individual Retirement Accounts

Even if you have a pension plan, you can have an **individual retirement account (IRA)** as well. This is a personal retirement account into which you can put a limited amount of money yearly. The earnings are not taxed until you retire.

Depending on your annual earnings, you can invest up to $2,000 a year in an IRA. One disadvantage of an IRA is that you are charged a penalty if you withdraw the money before you reach the age of 59½.

Some investors prefer to invest in *Roth IRAs.* Contributions to Roth IRAs are not deductible, but earnings are tax free. Depending on your situation, one type of account may be better for you than the other.

Plans for the Self-Employed

Do you plan to work for yourself? If so, a Keogh plan or a simplified employee pension may be the right type of plan for you. Both have the tax-deferment advantage of an IRA.

- With a **Keogh plan** (pronounced KEE-oh), you can invest up to 25 percent of your yearly earnings (up to $35,000) each year for retirement. There are special rules for setting up a Keogh account, so you should

interNET CONNECTION

Investing in a CD
You have $2,000 that you would like to invest in a certificate of deposit (CD). You know that banks have different interest rates and terms, and you would like to find more information

Connect:
- Visit the Web sites of three financial institutions in you area. Find out what their current interest rates and terms are for CDs. Check rates for one-year and five-year CDs, and see if there are penalties for early withdrawal.
- Write a one-paragraph summary of the CD that you chose, and explain why you chose that CD.

check with an accountant before you create one.

- A **simplified employee pension (SEP)** is a simpler tax-deferred retirement plan than the Keogh but one that also offers tax savings. It, too, is for the self-employed. Individuals can set aside as much as 15 percent of their yearly earnings, up to $30,000. (Owner-employees can set aside up to 13 percent.) A SEP account is easier to establish and maintain than a Keogh account, and some people prefer it for that reason.

SECTION 21.1 REVIEW

✓ Key Concept Checkpoint

Comprehension
1. Why might someone who is just starting out prefer a regular savings account to a CD?

2. Explain why you should start contributing to a retirement plan as soon as you can.

Critical Thinking
3. Why do some people find it difficult to save for retirement?

Checking Accounts and Other Banking Services

"Will that be cash, check, or charge?" This question is asked countless times each day. Just what are checks, and how do they work?

Checking Accounts

A check is a written document that authorizes the transfer of money from a bank account to a person or business. Most businesses and individuals rely on checks. For paying bills, they are easier and safer than cash. They also simplify record keeping.

Types of Checking Accounts

You open a checking account at a bank or credit union by depositing money into the account. To make a deposit, you fill out a deposit slip. Deposit slips are available in all bank branch offices. You will also receive a supply of deposit slips with your checks.

You can write checks up to the amount of your balance. Whether you gain interest on your balance or have to pay fees depends on the bank and the type of account you have.

A *regular checking account* often requires no minimum balance. However, it rarely earns interest, and you are usually charged a monthly fee for maintaining it. This fee may be a flat monthly rate ($4 to $8 a

Banking Wisely Choices about where to bank depend on many different factors. *What factors do you think are most important in choosing a bank?*

month, for example) or a charge for each check you write. A *NOW account* (negotiable order of withdrawal) pays interest on your deposits. However, you must keep a minimum balance in the account, usually at least $500. A *Super-NOW account* is similar to a NOW account except that the interest rate and minimum balance required are both higher.

Managing Your Checking Account

Having a checking account allows you to write checks when you need to pay bills or buy groceries. When you write a check, you must fill it out completely and accurately. (*Figure 21.3* shows how to do this.)

Sometimes you will receive checks. Your employer, for example, will probably pay you with a check. Normally, you will take the check to your bank to deposit it or cash it. To complete either transaction, you must **endorse** the check—sign your name on the back.

Although issuing checks will probably always be a popular method for paying employees, many employers now prefer to use direct deposit. *Direct deposit* is the electronic transfer of payment from a company to an employee's checking or savings account.

If your company uses direct deposit, your employer will provide you with a voided check, called an advice of debit, instead of a paycheck. An advice of debit is a standard paycheck that has been voided and stamped "Non-Negotiable." When balancing your checkbook, always enter the amount that is indicated on your advice of debit as if it were a "regular" paycheck.

Keeping Track of Your Account

If you write checks for more money than you have in your account, the account will be *overdrawn*. Banks charge a high fee for overdrawn checks. They may also send a check back to the business that

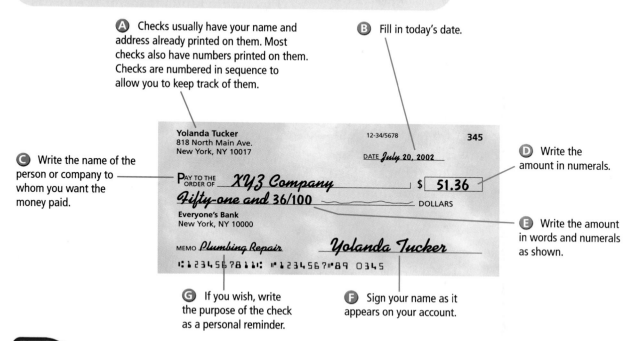

FIGURE 21.3

Using a Checking Account A checking account makes paying your bills convenient and safe. It also helps you track your expenses and manage your budget. A check authorizes your bank to take money from your account for payment to someone else. Be sure to write your checks clearly and completely.

Ⓐ Checks usually have your name and address already printed on them. Most checks also have numbers printed on them. Checks are numbered in sequence to allow you to keep track of them.

Ⓑ Fill in today's date.

Ⓒ Write the name of the person or company to whom you want the money paid.

Ⓓ Write the amount in numerals.

Ⓔ Write the amount in words and numerals as shown.

Ⓕ Sign your name as it appears on your account.

Ⓖ If you wish, write the purpose of the check as a personal reminder.

Yolanda Tucker
818 North Main Ave.
New York, NY 10017

12-34/5678   345

DATE *July 20, 2002*

PAY TO THE ORDER OF __*XYZ Company*__ $ | 51.36 |

Fifty-one and 36/100 _____ DOLLARS

Everyone's Bank
New York, NY 10000

MEMO *Plumbing Repair*   *Yolanda Tucker*

⑈1234567811⑈ ⑈1234567⑈89 0345

FIGURE 21.4

CHECK REGISTER

NUMBER	DATE	DESCRIPTION OF TRANSACTION	PAYMENT/DEBIT (-)		CODE*	FEE (−)	DEPOSIT/CREDIT (+)		$ BALANCE	
									172	16
343	7/15	Bob's Service Station	$ 24	36		$	$		24	36
		oil change							147	80
344	7/15	General Service Co.	72	14					72	14
		heater contract							75	66
	7/16	ATM transfer					200	00	200	00
		from savings							275	66
	7/17	Deposit					424	62	424	62
		paycheck							700	28
345	7/20	XYZ Company	51	36					51	36
		plumbing repair							648	92
	7/20	ATM withdrawal	40	00					40	00
		gift for James							608	92

▲ **Balancing Act** Each time you make any transaction involving your checking account, immediately record it in your check register. Add or subtract the transaction from your previous balance in the final column. *Why is it important to keep your balance current?*

submitted it for payment, causing you embarrassment. For these reasons, keep track of your account.

When you purchase your checks, you will get a **check register**, a small booklet for tracking your account. (See *Figure 21.4* on page 425.) Record all checks, deposits, fees, interest charges, and other transactions in the check register. Add and subtract amounts immediately so that you know exactly how much is in your account at any time.

Each month, you will get a statement of your account. You will need to reconcile the statement with your check register. To **reconcile** two items means to make them agree.

Using Other Banking Services

Banks offer additional services to help you manage your money.

- **Electronic funds transfer (EFT)** is the transfer of money from one bank account to another by electronic means rather than cash. Examples of EFT include direct deposit of payroll checks, withdrawals from ATMs, and purchases made with *debit cards*, also known as check cards, which automatically withdraw the amount of your purchase from your bank account.

Creative BUSINESS PRACTICES

United Auto Workers
Providing Employee Assistance Programs

The United Auto Workers (UAW), is a union that represents more than one million active and retired workers in a variety of industries. One of the purposes of the UAW is to negotiate wages and benefits, such as employee assistance programs, for its members.

Employee assistance programs, known in the union as work/family programs, help workers cope with personal or work-related problems. Third-party contractors offer employees financial and legal services, drug and alcohol abuse programs, marital and family counseling, and other confidential help paid for by their employers.

The UAW believes that third-party contractors are more effective because they can be strictly confidential. The UAW has found that employers' health insurance and workers' compensation costs are lower when problems are handled early on through employee assistance programs.

Critical Thinking
How does an employee's work life affect his or her personal life?

Link and Learn
For more information about the UAW, visit the union's Web site, via the link on the *Succeeding in the World of Work* Web site at **www.careers.glencoe.com**.

Online Banking

Another increasingly popular service is **online banking**. Online banking lets you manage your money from your own home computer, or from anywhere you can find online access. Most online bankers choose to use this service because it allows them to save time. Most banks offer online service at no extra charge.

In the past, some people were reluctant to try online banking because they feared hackers would be able to gain access to their private financial information. However, recent advances have made online banking much safer. Most of the institutions that offer online banking services have instituted a wide range of safety precautions.

For instance, if you choose to bank online, you will be assigned a special ID and password, which will protect your account from unauthorized users. Furthermore, online banking services use encryption to protect patrons' accounts. This technology scrambles your account information, making it impossible for anyone other than your banking service to read your financial data. Firewalls, computers or computer software that prevents hackers from accessing a company's local area network or intranet, are also used as a security precaution by most banking institutions.

Aside from being an efficient time-saving device, online banking also has the advantage of being comprehensive. Accessing your online account instantly brings up each and every transaction that has occurred over the past month or more and gives descriptions of the transactions, including the date processed, the amount, even where it took place.

Some online banking services also offer additional options for additional fees, such as the ability to pay your bills directly from your account. With this option, you inform the bank which bill you wish to pay online, and the bank automatically deducts the amount from your account each month.

Finally, with online banking you can access your account even when you are somewhere where your bank does not have a presence. Because online banking can be conducted anywhere, having a bank that lacks ATMs where you are traveling does not stop you from accessing your account.

SECTION 21.2 REVIEW

✔ Key Concept Checkpoint

Comprehension

1. Why might you choose a regular checking account instead of a NOW account?

2. Why must you write the amount of a check in both numerals and words?

3. Why is it important to reconcile your check register and bank statement?

Critical Thinking

4. What options do you have for conducting your banking transactions? Can they be used together, or must you choose only one method?

CAREER FOCUS

CAREER FACTS

Education or Training Most photojournalism jobs require photography experience and a bachelor's degree in journalism or photography.

Aptitudes, Abilities, and Skills Creativity and a good eye are essential, as are good people skills, determination, and ability to work independently and with others.

Career Outlook Employment is expected to increase more slowly than average, with keen competition.

Career Path A photojournalist may start as an assistant and then move on to a job as photographer or editor for a magazine or newspaper, or go on to start a private business or teach.

What is your key to success?

"Tenacity—I don't give up easily. This is a competitive business, and you have to work hard to get your first break. You also have to be tenacious to get a good photo. Creativity is another asset to me. The best shots are usually the ones you don't plan."

What does your job entail?

"I photograph news as it happens, wherever it happens. My job is to find the human angle to a story— a face or a scene that hooks the reader. I usually work with a print journalist, but sometime I'm sent to cover a story on my own. Then I also interview people and get all the facts of a story."

What do you like most about your work?

"The variety and the pace. Because I work at a small city paper, I get to cover a wide range of events. One day I might be taking photos of a high school graduation, and that same night I might be covering a crime scene."

What kind of training do you recommend for students?

"Learning how to see is the best training a photojournalist can have. Technical knowledge of photography is obviously extremely important, but it's even more important to develop a good eye. I also recommend getting as broad an education as possible. Photojournalism isn't just about taking pictures. You've got to have a broad knowledge about the world, plus people skills and writing skills to gather and write the news."

> **Critical Thinking** Why does a photojournalist have to be able to work both independently and as part of a team?

Using Credit Wisely

Now and then, life has a way of demanding more money than you have on hand. One way to obtain that money is through credit. **Credit** is a sum of money a person can use before having to reimburse the credit lender. It allows the person to receive a good or service now but to pay for it later. When you use credit, you are really taking out a loan.

Understanding Credit

Most businesses that sell a good or service offer credit. Car dealers, department stores, appliance dealers, and even some doctors offer credit. In fact, some companies (such as VISA and MasterCard) are in business just to extend credit.

Types of Credit

The most common type of credit is that offered through a credit card. A *credit card*, issued by a bank or other financial institution, allows the cardholder to charge amounts in many different places. The lender issues you a plastic card stamped with your name and account number. Usually, you are given a *credit limit*. This is the maximum amount you can charge against your account.

WHAT YOU'LL LEARN

- The different types of credit
- The advantages and disadvantages of using credit
- How to compare credit costs

WHY IT'S IMPORTANT

Understanding credit will allow you to avoid getting too deeply in debt.

KEY TERMS

- **credit**
- **application fee**
- **down payment**
- **finance charge**
- **annual percentage rate (APR)**
- **credit bureau**

Many businesses offer consumers charge accounts. A charge account is similar to a credit card account. In this case, the business issues the credit and often a credit card that can be used only at the company, or store, that issued it. When you buy an item, you charge it to your account. Each business sets the terms for its charge accounts.

Loans are another type of credit. People get loans from banks, credit unions, and other financial institutions to make large purchases. Car loans and mortgages are typical consumer loans.

Most loans are *installment loans*, in which you receive the money as a lump sum and pay it back in regular (usually monthly) payments called installments. You may have to pay an **application fee**, an amount of money charged to apply for the loan. Usually, you also have to make a **down payment**, a sum (usually a percentage of the total payment) paid at the time of the purchase.

Secured loans are guaranteed by *collateral*, an asset such as the borrower's home or car. If the borrower defaults on the loan—that is, fails to pay it—the lender can take the collateral. Unsecured loans do not require collateral.

Disadvantages of Credit

While the advantages of credit are clear to most people, credit also has at least two disadvantages. First, lenders charge a **finance charge**, which is a fee based on the amount of money you owe. Finance charges are based on a particular interest rate and can be figured in a number of ways. (The cost of credit is described in the next section.)

The second disadvantage of credit is the risk of overusing it. If you accumulate too much debt, you may not be able to make timely payments. You may lose your collateral on secured loans. Your financial reputation will also suffer.

Use credit when you need to, but avoid overusing it. People with credit problems can find help through organizations such as American Consumer Credit Counseling and the Consumer Credit Counseling Service.

Instant Approval Most stores have a service that allows them to process a purchase with your credit, debit, or ATM card immediately after you swipe your card through a machine. *What tasks do you think this machine performs?*

Seeking Counsel Talking with someone from a credit counseling service can help you work out credit problems effectively. *What might be the consequences of ignoring credit problems?*

CAREER CHECKLIST

Maintaining a Banking and Credit Account...

✔ Keep track of all ATM withdrawals and purchases as well as any checks written.

✔ Avoid using banks that charge high ATM fees.

✔ Establish a set of savings goals and create a plan to help you reach them.

✔ Avoid charging items when you do not have the money to cover the cost.

✔ Save your withdrawal and credit card receipts to match up with your statement.

✔ Never invest money in any venture that is not documented or legitimate

✔ Know your rights in regard to your bank and credit.

✔ Investigate your options for tax-free savings and retirement plans, such as a 401(k).

The Costs of Credit

Credit costs vary widely. Your best bet is to shop around. Not all companies compute costs in the same way or charge the same amounts.

- *Annual fees* Many credit card companies charge an annual fee or a membership fee. The amount is fixed and is charged to your account no matter how often you use the card.

- *Finance charges* If you pay off your entire balance every month, you will not incur finance charges, which are interest on your unpaid balance. Finance charges commonly amount to 1.5 percent of your balance per month, or 18 percent per year. The Federal Truth in Lending Act requires lenders to state the cost of the interest as an **annual percentage rate (APR)**. This is the yearly cost of the loan, expressed as a percentage. An APR allows you to compare the costs of credit from different lenders.

Most credit cards have a *grace period.* This is a time during which interest is not charged. With most credit cards, if you pay the entire amount by the due date stated on your first bill, you are not charged interest or any other finance charges.

Credit Agreements and Reports

When you apply for credit, you must complete a *credit application.* This form asks for details about your salary, bank accounts, and credit history. Before your application is approved, the lender will usually check with a credit bureau. A **credit bureau** is an agency that collects information on how promptly people and businesses pay their bills. The credit bureau provides this information, in the form of a credit report, to businesses that request it.

The credit bureau gives you a *credit rating,* a numerical rating that indicates how likely you are to pay your bills. If you have a poor credit rating, you may be denied a car loan or a mortgage. Make a habit of checking your credit rating regularly. You can do this by contacting a credit reporting agency such as Equifax, Trans

Living Large It can be tempting to use a credit card to buy items on the spur of the moment. *How could you prevent yourself from overusing credit?*

Union, or Experian and paying a fee. Errors sometimes occur, and you will want to see that the credit bureau corrects them as soon as possible.

SECTION 21.3 REVIEW

✓ Key Concept Checkpoint

Comprehension
1. Why is a credit card more convenient for everyday purchases than a loan?

2. Why is it easy for some people to get into financial trouble when they have credit cards?
3. Why do businesses check with credit bureaus before extending credit to individuals?

Critical Thinking
4. Do you think credit companies want you to use credit responsibly or irresponsibly? Why?

KEY TERMS
dividend (p. 419)
certificate of deposit (CD)
(p. 419)
401(k) plan (p. 421)
individual retirement
account (IRA) (p. 422)
Keogh plan (p. 422)
simplified employee
pension (SEP) (p. 422)

SECTION 21.1

- Saving your money in an interest-bearing account puts it to work for you. When interest is compounded, your savings will grow even more quickly. (p. 418)

- You can save money by depositing it in a savings account or money market account or fund. You can also buy savings bonds and certificates of deposit. (p. 419)

- You should start saving for your retirement as soon as possible. Participating in a pension plan is a good way to begin. In addition, you will probably want to contribute to an individual retirement account (IRA) or a 401(k) plan. For self-employed people, Keogh plans and simplified employee pension (SEP) plans allow tax-deferred savings. (pp. 419–422)

endorse (p. 424)
check register (p. 426)
reconcile (p. 426)
Electronic Funds Transfer
(EFT) (p. 426)
online banking (p. 427)

SECTION 21.2

- With a checking account, you deposit money and then write checks on your balance. (pp. 423–424)

- Track your account with a check register. Reconcile it monthly against your statement. (pp. 425–426)

- Electronic funds transfer and banking online make banking more convenient. (pp. 426–427)

credit (p. 429)
application fee (p. 430)
down payment (p. 430)
finance charge (p. 430)
annual percentage rate
(APR) (p. 431)
credit bureau (p. 432)

SECTION 21.3

- Credit through credit cards, charge accounts, and loans, allows you to buy something now and pay for it later. (pp. 429–430)

- Disadvantages of credit include finance charges and the possibility of taking on too much debt. (p. 430)

- The costs of credit include fees and finance charges. (p. 431)

- A credit bureau tracks how timely debts are paid. (p. 432)

Reviewing Key Terms

1. Write a brief speech giving advice on banking and credit to a person your age. Use each of the following terms.

- dividend
- certificate of deposit (CD)
- 401(k) plan
- individual retirement account (IRA)
- Keogh plan
- simplified employee pension (SEP)
- endorse
- check register
- reconcile
- credit
- application fee
- down payment
- finance charge
- annual percentage rate (APR)
- credit bureau

Recalling Key Concepts

2. You agree to keep your money deposited for a specific length of time in a ____.
   (a) certificate of deposit
   (b) money market mutual fund
   (c) checking account

3. Only self-employed workers can open a ____.
   (a) money market deposit account
   (b) CD (c) Keogh plan

4. When you compare a checking account statement with your check register to make sure they agree, you are ____ your checking account.
   (a) reconciling (b) overdrawing
   (c) transferring

5. The most common type of credit vehicle is a ____.
   (a) SEP (b) charge account
   (c) credit card

6. Credit can be costly because of ____.
   (a) credit bureaus
   (b) high interest rates
   (c) credit ratings

Problem Solving

7. What factors might help you choose between a very safe investment with a low interest rate and a riskier investment with a higher interest rate?

8. How can you use your checking account to keep track of your spending habits?

9. Why do you think most businesses offer credit to their customers?

10. Explain which is the wiser strategy: to save $100 a month in a savings account or to repay $100 a month toward a credit card debt of $1,200.

Work-Based Learning

Thinking Skills Problem Solving

11. Imagine that you earn a good salary but have allowed the balances on several credit cards to get too high. Suggest two actions you might take to begin solving your problem.

Interpersonal Skills **Negotiating to Arrive at a Decision**

12. Your sister has asked you to cosign a loan to help her buy a car. By cosigning, you are stating that if she can't repay the loan, you will. You don't think your sister can repay the loan. How do you handle this situation without harming your relationship with your sister?

School-Based Learning

Math **Calculate Interest**

13. Steve's bank pays an annual interest rate of 2.8 percent on savings accounts. The interest is compounded monthly. If Steve deposits $1,000 in a savings account, how much interest will he earn in three months?

Family and Consumer Sciences **Use Documentation**

14. A credit card company has refused to issue Howard a credit card, claiming that he has a bad credit rating. Howard is sure that the credit card company made a mistake. What documentation should Howard have when he calls the credit bureau to check his credit report?

Role Play

15. Credit Counseling

Situation Your younger friend recently got her first job, and has just dropped by to brag about how well she's doing. You soon find out that she is close to her limit on one credit card and isn't sure how to use her check register.

Activity Role-play a conversation in which you explain to your friend the basics of managing her finances. Explain why she shouldn't spend more than she makes, and how she should handle her checking account.

Evaluation You will be evaluated based on how well you meet the following performance indicators:

- Offer accurate and useful information about spending and money management habits
- Present your advice in a constructive and friendly manner
- Correctly answer any questions your friend may have

16. Choosing a Credit Card

Compare the advantages and disadvantages of five credit cards. Take into account fees, APR, and other factors. Make a chart comparing the cards and write a paragraph telling which would be best for you and why.

Connect Using the Internet, investigate at least three options for rescuing bad credit. Write a paragraph explaining how each works and the effect it would have on your credit.

Chapter 22

Buying Insurance

Section 22.1
Insurance Basics

Section 22.2
Home and Automobile
Insurance

Section 22.3
Health and Life
Insurance

CHAPTER OBJECTIVES

After completing this chapter, you will be able to

- Define some common insurance terms.
- List some ways to lower insurance costs.
- Describe the basic types of health, auto, and life insurance coverage.
- Explain the importance of owning home insurance.
- Distinguish between group and individual health insurance plans.

JOURNAL

Personal Career Plan

Write a short journal entry identifying the kinds of insurance you now have, and why. After you have studied this chapter, reread your journal entry and add a follow-up, explaining the kinds of insurance you expect to buy in the next few years.

Personal Career Project

Talk to at least two adults about what kinds of insurance they have, how long they've had each plan, and why they chose each type. Create a list of things to remember when you start looking for insurance. Record your findings in your journal.

Insurance Basics

When was the last time you made plans, only to have them changed by an unexpected event? One thing is certain in life: No matter how carefully we plan, some things go wrong. A driver backs into your new car. While you are at work, your television set is stolen. You break an arm and need emergency surgery.

How can you plan for life's unexpected events? One way is to buy insurance. When you purchase insurance, you pay an agreed-upon amount of money to an insurance company. The company in turn agrees to pay for losses caused by such events as automobile accidents, theft, or injuries that might otherwise ruin you financially.

The Language of Insurance

Remember when you first used a computer? You had to learn "computerese"—the language of computers. The same is true of insurance. The terms below are part of the language of insurance.

Insurance Policy

When you buy insurance, you'll receive an insurance policy. An **insurance policy** is a legal contract between a person buying insurance (a *policyholder*) and an insurance company. The policy explains:

- who is covered,
- types of losses for which the company will pay,
- amounts the company will pay, and
- the cost of the insurance.

An insurance policy is long and technical. In spite of this, you should read it carefully and ask questions about any unclear parts before you sign it.

Insurance Coverage

An insurance policy describes a policyholder's coverage. Insurance *coverage* refers to losses that an insurance company agrees to cover. The amount of coverage is the actual dollar amount that will be paid by the company in case of a loss.

All insurance policies have a list of *exclusions*. These are losses or risks that are not covered.

Benefit and Beneficiary

Money paid by an insurance company for a loss is called the *benefit*. In most cases the benefit is paid to the *beneficiary*, who is usually the policyholder.

Premiums

The amount a policyholder pays an insurance company is known as the **premium**. You can usually pay premiums in installments rather than all at once.

Deductibles

When you buy most types of insurance coverage, you agree to pay a deductible. A **deductible** is the portion of a loss that you pay before the insurance company pays the remaining cost. The higher the deductible that you pay, the lower the cost of your premiums.

Claim

How does an insurance company know to pay you for a loss? You file a **claim**, an oral or written notice to the insurance company.

Choosing Wisely Even though it takes time to read an insurance policy, you should understand its terms fully before you buy the coverage it provides. *Why do you think it is as important to understand what a policy does not cover as what it does cover?*

Kinds of Insurance

You can buy insurance for almost anything. It's possible to purchase marine insurance, space flight insurance, and dread-disease insurance. Professional dancers can have their legs insured. Concert pianists can have their hands insured.

Government Insurance Programs

These programs provide coverage if you lose your job (unemployment insurance), are injured on the job (workers' compensation), or qualify for health coverage (Medicare, Medicaid). See Chapter 23, Types of Benefits.

Holding Down Insurance Costs

How do you shop for big items such as a car or stereo system? Taking time to shop around can save you money when buying insurance. This is where workplace skills such as reading, math, decision making, problem solving, and reasoning are especially helpful. Here are several tips for controlling insurance costs:

- Know what type of insurance you want.
- Call several insurance agencies in your area to ask about coverages and costs.
- Ask about differences in premium costs with different deductibles. Consider paying higher deductibles in order to lower your premium costs.
- Don't buy more coverage than you need or less coverage than you need.

Like all industries, the insurance industry is in business to make money. Therefore, companies are less willing to insure you if they believe you are more likely to use the insurance.

For example, people with poor driving records often pay high premiums for auto insurance. Younger drivers also pay high premiums because statistics have shown that they are involved in more accidents. In some cases, insurance companies may refuse to insure a driver altogether.

Life insurance premiums are determined based on a similar philosophy. If you smoke, are overweight, or have a chronic illness, you will probably have a hard time finding affordable insurance.

SECTION 22.1 REVIEW

✔ **Key Concept Checkpoint**

Comprehension

1. Explain the difference between a premium and a deductible.

2. Imagine that you are drawing up a new budget for the coming year. Describe three ways to save money on your insurance costs.

Critical Thinking

3. Do you think it is ethical for an insurance company to refuse to cover someone? Why or why not?

Home and Automobile Insurance

What are your insurance needs? If you're like most people, you'll need only the basics: home, automobile, health, and perhaps life insurance.

You will want to be sure you have the right protection and that you do everything necessary to keep your coverage up-to-date. It is important to understand how insurance works because a great deal of money will be at stake.

Home Insurance

If you decide to rent an apartment, you'll need renter's insurance. This type of insurance covers your belongings up to a set amount, minus your deductible. *Figure 22.1* on page 442 shows one way to keep track of your belongings in case you need to file a claim.

If you decide to buy a house or condominium, you'll purchase homeowner's insurance. This type of coverage protects your house and its contents against losses due to fire and theft. It generally does not cover floods or earthquakes. Supplemental insurance is available to cover these risks.

Automobile Insurance

Many states require by law that drivers have insurance. You can find out about a state's requirements from the insurance commissioner or motor vehicle division.

FIGURE 22.1 — INVENTORY OF PERSONAL PROPERTY

Item	Purchase Price	Date of Purchase	Item	Purchase Price	Date of Purchase
Electronic Items:			**Collections:**		
TV					
CD Player					
Stereo			**Other Valuables:**		
Camera					
Computer					
			Furniture:		
Jewelry:					
Watch			**Silverware, Dishes, Glassware:**		
Ring					
Sports Equipment:			**Electrical Appliances:**		
Musical Instruments:			**Linens:**		
Clothing:					
Tools:					

▲ **Keeping Track** When you buy renter's or homeowner's insurance, make an inventory of your possessions, and keep receipts for items of value. Update your records annually. What other kinds of items would you include on a list such as this? *Why is it also a good idea to photograph or videotape your possessions?*

Types of Coverage

When you buy a standard automobile insurance policy, you usually buy several different kinds of coverage. Each type of coverage insures your car and you for a different kind of loss, damage, or injury.

Liability Insurance What if you're involved in an accident that's your fault? **Liability insurance** covers damage or injury for which you're responsible. This includes injuries suffered by the driver and passengers in the other car and by passengers in your car. It also covers property damage to the other car. Liability insurance doesn't cover your injuries or property damage to your car.

Medical Payments Insurance If you suffer injuries in an auto accident, whether or not it's your fault, *medical payments insurance* will cover your medical expenses. Medical payments insurance also covers medical expenses of your passengers. This insurance is limited though. For example, many policies cover only up to $5,000 in medical expenses per person. Liability insurance will cover expenses beyond the maximum amount per person of medical payments coverage.

Collision Insurance In an accident that's your fault, **collision insurance** covers the cost of repairs to your car. It also covers damage to your car if you're in an accident caused by a driver who is not insured. *Figure 22.2* on pages 444-445 provides advice on what to do in case you're involved in an auto accident.

Comprehensive Insurance **Comprehensive insurance** covers your car for reasons other than a collision. These reasons include theft, fire, and vandalism.

Uninsured Motorist Insurance You can buy *uninsured motorist coverage* to protect yourself against drivers who do not have liability insurance. This coverage is optional. You may not need it if you have medical payments or health coverage.

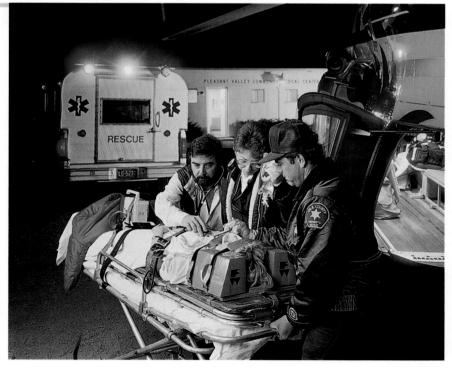

Under Cover Liability insurance protects you against claims or lawsuits by people whose cars are damaged and who are injured in an accident that is your responsibility. *Why is it important to have as much auto liability insurance as you can afford?*

FIGURE
22.2

Handling Auto Accidents
Sooner or later, you are likely to be involved in an automobile accident. If and when this happens, you should stay calm, check all parties for injuries, report the accident to the police, record important information, and call your insurance company.

B **Check for Injuries** If you are not injured, get out of your car to see whether the driver and any passengers in the other car are injured. Make sure that you are out of the way of passing vehicles.

A **Stay Calm** When you're involved in an auto accident, try to stay calm so that you can think clearly. Move your car to the side of the road, if possible, away from traffic.

C **Report the Accident to the Police** Call the police to report the accident. Request an ambulance if someone is injured.

D **Record Important Information** When the police arrive, be prepared to show your driver's license, auto registration, and proof of insurance. As clearly as possible, explain to the police officer the facts as you saw them. If you and the other driver disagree over the incident, avoid arguing. Exchange driver's license numbers and names of auto insurers with the other driver.

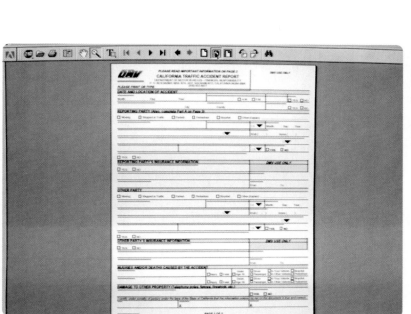

E **Report the Accident to the DMV** As soon as possible, call your insurance company to report the accident and file a claim. Also fill out a traffic accident report form at the DMV if your state requires it.

ETHICS *in Action*

Reporting Injuries Last week you hurt your neck at the gym, and it still feels achy. Today you were involved in a minor automobile accident. There is no damage to your car, but your friend tells you that you should sue the other driver for your neck injury. He says that a doctor won't know if you hurt it at the gym or in the accident. Your friend's suggestion is tempting because you don't have medical insurance to pay for treatment for your neck.

THINK ABOUT IT

Will you tell your insurance company that your neck was injured in the accident? Why or why not?

Systems of Automobile Insurance

When people are in automobile accidents, they sometimes disagree about who is at fault. To limit delays and disagreements, some states have passed laws establishing a *no-fault system*. This means that policyholders have their claims paid by their own insurance companies, no matter who is at fault.

Buying Automobile Insurance

Automobile insurance can be costly. You will want to get the best possible policy for the right amount of coverage.

FIGURE 22.3 **EXAMPLES OF AUTO INSURANCE DISCOUNTS**

Defensive driving courses	10 percent discount on liability, collision, medical payments, and personal injury protection*
Airbags and other passive restraints	15 percent discount on medical payments and personal injury protection (driver's side); 30 percent discount on medical payments and personal injury protection (both sides)
Drug/alcohol education	15 percent discount on liability, collision, medical payments, and personal injury protection
Antitheft devices	Reduces comprehensive premium; amount of discount varies by device and county
Two or more cars on policy	5 percent discount on liability, collision, medical payments, and personal injury protection

*Personal injury protection pays the same as medical payments, plus 80 percent of lost income and the cost of hiring someone to take on household and caregiver responsibilities of an injured person. The coverage is the same as with medical payments insurance.

▲ **Smart Shopping** It pays to check with several insurance companies to find out about available discounts on auto insurance. *Why do you think some companies offer discounts for drug and alcohol education?*

There are several ways to control or lower the cost of your auto insurance premiums. They include the following:

- *Shop around.* Try to get prices from at least three different companies.

- *Drive carefully.* Some companies offer safe-driver discounts to policyholders with good driving records.

- *Take driver education classes.* Some companies give discounts to drivers who take driver education courses.

- *Buy only the coverage you need.* If you have health insurance coverage, you may not need medical payments coverage or uninsured motorist protection. Also, if the premium is more than 10 percent of your car's value, think twice about buying collision coverage.

- *Raise your deductibles.* If you have a good driving record and can afford higher deductibles, this will save you money.

- *Take advantage of insurance discounts.* Some insurance discounts are required by state law; others are optional. **Figure 22.3** provides examples of auto insurance discounts.

CAREER CHECKLIST

When Purchasing Insurance...

☑ Research your needs and different options.

☑ Compare quotes from different agencies before choosing one.

☑ Ask your agent to explain all deductibles and coverage options involved in your plan.

☑ Keep all documents and receipts relating to insurance policies and claims.

☑ Always carry your information for health and auto insurance— you never know when you may need it!

☑ Never let someone else use your insurance plan illegally.

☑ Follow up on all claims.

☑ Be careful to not allow any lapse in insurance coverage.

SECTION 22.2 REVIEW

Key Concept Checkpoint

Comprehension

1. Why is it important to purchase home insurance?

2. Which of the five types of auto insurance coverage would you most likely select if you were buying a new car? Explain your reasoning.

3. How might you influence the cost of your auto insurance premiums even before you buy a car?

Critical Thinking

4. If you were driving 15 miles per hour over the speed limit, and you ran into a car turning in front of you, with whom would an insurance company find fault?

CAREER FOCUS

CAREER FACTS

Education or Training All public school teachers must obtain teaching licenses in addition to completing a bachelor's degree program and an approved teacher-training program that includes student teaching.

Aptitudes, Abilities, and Skills Strong communication skills and an aptitude in the specific subject are necessary, as is the ability to motivate students, inspire trust, and maintain a positive classroom environment. Teachers must also be organized, dependable, patient, creative, and committed.

Career Outlook Average job growth is expected through 2008 for secondary school teachers, with some variation by location and subject area.

Career Path Teachers may go on to become school librarians, reading specialists, curriculum specialists, guidance counselors, school administrators, or supervisors.

What is your key to success?
"I am very familiar with the subject matter I teach, and keep myself up-to-date on new developments in my field. I am also very patient. I teach students of all different academic abilites, and having patience allows me to work with all of them until they have grasped the material."

What does your job entail?
"My most important job duty is to create effective lesson plans to reach all of my students. I plan activities that are realistic for my struggling students as well as challenging for my high achievers. I also create and grade tests, homework, and projects. I speak with parents and meet with other teachers and staff to discuss school issues."

What do you like most about your work?
"The most rewarding part of being a teacher is seeing my students grasp a scientific concept and succeed in biology. I also enjoy the variety that the job offers—one week I might have only homework to grade, but the next week I might have 120 exams to grade with all different types of questions, including essays."

What kind of training did you have?
"I received my bachelor's of science degree in biology, which gave me the content knowledge I need. I then worked for a master's degree in education, learning the necessary education theories and teaching practices. As part of my master's program, I was required to do a semester of student teaching under the supervision of a licensed teacher."

Critical Thinking What skills and abilities do you have that would make you a strong teacher?

Health and Life Insurance

So far, you've thought about planning for unexpected events involving your belongings and your car. Now you'll consider coverage for your most basic possessions: your health and your life.

Health Insurance

The cost of health care in the United States is rising. How can you ensure that your medical costs stay within your budget? You may be able to participate in a health insurance plan provided by your employer. You can also learn about types of coverage and the advantages and disadvantages of each.

Types of Coverage

As with auto insurance, health insurance coverage varies. Types of health coverage fall within three major categories.

Major Medical Coverage As with other types of health insurance, **major medical coverage** includes hospital and surgical expenses, doctor visits, prescription drugs, and medical tests. It differs from other types because it requires you to pay a deductible and **coinsurance,** which is a percentage of your medical expenses. An advantage of major medical coverage, though, is that you're able to choose any hospitals and physicians you prefer.

WHAT YOU'LL LEARN

- How to compare basic types of health and life insurance
- How to distinguish between group and individual health insurance

WHY IT'S IMPORTANT

Knowing what to look for when you shop for insurance will help you get the best plan for your money.

KEY TERMS

- major medical coverage
- coinsurance
- term life insurance
- face value
- cash-value life insurance
- whole life insurance

Health Maintenance Organizations Unlike major medical coverage, a *health maintenance organization (HMO)* is a type of health coverage with no deductibles. Members usually pay a small *copayment* for doctor visits. In an HMO, checkups and well-baby care are covered, but your choice of physicians is limited.

Preferred Provider Organizations Do you prefer a wider choice of doctors than you would have with an HMO? Then a *preferred provider organization (PPO)* may be for you. PPOs offer some of the low-cost advantages of HMOs while allowing more freedom of choice of doctors. With a PPO you often pay higher premiums and higher copayments than you would with HMO coverage.

One limiting factor in the HMO is its gatekeeper system. In an HMO, you choose a primary doctor, usually a general practitioner, and can only see another doctor at the recommendation of the primary. With a PPO, any doctor in the program is available.

Although group health plans, such as HMOs and PPOs, make health insurance affordable, they present disadvantages. These plans are run by insurance companies that have been known to consider their finances before their medical responsibilities.

For instance, HMOs or PPOs may discourage doctors in their networks from prescribing costly treatments or surgical procedures if there is a chance that such measures may not be absolutely necessary. At times, people have even had to take their HMO or PPO to court to receive care.

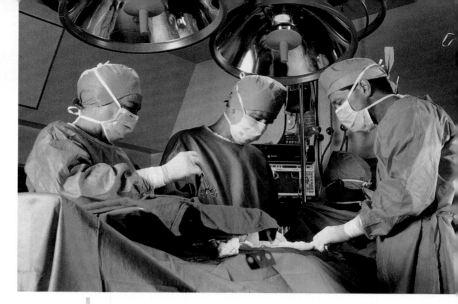

Costly Care Health-care costs are rising. *What would be the best health-care provider option for you? Why?*

Types of Plans

You can buy health insurance through a group plan or an individual plan. Most people in the United States belong to group plans, either through their employers or through associations such as trade or alumni associations.

Group Plans Most group plans are offered through employers. Group plans

Finding Health Insurance
Your new job—even though it offers a nice salary—doesn't include health insurance. You are healthy, 21 years old, have no dependents, and you need to find a health insurance plan.

Connect
- Research two health insurance companies that serve your local area and visit their Web sites. Compare the premiums, deductibles, and prescription drug benefits of their plans.
- Write a one-paragraph summary of the costs and benefits of the plan you chose and why you chose that plan.

keep premium costs down by spreading the risk over a large number of people. These plans usually have a deductible, coinsurance, and major medical coverage.

Individual Plans People not enrolled in a group plan can buy insurance coverage through an individual plan. This may include students living on their own, self-employed workers, or retirees. Such coverage can be expensive.

Disability Coverage

Suppose that you become ill and can't return to work for a month or two. How would you pay your bills? Disability insurance pays you a percentage of your salary.

Short-term disability insurance usually covers you for only a few months.

Long-term disability insurance can pay for a lifetime of missed work.

Life Insurance

If others in your household, such as a spouse and children, count on your salary, life insurance will provide money to them in case you die. Some employers offer life insurance as a benefit, but many people buy additional coverage as well.

Types of Life Insurance

There's a wide and confusing array of life insurance choices. It's important to understand each type. The two basic types of life insurance are term life insurance and cash-value life insurance.

Creative BUSINESS PRACTICES

Sylvan Learning Systems, Inc.
Offering Online Benefits

Sylvan Learning Systems, Inc. provides personalized tutoring services to students of all ages and skill levels. The Baltimore, Maryland-based company operates more than 900 Sylvan Learning Centers in North America and Asia, as well as eSylvan, an Internet-based tutorial service.

Sylvan Learning offers its 7,000 employees 24-hour-a-day online access to their benefits information via the company's intranet. For core benefits such as health insurance and retirement accounts, employees can learn the current details of the plans, update their information, and view transactions.

The system gives employees more control over their benefits plans. Sylvan gets lower administrative costs and a human resources department that can focus on other issues.

Critical Thinking

How do you think online access to benefits affects employees' relationships with human resources personnel?

Link and Learn

For more information about Sylvan Learning Systems, visit the company's Web site via the link on the *Succeeding in the World of Work* Web site at **www.careers.glencoe.com**.

Term Life Insurance   Of the two types of life insurance, term is less costly. **Term life insurance** simply protects your dependents if you die. It has no cash value and provides coverage for a set number of years. If you should die, the beneficiary receives an amount of money known as the **face value** of the policy.

Cash-Value Life Insurance   The second basic type of life insurance, **cash-value life insurance**, is part insurance and part investment. You can borrow money against the total amount of premiums paid on a cash-value policy. One kind of cash-value life insurance is whole life insurance. **Whole life insurance** works in part like term life insurance but has a savings component. With whole life insurance, you can build a reserve of money that you can borrow against or collect when you retire.

Buying Life Insurance

As with other types of insurance, when you buy life insurance, you'll purchase a policy and pay premiums to an insurance company. The company agrees to pay a benefit to your beneficiary if you die. The premium amount will depend on factors such as your age, your health, and the type of policy you buy. Here are some questions to consider before buying life insurance:

- *Should you buy life insurance?*   If someone depends on you for your earning power, you should have life insurance. If you have no dependents, you may not need the insurance.

- *How much life insurance do you need?*   This depends on how old you are, whether you have dependents, how much your family will need to pay off your debts if you die, and how much insurance you can afford.

- *What are some tips on buying life insurance?*   Take the time to shop around for life insurance, just as you would when buying a car. Life insurance prices vary widely. Don't make your decision solely on an agent's advice. Talk to others and take advantage of consumer guides.

SECTION 22.3 REVIEW

✔ Key Concept Checkpoint

Comprehension
1. What are the advantages and disadvantages of major medical coverage, HMO coverage, and PPO coverage?
2. If your employer doesn't offer health insurance, what choices do you have in buying health insurance?
3. Explain the difference between term life insurance and whole life insurance.

Critical Thinking
4. What might happen if you received a serious injury and you had no health insurance?

KEY TERMS
insurance policy (p. 438)
premium (p. 439)
deductible (p. 439)
claim (p. 439)

SECTION 22.1

- Although insurance policies are long and complex, it pays to learn the language of insurance. (pp. 438–439)
- You can hold down your insurance costs by shopping around, buying only the coverage you need, and seeking discounts. (p. 440)

liability insurance (p. 443)
collision insurance (p. 443)
comprehensive insurance (p. 443)

SECTION 22.2

- Home insurance protects your valuables whether you own or rent. (p. 441)
- The five major types of auto insurance are liability, medical payments, collision, comprehensive, and uninsured motorist coverage. (p. 443)
- Staying calm will help you manage an accident. (pp. 444–445)
- You can lower your auto insurance premiums by shopping around, driving safely, taking driver education courses, buying only the coverage you need, and raising your deductibles. (p. 447)

major medical coverage (p. 449)
coinsurance (p. 449)
term life insurance (p. 452)
face value (p. 452)
cash-value life insurance (p. 452)
whole life insurance (p. 452)

SECTION 22.3

- The cost of health care is rising, but you have choices in limiting what you pay for coverage. (p. 449)
- Three basic types of health-care coverage are major medical coverage, HMO coverage, and PPO coverage. (pp. 449–450)
- Types of health insurance plans are group and individual plans. (pp. 450–451)
- Life insurance provides benefits for your dependents. (p. 451)
- Two broad categories of life insurance are cash-value and term life insurance. (p. 452)

Reviewing Key Terms

1. Write one paragraph each about insurance basics, auto insurance, health insurance, and life insurance. Use the terms below in your paragraphs.
   - insurance policy
   - premium
   - deductible
   - claim
   - liability insurance
   - collision insurance
   - comprehensive insurance
   - major medical coverage
   - coinsurance
   - term life insurance
   - face value
   - cash-value life insurance
   - whole life insurance

Recalling Key Concepts

2. Insurance premiums are paid by ____.
   (a) an insurance company
   (b) a policyholder to an insurance company
   (c) an insurance company to a beneficiary

3. One way to lower your insurance costs is to ____.
   (a) raise your risk
   (b) lower your deductibles
   (c) raise your deductibles

4. The type of automobile insurance that covers the cost of repairs to a car that you run into in an accident is ____.
   (a) comprehensive (b) collision
   (c) liability

5. You are likely to pay lower auto insurance premiums if you ____.
   (a) buy a less expensive car
   (b) buy more coverage than required by law
   (c) lower your deductibles

6. Which type of health insurance requires policyholders to pay coinsurance? ____.
   (a) an HMO (b) a PPO
   (c) major medical coverage

7. Whole life is a type of ____ life insurance.
   (a) face value (b) cash-value (c) term

Problem Solving

8. Why do you think most insurance policies provide for a deductible?

9. Which type of auto insurance coverage do you think is most important?

10. Why should you buy health insurance even if you're well and practice a healthy lifestyle?

Work-Based Learning

Basic Skills Writing

11. As a writer for a consumer magazine, you are preparing an article on the relationship between lower auto insurance rates and automobile safety features. Research existing safety features on a variety of cars. Include information on the development of future auto safety features. Prepare a list of these, with a brief description of their functions.

School-Based Learning

Social Studies **Research Insurance Requirements**

12. Kai is a supervisor for an electronics company. The company wants him to spend a year training new supervisors in its plant in Monterey, Mexico. Kai will use his own car while he lives in Mexico. Use the Internet and sources such as *Birnbaum's Mexico* to research insurance requirements for using your own car in Mexico.

Math **Calculate Insurance**

13. On her way to work one morning, Carla slipped on an icy sidewalk and broke her arm. The total cost for medical treatment was $1,000. Carla has major medical coverage through her employer. Her deductible is $500, and coinsurance is 20 percent. Of the medical costs for her broken arm, how much will Carla have to pay?

Role Play

14. The Need for Insurance

Situation Your best friend just bought a car, and came over to take you for a ride. While you're talking, your friend tells you that he doesn't plan on buying insurance. He says that if he gets into an accident while uninsured, the other driver's insurance will pay for everything as long as it's not his fault. In the mean time, he'll save some money.

Activity Role-play a conversation in which you explain to your friend that,

while he may be technically right, he's missing a few key points about why he should have insurance coverage—and he's probably behaving illegally.

Evaluation You will be evaluated based on how well you meet the following performance indicators:

- Accurately explain how different types of auto insurance work
- Effectively inform your friend of the safety risks he is taking
- Correctly answer any questions your friend may have

15. Compare Employee Plans
Call the human resources departments of at least two companies, and find out what insurance plans they offer for their employees. Find out the type of plan, how much each employee must pay, and how long one has to work at the company to qualify for the plan. Summarize your findings in a brief essay.

Connect Research online the specific differences between an HMO and a PPO. Which gives you more flexibility? Which costs less? What factors might influence how the plan works for you? Write a paragraph detailing which plan you would choose and why.

Chapter 23

Taxes and Social Security

Section 23.1
All About Taxes

Section 23.2
All About Social
Security

CHAPTER OBJECTIVES

After completing this chapter, you will be able to

● Describe the tax system and the obligations it imposes on you.

● Complete a federal tax return.

● Describe how the Social Security system works.

● Identify Social Security benefits and state social insurance benefits.

● Explain the main problems facing the Social Security system today.

JOURNAL

Personal Career Plan

Imagine that you are thinking about retiring after 45 years in your career. You have saved some money and have paid into Social Security. You could even continue working part-time if needed. Write a journal entry about your options. Do you think you'll have to keep working part-time?

Personal Career Project

Talk to several adults who have recently retired, or who are considering retiring. How have they prepared for leaving the workforce? How much have they relied on Social Security? Record in your journal how their experiences and feelings change your projections about your own retirement?

All About Taxes

What do you think of when you hear the word *taxes*? The extra charge that's added to your bill when you buy a CD? The money your employer takes out of your paycheck each week? It's all money that comes out of your pocket and goes to the government, and it really adds up. You do get a great deal out of the taxes you pay, though. Think about it. What benefits from paying taxes can you name? How many have you enjoyed today?

Understanding Taxes

You may think that the whole topic of taxes is confusing. Actually, the general structure and workings of our tax system are easy to understand.

First of all, *taxes* are payments that you make to support the government and to pay for government services. There are three levels of government: federal, state, and local. The federal government runs the country as a whole. State governments manage the 50 states. Local governments govern counties, cities, and towns. All three levels of government need money to operate, so you must pay taxes to all three.

The **Internal Revenue Service**, or **IRS**, is the agency that collects federal taxes and oversees the federal tax system. The IRS now has a Web site that provides all of its standard forms, including forms for filing taxes. These forms can be completed online and then printed and mailed to the IRS. Taxes paid to the IRS go into the U.S. Treasury.

Long-Term Investments The federal government has spent billions of tax dollars on space exploration. *Do you think this is a wise use of funds? Why or why not?*

Types of Taxes

There are many kinds of taxes. The following are common ones.

- *Income taxes*   You pay income tax on your income, or the money you make. This income may come from working or from other sources, such as the interest your bank pays you on your savings, or it may come from profit you make on selling real estate. Income taxes are the federal government's main source of money.

Income tax is calculated as a percentage of the taxable income you earn. (*Taxable income* is your income after you subtract certain permitted amounts.) At the present time, the federal income tax ranges from 15 to 39.6 percent. In general, the greater your taxable income, the higher the rate of income tax you must pay. Your employer will **withhold**, or take out, money from your paychecks to pay income tax due on your wages.

In most states, people also pay state income tax. Many cities also have income taxes. State and local income tax rates vary, but they're generally much lower than federal rates.

Self-employed people have added responsibilities because they don't have employers to withhold their taxes. If you are self-employed, you will be required to withhold your own taxes. Generally, the IRS requires self-employed individuals to pay income taxes quarterly (four times a year) based on the income they estimate they will make that year. It's important to remember to set aside money for your taxes. You wouldn't want to face a potentially large tax bill without having the money to pay it!

- *Social Security taxes* Workers pay Social Security taxes so that they can receive benefits when they retire. (You'll read more about Social Security on pages 471–474.) Like income taxes, Social Security taxes are figured as a percentage of the money you earn.

Employers withhold money from paychecks to pay Social Security taxes, just as they do for

FIGURE
23.1

SAMPLE PAY STUB

MICHAELS, LISA N
0987426143

(STATEMENT OF EARNINGS AND DEDUCTIONS.
DETACH AND RETAIN FOR YOUR RECORDS. NON-NEGOTIABLE)

DESCRIPTION	RATE	HOURS	EARNINGS	YEAR TO DATE
REGULAR EARNING		54 00	380 50	2 280 05

	TAXES/DEDUCTIONS	YEAR TO DATE
FEDERAL	23 03	138 18
STATE	4 29	25 74
SOCIAL SECURITY	7 20	43 20
MEDICARE	5 45	32 70

NOT ELEGIBLE FOR LEAVE ACCRUALS

	EARNINGS	TAXES	DEDUCTIONS	NET PAY	PAY PERIOD	WARRANT NO	AMT OF WARRANT
CURRENT	380 50	39 97	0	340 53	BEGIN 03-19	22072196	338 90
YEAR TO DATE	2 280 05	239 82	0	2 040 23	END 04-02		

▲ **Don't Forget Your Taxes** **Gross pay** is the total amount you earn. **Net pay,** sometimes called take-home pay, is the amount that remains after money has been deducted for various taxes. *How much money did the employer withhold from this paycheck? If you are preparing a monthly budget, should you plan on using your gross pay or your net pay? Why?*

CONNECTION

Tax Break
You earned $31,000 last year. You are calculating your last year's income taxes and know that your tax rate increases as your income increases.

Connect
• Go to the Internal Revenue Service's Web site and locate the tax tables that you need. Find the income break points for the different tax rates.
• Calculate the tax on your income from last year. Write a one-paragraph summary of what you learned from visiting the IRS Web site.

income taxes. Your paycheck stub shows the money withheld in a box labeled "FICA," which stands for Federal Insurance Contribution Act, or Social Security. See *Figure 23.1.*

• *Sales taxes* When you buy something, the salesperson may add sales tax to the price. This tax goes to the state or local government. Almost every state has a sales tax.

Sales tax is calculated as a percentage of the price of an item. The tax rate varies from state to state. See *Figure 23.2,* which shows the various state sales tax rates. In addition to state taxes, local sales taxes may be added to the cost of items you purchase.

FIGURE
23.2

SALES TAX BY STATE

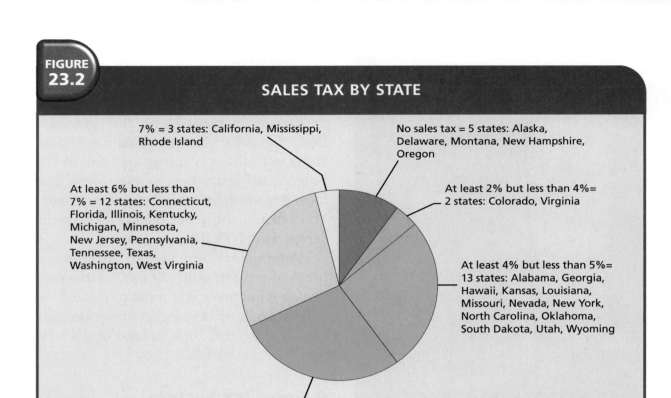

7% = 3 states: California, Mississippi, Rhode Island

No sales tax = 5 states: Alaska, Delaware, Montana, New Hampshire, Oregon

At least 6% but less than 7% = 12 states: Connecticut, Florida, Illinois, Kentucky, Michigan, Minnesota, New Jersey, Pennsylvania, Tennessee, Texas, Washington, West Virginia

At least 2% but less than 4%= 2 states: Colorado, Virginia

At least 4% but less than 5%= 13 states: Alabama, Georgia, Hawaii, Kansas, Louisiana, Missouri, Nevada, New York, North Carolina, Oklahoma, South Dakota, Utah, Wyoming

At least 5% but less than 6% = 15 states: Arizona, Arkansas, Idaho, Indiana, Iowa, Maine, Maryland, Massachusetts, Nebraska, New Mexico, North Dakota, Ohio, South Carolina, Vermont, Wisconsin

SOURCE: Sales Tax Institute.com

▲ **State Revenue** Sales tax is the chief source of revenue for most state governments. Sales tax is calculated on purchase price. For example, if you buy a $10.00 book and the sales tax rate is 5 percent, you'll pay $10.00 plus 50¢ (5% × $10 = 0.50), or $10.50. In some states, some items (for example, clothing or other necessities) are free from sales tax. *What is the sales tax rate in your state?*

- *Property taxes* The main source of money for local governments is property taxes. These taxes are based on the value of property—generally land and buildings.

Where Do Your Tax Dollars Go?

Each year, federal, state, and local governments take in billions of dollars in taxes. Where does this money go? Here's just a partial list of services paid for in full, or in part, by your tax dollars:

- *education*, including public schools and libraries;
- *transportation*, ranging from roadways and mass transit to dams and airports;
- *safety*, including law enforcement and fire protection;
- *health*, ranging from hospitals to medical research studies;
- *military services*; and
- *postal services*.

Taxes at Work Local services, such as fire and police protection, are paid for primarily through local taxes. *What other services does your community provide?*

It's Your Responsibility

When you go out to eat with friends, you split the bill. As a citizen, you also have to split the bill for the services the government provides.

Since we all share in the benefits, we should all contribute our fair share of taxes. That seems reasonable. The problem is that people disagree on what's fair. Some taxpayers think that rich people should pay a larger share of their income than low or middle income people. Some object to paying for services they don't use. Some disagree with the way the government spends money.

Making everyone happy is impossible. Does that mean that you just have to go along with the way things are? Not at all. You can influence how federal, state, and local governments spend your tax money. You can also influence the tax laws themselves. How? That's easy: vote.

Voters elect representatives at every level of government. These lawmakers decide what taxes you must pay and how your tax money is spent. It's your responsibility as a citizen to vote for officials who represent your beliefs.

A Good Tax System

Suppose it were up to you to design a tax system. What kind would you create? Lawmakers have argued over this question for decades, and the debate goes on. Still, most people agree that a good tax system has certain features.

- A tax system should be fair. Everyone who is able to pay should pay his or her fair share.

- Tax laws should be clear and simple. Many people think that the present system is too complicated. There are too many rules and tax forms.

- Taxes should be collected at a convenient time when most people are able to pay.

- A tax system should be stable. Taxpayers should know in advance how much they'll owe. If tax laws are always changing, people can't predict how much money to budget for taxes.

- A tax system should be flexible. When necessary, the government should be able to adjust the tax system to bring in more or less income. For example, during a war, the government may need to raise more money.

Understanding Federal Income Tax Returns

You've probably heard stories about people who got in trouble over their taxes. Maybe they didn't file their tax return on time. Maybe an audit, or review of their taxes by the IRS, revealed that they had failed to report some of their income. These kinds of mistakes can lead to hefty fines. So should you worry about your taxes? No, but you should understand that the IRS takes tax paying seriously. You've got to do it, and you need to do it right. If you make an honest effort, though, you have little to worry about.

To pay federal income tax, you must complete and file an income tax return each year. An **income tax return** is a form that shows how much you earned from working and made from other sources. It also shows how much tax you owe. If your employer withheld more money from your paychecks than you owe, you'll get a tax refund. If your employer didn't withhold enough, you'll have to pay the difference.

Creative BUSINESS PRACTICES

Chick-Fil-A
Never on Sunday

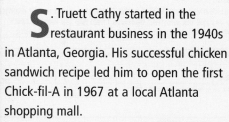

S. Truett Cathy started in the restaurant business in the 1940s in Atlanta, Georgia. His successful chicken sandwich recipe led him to open the first Chick-fil-A in 1967 at a local Atlanta shopping mall.

Still owned by Mr. Cathy and his family, Chick-fil-A is now the second largest chicken restaurant chain in the country. Because the Cathy family does not have to answer to investors, they can operate the company with more flexibility. For example, Mr. Cathy's religious beliefs have led him to close his restaurants on Sundays. He will not allow Chick-fil-A units—whether operated by the chain or licensees—to open on Sundays.

With its Sundays-off policy, Chick-fil-A attracts overworked restaurant employees who are guaranteed at least one day off a week. If the employees and franchisees do not share Mr. Cathy's religious convictions, they still appreciate the time off.

Critical Thinking

Do you think that companies should be influenced by their owners' personal lives? Why or why not?

Link and Learn

To read more about Chick-fil-A restaurants, visit the company's Web site via the link on the *Succeeding in the World of Work* Web site at **www.careers.glencoe.com**.

FIGURE 23.3

FORM W-4

Personal Allowances Worksheet (Keep for your records.)

A Enter "1" for **yourself** if no one else can claim you as a dependent . . . . A _____

B Enter "1" if:
- You are single and have only one job; or
- You are married, have only one job, and your spouse does not work; or
- Your wages from a second job or your spouse's wages (or the total of both) are $1,000 or less.

. . **B** _____

C Enter "1" for your **spouse**. But, you may choose to enter -0- if you are married and have either a working spouse or more than one job. (Entering -0- may help you avoid having too little tax withheld.) . . . . **C** _____

D Enter number of **dependents** (other than your spouse or yourself) you will claim on your tax return . . . . . . **D** _____

E Enter "1" if you will file as **head of household** on your tax return (see conditions under **Head of household** above) . **E** _____

F Enter "1" if you have at least $1,500 of **child or dependent care expenses** for which you plan to claim a credit . . **F** _____

G **Child Tax Credit:**
- If your total income will be between $18,000 and $50,000 ($23,000 and $63,000 if married), enter "1" for each eligible child.
- If your total income will be between $50,000 and $80,000 ($63,000 and $115,000 if married), enter "1" if you have two eligible children, enter "2" if you have three or four eligible children, or enter "3" if you have five or more eligible children . . **G** _____

H Add lines A through G and enter total here. **Note:** *This may be different from the number of exemptions you claim on your tax return.* ▶ **H** _____

For accuracy, complete all worksheets that apply.
- If you plan to **itemize or claim adjustments to income** and want to reduce your withholding, see the **Deductions and Adjustments Worksheet** on page 2.
- If you are **single**, have **more than one job** and your combined earnings from all jobs exceed $34,000, OR if you are **married** and have a **working spouse or more than one job** and the combined earnings from all jobs exceed $60,000, see the **Two-Earner/Two-Job Worksheet** on page 2 to avoid having too little tax withheld.
- If **neither** of the above situations applies, **stop here** and enter the number from line H on line 5 of Form W-4 below.

- **Cut here and give Form W-4 to your employer. Keep the top part for your records.** -

Form **W-4**
Department of the Treasury
Internal Revenue Service

Employee's Withholding Allowance Certificate

OMB No. 1545-0010

▶ **For Privacy Act and Paperwork Reduction Act Notice, see page 2.**

1 Type or print your first name and middle initial	Last name	2 Your social security number
Lisa N	Michaels	123 45 6789

Home address (number and street or rural route)
33 Clark Lane

3 ☒ Single ☐ Married ☐ Married, but withhold at higher Single rate.
Note: *If married, but legally separated, or spouse is a nonresident alien, check the Single box.*

City or town, state, and ZIP code
Greenville MA 01234

4 If your last name differs from that on your social security card, check here. **You must call 1-800-772-1213 for a new card** . . . ▶ ☐

5 Total number of allowances you are claiming (from line **H** above **OR** from the applicable worksheet on page 2) — **5** 0

6 Additional amount, if any, you want withheld from each paycheck — **6** $ _____

7 I claim exemption from withholding for 2000, and I certify that I meet **BOTH** of the following conditions for exemption:
- Last year I had a right to a refund of **ALL** Federal income tax withheld because I had **NO** tax liability **AND**
- This year I expect a refund of **ALL** Federal income tax withheld because I expect to have **NO** tax liability.
If you meet both conditions, write "EXEMPT" here . . . . ▶ **7** _____

Under penalties of perjury, I certify that I am entitled to the number of withholding allowances claimed on this certificate, or I am entitled to claim exempt status.

Employee's signature
(Form is not valid unless you sign it) ▶ *Lisa N. Michaels*

Date ▶ 8/10/03

8 Employer's name and address (Employer: Complete lines 8 and 10 only if sending to the IRS.)	9 Office code (optional)	10 Employer identification number

Cat. No. 10220Q

▲ **Withholding** All employees must fill out a Form W-4. *Why is it important to complete this form accurately?*

How does your employer know how much to withhold? Simple: by looking at the information you provide on a Form W-4, like the one in ***Figure 23.3.*** Completing this form is easy.

- Fill in your name, address, and Social Security number. Indicate whether you are married or single.

- Write the number of *allowances,* or deductions, you are allowed to claim. The higher the number, the less tax withheld. Use the "Personal Allowances Worksheet" on the Form W-4.

- Indicate whether you are *exempt*—excused—from having to pay tax.

- Sign and date the form.

How Do You File a Return?

In general, if you're single and earn at least $6,400 in a calendar year, you must file an income tax return. This figure changes from time to time, however. Check with the IRS for the current figure. You have to mail your tax return to the IRS by April 15.

To prepare your return, you'll need Form W-2. See **Figure 23.4.** Your employer will send this form to you. It shows how much money you earned and how much your employer withheld for taxes.

There are three basic federal income tax forms: 1040EZ, 1040A, and 1040. Form 1040EZ is the simplest one to fill out. It will probably work for you. These key terms will help you understand the tax forms:

- An **exemption** is a fixed amount of money that is excused from taxes. For example, in one recent year the IRS let each taxpayer claim a $2,500 personal exemption.

- A *dependent* is someone whom you support, such as a child.

FIGURE 23.4

FORM W-2

a Control number	22222	Void ☐	For Official Use Only ▶ OMB No. 1545-0008		
b Employer identification number 08-X1X0X1X				1 Wages, tips, other compensation **9175**	2 Federal income tax withheld **701.42**
c Employer's name, address, and ZIP code **ABC Painting Co., Inc. 432 Lomard Avenue Greenville, MA 01234**				3 Social security wages **9175**	4 Social security tax withheld **228.06**
				5 Medicare wages and tips **9175**	6 Medicare tax withheld **63.93**
				7 Social security tips	8 Allocated tips
d Employee's social security number 0X1-XX-1X00				9 Advance EIC payment	10 Dependent care benefits
e Employee's name (first, middle initial, last) **Lisa N. Michaels 33 Clark Lane Greenville, MA 01234**				11 Nonqualified plans	12 Benefits included in box 1
				13 See instrs. for box 13 **01000**	14 Other

15 Statutory employee ☐	Deceased ☐	Pension plan ☐	Legal rep. ☐	Deferred compensation ☐

f Employee's address and ZIP code

16 State Employer's state I.D. no. **MA 11-X1X0X1X**	17 State wages, tips, etc. **9175**	18 State income tax **402**	19 Locality name **GREENVILLE**	20 Local wages, tips, etc. **9175**	21 Local income tax **215**

Form **W-2** Wage and Tax Statement

Department of the Treasury—Internal Revenue Service

For Privacy Act and Paperwork Reduction Act Notice, see separate instructions.

Copy A For Social Security Administration—Send this entire page with Form W-3 to the Social Security Administration; photocopies are **not** acceptable.

Cat. No. 10134D

▲ **Wage and Tax Statement** Your employer will send you a Form W-2 in January. *What information on this form will help you prepare your income tax return?*

FIGURE
23.5

FORM 1040EZ

Department of the Treasury—Internal Revenue Service

Form 1040EZ **Income Tax Return for Single and Joint Filers With No Dependents**

OMB No. 1545-0675

Use the IRS label here

Your first name and initial: Lisa N Last name: Michaels

If a joint return, spouse's first name and initial / Last name

Home address (number and street). If you have a P.O. box, see page 12. / Apt. no.
33 Clark Lane

City, town or post office, state, and ZIP code. If you have a foreign address, see page 12.
Greenville MA 01234

Your social security number: 1 2 3 4 5 6 7 8 9

Spouse's social security number

Presidential Campaign (p. 12)
Note. Checking "Yes" will not change your tax or reduce your refund. Do you, or spouse if a joint return, want $3 to go to this fund? ▶

You ☐ Yes ☐ No   Spouse ☐ Yes ☐ No

Income

Attach Form(s) W-2 here. Enclose, but do not attach, any payment.

		Dollars	Cents
1	Total wages, salaries, and tips. This should be shown in box 1 of your W-2 form(s). Attach your W-2 form(s). 1	9,175	
2	Taxable interest. If the total is over $400, you cannot use Form 1040EZ. 2	63	
3	Unemployment compensation, qualified state tuition program earnings, and Alaska Permanent Fund dividends (see page 14). 3		
4	Add lines 1, 2, and 3. This is your **adjusted gross income.** 4	9,238	

Note. You must check Yes or No.

5	Can your parents (or someone else) claim you on their return? **Yes.** ✓ Enter amount from worksheet on back. **No.** ☐ If **single,** enter 7,200.00. If **married,** enter 12,950.00. See back for explanation. 5	3,900	
6	Subtract line 5 from line 4. If line 5 is larger than line 4, enter 0. This is your **taxable income.** ▶ 6	5,338	

Payments and tax

7	Enter your Federal income tax withheld from box 2 of your W-2 form(s). 7	701	
8a	**Earned income credit (EIC).** See page 15.		
b	Nontaxable earned income: enter type and amount below. Type _____ $ _____ 8a		
9	Add lines 7 and 8a. These are your **total payments.** 9	701	
10	**Tax.** Use the amount on **line 6 above** to find your tax in the tax table on pages 24–28 of the booklet. Then, enter the tax from the table on this line. 10	799	

Refund

Have it directly deposited! See page 20 and fill in 11b, 11c, and 11d.

11a	If line 9 is larger than line 10, subtract line 10 from line 9. This is your **refund.** 11a
▶ b	Routing number
▶ c	Type: ☐ Checking ☐ Savings d Account number

Amount you owe

12	If line 10 is larger than line 9, subtract line 9 from line 10. This is the **amount you owe.** See page 21 for details on how to pay. 12	98	

I have read this return. Under penalties of perjury, I declare that to the best of my knowledge and belief, the return is true, correct, and accurately lists all amounts and sources of income I received during the tax year.

Sign here
Keep copy for your records.

Your signature: Lisa N. Michaels
Date: 1/10/03   Your occupation: Programmer
Spouse's signature if joint return. See page 11.
Date   Spouse's occupation

For Official Use Only

May the IRS discuss this return with the preparer shown on back (see page 21)? ☐ Yes ☐ No

For Disclosure, Privacy Act, and Paperwork Reduction Act Notice, see **page 23.**   Cat. No. 11329W   Form **1040EZ**

▲ **Income Tax Return** Most young taxpayers can use Form 1040EZ for at least the first few years they file tax returns. *What form do you need to attach to Form 1040EZ?*

FIGURE
23.6

TAX TABLE

1040EZ Tax Table

If Form 1040EZ, line 6, is—		And you are—	
At least	But less than	Single	Married filing jointly
		Your tax is—	

11,000

At least	But less than	Single	Married filing jointly
11,000	11,050	1,654	1,654
11,050	11,100	1,661	1,661
11,100	11,150	1,669	1,669
11,150	11,200	1,676	1,676
11,200	11,250	1,684	1,684
11,250	11,300	1,691	1,691
11,300	11,350	1,699	1,699
11,350	11,400	1,706	1,706
11,400	11,450	1,714	1,714
11,450	11,500	1,721	1,721
11,500	11,550	1,729	1,729
11,550	11,600	1,736	1,736
11,600	11,650	1,744	1,744
11,650	11,700	1,751	1,751
11,700	11,750	1,759	1,759
11,750	11,800	1,766	1,766
11,800	11,850	1,774	1,774
11,850	11,900	1,781	1,781
11,900	11,950	1,789	1,789
11,950	12,000	1,796	1,796

▲ **Taxes Owed** Using a tax table is easy. First, find the line that corresponds to your taxable income. Then find the column that corresponds to your status—single or married, for example. Your tax is the amount shown where the income line and status column meet. *If you're single and your taxable income was $11,200, how much tax would you owe?*

- A **deduction** is an expense that you are allowed to subtract from your income. Examples may include medical or business expenses. The less taxable income you have, the less tax you'll have to pay.

To relieve themselves of paying excessive taxes, many people try to reduce the amount of income they report. Putting money into a 401(k) retirement fund or IRA, or donating to a charitable organization are legal ways to reduce your taxable income. Some taxpayers resort to illegal methods to lessen their taxable income. These methods are known as *fraud* or *tax evasion.*

The most common form of tax evasion is in not declaring income in the annual tax return. To deter illegal tax reporting, the IRS performs random *audits*. During an audit, the IRS requires a business or individual to prove that the information on a tax return is accurate.

You can probably file Form 1040EZ if you meet the following qualifications.

- You're single and earned less than $50,000 during the year. (Check each year with the IRS about the current maximum earnings.)

- You had no other income, such as taxable interest or dividends totaling more than $400.

- You are not claiming an exemption for being over 65 or for being blind.

- You have no dependents.

Check with the IRS for additional requirements for using Form 1040EZ.

Figure 23.5 shows Form 1040EZ. Completing this form involves several basic steps.

- Add up your total income from working and from other sources.

- Subtract your **standard deduction** and personal exemption.

- Use the tax table to find out how much tax is due on your income. ***Figure 23.6*** shows a portion of the table. By comparing this amount with the taxes withheld on your Form W-2, you'll see whether you owe more taxes or will get a refund.

As *Figure 23.7* shows, figuring your taxes isn't hard if you're organized. Need help? Don't worry. The IRS provides free publications that will help. You can also get help over the phone, via the Internet, and from tax-help books at the library. If you have a computer, you might try tax-preparation software. Alternatively, you can pay a tax-preparation service or an accountant to prepare your forms for you.

FIGURE 23.7

Filing a Federal Tax Return Filing a federal tax return is not difficult if you organize your information and follow instructions.

A **Assemble Your Records** Gather the necessary information. For example, you'll need Form W-2 and records of any other earnings, such as a statement of interest from your bank. If you've filed a tax return before, have a copy of your previous return on hand for reference.

B **Get the Forms** Obtain the tax form you'll need, such as a Form 1040EZ or 1040A, and the corresponding IRS instruction booklet. You can find forms and booklets at post offices, libraries, and most banks. You can also get them from the IRS. (The IRS even has a Web site from which you can download forms.) If you use a tax-preparation computer program, the software will probably include the forms you need.

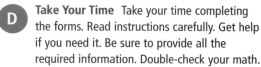

D **Take Your Time** Take your time completing the forms. Read instructions carefully. Get help if you need it. Be sure to provide all the required information. Double-check your math.

C **Consider Online Forms** If it would be easier to fill these forms out online, the IRS Web site allows you to choose a form, and fill it out on the site. This can save you time, help avoid handwriting problems, and make it harder to misplace the form.

E **Keep a Copy** Keep a photocopy of the completed tax return for your records. Attach any necessary forms (such as the W-2) to the original return, and send it to the IRS by April 15.

SECTION 23.1 REVIEW

✓ Key Concept Checkpoint

Comprehension

1. List five characteristics of a good tax system. Why are these features desirable?

2. How does the amount of money you earn and the amount withheld determine whether you owe income tax?

3. How will understanding such terms as exemption, dependent, and deduction help you complete a tax return?

Critical Thinking

4. Why do you think the taxation process involves so much paperwork?

CAREER FOCUS

Fred Helwig
Psychologist

CAREER FACTS

Education or Training A doctoral degree is required to work as a licensed clinical or counseling psychologist. A bachelor's degree is required to work as a psychologist's assistant at a community-based mental health program. Classes in biology, physical and social sciences, and statistics are helpful.

Aptitudes, Abilities, and Skills Emotional maturity and the ability to interact well with others are necessary. Excellent communication skills and the ability to work alone and as part of a team are also important.

Career Outlook Average job growth is expected through 2008.

Career Path Psychologists may go on to work for a specialized hospital, to form their own practice, or to teach at the college level.

What is your key to success?
"The key to my success is patience with clients, as well as objective listening and communication skills. Because listening to serious problems can be emotionally draining, it is also important to have outside activities to take my mind off work."

What do you like most about your work?
"I help people understand themselves better and help them develop healthy relationships with family and coworkers. My work is gratifying when I witness changes and have success stories. I also appreciate that I can arrange my own schedule. I see from 5 to 40 patients a week, which requires some variation in my schedule. Most people want to see me on evenings and weekends, so I have to work irregular hours."

What kind of training did you have?
"I have always had an interest in psychology and understanding how people work and what motivates them. I have a master's degree in psychology, and am currently working on my doctorate in psychology. In addition, I am certified as a Licensed Clinical Professional Counselor (LCPC) and Certified Alcohol and Drug Counselor (CADC)."

What training do you recommend for students?
"To practice in this field, students should earn a master's degree as well as certification. Knowledge of basic psychology is a benefit in any job, even if students decide not to stay in the field."

Critical Thinking Why is emotional maturity necessary to work as a psychologist?

All About Social Security

What does the term *Social Security* mean to you? Do you think of retired workers who depend on their Social Security checks to live? That's part of it, but there's more to Social Security than that. It's a program that provides benefits for people of all ages. For example, if a worker becomes disabled, Social Security will help his or her family cope with the loss of income.

How the Social Security Program Works

Where does the money that pays for Social Security benefits come from? Most of it comes from Social Security taxes. Both workers and employers pay these taxes. As you read earlier, employers deduct Social Security tax from your paycheck. Your employer matches your contribution. If you're self-employed, you must pay both the employee's and employer's share of the tax. (Currently, however, self-employed workers may deduct half of their Social Security tax from their federal income tax.)

Your Social Security Number

Do you know your Social Security number? Your parent or guardian probably got one for you when you were little. This is your permanent identification number. The government uses it to keep track of your contributions and work history. Your employer will ask you for this number. You'll also need to put it on tax forms.

WHAT YOU'LL LEARN

- How the Social Security system works
- How to identify four Social Security progam benefits and two state social insurance benefits
- The main problems facing the Social Security system today

WHY IT'S IMPORTANT

Understanding Social Security, which acts as a federal retirement safety net, will help you plan for your future.

KEY TERMS

- **work credits**
- **disabled worker**
- **Medicare**
- **unemployment insurance**
- **workers' compensation**

Mass Layoffs Many people lost their jobs during the Great Depression of the 1930s. Families suffered severe hardship. Congress passed the Social Security Act of 1935 to aid families whose members lost their jobs, were unable to work, or were retired. ***Do you know anyone who receives Social Security benefits? Why do they recieve Social Security?***

Becoming Eligible for Benefits

Once you begin working, you start to earn work credits. **Work credits** are measurements of how long you've worked. You must earn a certain number of credits to get Social Security benefits. You earn work credits for each year you work and pay Social Security taxes.

Types of Benefits

There are many different kinds of Social Security benefits. Some are for eligible people of any age.

- *Disability benefits* are paid to disabled workers. A **disabled worker** is someone who cannot work because of a physical or mental condition.

The amount of the benefit is based on the worker's average earnings.

- *Survivors' benefits* are paid to the family of a worker who dies.

- *Retirement benefits* are paid to workers who retire. Up to a certain amount, the higher your average yearly earnings, the higher your benefits. The retirement age for reduced benefits is now 62. The retirement age for full benefits is now 65. That age will gradually rise to 67 by 2027.

- *Health insurance benefits* are paid to people who need hospitalization or other medical care. These benefits, called **Medicare**, cover nearly everyone who is 65 or older.

Social Security is a federal program. As a worker, you're also entitled to benefits from two state-run social insurance programs. These are similar to Social Security. Their rules vary from state to state, however.

- **Unemployment insurance** provides temporary income to workers who have lost their jobs. To be eligible, you generally must have worked for a certain length of time and not have lost your job through your fault. Unemployment insurance is funded by taxes both the employer and employee pay.

Helping Older Americans Medicare helps people who are 65 and older meet the high costs of medical care. *Who pays for Medicare? How?*

CAREER CHECKLIST

When Paying Taxes...

- ☑ Study all forms that you fill out for your job, and check to ensure that they are filled out correctly.
- ☑ Understand what you claim on your tax forms and why—this will prevent you from making any errors.
- ☑ Review your pay stubs to make sure that you are being taxed correctly.
- ☑ Keep copies of all tax returns and other related documents.
- ☑ Seek professional help when filing your taxes if your taxes are complicated or you are eligible for deductions.
- ☑ Find the appropriate IRS tax forms online.
- ☑ Don't allow your employer to pay you without withholding taxes. You could end up owing a lot of money to the government!

- **Workers' compensation** benefits are paid to workers injured on the job and to dependents of workers killed on the job. These benefits may include medical care, disability income, and other benefits. Workers' compensation is funded by taxes the employer pays.

Tough Decisions It is the U.S. Congress's responsibility to solve the problem with Social Security. *What can you do to influence the decisions that are made?*

The Future of Social Security

If you follow the news, you know that Social Security is a "hot issue" these days. That's because the system has a big problem: it's going broke.

The Social Security taxes you pay provide benefits for workers who have already retired. When it's your turn to retire, younger workers will pay the taxes to fund *your* retirement.

Well, maybe. Here's the problem: People are living longer so they receive more benefits; and many are retiring earlier so they pay less into the system. At the same time, the U.S. birthrate is declining. This means that there will be fewer young workers around to support retired people in the future. The situation will worsen as the large number of workers now in their 40s and 50s reach retirement age. Before long, the money being paid out will exceed the amount coming in.

There are many proposed solutions to this problem. Some would increase taxes. Others would cut benefits. One way or another, the system needs to be changed. You can play a part in making these changes by staying informed and voting.

SECTION 23.2 REVIEW

✓ Key Concept Checkpoint

Comprehension

1. Why is it important to build up work credits?

2. Why is the program of benefits discussed in this section called Social Security?

3. What may happen to Social Security by the time you retire if the system isn't changed soon?

Critical Thinking

4. Do you believe that it is a good idea for a society to have a system like Social Security? Why or why not?

KEY TERMS
Internal Revenue
    Service (IRS) (p. 458)
withhold (p. 459)
income tax return (p. 463)
exemption (p. 465)
deduction (p. 467)

SECTION 23.1

- Taxes are payments that people must make to support federal, state, and local governments. Common taxes include income taxes, Social Security taxes, sales taxes, and property taxes. (pp. 458–461)

- Tax dollars pay for a wide range of services, such as education, transportation, and military services. (p. 461)

- You can influence the way that tax dollars are spent by voting for officials who represent your views. (p. 462)

- A good tax system should be fair, simple, convenient, stable, and flexible. (pp. 462–463)

- Your income tax return shows how much income you received and how much tax you owe. Form W-4 will tell your employer how much tax to withhold. Form W-2 will show how much you earned. (pp. 463–465)

KEY TERMS
work credits (p. 472)
disabled worker (p. 472)
Medicare (p. 472)
unemployment
    insurance (p. 473)
workers' compensation
    (p. 473)

SECTION 23.2

- The money for Social Security benefits comes chiefly from Social Security taxes paid by workers and employers. (p. 471)

- The government uses your Social Security number to keep track of your contributions and work history. (p. 471)

- You earn work credits each year that you work and pay Social Security taxes. You must earn a certain number of credits to become eligible for Social Security benefits. (p. 472)

- Social Security benefits include disability benefits, survivors' benefits, retirement benefits, and health insurance benefits. (p. 472)

- Two state-run programs that provide benefits for workers are unemployment insurance and workers' compensation. (p. 473)

- The Social Security system must be changed to keep the amount of money being paid out from exceeding the amount coming in. (p. 474)

Reviewing Key Terms

1. Write one paragraph about taxes and one paragraph about Social Security. Use the terms below.
   - Internal Revenue Service (IRS)
   - withhold
   - income tax return
   - exemption
   - deduction
   - work credits
   - disabled worker
   - Medicare
   - unemployment insurance
   - workers' compensation

Recalling Key Concepts

2. Which of the following is *not* a characteristic of a good tax system?

   (a) Everyone pays his or her fair share.

   (b) Tax rules are clear and simple.

   (c) Taxes are collected at the beginning of each year.

3. You'll have to pay additional income tax if ____.

   (a) your employer withholds too little tax

   (b) your employer withholds too much tax

   (c) you don't receive a Form W-2

4. Social Security taxes are paid by ____.

   (a) workers (b) employers

   (c) both workers and employers

5. Which one of the following benefits is *not* part of Social Security?

   (a) workers' compensation

   (b) survivors' benefits (c) Medicare

6. One reason why the Social Security system is in trouble is that ____.

   (a) fewer people are retiring

   (b) the birthrate is declining

   (c) the birthrate is increasing

Problem Solving

7. Do you believe that everyone should pay a fair share of taxes? Explain.

8. How does voting give all citizens an equal voice in deciding how their government spends tax dollars?

9. Your employer has recorded the wrong Social Security number for you. Why is it important to correct the error?

10. What is the drawback of having the Social Security taxes of younger workers pay for the benefits of older workers?

Work-Based Learning

Basic Skills Math

11. Suppose you bought an exercise machine for $161, books for $36, CDs for $32, and a watch for $45. If the state sales tax is 4 percent, how much did you spend?

Information Acquiring and Evaluating Information

12. It's time to file an income tax return, however, you're not sure which form to complete or how to complete it. Describe two ways to get answers to your questions.

School–Based Learning

Computer Science Research Tax Preparation

13. Amy works in the human resources department. Her supervisor has asked her to help run a workshop for new employees. Part of the workshop will focus on taxes and tax-preparation software. Research tax-preparation programs in the library, via the Internet, or by speaking to taxpayers who have used such programs. Are there any that you think Amy should recommend? Why or why not?

Math Calculate Social Security

14. In 1995, Daniel earned $22,490 as a paralegal aide. He got paid every two weeks. His employer withheld Social Security tax at a rate of 7.65 percent. How much did Daniel's employer withhold from each paycheck?

Role Play

15. Make Your Case

Situation You are a member of a non-profit organization dedicated to the reform of the Social Security system. You have set up a meeting with a senator from your state to convince him/her of your views.

Activity Role-play a conversation in which you explain your organization's position on Social Security, explaining how you feel the system should be reformed. Use your knowledge of both the tax system and the Social Security system to defend your organization's opinions.

Evaluation You will be evaluated based on how well you meet the following performance indicators:

- Defend your position by accurately using the realities of the tax and Social Security systems.
- Point out the flaws in the current system and the advantages of your proposal.
- Correctly answer any questions your Senator may have.

*inter*NET
CONNECTION

16. Social Security Debate
Research the current Social Security debate in Congress by reading recent articles from major newspapers. Contact your state representatives in Congress and ask their positions on the issue. Based on this issue, would you vote for your current representatives? Explain your opinions in a brief essay.

Connect Research online the different positions on Social Security. What do the Democrats say? the Republicans? the Libertarians? With whom do you agree?

Budgeting Time and Money in Your Career

✓ Overview

Soon you'll be responsible for all of your decisions regarding your time and money. Preparing for this challenge will simplify the transition from student to adult. You may be surprised by some of the choices and changes you'll have to make. Planning how you will spend your time and money now will enable you to gain satisfaction from your personal and professional life.

✓ Assignment

Conduct targeted research about the career field that you want to enter. Consider career choices with varying educational requirements. How many hours are involved in a typical work week? How much money can you expect to make? Will you need to work at night, during the day, both? Once you've conducted adequate research, plan a typical month in your life as an adult worker. Develop a monthly personal schedule that projects how much time you'll need for working, shopping, recreation, and other pursuits. Then estimate a monthly budget using an entry-level salary for your field. Don't forget to budget for expenses such as car insurance, utilities, rent, savings, and so forth. You will probably need to conduct research to find out the prices of many of the expenses that will become part of your daily life.

✓ Tools/Resources

To complete this assignment, you must conduct research using a variety of sources including the Internet and the library.

✓ Procedures

Using the ideas provided in the Helpful Hints section, conduct research to find out specifics about the salary and work hours of various careers in your chosen career field. Select the career that most closely matches your lifestyle desires, then create a budget. When planning your budgets, consult up-to-date resources to determine the prices of the items and resources you will need. When you've completed your budgets, write a one-page essay explaining how your perception of working full-time has changed.

✓ Report

Your final product for this lab should include two posters representing your monthly schedule and monthly budget reflecting your lifestyle goals and desires. Remember to use graphic elements such as pie charts and calendars whenever possible to make your project visually interesting.

You should also present a typed, one-page summary that discusses how your perceptions of adult life have changed as a result of this lab.

✓ Presentation and Evaluation

You will be evaluated based on

- Depth of planning and research presented in budgets
- Presentation and neatness
- Accuracy of data and projections

Your report will be evaluated based on

- Depth of reflection expressed
- Grammar and mechanics

✓ Personal Career Portfolio

Print out a copy of your completed report to include in your personal career portfolio.

HELPFUL HINTS

Things to Consider

When anticipating how to budget your time, consider how much time you'll need to devote to the following activities:

- Work (including commute)
- Grocery shopping
- Cleaning
- Errands
- Paying bills
- Shopping for clothes and gifts
- Errands
- Exercising
- Recreation
- Staying in touch with friends and family
- Reading
- Seeking additional schooling
- Miscellaneous activities

When developing your monthly budget, think of how much money you'll need to reserve for the following expenses:

- Rent/mortgage
- Groceries
- Clothing
- Recreation/entertainment
- Health care
- Car expenses
- Homeowner's/renter's insurance
- Cable
- Utilities
- Tuition
- Savings
- Investment/retirement savings
- Gifts

Lifelong Learning

Portfolio Project

Choosing a Second Career Many people pursue second careers after retirement. For instance, a retired teacher many choose to become a museum tour guide, while a retired engineer may opt to teach high school science. Such opportunities for personal growth actually help people live longer, happier lives. Think about something that you might enjoy doing after retirement. Conduct some research about this career. Is it a suitable choice for a retired person? How would this career help you enjoy your retirement years? Explain your findings in a two-page essay.

CAREER LAB PREVIEW

Putting It All Together: Developing a Plan to Achieve Success Throughout Life

As part of this unit, you will create a career time line. You'll identify realistic career and personal goals and plot short- and long-term strategies for achieving your ideals, then present them to the class. Later, your time line will enable you to keep track of your progress through the world of work!

Chapter 24

Adapting to Change

Section 24.1
Managing Your Career

Section 24.2
Changing Jobs or Careers

CHAPTER OBJECTIVES

After completing this chapter, you will be able to

- Identify ways to prepare yourself for the future.

- Describe actions and behaviors that lead to promotions

- Explain why workers may want to change jobs, and describe strategies for seeking a new job or career.

- Describe steps to take if you lose your job.

JOURNAL

Personal Career Plan

Imagine that you hold a job that is an important step toward your career goal. Now you've been offered a promotion that will take you away from your familiar responsibilities and friendly colleagues. In your journal, list the advantages and disadvantages of this job change.

Personal Career Project

Interview two adults who have successful careers. Ask them about their original goals and the paths their careers have taken. Did they meet their orginal goal? If not, why. In your journal, write whether you think you will alter your career goals and why.

Managing Your Career

WHAT YOU'LL LEARN

- How to prepare yourself for the future
- The qualities, actions, and behaviors that will help you achieve promotions

WHY IT'S IMPORTANT

When you enter the work force you'll be expected to understand the standard practices and procedures used at most places of employment.

KEY TERMS

- **downsizing**
- **promotion**
- **seniority**
- **perseverance**

Think back over your high school years. How have you changed? In the years ahead, changes will continue to occur. Your skills and interests will keep expanding in new directions. New career possibilities will emerge. The world of work will change, too. Changes at work may open even more doors. Can you predict these changes? No. You *can*, however, prepare yourself to respond to them.

Preparing for the Future

Today's workplace offers challenges that earlier generations of workers did not face. First of all, the job market changes quickly. Jobs that once employed a majority of the population have become much less significant. ***Figure 24.1*** shows the ten jobs that experts predict will grow fastest through the year 2008.

Tracking employment trends is one way to prepare for the future. What else can you do?

Thinking in New Ways

You may know people who took jobs when they were young and stayed with the same company for their entire working lives. Forty years ago, that was typical. Today it is not. As you learned in the first chapter of this book, the average American will have more than eight different jobs by the age of 32. People can expect to change employers several—perhaps many—more times before they retire. What does this mean?

It means that your career and your job security are in your own hands. That can be to your advantage—if you use your self-management skills.

The new world of work is a leaner place than ever before. Many companies have gone through **downsizing**, the elimination of jobs in a company to promote efficiency or to cut costs. Some people end up losing their jobs from downsizing. Everyone, however, is affected. When, for example, management jobs are cut, individual workers acquire additional responsibilities. That can mean more job satisfaction. Yet it can also mean more work and greater demands on those workers.

Keeping Up

Luckily, the company you work for wants you to meet these demands at least as much as you do. To help workers, many of today's companies invest heavily in employee training and education. AT&T, for example, spends about $1 billion annually on training. The average AT&T employee receives a little more than a week of training every year. At your job, make use of all opportunities to keep your skills and knowledge up-to-date. In other words, become a *lifelong learner*.

The competitive global market puts added demands on workers. Businesses want to maintain the state of the art. These

FIGURE 24.1

THE TEN FASTEST GROWING OCCUPATIONS: 1998–2008

Occupation	Employment in 1998	Projected Employment in 2008	Percentage Change 1998-2008
Computer engineers	299,000	622,000	108
Computer support specialists	429,000	869,000	102
System analysts	617,000	1,194,000	94
Database administrators	87,000	155,000	77
Desktop publishing specialists	26,000	44,000	73
Paralegals and legal assistants	136,000	220,000	62
Personal care and home health aides	746,000	1,179,000	58
Medical assistants	252,000	398,000	58
Social and human service assistants	268,000	410,000	53
Physician's assistants	66,000	98,000	48

SOURCE: U.S. Bureau of Labor Statistics, *Economic and Employment Projections, 1998-2008*, November 1999.

▲ **Emerging Opportunities** This table shows the ten jobs that experts believe will grow fastest through the year 2008. *Which job is expected to grow at the highest rate? Even if the prediction is accurate, why can't a person count on a job in this field?*

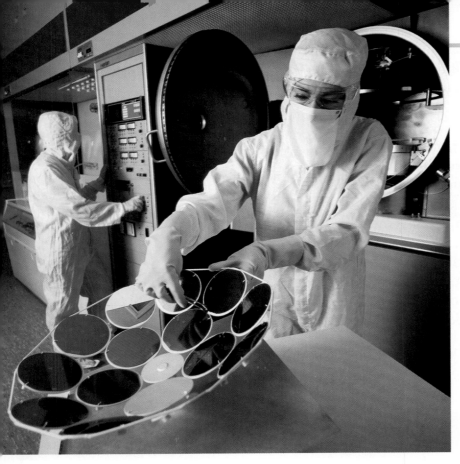

companies require workers with state-of-the-art knowledge and skills.

Since no one can predict with certainty what new technology will appear, you should develop solid reading, writing, math, speaking, and listening skills. These skills will give you the basic tools for absorbing new technology.

When new technology appears in your workplace, get involved right away. Volunteer for training sessions or tasks that will give you hands-on training. Take technology courses at community colleges and vocational and technical centers. Many companies offer paid tuition for employees who want to take courses in areas related to their jobs.

Growing in Your Job

Continuing to update and improve your skills and knowledge will make you valuable to your employer. It may also help you earn a promotion. A **promotion** is a job advancement to a position of greater responsibility and authority. Promotions will offer new challenges. Usually promotions also bring increased income.

Who Gets Promoted?

The people who earn promotions are the people who have shown their supervisors that they can handle additional responsibility and authority. What qualities and behaviors do employers look for?

- *Seniority* **Seniority** is the position or prestige you achieve by working for an employer for a sustained length of time. Greater seniority is usually thought of as indicating greater experience and dependability.

- *Knowledge and competence* Employers want workers who know how to do their jobs, even if the new job requires different skills. Employers also look for workers who go a step beyond this—workers who excel. These employees are likely to do well in jobs with more responsibility.

- *Willingness to learn* Employers promote workers who show they want to increase their knowledge and skills.

- *Initiative* You'll probably advance in your career if you make it clear to your supervisor that advancement is an important goal for you. A good time to talk about career goals is during your performance evaluation. Avoid giving the impression that you want to get out of your current job, however. Emphasize that you want more responsibility and challenge.

Creative
BUSINESS PRACTICES

Red Hat, Inc.
Web-Based Performance Reviews

Red Hat, Inc. develops and manages the Linux computer operating system and other Internet-based technology, such as secure Web servers. It's only natural that Red Hat, based in Durham, North Carolina, would make the move from paper to Web-based employee performance appraisals.

As part of Red Hat's program, employees enter goals and regularly record their progress in a performance management system, which can be accessed online. Managers log on to monitor their employees' goals and comment about their performance.

Because managers and employees update the system frequently, performance is tracked consistently. This makes formal yearly performance reviews more comprehensive, because managers tend to evaluate employees based on their progress documented throughout the year.

The Web-based performance management system also benefits the Red Hat company, because executives can easily see if the company is on track to meet its goals.

Critical Thinking

Do you think a Web-based performance system can help make employees more productive? Why or why not?

Link and Learn

To read more about Red Hat, Inc., visit the company's Web site via the link on the *Succeeding in the World of Work* Web site at **www.careers.glencoe.com**.

- *Perseverance* **Perseverance** is the quality of finishing what you start. Employers want to know that you will see a job through to completion.

- *Cooperativeness* When you have more responsibility, you'll have to cooperate with more people. Employers want people who can get along well with others.

- *Thinking skills* When considering whom to promote, employers look for people who can think through situations and solve problems.

- *Adaptability* Employers want workers who can adapt to new situations and a changing business.

- *Education and training* Employers promote people who have the training needed for the new job.

Handling Your New Responsibilities

Getting a promotion may change your work life in many ways. Often it means you'll become a supervisor. Then you will be responsible for both your own work and the work of others. Look back at Chapter 14 to remind yourself of the qualities of a good supervisor.

Be aware that as a supervisor your relationships with your former coworkers will change. You'll be the boss. You must oversee their work and give direction. You will review their performance. It may be difficult to have close friendships with people you supervise. Be sure you are prepared for these changes.

Keeping Pace with Change Learning should not end with high school or even college. Workers must keep up-to-date on the latest information in their fields. *How can further education give you greater confidence?*

Work Etiquette If you want to decline a promotion, talk to your supervisor face-to-face. ***Why do you think this is important?***

Declining a Promotion

Being offered a promotion is always a good thing. It shows you've earned your employer's trust and appreciation. Not every promotion, however, is right for you. Perhaps the promotion requires too many personal sacrifices. For example, you might be asked to travel more than you want or to take on responsibilities you don't feel ready for.

It's OK to decline a promotion. Most employers will respect your judgement. Avoid closing the door on future offers, however. Even if this promotion is not right, the next one might be. Let your supervisor know your specific reasons for declining a promotion. Leave your supervisor with the impression that you like your work and want to be considered for future promotions.

SECTION 24.1 REVIEW

✔ Key Concept Checkpoint

Comprehension

1. How will continuing your education help you be prepared for changes in the workplace?

2. Why is it important to let your supervisor know you're interested in a promotion?

Critical Thinking

3. What should you do if you are repeatedly passed over for promotions?

CAREER FOCUS

CAREER FACTS

Education or Training
A bachelor's degree with a focus on Web design is helpful, as well as an internship in the field. Web designers must be familiar with HTML (HyperText Markup Language), Adobe Photoshop, and Adobe Illustrator.

Aptitudes, Abilities, and Skills
Knowledge of Web development and e-commerce, along with strong people skills, good organizational skills, and the ability to work as a member of a team are essential.

Career Outlook   Average job growth is expected through 2008.

Career Path   Web designers may choose to become Web programmers, Web producers, project managers, or system administrators.

What is your key to success?
"My keys to success are my creativity and attention to detail. Users like to visit Web sites that are visually pleasing and easy to use."

What does your job entail?
"I develop a variety of Web sites. I am involved in all aspects of a site launch from start to finish. My duties include defining the overall structure, choosing and implementing the graphic look, defining the content, and managing and supporting the content managers who provide the everyday maintenance."

What skills are most important to you?
"Technical skills, such as a general knowledge of computers, networks, the Internet, and some programming languages (HTML, XML, JavaScript), are just as important as people skills. Clients often don't know exactly what they are looking for, and it is up to the Web designer to ask questions and present options."

What do you like most about your work?
"My job gives me the ability to be creative and to turn ideas and concepts into a finished product. I gain the most satisfaction from my job when a Web site I produce exceeds the client's expectations."

How did you get into Web design?
"After I graduated from college with a finance degree, I worked as a financial systems consultant for a small company. A coworker was working on a Web site for a nonprofit event and needed some help with the design and layout. I ended up working on the project and realized that Web design was the right field for me."

> **Critical Thinking**   How can you gain experience in computer programming languages such as HTML if your school does not offer relevant classes?

Changing Jobs or Careers

As you know, you are likely to change employers several times during your work career. Sometimes you may choose the change because you want to seek new opportunities. At other times, the change may be forced on you by events beyond your control.

Why Change Jobs?

Changing your job should never be a snap decision. Before making a change, you should analyze what is missing from your current job and what you want from a new one. Always make sure you have thought through the change carefully.

Because You're Not Happy

When you are unhappy at work, a job change may be one solution. *Figure 24.2* on page 492 is a checklist of danger signs. Use it to evaluate your situation.

Before giving up on your job, however, consider whether there might be a way to stay and solve the problem. If you decide to stay, set work goals for yourself. What do you want to achieve in your job—a pay raise, a promotion, new responsibilities or challenges? How long will you give yourself to reach your goals?

Because You Want to Grow

It is possible to outgrow your job. Perhaps you feel unfulfilled and unchallenged. Perhaps you have discovered that what you are doing isn't really what you want to do. In these cases, a job change may be what you need.

FIGURE
24.2

SIGNS OF TROUBLE CHECKLIST

- [ ] Do my coworkers ignore me or leave me out?

- [ ] Do I feel that I'm wasting my time?

- [ ] Do I find myself daydreaming what my life would be like without this job?

- [ ] Is being sick a relief to me because I don't have to go to work?

- [ ] Do I seem to always be making someone at work angry or upset?

- [ ] Do I feel as though I don't have a future with the company or a chance for advancement?

- [ ] Do I have trouble sleeping because I'm worried about my job?

▲ **Evaluate Your Position** Use this checklist to evaluate your level of job satisfaction. Answering yes to any of these questions indicates that you should reassess your situation. Changing your job isn't necessarily the answer, however. *How might you solve a work problem if you plan to stay?*

ETHICS *in Action*

Evaluating Loyalty You have worked as an assistant to the elderly owner of a small eyeglass shop for several years. You have become close to the owner, helping him with tasks around his house and even inviting him to your family's home for holidays. Because he has no children, the owner says he will leave the shop to you when he passes away. Yesterday, the manager of a new eyeglass shop offered you a position that pays double your current salary. You told him you would get back to him soon.

THINK ABOUT IT
What are the pros and cons of taking the job at the new store? What will you decide?

Because Your Job Is Terminated

There are times, of course, when a job change is forced on you. Downsizing, corporate restructuring, and global economic factors have created a working world in which little is constant except change.

You *can* prepare for an unexpected job loss. Stay alert to signs of trouble. These include signals that your supervisor is displeased with your work or that the company is not doing well. Read newspaper articles and magazines about your industry to detect industry trends.

Making the Change

When you decide to make a career or job change, put your decision-making skills to work. First you have to define your needs or wants.

Focusing Your Search

Consider where you want to look for a new job. Here are three possible ways to focus your search.

- *Same job, new company* If you like what you're doing, explore similar positions with other companies. You already know you have the right skills for the job. A different company, however, may offer better opportunities.

- *New job, new company* What if you have the right skills for your

job but you really don't like it? That happened to Lisa Von Drasek. She was working in book sales when a layoff forced her to do some rethinking. She suddenly realized she didn't feel fulfilled in her career. She wanted a job that would allow her to make a difference in the world. When a friend suggested library school, Von Drasek was skeptical. After talking with several librarians, however, she signed up for a master's program.

Today she's a children's librarian at the Brooklyn Public Library. Every day, she sees young teen mothers, recent immigrants, and others discover the world of books. She has even developed her own children's

Staying Informed Keeping up with business news can bring early warnings of trouble in your industry or company. It can also bring news of better times to come. *What are some examples of business news that could affect employment in your area?*

writing program. "The kids run up to my desk and say, 'When are we going to write?'" she says. "I make a difference."

- *Starting over* A third possibility is to turn a hobby or interest into a career. Geoffrey Macon had spent 17 years in the banking industry. When a combination of health problems and corporate restructuring cost him his job, he turned his career in a different direction. Macon had always had a passionate interest in ethnic art. He became an entrepreneur, designing, manufacturing, and selling plates and other tableware based on ethnic designs.

What's Different This Time Around?

In this book, you have been introduced to many job search strategies. Chapter 2, for example, talked about career decision making. Chapter 3 gave tips on researching careers. Chapter 6 provided basic information on finding and applying for a job. Chapter 7 covered interview techniques. The main focus in these chapters was on choosing your career and landing your first job. The advice is just as useful when you are finding a new job or changing your career. You will still need to research jobs, apply for jobs and make a great impression in an interview.

Making Work Enjoyable These entrepreneurs have turned a personal interest into a way of making a living. *What interest of yours might you turn into a business?*

In addition, consider the following points:

- Because you've been out in the world of work, you have much more data available to you. What are your skills? Which tasks have you enjoyed most?

- Consider how you can use proven skills in new ways. Suppose you have been a receptionist. Your telephone skills could be used in marketing. Your ability to remain in control when all the lines are flashing could be valuable in retail sales.

- List jobs or careers that you might like. What are the pros and cons of each? How can your skills and interests be applied to them?

- Research jobs in which you are interested. You have probably built up a network of people at your current job. Use these contacts to explore new directions.

- Try to arrange your interviews so that you don't miss work.

- Don't burn your bridges with your present employer. You don't want to lose your current job until you've landed a new one. Besides, you never know when your old contacts will once again be valuable to you.

- When you've found a new job, give proper notice to your current employer. **Notice** is an official written statement that you are leaving the company. Most people prepare a formal letter of resignation. Businesses usually have a policy stating how long they expect employees to work after giving notice.

CAREER CHECKLIST

Facing A Career Change...

- ✔ Keep your long-term goals in mind when you consider making a career change.
- ✔ Remember that many successful individuals make changes in their career paths.
- ✔ Never fear moving on to a more challenging job—that is the best move you can make!
- ✔ View change as a positive way to learn more about yourself and your interests.
- ✔ Apply skills and knowledge you've already acquired when you start a new job.

- Don't tell coworkers about your job hunt. Always inform coworkers about the new job *after* you've given notice.

- Don't lose steam at work. People will remember if you slack off during your last two weeks. Leave a good impression.

- Let people outside the company know what's happening. Tell clients or other business contacts that you are leaving. Don't criticize the company, however, no matter how disappointed or angry you feel. Doing so will only make you seem petty, and it could lose you a future job.

Dealing with a Job Loss

Most people are laid off or have their jobs terminated at least once during their working careers (See **Figure 24.3**). It is always a painful experience. If it happens to you, you may feel depressed, embarrassed, resentful, angry, afraid, or discouraged.

FIGURE 24.3 Losing a Job If you lose your job, you may think you have nothing to do. That's not true! You'll be working full-time getting a new job.

A **Ask Questions** Your first response to the news of the job loss may be a powerful negative emotion such as anger or sadness. As soon as you have your emotions under control, talk with your supervisor. Ask about job-search services available through your employer, severance pay (money that may be offered to employees who are dismissed), funds from profit-sharing or pension plans, payment for unused vacation time, and terms for extension of your health insurance coverage.

B **Review Your Budget** Next, review your financial situation. Figure out how much money you have to live on. Then prepare a budget so you know you can pay for the things you must have. Find ways to cut back on your expenses.

C **Apply for Benefits** In most cases, workers who lose their jobs can get unemployment benefits. These checks will help you get by until you find your next job. Every state has its own guidelines for applying for unemployment compensation. Most states require official documentation of your termination, such as the example shown above.

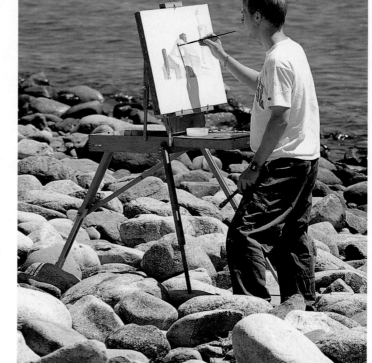

D **Look for a New Job** Update and improve your résumé. Remember that it should be brief and to the point. Ask several people to read it over, and consider having it printed professionally. Use every strategy you can think of in your job search. These include networking, contacting employment agencies, using job search Web sites, and reading the classified ads.

E **Seize the Opportunity** Stay positive as you go for interviews. Remember that a job loss can be a good opportunity to find a better job or to follow your dreams.

These are valid emotions, and you shouldn't be ashamed of feeling them. However, don't let them overwhelm you. Try to remain positive. Look on the event as an opportunity to start over. Perhaps, like Lisa Von Drasek or Geoffrey Macon, you may be able to do what you've always wanted. You may even be able to earn a better income than you did before.

Changing Careers

You've decided to switch careers and make teaching children your next goal in life. You have a college degree—but not in education—so you need to find out what you need to do to become a teacher.

Connect

- Find your state's Board of Education on the Internet. Research the requirements for teachers.
- Write a one-page report on what you will do to start your new career and how your experience might be helpful to you as a teacher.

Seeking a New Job Try to be open-minded when you are looking for a new job. You might find that your skills apply to some very interesting jobs. *What kinds of skills would be important in the job pictured here?*

SECTION 24.2 REVIEW

✓ Key Concept Checkpoint

Comprehension

1. Why is the desire for personal growth a good reason to change jobs.
2. What are some of the unique aspects of looking for a job when you already have one?

3. Why is it important to keep a positive attitude when you have lost your job?

Critical Thinking

4. Why might a supervisor choose to demote an employee instead of firing that person?

KEY TERMS
downsizing (p. 485)
promotion (p. 486)
seniority (p. 487)
perseverance (p. 488)

SECTION 24.1

- You can prepare for the future by tracking employment trends and managing your own career (pp. 484–485)

- Many businesses are downsizing, or eliminating jobs to cut costs. Some employees lose their jobs, and others gain new responsibilities. (p. 485)

- Businesses help employees meet the demands of the workplace by offering training and paying for education. (pp. 485–486)

- Continuing to update your skills and knowledge may also help you get a promotion. (p. 486)

- Employers look for many different qualities and behaviors when selecting employees to promote, including competence, willingness to learn, initiative, and adaptability. (pp. 486–488)

- Getting a promotion may change your relationships with coworkers. Be prepared for this change. (p. 488)

- If a promotion is not right for you, decline it. Keep your options open, however. Let your employer know you are open to future offers. (p. 489)

KEY TERM
notice (p. 495)

SECTION 24.2

- You may choose to change jobs for a number of reasons, including unhappiness in your job, the desire to grow, or termination of your job. (pp. 491–492)

- Focus your job search. You might look for a job like the one you have but with a different company. You might look for a job that will use your current skills but in a different field. You might look for a job that involves a hobby or personal interest. (pp. 493–494)

- You will use many of the job search strategies that you learned in previous chapters. This time, however, you have more information about yourself and your skills. (pp. 494–495)

- If you lose your job, first find out what your former employer is offering to you at termination. Then assess your financial situation, and arrange for unemployment benefits. Update and improve your résumé. Stay positive as you go for interviews. (pp. 496–498)

Reviewing Key Terms

1. Write a checklist of ways to manage your career. Use each of the following terms.
   - downsizing
   - promotion
   - seniority
   - perseverance
   - notice

Recalling Key Concepts

Determine whether each statement is true or false. Rewrite any false statements to make them true.

2. In today's workplace, your career and your job security are mainly in your own hands.

3. Businesses do little to help employees keep their job skills current.

4. When promoting workers, employers consider such factors as seniority, initiative, and perseverance.

5. If you have problems with your coworkers or supervisor, the only thing you can do is find a new job.

6. Emotions such as fear or sadness are normal when you lose your job.

Problem Solving

7. How can tracking employment trends help you manage your own career?

8. How can skills in reading, writing, math, speaking, and listening help you keep up with new technology?

9. You have learned that you can either adjust to a negative work situation or decide to make a job change. List two possible benefits and two drawbacks to each choice.

10. Suppose you find a new job, and you know that you will never want to work for your former employer again. Why is it still a good policy not to criticize your former employer?

11. Why should you examine your financial situation soon after finding out about a job loss?

Work-Based Learning

Basic Skills Writing

12. Write a letter of resignation that includes a gracious opening, a body stating the reason for leaving and notification of the last day you plan to be on the job, and a cordial closing.

Interpersonal Skills Exercising Leadership

13. You have received a promotion, and you now supervise Carrie, a coworker who is also a good friend. Carrie has begun coming in to work late, leaving early, and not performing as well on the job as before. When you talk with her, she says: "What's the big deal? I thought you were my friend. You sure have changed since you became a boss." What should you say?

School-Based Learning

Human Relations Express Interest

14. Margo is an admissions clerk in a health-care center. She has held the job for three years. A better position in the department has become available, and Margo thinks she is qualified for the promotion. Her supervisor, however, has not offered the position to her. Margo feels overlooked and also a little angry. What should she do?

Computer Science Select Technology

15. Miguel is an equipment specialist for a construction firm. His supervisor has asked him to recommend a laptop computer that engineers can take with them to the work site. Create a list of features Miguel might look for in a laptop that would make it suitable.

Role Play

16. Declining a Promotion

Situation You work as a senior accountant at a large advertising firm. You've worked hard and have done a good job for your employer over the past five years. The president of the company is impressed with your job performance and would like to make you the company's controller. Although you are flattered by the offer, you are happy with your current position and don't want the added responsibility of being in charge of the company's finances.

Activity With a partner, role-play a situation in which you refuse the president's promotion. Show a good way and a poor way to decline a promotion. Present your role plays to the class.

Evaluation You will be evaluated based on how well you meet the following performance indicators:

- Present valid, positive reasons for declining your employer's offer of a promotion
- Conduct yourself maturely and professionally during your conversation with your employer

17. Conduct an Interview

Talk to a person who has been laid off or downsized at some point. Ask the person about matters relevant to his/her loss of employment, including warning signs and severance pay. Ask your interviewee about strategies that he/she used to survive financially. Record your findings in your journal.

Connect Using the Internet, research the economic factors that trigger companies to lay off workers or downsize. Then research actions that some major corporations take to ease the blow of downsizing.

Chapter 25

Balancing Work and Personal Life

Section 25.1
Setting Up Your Own Household

Section 25.2
Managing Work, Family, and Community Life

CHAPTER OBJECTIVES

After completing this chapter, you will be able to

- Decide on a place to live, organize your living space, and establish good housekeeping habits.

- Describe ways of balancing your work and personal life.

- Identify some family-friendly employment practices.

- Participate in your community as a voter and volunteer.

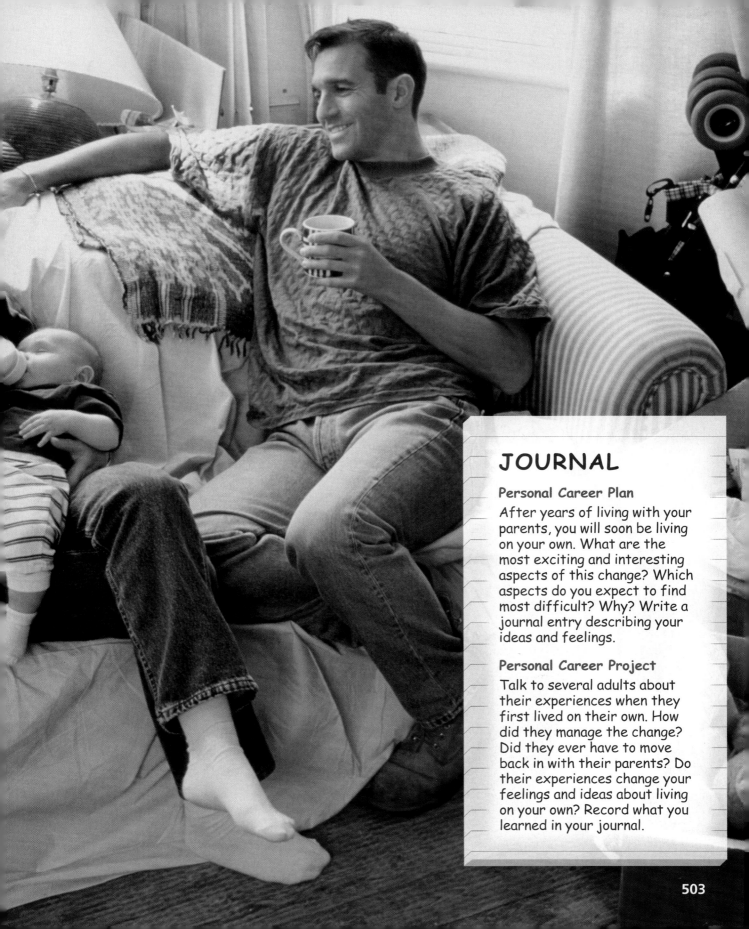

JOURNAL

Personal Career Plan

After years of living with your parents, you will soon be living on your own. What are the most exciting and interesting aspects of this change? Which aspects do you expect to find most difficult? Why? Write a journal entry describing your ideas and feelings.

Personal Career Project

Talk to several adults about their experiences when they first lived on their own. How did they manage the change? Did they ever have to move back in with their parents? Do their experiences change your feelings and ideas about living on your own? Record what you learned in your journal.

503

Setting Up Your Own Household

You've planned your career, you've landed your first job, you've drawn your first paycheck. What's the next step? For many people, it's finding their own place to live. One of the most exciting decisions you'll ever make is choosing where you'll live.

To Move or Not to Move

Depending on your personal situation, you may be ready to move into a place of your own. Before settling on this plan, though, weigh the pros and cons of living at home.

As you may have guessed, living at home is much less expensive. Even if your parent(s), relative(s), or guardian(s) charge you room and board, you'll still probably be paying less than you would to rent an apartment. In addition, you won't have to buy your own furniture, and you can probably save money on food and laundry as well. On the negative side, living at home means you won't be able to make all your own decisions, and privacy may become a serious issue.

Now consider the pros and cons of having your own place. For most people, being more independent is the number one factor. The challenge of being on your own, the enjoyment of fixing up your own place, your sense of individual pride and responsibility—these are part of the joy of drawing a paycheck!

On the other hand, you'll have to pay the monthly rent, although you might reduce the expense by having roommates. Even good roommates, though, will complicate your life. You'll have to adapt to other people's personalities and habits. *Figure 25.1* provides a questionnaire for assessing potential roommates.

If you decide to move, choose the location carefully. These questions may help you evaluate possible areas:

- How far will I have to **commute**, or travel, to get to my job?

- Is the area safe?

- Is it close to public transportation?

- Is it close to my friends and family?

- Is it near places I go to for recreation and entertainment?

Surviving the Transition When you move into a place of your own, you accept new responsibilities and face new problems. It can be a stressful time. *How can your parents and friends help you through such a time?*

FIGURE 25.1

ROOMMATE QUESTIONAIRE

- Do you have a regular income?

- What hours do you work?

- When do you go to bed? Wake up?

- Do you drink alcohol?

- Do you smoke?

- Will you ever have friends and family staying with you? If so, who?

- Do you like to cook?

- Do you watch a lot of television? What programs? What hours?

- Do you listen to music much? If so, what kind(s) of music?

- Do you play a musical instrument? What kind(s) of music? Do you practice at home? If so, when?

- Do you have a pet or want one? If so, what kind?

- What kind of parties do you like to have and how often?

- Do you enjoy time alone? If so, how much and how often?

- What kind of housekeeper are you?

- How long do you think you'll want to share a place?

▲ **Compatibility Check** Learning details about a potential roommate before sharing an apartment is essential. *Why would it be helpful to ask these questions even of someone you know?*

Money Matters

After you find a place you like, prepare a budget. Estimate how much you will have to spend each month to live on your own. You may want to review budgeting in Chapter 20.

Remember that the amount you budget needs to include more than the monthly rent. You may have to pay a monthly maintenance fee. You'll also have to pay for **utilities**—services for your dwelling, including the cost of electricity, gas or oil heat, and perhaps water. In addition, you will have telephone costs and probably cable TV costs.

You can't predict exactly how much your utility costs will be. Some may be included in your monthly rent, and heating and electricity costs can vary widely. However, most utility companies can provide you with estimates based on other households in your neighborhood. Talk to your friends and neighbors, too, so that your monthly bills don't turn out to be an unpleasant surprise. Use your estimated monthly expenses as a guide to identify places you can afford.

Choosing Wisely When young people move into their first apartment, they often don't have a lot of money. *What can you do if you can't afford a place where you would feel comfortable and safe?*

FIGURE 25.2 — RENTAL PROPERTY CHECKLIST

Inside Areas
- Halls and stairways
  - _____ What condition are they in?
  - _____ Can you use them safely and conveniently when your arms are loaded with groceries?
  - _____ Does someone clean them regularly?
  - _____ Are there at least two exits?
- Cleanliness
  - _____ Is the apartment clean?
  - _____ Is the rental property clean?
- Room configuration
  - _____ Do you like the floor plan?
  - _____ Will there be enough privacy if you have a roommate?
- Storage
  - _____ Is there enough storage space?
  - _____ How many closets are there?
- Kitchen
  - _____ Do all the appliances work?
  - _____ Do the cabinet doors and drawers work?
  - _____ Is there enough space in the cabinets?
  - _____ Are the faucets and sink in good condition?
- Bathroom
  - _____ Is there a shower?
  - _____ Is there a bath?
  - _____ Are the faucets, sink, shower/bath in good condition?

- _____ Is there good water pressure?
- _____ Will there be plenty of hot water?
- Windows and screens
  - _____ Do the windows fit snugly and work smoothly?
  - _____ Do the windows have locks?
  - _____ Are there screens?
- Doors
  - _____ Are the doors sturdy and secure?
  - _____ Do they have dead bolts?
- Laundry facilities
  - _____ Are there washers and dryers in the building or in the complex?

Outside Areas
- Neighborhood
  - _____ Is it safe?
  - _____ Is it quiet?
  - _____ Is it clean?
- Parking
  - _____ Is there enough parking?
  - _____ Is parking convenient?
  - _____ Is the parking area safe?
- Safety
  - _____ Is the area around your building or complex well lighted?
  - _____ Is the general area safe at night?

▲ **Look Before You Leap** Make copies of this checklist, and complete them as you visit different rental properties. Use the checklist to compare places that interest you. *Which items are most important to you? Why?*

Remember one of the most important elements you've learned about decision making—gather all the information you can. Before deciding on a place to live, inspect it thoroughly. *Figure 25.2* presents a useful checklist of things to look for. Use it to compare places and to choose the one that's best for you.

When you're ready to sign on the dotted line, be sure you understand the following items:

- *Lease*   Usually, owners will ask you to sign a lease. This written agreement spells out the responsibilities of the owner and *tenant*, or the person renting the property.

- *Rent and due date*   How much is the rent? When is it due? Is there a penalty for late payment?

- *Security deposit*   How much is the security deposit? A **security deposit** is money you pay the owner before you move in; often, it's equal to one or two months' rent. The deposit is held to cover potential damage while you live in the dwelling. If no damage occurs, the security deposit should be returned to you when you move out.

- *Landlord's responsibilities* Which repairs and maintenance jobs (such as cleaning hallways) are the landlord's responsibility? Which are your responsibility?

- *Utilities* Are any of the utilities included in the monthly rent?

Settling in and Getting Connected

As soon as possible after signing your lease, measure the rooms and begin deciding where your furniture will go. Measure doorways and check angles to make sure larger pieces of furniture will fit into your new place. Note the placement of outlets, phone jacks, and cable for the television. Do not put furniture above or in front of hot or cold air registers. Avoid placing electronics in front of windows; doing so will protect such equipment from wear and tear caused by temperature changes and from possible theft.

Give some thought to the most comfortable furniture arrangement. You may want a quiet area for a desk or computer. You may want to be able to see the television from rooms other than the living room. The more forethought you give the arrangement of things, the easier life will be in the long run.

You might try drawing the rooms to scale on paper. For example, an inch on paper might equal a foot of floor space. By measuring your furniture and drawing it to scale, you can plan where the largest pieces will fit and decide on new items you'll need.

You'll also have to make arrangements with your utility companies, telephone company, cable TV company, and so on to have services turned on. Call each company as soon as you sign your lease. Tell their representatives when you want service to begin and schedule appointments so that you can be present when the service people arrive.

Friendly Support Although moving is hard work, it can be fun. *What are some advantages in getting friends to help with the move?*

Don't forget to report your new address to the post office. Your mail will be forwarded to your new address, beginning on the date you specify. You might also want to get a stack of postcards from the post office and send your new address to family, friends, and business acquaintances.

Housekeeping Habits

What makes a household work on an everyday basis? Routines are a large part of the answer. One of the biggest favors you can do for yourself is to establish a few basic housekeeping habits.

At the top of the list—pay your bills on time. Most bills arrive with a due date, the date by which the payment must be received. Don't bury your bills under piles of other mail. Consider buying a file or bill holder so that envelopes don't get lost or forgotten. Paying your monthly bills on time not only gives you a good credit record (valuable when you need a loan), but it will also undoubtedly save you money on late fees and credit card finance charges.

Set aside a small amount of time on a regular basis for housecleaning. If you wait until you need a bulldozer to straighten up your rooms, the job will seem much harder than it really is. You can raise the quality of your life a great deal by regularly seeing to such simple jobs as washing the dishes and sweeping the floor.

The same basic rule applies to doing the laundry. Don't wait until the pile looks like Mt. Everest. Doing a load of laundry every few days will not only keep your living space looking better, you'll actually have more choices of clothes to wear!

Cook healthful meals and try to eat at regular times. A steady diet of fast food will not only rob you of energy, but it will also cost much more than cooking for yourself. Keep a list handy of groceries and other household items you need to buy. Jot things down when you notice you need them. That way, you won't run out of necessary items, and when you shop for groceries, you'll know what you need and won't buy items you already have. You'll be surprised at how these few housekeeping routines can actually save you time and money.

SECTION 25.1 REVIEW

✔ Key Concept Checkpoint

Comprehension

1. Why might it be a good idea to live at home until you are established in your job?

2. Why should you call the utility, telephone, and cable TV companies as soon as you sign your lease?

3. Which housekeeping habits do you think are the easiest to maintain? Which ones may be more difficult?

Critical Thinking

4. How can keeping a clean house improve your quality of life?

CAREER FOCUS

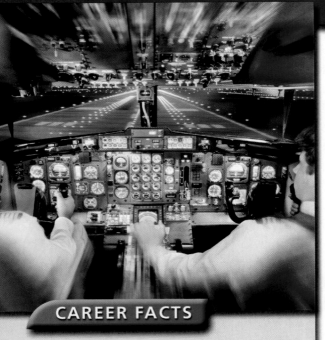

CAREER FACTS

Education and Training A commercial pilot's license is necessary, along with an instrument rating from the FAA. Most commercial airlines require pilots to have a college degree.

Aptitudes, Abilities, and Skills Pilots must have 20/20 vision, good hearing, good hand-eye coordination, good reaction skills, and strong decision-making skills.

Career Outlook Employment is expected to increase more slowly than average through 2008, and competition will be keen.

Career Path Many pilots start as flight instructors to gain flying hours, then go on to fly chartered planes. Some pilots become flight engineers, first officers, and captains.

What is the key to your success?

"The most important part of being a pilot is attention to detail. Pilots are required to know a lot about the airplanes they fly and understand how every part works."

What does your job entail?

"My job requires more than just the obvious flying of an airplane. As captain, I am responsible for ensuring the safety of passengers. I review the weather at the departure and destination cities, as well as along the flight route. I order the fuel, ensure that the airplane has been properly maintained, and make sure that the flight attendants have the equipment they need."

What training did you have?

"When I was four years old, I set my mind on being a pilot. When I eventually went to college, I studied aeronautics to learn how airplanes fly. I also took flying lessons. As an airline pilot, I am constantly training."

What do you like most about your work?

"I love landing the plane—it's the most challenging part of my job. A smooth landing is like hitting a home run. It requires me to synthesize all of the flying skills that I've developed. I also love my job because it enables me to travel and see the world. My job pays me to see beautiful places and meet new people all the time. The view from the flight deck is better than from any office building."

> **Critical Thinking** What do you think is the most challenging part of being a pilot? What do you think is the most rewarding?

Managing Work, Family, and Community Life

A job can take up a good deal of your time and energy. However, just as you wouldn't eat only one kind of food, you shouldn't let one aspect of your life dominate all the others. Balance is as essential to your personal life as it is to your diet. Knowing how to balance your work and your personal life is key to successfully managing your career.

Enriching Your Personal Life

You have a responsibility to yourself as well as to your job. Fulfilling that personal responsibility can bring about the feeling of life success that you value most of all. Here's a good rule of thumb: No matter what happens at work, don't forget what you're working for.

Strive to balance your work life and your commitments to yourself, your family, friends, and the community. By doing so, you will be successful in reaching your career goals as well as your personal goals in life. The pressures of a job can sometimes seem to overshadow the other aspects of your life, but in the long run, the time you spend outside of work will prove at least as valuable as the time you spend on the job. The right balance will make you happier, healthier, and probably even more satisfied with your work.

WHAT YOU'LL LEARN

- How to balance your work life and your personal life
- Strategies for meeting family responsibilities
- Some family-friendly employment practices
- How to participate in your community as a voter and volunteer

WHY IT'S IMPORTANT

Living independently is a complicated juggling act that requires preparation, strategy, and knowledge.

KEY TERM

- **register**

Get on Your Feet People must have time to play in order to remain mentally and physically healthy. *Why is it important to make time for physical activities such as soccer or dancing?*

Expand Your Circle of Friends

Since you spend so much time at work, you'll form friendships with coworkers. That's good, but you should also focus on developing friendships outside of work. This is a key to avoid keeping work at the center of your life. How can you expand your circle of friends?

Join a group. Get involved with an organization that interests you, such as an environmental association, arts group, or charity. Sign up for a sports league. Join a book group at a local bookstore. Take up a hobby or enroll in evening classes at a local community college.

Family Responsibilities

The biggest challenge for working parents is finding time for both work and home. They're torn between job responsibilities and the needs of their children. Life often becomes a delicate balancing act, and every hour can seem accounted for. When anything happens to upset the balance, there's a scramble to pick up the pieces. It can be tough on the parents and on the children. Magda Cosner knows about these difficulties.

Cosner is a Miami police officer. After returning to work from maternity leave, her schedule worked well—for a while. Now her department is going to change her schedule. "I'm going to have to start coming in at 6:30 in the morning instead of 8:30," Cosner explains. "That's going to cause a problem with the kids—they'll have to be up at 5:30. My husband's very helpful with the kids ... but he's a police officer, too, and with my new schedule, we're not going to have a day off together anymore."

There are no easy solutions to problems such as these. However, careful planning and communication are a start. They can enable families to build on the love for one another that is the foundation of their relationship.

People Need People

Everyone needs to share thoughts and feelings. The very act of talking and listening creates a bond between people and makes it easier to deal with problems. Make listening to the needs of your spouse or roommate a major priority. Communication is the key. Listen to what others have to say, what problems they're facing, what interests them. When work and other obligations present problems, keep the lines of communication open.

Be considerate of each other. Pay attention to the little things that can make life more pleasant for everyone in your household. This can mean anything from turning off lights to adjusting mealtimes. If you know that someone has a pet peeve, do what you can to avoid it.

Don't forget how good it feels to receive praise and encouragement. An enthusiastic word goes a long way toward keeping a relationship strong.

Children have many needs. They need to be fed, clothed, bathed, taken to activities, and helped with homework. That's just part of it. They need to be loved, and love takes time and energy. Make time for talking, playing, and being together.

Taking Time Out Caring for children's emotional needs is as important as caring for their physical needs. *Why is it important for parents to play with their children every day, not just on weekends?*

A Balancing Act

There are no easy rules for balancing your responsibilities to your job and to your family. Everyone's situation is different. However, *Figure 25.3* provides a few hints that you can apply in your own way.

Help from Employers

You might think your company is the last place to look for help in managing your family life. In fact, employers are realizing that it is to their benefit to help families. Studies show that employees who are under less family stress are more loyal and more productive. What kind of help do employers offer? Benefits vary from company to company, but here are a few:

- *Flextime* You can work the schedule that's best for you and your family.

- *On-site day care* It's sometimes easier to bring children to work with you than to take them elsewhere. You can also visit them during your breaks or at lunchtimes.

- *Family-friendly training for managers* Many companies train their managers to be sensitive to the family needs of their staff. As a result, you may find it easier to make special arrangements to balance your job responsibilities and your family's needs.

FIGURE 25.3 **Balancing Your Job and Family Responsibilities** Putting extra effort into balancing work and family responsibilities will undoubtedly lead to greater personal satisfaction.

A **Be Realistic** Accept the fact that you will have to make compromises in your job and your family life in order to make time for both. At the same time, don't build up resentment—do at least some of the things you want to do. When possible, leave work on time so that you have enough free time in the evenings.

B **Share the Work** Share family duties and household chores so that no one person has to do them all.

C **Don't Overschedule Your Nonwork Time** Allow for free time to spend doing something you enjoy with your family.

D **Keep Your Promises** If you say you'll be somewhere or do something, stick to your word.

Safe and Secure On-site day care centers are one of the most popular employee benefits for working parents. *How do such day care centers help parents concentrate on their jobs?*

*inter*NET CONNECTION

Register to Vote
You will soon turn 18 and would like to register to vote so you can take part in the November election.

Connect
• Visit the Web site of the Board of Elections in your city. Find out what you need to do to register to vote.
• Make a list of the different ways your city registers voters. Write a one-paragraph summary telling which way you plan to register to vote and why it's important to register.

Your Responsibilities as a Citizen

As you move into the world of work and get your own place to live, your responsibilities as a citizen will grow. You'll be a working adult, a taxpayer, and a voter.

Being Informed

As a citizen, your community is your responsibility. You need to stay informed on issues and events.

Read the newspaper. Listen to radio and television news reports. Talk to your neighbors to learn what they think about issues. The skills of reading, listening, and speaking and the competencies of acquiring and using information will help you as a citizen. Then you can put your knowledge to work by voting.

Voting

Voting is your most important obligation as a citizen. Your vote helps decide who our leaders will be and what laws we will live by. Don't let other people make these decisions for you.

Before you can vote, you must be at least 18 years old and **register**, or officially sign up as a qualified voter. Methods for registering vary from place to place. To find out how it is done in your area, call the League of Women Voters, your county election commission, or the county registrar's office.

Use Your Vote To cast an informed vote, you have to prepare for an election by learning about the candidates and issues. *How important is your vote? Will it matter in an election in which thousands or millions of people vote? Explain.*

BALLOTS

Creative
BUSINESS PRACTICES

Johnson & Johnson
Helping Balance Work and Family

Johnson & Johnson, maker of baby products and other health care items, believes families—especially those of its employees—are important. The New Brunswick, New Jersey-based company has a commitment to make employees' lives easier with its "Balancing Work and Family" program.

Johnson & Johnson offers benefits to parents that are rarely found at other companies. New moms and dads can take up to 52 weeks off. Employees enjoy a flexible leave policy that allows them to take off as much time as needed to resolve family matters. The company allows its managers to telecommute.

For those who work on site, Johnson & Johnson has six child development centers at its offices in New Jersey and Pennsylvania.

These centers provide child care for over 900 children of employees during the work week and on holidays.

Johnson & Johnson also offers resources and referral programs for new home or car buying, home repairs, adoption, and elder care.

Critical Thinking
What other benefits do you think would be helpful to working parents?

Link and Learn
To read more about Johnson & Johnson's "Balancing Work and Family" program, visit the company's Web site via the link on the *Succeeding in the World of Work* Web site at **www.careers.glencoe.com**.

Doing Your Part

Actively participating in your community is not only a responsibility, it's also a way to genuinely enrich your life. By engaging in volunteer work, you'll widen your circle of friends, learn new skills, and make your community a better place in which to live.

How can you get involved? Think of the activities you enjoy and the concerns that are important to you. Call the organizations that promote those activities and ask if they offer volunteer opportunities. Talk to people, ask questions, attend some meetings. Just remember that whether you're interested in restoring old buildings, reading to the blind, or coaching basketball, you've got a lot to give.

One Final Word: Give It All You've Got!

Whatever career you follow, whatever your family situation, live as fully as you can. Your job and your loved ones may take you to places you can't even imagine now. Above all, enjoy what you do. At work and at home, you get out of life as much as you put into it.

CAREER CHECKLIST

Moving Forward on Your Career Path...

- ✔ Keep your job a priority, but don't let it consume you.
- ✔ Make time for your personal interests and hobbies.
- ✔ Make sure your ultimate goals are at the forefront of your job and personal life.
- ✔ Take charge and be responsible for your actions.
- ✔ Be proud of your successes and maintain a positive outlook and healthy self-esteem.
- ✔ Always challenge yourself to reach your highest limits.
- ✔ Ask for more responsibilities at work and seek new ways to expand your job skills.
- ✔ Maintain your job journal to see how you grow throughout your career.

SECTION 25.2 REVIEW

Key Concept Checkpoint

Comprehension

1. How can making time for yourself make you more productive at work?
2. Why should you treat time scheduled with your family with the same importance as you treat work?
3. Why are people frequently more productive when they work for a family-friendly company?

Critical Thinking

4. Which employee benefits are most important to you? Why?

KEY TERMS
commute (p. 505)
utilities (p. 506)
security deposit (p. 507)

SECTION 25.1

- Setting up your own household is a major life change. Before moving out, be sure that staying at home for a while isn't better for you. Consider the pros and cons of having your own place. (pp. 504–505)

- Prepare a budget to estimate how much you'll have to spend on your own place. (p. 506)

- Choose a location that fits your needs, values, and budget. (p. 506)

- Before you sign a lease, be sure you understand all the costs and responsibilities involved. (pp. 507–508)

- Plan how your furniture will fit in your apartment. (p. 508)

- Make your life easier by establishing some good house-keeping habits. (p. 509)

KEY TERM
register (p. 516)

SECTION 25.2

- Balance your work time and your personal time. (p. 511)
- Develop friends outside of work by joining groups. (p. 512)
- Fulfilling responsibilities to both your job and your family can be difficult. Communication is the key. A few rules of thumb include being realistic, sharing family duties, and keeping your promises. (pp. 512–515)
- Employers sometimes help people manage their family lives by offering flexible work schedules and on-site day care centers. (p. 514)
- Voting is a citizen's most important duty. Before you can vote, you must register. (p. 516)
- Participate in your community by joining volunteer organizations. (p. 518)

Reviewing Key Terms

1. Write a paragraph describing how you will handle finding and living in your own place. Use the terms below in your paragraph.
   - commute
   - utilities
   - security deposit
   - register

Recalling Key Concepts

Determine whether each statement is true or false. Rewrite any false statements to make them true.

2. There are some advantages to living at home for a while after graduating from high school.

3. It's wiser to leave all housekeeping chores for the weekend.

4. Your responsibilities at work are the most important ones you have.

5. Having coworkers as friends is good, but you should try to have friends outside of work too.

6. Your only responsibility as a citizen is to vote.

Problem Solving

7. Why should you carefully evaluate anyone whom you are considering as a roommate?

8. Which is most important to you when choosing a place to live—being close to work, the amount of the rent, or living in a safe neighborhood? Why?

9. What's wrong with making friends from work the center of your social life?

10. When a job takes up a good deal of your time, why is it especially important to schedule time with your family and friends?

11. Why do you need to be well informed to fulfill your responsibility as a voter?

Work-Based Learning

Basic Skills Knowing How to Learn

12. Imagine that a proposition is on the ballot for the next election. The proposition calls for a special tax to support state parks. What are three sources of information you might use to form your decision about how to vote on this issue?

Resources Allocating Money

13. You have take-home pay of $1,600 per month. You have a monthly car payment of $150. Your car insurance is $650 every six months. Estimate additional expenses for food, entertainment, clothes, gas and repairs for your car, laundry, and so on. (Refer to Figure 20.2 for any expense categories you may have forgotten.) Base your estimates on your actual spending habits. Use these figures to create a personal budget. Use the budget to figure out how much you can afford to spend on rent and utilities each month.

School-Based Learning

Math Make Financial Decisions

14. You and your roommate have just rented an apartment together. The only furniture you have is bedroom furniture, which you each brought from home. You each have $500 to contribute toward furnishing the new apartment. What should you buy? Make a list of items you need. Then go shopping to find the best prices on those items. Finally, select the items you need most and can afford to buy right now.

Social Studies Research Clubs

15. Sandra has recently taken a job that requires her to move to your city. Except for her new coworkers, she doesn't know anyone there. She has decided she will join an organization or club in order to make new friends. Sandra enjoys dancing, photography, and art. What organizations might she join? Do research to find those related to her interests.

Role Play

16. Balance Work and Personal Life

Situation You've been out in the real world for a few years now. A younger friend of yours has just graduated from college and started a new job. He has confided to you that he's feeling overwhelmed by his professional responsibilities. He wants to do a good job, but doesn't want to sacrifice his personal life and free time.

Activity Role-play a conversation with your friend in which you explain how to balance conflicting priorities. Remind him where his priorities should lie, and in what order. Help him to see how to live the balanced life he desires.

Evaluation You will be evaluated based on how well you meet the following performance indicators:

- Understand the conflicting motivators in your friend's situation
- Present strategies for balancing professional and personal demands
- Answer any questions that your friend may have

interNET CONNECTION

17. Finding an Apartment

Make a detailed list of things you would look for in an apartment. Using your local classified ads, locate at least three possibilities in your area. Call the landlord or visit each apartment to find out which apartment would be best for you. Choose one apartment, and write a short paragraph explaining your selection.

Connect Visit at least two Web sites that list apartments for rent. You may want to look at the online version of your local newspaper. Choose at least two apartments that would suit you and follow up on each to find out more.

CAREER LAB
Real-World Workshop

Putting It All Together: Developing a Plan to Achieve Success Throughout Life

✓ Overview

Imagine where you would like to be in 20 years. What industry would you like to work in? What job title do you expect to have? Where do you want to live? What kind of personal goals do you desire to achieve? It's impossible to know exactly how the future will turn out, but plotting solid goals and strategies will enable you to have more control over your life. Remember: goods things usually just don't "happen," they're the result of hard work and planning!

✓ Assignment

In Unit 1, you chose a career and mapped out the steps you would take to prepare for that career. Now, at the close of Unit 7, you've had the opportunity to conduct a lot more career exploration. Your goals have probably changed since the time that you put together your first plan. Revisit your career plan, and redesign or refine it using everything you've learned. This time, you will present your plan as a time line, including your personal and financial goals, such as buying your first house, along with your career goals. To formulate a comprehensive and specific plan, you'll need to conduct research. Finally, you will present your time line to the class.

✓ Tools/Resources

To complete this assignment, you'll need to consult your school counselors, library reference materials, the Internet, adult professionals in your desired field, companies where you might gain employment, real estate agents, financial advisors, and so forth. The more extensive your research, the more realistic and useful your time line will be.

✓ Procedures

Using the ideas presented in the Helpful Hints feature, follow the steps listed below to create your time line.

- Carefully scrutinize your career profile from Unit 1. What do you want to change? Which elements of your time line are still relevant to your current goals?
  - Organize your plan as a time line and address any gaps or changes. You may need to add many new goals or steps.
  - Conduct research to find out about necessary training and education required for members of your new desired career field. Be sure to include high school courses relevant to the career.

- Seek information about internships and volunteer opportunities so that you can start working on your goals immediately.
- Add your personal goals to your time line, and note if they require you to adjust your career plans.
- Make your time line aesthetically appealing. Create an original, colorful, and attractive poster, and prepare a 15-minute presentation.

✓ Report

Your final product for this lab should include a poster that features your time line and text explains your personal and career goals. Finally, you will give an oral presentation to the class.

✓ Presentation and Evaluation

You will be evaluated based on

- Development of comprehensive, realistic short- and long-term goals based on thorough research
- Creativity and neatness
- Quality of presentation
- Evidence of growth and maturity in devising second career time line
- Application of skills and knowledge presented in text

✓ Personal Career Portfolio

Save your time line with the other materials you've prepared for your personal career portfolio.

HELPFUL HINTS

Sources for Advice

When faced with the prospect of deciding your future, it's hard to know where to start. To make your task less overwhelming, try using some of the following "start-up" approaches:

- Talk to an adult whom you respect. Ask this person how he or she arrived at his or her current station in life.

- If you don't know of an adult who can provide the right kind of help, ask your school guidance counselor for a referral.
- Consider taking a formal career interest and aptitude assessment test.
- Focus on gaining appropriate training and education as your first goal.

Glossary

ability A skill a person has already developed. (p. 36)

access To find and use information. (p. 367)

active listening Listening with full attention. (p. 301)

addiction The physical or psychological need for a substance. (p. 217)

affirmative action Action to give those who have suffered discrimination a fair chance. (p. 239)

agenda A list of items to be addressed at a meeting. (p. 288)

allowances Deductions. (p. 464)

analogy A problem-solving strategy in which a person says one thing is like another in order to suggest a solution. (p. 328)

annual percentage rate (APR) The amount of interest for one year, expressed as a percentage. (p. 431)

application fee An amount of money charged to apply for a loan. (p. 430)

apprentice Someone who learns how to do a job through hands-on experience under the guidance of a skilled worker. (p. 99)

aptitude One's potential for learning a certain skill. (p. 36)

arbitration A hearing at which both sides present evidence and witnesses to an arbitrator, who issues a written decision, just as a judge or jury would do. (p. 245)

arrogance An excessive display of self-regard. (p. 201)

assertiveness The confident presentation of oneself and one's abilities. (p. 200)

asset Anything of value that a person or business owns. (p. 82)

assumptions Beliefs a person takes for granted. (p. 328)

attitude A person's basic outlook on life. (p. 194)

audience One or more persons who receive information. (p. 297)

audit A process through which the IRS asks a business or individual to prove that the information on their tax return is correct. (P. 467)

bait and switch The fraudulent practice of advertising a bargain item that is not available for sale in the advertiser's store; when customers arrive, a salesperson tries to talk them into a more expensive item. (p. 390)

balance sheet A summary of a business's assets, liabilities, and owner's equity. (p. 82)

beneficiary The person who receives a benefit from an insurance company. (p. 439)

benefit Money paid by an insurance company for a loss or some occurrence. (p. 439)

benefits Forms of reward for employment beyond salary, including health insurance, paid vacation and holiday time, and retirement plans. (p. 61)

body language The posture, gestures, and eye contact people use to express themselves nonverbally. (p. 136)

brainstorm To think creatively without evaluating ideas until later. (p. 326)

broadband access High-speed Internet access, usually using telephone or cable TV lines. (p. 307)

budget   A plan for saving and spending money based on one's income and expenses. (p. 398)

business cycle   The movement of the economy from good times to bad and back to good; includes a peak or boom, a contraction, a trough, and an expansion. (p. 384)

business plan   Specific information about a business's product(s), location, employees, organization, marketing plan, and competitors. (p. 80)

cafeteria plan   A plan that allows employees to choose the benefits they want. (p. 167)

career   A series of related jobs built on a foundation of interest, knowledge, training, and experience. (p. 5)

cash flow statement   A monthly plan that shows when a business anticipates cash coming in and being paid out. (p. 82)

cash-value life insurance   Part insurance and part investment, in which you can borrow money against the total amount of premiums paid on a cash-value life insurance policy. (p. 452)

cause and effect   What happened and what made it happen. (p. 299)

certificate of deposit (CD)   A type of investment in which a person deposits a specific amount of money for a fixed amount of time at a stated interest rate. (p. 419)

check register   A small booklet that allows one to keep track of the money in one's checking account. (p. 426)

chronological résumé   A résumé organized in reverse time order. (p. 122)

civil law   The type of law that pertains to arguments in which one person (or company) claims that another person (or company) has violated rights or neglected responsibilities. (p. 242)

claim   An oral or written notice given to an insurance company to collect for a loss or a certain occurrence. (p. 439)

coinsurance   The percentage of major medical expenses that a policyholder is required to pay. (p. 449)

cold call   A blind telephone call—a call that is not the result of a lead or a referral—that is made to discover whether there is a job opening or to gain a contact. (p. 116)

collateral   An asset such as a house or a car that could be taken by the lender if a loan is not repaid as promised. (p. 430)

collective bargaining   Using the power of numbers (the workers in a union) to negotiate for better wages, increased benefits, better safety rules, and other job improvements. (p. 236)

collision insurance   Insurance that covers damage to a policyholder's car caused by an accident. (p. 443)

commission   Earnings based on how much a worker sells. (p. 165)

communication   The exchange of information between senders and receivers. (p. 296)

commute   To travel to and from one's job. (p. 505)

company culture   The behavior, attitudes, values, and habits of the employees and owners of a company that are unique to that particular company. (p. 156)

comparison and contrast   The pointing out of similarities and differences. (p. 299)

compensatory time   Paid time off from work, instead of cash, in exchange for working overtime. (p. 235)

compounded   Paid interest on money originally invested and also on any interest that has already been added. (p. 418)

comprehensive insurance   Insurance that covers damage to a policyholder's car for reasons other than a collision. (p. 443)

GLOSSARY

Glossary

compromise To settle a dispute by having each party give up something. (p. 268)

confidentiality The keeping of secrets from people who are not supposed to know them. (p. 185)

conflict resolution A problem-solving strategy for settling disputes. (p. 268)

consequence An effect or outcome. (p. 319)

constructive criticism Criticism presented in a way that can lead to learning and growth. (p. 204)

consume To buy and use goods and services. (p. 381)

consumer fraud Dishonest business practices used by people trying to trick or cheat consumers. (p. 389)

consumers Individuals who buy and use goods and services. (p. 381)

contact list A list of people one knows and will contact to build a network. (p. 113)

contingency fee A lawyer's fee based on a percentage of the amount of money that a client wins in a court case. (p. 248)

continuing education Programs offered by high schools, colleges, and universities that are geared toward adult students. (p. 101)

convenience benefits Benefits that make workers' lives easier. (p. 167)

cooperativeness A willingness to work well with everyone on the job to reach a common goal. (p. 174)

cooperative program A program combining school and work in which a local employer teams with a school, hiring students to perform jobs that are taught in school classes. (p. 54)

copayment The amount of money an HMO member pays for each service from a health-care provider. (p. 450)

copyright The legal right of authors or other creators of works to control the reproduction and use of their works. (p. 350)

corporation A business owned by people who buy part of, or shares in, the company. (p. 79)

coverage Losses or events that an insurance company will insure against. (p. 439)

cover letter A letter a job seeker sends along with a résumé to introduce the job seeker to an employer. (p. 125)

credit A sum of money a person can use before having to reimburse the credit lender. (p. 429)

credit application A form that a person must complete when seeking credit; it asks for details about the person's job, salary, bank account(s), and credit history. (p. 432)

credit bureau An agency that collects information on how promptly people and businesses pay their bills. (p. 432)

credit card A card usually issued by a bank or other financial institution that allows the holder to charge amounts of purchases in many different places. (p. 429)

credit limit The maximum amount of money a person can charge against an account. (p. 429)

credit rating An estimate made by a credit bureau that tells how likely an individual is to pay his or her bills. (p. 432)

credit union A not-for-profit financial institution similar to a bank; people who belong share a common bond. (p. 418)

criminal law The type of law under which the government charges an individual or organization with committing a crime. (p. 246)

criteria Standards of judgment. (p. 318)

cross-functional team   A group of people from two or more departments or areas of expertise who work together toward a common business goal. (p. 278)

customer   Anyone who receives the results of your work, according to TQM. (p. 282)

customer relations   The use of communication skills to meet the needs of business customers or clients. (p. 296)

data   Information, knowledge, ideas, facts, words, symbols, figures, statistics. (p. 34)

database   A software program in which information is stored in tables and can be sorted and combined in different ways. (p. 345)

debit card   Also known as a check card; a card that automatically withdraws the amount of a purchase from your bank account (p. 426)

decision-making process   A logical series of steps used to identify and evaluate possibilities and arrive at a workable choice. (p. 24)

deductible   The portion of the cost of a loss that an insurance policyholder pays before the insurance company pays the remaining cost. (p. 439)

deduction   An expense, such as certain medical or business costs, that taxpayers are allowed to subtract from their income when figuring the amount of tax they must pay. (p. 467)

defensiveness   The guarding of oneself emotionally against negative opinions. (p. 205)

defined-benefit plan   A type of pension plan that provides a fixed amount of money at a person's retirement. (p. 421)

defined-contribution plan   A type of pension plan in which the employer contributes a set amount of money to the plan each year; also called profit-sharing plan. (p. 421)

delegating   Assigning tasks to other people. (p. 364)

deliberate   Purposeful. (p. 243)

dependent   Someone, such as a child, who relies on another person for support. (p. 465)

depression   A very serious recession, or downturn in the economy. (p. 384)

desktop publishing   The use of computers and special software to create professional-looking printouts; uses include reports, brochures, newsletters, invitations, and greeting cards. (p. 346)

direct deposit   The electronic transfer of payment from a company to an employee's banking account. (p. 424)

directory   A special computer file that contains the names of a group of files on a broad topic; also called a folder. (p. 370)

disabilities   Conditions that include visual or hearing impairment, mental illness, or paralysis. (p. 238)

disabled worker   Someone who cannot work because of a physical or mental condition. (p. 472)

discrimination   Unequal treatment based on such factors as race, religion, nationality, gender, age, or physical appearance. (p. 237)

disputes   Disagreements. (p. 242)

distributing   Making goods and services available, such as by selling or delivering, to the people who need or want them. (p. 380)

diversity   Variety. (p. 269)

dividend   A portion of a fund or an organization's profits. (p. 419)

down payment   The amount of money paid at the time something is purchased through an installment loan. (p. 430)

Glossary

downsizing The elimination of jobs in a company to promote efficiency or to cut costs. (p. 485)

downtime Periods of time when nothing is scheduled. (p. 362)

drug-testing programs Programs designed to detect illegal drug use. (p. 218)

e-commerce The buying and selling of goods and services on the Internet, especially the World Wide Web. (p. 349)

economics The study of how a group produces, distributes, and uses its goods and services. (p. 380)

economic system A country's way of using resources to provide the goods and services people want and need. (p. 380)

economy The ways in which a group produces, distributes, and consumes its goods and services. (p. 11)

Electronic Funds Transfer (EFT) The transfer of money from one bank account to another by electronic means, rather than cash. (p. 426)

e-mail Electronic mail; messages sent from computer to computer. (p. 307)

emergency fund Money people put aside for needs they cannot anticipate. (p. 404)

empathize To see someone else's point of view and to imagine oneself in his or her situation. (p. 263)

endorse To sign one's name on the back of a check before depositing or cashing it. (p. 424)

enthusiasm Lively interest or eagerness. (p. 198)

entrepreneur Someone who starts and then runs a business. (p. 68)

enumeration The listing or citing of key points when speaking or writing. (p. 299)

enunciation The clear and separate vocalization of each sound in a word. (p. 300)

equity The savings an entrepreneur invests in his or her business. (p. 82)

ergonomics The applied science that attempts to design work areas that are safe, comfortable, and efficient. (p. 223)

ethics The moral rules of society; the values that help people decide what is right and what is wrong. (p. 181)

etiquette Good manners; the rules of polite behavior in dealing with other people. (p. 266)

evaluation The comparison and contrast of data or possible outcomes to decide which is the best choice. (p. 88)

exclusions Losses or risks not covered by an insurance company. (p. 439)

exempt Excused from something, such as having to pay taxes. (p. 464)

exempt employees Workers who are not eligible to earn overtime pay; generally, those who earn salaries. (p. 165)

exemption A fixed amount of money that is excused from taxes. (p. 465)

expenses Money that must be paid out. (p. 400)

exploratory interview A short, informal talk with someone who works in a career one finds appealing. (p. 54)

face value The amount of a death benefit that an insurance company pays. (p. 452)

facilitator A leader who helps a team work more smoothly by coordinating its tasks. (p. 280)

fax Facsimile; a copy or replica of a message received over telephone lines. (p. 307)

felony A serious crime, such as murder or rape, punishable by imprisonment or death. (p. 246)

finance charges Fees that lenders charge that are usually based on the amount of money owed. (p. 430)

financial plan A description of a business's start-up costs, operating expenses, and other costs for its first few months of operation. (p. 81)

financial responsibility Accountability in money matters. (p. 409)

first aid Actions taken in a physical emergency before help arrives. (p. 225)

fixed expenses Expenses that people have already agreed to pay and that must be paid by a particular date. (p. 400)

flexible expenses Expenses that come irregularly or that people can adjust more easily than fixed expenses. (p. 400)

flextime An arrangement in which workers construct their own work schedules. (p. 59)

fluctuate To go up or down, as prices do in a free-enterprise system. (p. 383)

Food Guide Pyramid A guideline created by the U.S. Department of Health and Human Services to show people the nutrients they need each day. (p. 215)

401(k) plan A type of pension plan in which an employee contributes a specific portion of his or her salary to the plan each year; employers may match the contribution. (p. 421)

franchise The legal right to sell a company's goods or services in a particular area. (p. 75)

free enterprise A type of economic system in which individuals or individual businesses buy and sell and set prices with little intervention by the government. (p. 381)

functional team A group of people from one company department or area of expertise who work together toward a common business goal. (p. 278)

gender Sex, either male or female. (p. 237)

generality A broad or indefinite statement. (p. 298)

generalization A broad law, statement, or principle. (p. 299)

generic products Products without brand names that usually have plain packaging and are not advertised as brand-name products are. (p. 388)

global economy The worldwide linkage of national economies. (p. 11)

globalization The establishment of worldwide communication links between people and groups. (p. 337)

goods Items that people buy. (p. 11)

goods-producing industries Industries that provide goods, such as stereo systems, cars, and buildings. (p. 17)

goodwill The loyalty of existing customers. (p. 75)

gossip Idle talk or rumor, especially about the personal affairs of others. (p. 207)

grace period A time during which interest is not charged on a loan. (p. 432)

gross domestic product (GDP) The total dollar value of all goods and services produced in a country during one year. (p. 385)

gross pay The total amount of money a person earns. (p. 460)

gross profit The difference between the cost of a good or service and its selling price. (p. 82)

Glossary

H

health maintenance organization (HMO) A health-care plan that has no deductibles but that usually requires a copayment and offers limited physician choice. (p. 450)

hot call A telephone call made to a referral or to follow up on a lead. (p. 115)

hourly wages Pay that is based on a fixed rate for each hour worked. (p. 164)

income Money one receives. (p. 400)

income statement A document showing how much money a business earned or lost during a specified period of time. (p. 82)

income tax return A form that shows how much income a person received from working and other sources and how much tax that person must pay. (p. 463)

indictment Under criminal law, a list of charges the government brings against an individual or organization. (p. 246)

individual career plan A planned course of action leading to a career goal. (p. 93)

individual retirement account (IRA) A personal retirement account into which a working person can put a limited amount of money each year; a portion or all of this money may be tax deferred until the person retires, depending on his or her annual earnings. (p. 422)

inflation A sharp increase in the average price of goods and services. (p. 385)

inflection A change in the pitch or loudness of one's voice, often used for emphasis. (p. 299)

initiative A willingness to do what is necessary without having to be told to do it. (p. 176)

installment loans Loans in which people receive money in a lump sum and pay it back in installments, or regularly scheduled payments. (p. 430)

insurance policy A legal contract between a person buying insurance and an insurance company. (p. 438)

interest The money that banks pay depositors for the use of their money. (p. 418)

interests Favorite activities. (p. 4)

Internal Revenue Service (IRS) The government agency that collects federal taxes and oversees the federal tax system. (p. 458)

Internet A worldwide electronic community in which millions of computers and computer users are linked. (p. 117)

Internet job services Web sites, newsgroups, and bulletin boards created by trade organizations, companies, and individuals specifically for job recruitment and career research. (p. 53)

internship A formally defined temporary position, usually unpaid, that often requires a longer-term commitment than volunteering. (p. 55)

interpret To make sense of; to translate. (p. 300)

interview A formal meeting in which a job seeker and an employer meet face-to-face to discuss possible employment. (p. 132)

GLOSSARY

jargon   The vocabulary of a particular trade, profession, or group. (p. 306)

job   Work that a person does for pay. (p. 5)

job application   A document that job seekers fill out so that employers can use it to screen applicants. (p. 120)

job lead   Information about a job opening. (p. 112)

job market   The demand for particular jobs. (p. 11)

job shadowing   Following a worker on the job for a few days to learn the routine. (p. 55)

Keogh plan   A retirement plan for self-employed people in which a certain percentage of one's earnings can be invested and is tax deferred until one retires. (p. 422)

keywords   Descriptive words that tell a computer what to search for. (p. 117)

labor contract   A legal agreement between an employer and a union, specifying wages, benefits, working conditions, hours, and grievance procedures for union members. (p. 236)

laptop   A small, briefcase-size portable computer. (p. 339)

layoff   Job termination that results when a company's business slows. (p. 168)

leadership style   How a person behaves when he or she is in charge of other people. (p. 286)

learning styles   The different ways that people naturally think and learn. (p. 37)

lease   A contract to use something for a specified period of time. (p. 74)

liability   A debt owed by a person or a business. (p. 82)

liability insurance   Insurance that covers damage or injury for which a policyholder is responsible. (p. 443)

liable   Responsible. (p. 242)

lifelong learner   A person who makes use of all opportunities to keep his or her skills and knowledge up-to-date. (p. 485)

lifestyle   The way a person uses his or her time, energy, and resources. (p. 6)

lifestyle goals   The ways in which a person wants to spend his or her time, energy, and resources in the future. (p. 30)

listserv   An e-mail network that links professionals who work in a specific industry. (p. 114)

major medical coverage   Insurance that covers hospital and medical expenses, allowing for full choice of hospitals and doctors but requiring a deductible and coinsurance. (p. 449)

marketing   The process of getting goods and services to consumers; includes the packaging, shipping, advertising, and selling of goods and services. (p. 383)

market outlook   The potential for future sales. (p. 75)

marketplace   The entire realm of trade and business; the "place" where buying and selling go on. (p. 383)

mediation   A process in which two opposing people or organizations present their cases to a neutral panel or person who helps them reach a compromise or an agreement. (p. 245)

GLOSSARY

Glossary

medical payments insurance Insurance that covers medical expenses of a policyholder and his or her passengers involved in an auto accident. (p. 443)

Medicare A part of the Social Security program that provides health insurance benefits to people who need hospitalization or other medical care. (p. 472)

mentors Experienced coworkers who act as guides or informal teachers for new employees. (p. 159)

minimum wage The lowest hourly wage that an employer can legally pay for a worker's services. (p. 234)

minutes The written record of what is said and done during a meeting, kept by the secretary. (p. 288)

misdemeanor A crime, such as shoplifting, that is less serious than a felony. (p. 246)

mission A company's overall goal. (p. 278)

modem A device that translates data from a computer into digital signals that can travel over telephone lines. (p. 307)

negligence Disregard. (p. 243)

net pay The amount of income left after taxes and other deductions are taken out. (p. 460)

net profit The amount of money left after operating costs are subtracted from the gross profit. (p. 82)

networking Communicating with people one knows or can get to know to share information and advice. (p. 112)

net worth The difference between the assets of a business and its liabilities. (p. 82)

new business Any topic brought before the participants of a meeting for the first time. (p. 288)

no-fault system A system of insurance in which insurance companies pay for their policyholders' damage no matter who is at fault in an accident. (p. 446)

nonexempt employees Workers who are covered by a law that entitles them to earn overtime pay. (p. 165)

notice An official written statement that one is leaving a company. (p. 495)

NOW account A negotiable order of withdrawal; a type of checking account that pays interest on deposits but requires a minimum balance. (p. 424)

nutrients The substances in food that the body needs to produce energy and stay healthy. (p. 214)

Occupational Safety and Health Administration (OSHA) The branch of the U.S. Department of Labor that sets job safety standards and inspects job sites. (p. 222)

online banking A banking service that lets you manage your bank account from a remote computer. (p. 427)

on-the-job training On-site instruction in how to perform a job. (p. 99)

operating expenses The costs of doing business. (p. 81)

orientation A program that introduces new employees to their new company and its policies, procedures, values, and benefits. (p. 158)

outsourcing A practice in which businesses hire other companies or individuals to produce their services or goods. (p. 14)

overdrawn An account in which checks have been written for more money than is in the account. (p. 424)

overtime   Extra pay for each hour worked in excess of 40 hours per week. (p. 164)

parliamentary procedure   Strict rules of order for conducting a meeting. (p. 287)

partnership   A business arrangement in which two or more people share ownership. (p. 78)

passbook account   A savings account with which one receives a booklet in which to record transactions. (p. 418)

pending   Temporarily on hold. (p. 367)

pension plan   A benefit that builds a retirement fund for each worker. (p. 167)

people   A category that describes careers that involve working with people and animals. (p. 34)

performance bonuses   Rewards given to workers for high levels of performance. (p. 166)

performance reviews   Meetings between an employee and his or her supervisor to evaluate how well the employee is doing his or her job. (p. 167)

perseverance   The quality of finishing what one starts. (p. 488)

personal career profile form   A chart in which one can arrange what one has learned about oneself and what one has learned about a possible career side by side, along with a number indicating how closely the two match. (p. 88)

personality   The combination of an individual's attitudes, behaviors, and characteristics. (p. 37)

policyholder   A person who buys insurance. (p. 438)

positive self-talk   The use of positive statements to "outtalk" one's negative inner voice. (p. 197)

preferred provider organization (PPO)   A health-care plan similar to an HMO, with more choice of physicians but with higher premium and copayment costs. (p. 450)

prejudice   An unjustifiable negative attitude toward a person or group. (p. 187)

premium   The amount of money a policyholder pays for insurance. (p. 439)

presentation software   Software that allows a user to combine visual aids, outlines, graphics, and data in an interactive slide show. (p. 344)

previewing   Reading only the parts of a document that outline or summarize its contents. (p. 309)

prioritize   To put in order from first to last or from most important to least important. (p. 321)

probation   The period after an employee is first hired, when he or she is "on trial." (p. 168)

problem solving   A technique involving the use of thinking skills to suggest solutions to problems or situations, such as theoretical ones posed by an interviewer. (p. 141)

procrastinate   To put off deciding or acting. (p. 321)

producers   Companies or individuals who make or provide goods and services. (p. 381)

producing   Creating goods or services. (p. 380)

professionalism   A mature approach and appropriate behavior in regard to one's job. (p. 203)

profit-sharing plan   A program that gives workers a portion of their company's profits. (p. 166)

Glossary

promotion   A job advancement to a position of greater responsibility and authority. (p. 486)

pronunciation   How the sounds and stresses of a word are voiced. (p. 300)

purpose   An overall goal or aim. (p. 297)

recession   A six-month or longer period when the economy does not grow. (p. 384)

reconcile   To compare items and make them agree; used to refer to a checking account statement and check register. (p. 426)

record keeping   Organizing and maintaining records, often of one's income and spending. (p. 402)

redeem   To cash in. (p. 419)

references   People who will recommend applicants to an employer. (p. 121)

referral   Someone to whom one has been directed who may have information about a job or job opening. (p. 113)

register   To officially sign up as a qualified voter. (p. 516)

regular checking account   A type of checking account that usually does not require a minimum balance but generally charges service fees. (p. 423)

repetitive stress injuries   Injuries caused when the same motions are performed over and over. (p. 223)

resources   Time, money, material, information, facilities, and people needed to get a job done. (p. 317)

responsibility   A willingness to accept an obligation and to be accountable for an action or situation. (p. 177)

résumé   A brief summary of a job seeker's personal information, education, skills, work experience, activities, and interests. (p. 122)

revenue   Income from sales. (p. 82)

role-playing   Acting out a role in a make-believe situation, usually at the request of another person for the purpose of evaluation. (p. 140)

Roth IRA   An individual retirement account for which contributions are taxed, but earnings are tax-free. (p. 422)

salary   A fixed amount of pay for a certain period of time, usually a month or a year. (p. 165)

scan   A method of electronically copying a document into a computer. (p. 124)

schedule   A list or chart showing when tasks must be completed. (p. 359)

school-to-work programs   Programs that bring local schools and businesses together so that students can gain work experience and training. (p. 115)

security deposit   Money a tenant pays a property owner before moving in, usually equal to one or two months' rent. (p. 507)

sedentary   A type of activity in which most of one's time is spent sitting. (p. 215)

self-concept   The way one sees oneself. (p. 37)

self-directed   Responsible for choosing one's own methods for reaching a goal. (p. 276)

self-esteem   Recognition and regard for oneself and one's abilities. (p. 197)

self-management   The act of making oneself do what is necessary to build a better career. (p. 178)

self-starters   Workers who work without having to be told what to do. (p. 277)

seniority   A position or prestige achieved by working for an employer for a sustained length of time. (p. 487)

service learning   Programs in which students do community service—such as helping to clean up urban neighborhoods—as part of their schoolwork. (p. 55)

service-producing industries   Industries that provide services for a fee. (p. 17)

services   Activities done for others for a fee. (p. 11)

settlement   A mutual agreement that does not state that either party in a dispute is right or wrong. (p. 244)

sexual harassment   Any unwelcome behavior of a sexual nature. (p. 239)

shareholders   The owners of a company who buy shares, or parts, of the company and earn a profit based on the number of shares they own. (p. 79)

simplified employee pension (SEP)   A tax-deferred retirement plan for the self-employed that is simpler and easier to set up and maintain than a Keogh plan. (p. 422)

skills   Developed abilities. (p. 4)

skills résumé   A résumé organized around skills and accomplishments rather than time order. (p. 122)

skimming   Reading quickly for main ideas and key points. (p. 310)

small-claims court   A court that handles disputes over relatively small amounts of money and does not require lawyers. (p. 244)

Social Security   A government program that provides benefits for people of all ages. (p. 471)

Social Security number   A number issued by the federal government that one needs in order to get a job. (p. 120)

sole proprietorship   A business that is completely owned by one person. (p. 78)

spreadsheet   A software program that arranges data in rows and columns; often used for keeping accounts payable records and projecting expenses. (p. 345)

standard deduction   A set amount of money taxpayers may subtract from their income when figuring how much tax they must pay; amount is set by the IRS and based on itemized deductions claimed by thousands of "average" taxpayers. (p. 467)

standard English   The form of writing and speaking taught in school and used in newspapers and on television news programs. (p. 120)

standard of living   A measure of quality of life based on the amount of goods and services individuals can buy. (p. 386)

start-up costs   The expenses involved in beginning a business. (p. 73)

statement account   A savings account with which a person receives a computerized statement of transactions, usually monthly. (p. 418)

stereotype   An oversimplified and distorted belief about a person or group without attention to individual differences. (p. 269)

stress   Emotional and physical tension resulting from the body's natural response to conflict. (p. 142)

strike   A suspension of work called by a union against an employer to coerce the employer to accede to collective bargaining demands. (p. 236)

strike fund   Money collected by a union to pay workers who are on strike. (p. 236)

style   An individual way of expressing oneself. (p. 306)

subdirectories   Smaller groupings of files within a computer directory. (p. 370)

subject   A main topic or key idea. (p. 298)

Glossary

summons An order to appear in court. (p. 243)

Super-NOW account An enhanced version of the NOW account; a checking account that pays a higher interest rate than a NOW account but also requires a higher minimum balance. (p. 424)

tact The ability to say and do things in a way that will not offend other people. (p. 259)

tax evasion Also known as fraud; using illegal methods to avoid paying taxes. (p. 467)

taxable income A person's income after he or she subtracts certain permitted amounts of money for tax-figuring purposes. (p. 459)

taxes Payments made to support the government and to pay for government services. (p. 458)

team An organized group that sets goals, makes decisions, and implements actions. (p. 14)

team planning A process that involves setting goals, assigning roles, and communicating regularly. (p. 278)

technological literacy Knowing about and being able to use technology effectively. (p. 340)

telecommuting Using modern technology—especially computers, fax machines, and telephones—to perform a job at home. (p. 14)

teleconferencing Holding discussions among people in different locations by electronic means. (p. 337)

tenant A person renting a property. (p. 507)

terminate To end a worker's employment. (p. 168)

term life insurance Insurance that provides money to the policyholder's dependents or other beneficiaries if he or she dies. (p. 452)

things Physical objects of any size, such as intruments, tools, machinery, equipment, raw materials, and vehicles. (p. 34)

time line A type of chart that shows the order in which events occur in time. (p. 359)

tone Manner or mood, as in writing. (p. 305)

total quality management (TQM) A theory of management that carefully coordinates company efforts to achieve customer satisfaction and continuous product improvement; also called "Commitment to Quality." (p. 282)

tracking schedule A chart that identifies the people who will be working on each part of a project and when they will start and finish. (p. 280)

trade school A privately run institution that trains students for particular types of jobs. (p. 100)

unemployment insurance A state-run social insurance program that provides some temporary income to workers who have lost their jobs. (p. 473)

unfinished business Any topic brought before the participants of a meeting for at least the second time. (p. 288)

uninsured motorist coverage Insurance that provides coverage for damage or injuries caused by a driver who is at fault in an auto accident and does not have liability insurance. (p. 443)

utilities Services for one's dwelling, including electricity, heat, and water. (p. 506)

values The principles a person wants to live by and the beliefs that are important to that person. (p. 31)

vocational-technical center A school that offers a variety of skills-oriented programs. (p. 100)

warranty A guarantee that a product meets certain standards of quality. (p. 392)

whole life insurance A type of cash-value insurance with a savings component, which can build a reserve of money that a policyholder can borrow against or collect when he or she retires. (p. 452)

withhold Deduct, as money from a paycheck. (p. 459)

word processing Using any software program that creates text-based documents. (p. 344)

work credits Measurements of how long a person has worked, a certain number of which the person must earn in order to become eligible for Social Security benefits. (p. 472)

work environment The social and physical surroundings of a job, which can affect a worker's well-being. (p. 59)

workers' compensation A state-run social insurance program that provides benefits to workers injured on the job and to dependents of workers killed on the job. (p. 222, p. 473)

work permit A document needed by workers under 16 and sometimes by those under 18, showing that the young person knows about restrictions on the hours young people can work and the kinds of jobs they can hold. (p. 120)

GLOSSARY

Index

Page numbers in *italics* refer to illustrations.

INDEX

INDEX

National Career Development Curriculum

The **National Career Development Guidelines** help schools and government agencies plan quality career guidance and counseling programs. The guidelines were developed by the National Occupational Information Coordinating Committee, a federal interagency committee that promotes the development and use of occupational and labor market information.

Career development has become increasingly important to youths and adults who are preparing to work in a society that is characterized by changing technologies, job distributions, economic outlooks, employer requirements and expectations, and family structures. Educators, employers, parents, youths, and adults are demanding comprehensive programs that will lead students of all ages through a sequential process of career development that will enable them to succeed in the future workplace. To respond to this need, state and professional associations, as well as national leaders, practitioners, and career development experts, have collaborated to develop the National Career Development Guidelines.

The guidelines contain 12 competencies that relate to three areas of career development: self-knowledge, educational and occupational exploration, and career planning. The competencies are:

Self-Knowledge
1. Knowledge of the importance of self-concept
2. Skills to interact with others
3. Awareness of the importance of growth and change

Educational and Occupational Exploration
4. Awareness of the benefits of educational achievement
5. Awareness of the relationship between work and learning
6. Skills to understand and use career information
7. Awareness of the importance of personal responsibility and good work habits
8. Awareness of how work relates to the needs and functions of society

Career Planning
9. Understanding how to make decisions
10. Awareness of the interrelationship of life roles
11. Awareness of different occupations and changing male/female roles
12. Awareness of the career planning process

Photo Credits